Becoming the Pearl-Poet

STUDIES IN MEDIEVAL LITERATURE

Series Editor: Albrecht Classen, University of Arizona

Studies in Medieval Literature invites scholars to publish their most powerful, exciting, and forward-looking studies, which will thus become an excellent platform for Medieval Studies at large.

Recent Titles

Becoming the Pearl-Poet

Perceptions, Connections, Receptions

Edited by

Jane Beal

LEXINGTON BOOKS
Lanham • Boulder • New York • London

Published by Lexington Books
An imprint of The Rowman & Littlefield Publishing Group, Inc.
4501 Forbes Boulevard, Suite 200, Lanham, Maryland 20706
www.rowman.com

6 Tinworth Street, London SE11 5AL, United Kingdom

British Library Cataloguing in Publication Information Available

Library of Congress Cataloging-in-Publication Data Available

Names: Beal, Jane, editor.
Title: Becoming the Pearl-poet : perceptions, connections, receptions / edited by Jane Beal.
Description: Lanham : Lexington Books, [2022] | Series: Studies in medieval literature | Includes bibliographical references and index. | Summary: "From Becoming the Pearl-Poet, students and scholars alike can learn about the Pearl-poet and the five poems attributed to him, Pearl, Cleanness, Patience, Sir Gawain and the Green Knight, and St Erkenwald, exploring key ideas that will inform a deeper understanding and appreciation of this medieval English writer's work" —Provided by publisher.
Identifiers: LCCN 2022033531 (print) | LCCN 2022033532 (ebook) | ISBN 9781793646750 (cloth) | ISBN 9781793646774 (paper) | ISBN 9781793646767 (epub)
Subjects: LCSH: English poetry—Middle English, 1100–1500—History and criticism. | LCGFT: Literary criticism. | Essays.
Classification: LCC PR1972.G353 B43 2022 (print) | LCC PR1972.G353 (ebook) | DDC 821/.1—dc23/eng/20220908
LC record available at https://lccn.loc.gov/2022033531
LC ebook record available at https://lccn.loc.gov/2022033532

In loving memory of my brother, my Dreamer,
Abraham Lincoln Jeremiah Beal
February 12, 1979–October 29, 2021

Amen, amen dico vobis:
nisi granum frumenti cadens
in terram mortuum fuerit,
ipsum solum manet.
Si autem mortuum fuerit,
multum fructum adfert.

John 12:24
Biblia Sacra Vulgata

Contents

Acknowledgments

This book, *Becoming the Pearl-Poet: Perceptions, Connections, Receptions*, has been a labor of love in a time of trial. During the worldwide coronavirus pandemic (2019–2022), the contributors to this volume made tremendous efforts to write, research, revise, and edit the chapters that readers will find in the pages of this volume. I am honored to be in the company of such dedicated scholars, who overcame significant challenges and hinderances to produce this book with me. I am grateful to all of them: Elizabeth Allen, Kristin Bovaird-Abbo, John Bowers, Ethan Campbell, Nancy Ciccione, David Coley, Michael D. C. Drout, Joel Fredell, Jonathan Gerkin, Grace Hamman, Scott Kleinman, Kenna Olsen, Corey Owen, Jonathan Quick, and Mickey Sweeney. I wish to acknowledge especially Kenna, Mickey, and John, who took on key editorial tasks in addition to writing their own chapters. Their sharp eyes and attentive editing skills have strengthened our book.

I am thankful for the editors at Lexington Books, a division of Rowman & Littlefield, beginning with Albrecht Classen, who is the editor of the publisher's Studies in Medieval Literature series. Professor Classen is not only one of the most productive scholars in the history of medieval literary and cultural studies, but also an entirely collegial editor, ally, and friend. Albrecht, thank you for your essential role in bringing this book through the publication process so that it can reach a wide audience of interested students and scholars. I am very thankful for acquisitions editors Megan Conley and Holly Buchanan, too. They oversaw the contract process and manuscript delivery. Holly, your boundless patience and kindness is deeply appreciated.

The collaborative, scholarly enterprise represented by this book has been nurtured and fostered by opportunities to present, discuss, and debate ideas and interpretations of the *Pearl*-poet at the International Congress on Medieval Studies (ICMS), held annually at the University of Western Michigan in Kalamazoo, Michigan, and the International Medieval Congress (IMC), held annually at the University of Leeds in England. To the presidents and vice presidents of the international Pearl-Poet Society, who have organized so many of the conference sessions and roundtables in which I and the other contributors to this volume have participated over the years: thank you kindly. Like each of you, four colleagues with whom I meet regularly in Leeds have helped me as the editor of this book: Ashley Bartelt, Catherine Batt, Kimberly Jack, and Mickey Sweeney. I thank you not only for your intellectual brilliance, but also for your friendship in all matters concerning our divine poet.

Many universities have contributed to the creation of this book, by gainfully employing several of the writers, and I wish to especially thank my own: the University of La Verne. The research for my chapter in this volume was supported by a grant from the Provost's Office, approved by our past provost, Dr. Jonathan Reed. The grant enabled me to study the Pearl Manuscript, Cotton Nero A.x, in the British Library, to view the Hereford Mappa Mundi *in situ* in Hereford Cathedral, and to present my findings at the International Medieval Congress in England. In addition, in 2020, Dr. Jonathan Reed, President Devorah Lieberman, and the Board of Trustees approved my tenure and promotion to full professor at our university, for which I am profoundly thankful. This support and security of employment undergirds my ability to make progress in my scholarly work and to pass on the benefits to my students and other scholars. President Liberman, I especially thank you for all that you have done to lead our university through the storms of the past few years. You have my highest admiration and deepest gratitude. *Per ardua ad astra.*

Other colleagues in the College of Arts and Sciences at my university have provided support for my work on this book. In 2022, Dean Shannon Mathews, in partnership with our new Provost Kerop Janoyan and Associate Deans Ngoc Bui and Gerard Lavatori, granted a course release/workload exchange to me for scholarship, which has helped me to make further progress. Dean Mathews, I greatly thank you for your support, which is inestimable: I truly value it. To my colleagues in the English Department, thank you as well. While serving as your chair, and working on this book, I have found you to be true allies and friends. Jeff, Cathy, Laurie, Kara, and Clara, may you be ever blessed. Melanie, I always appreciate your service to our department.

I thank my students, too, because they inspire me. My special thanks go to English major Sara Winsky, who was my undergraduate research assistant for this book. Together, we discussed each and every chapter in detail, working through questions, ideas, and editorial corrections and formatting. Sara's joyful personality, quick thinking, and constant companion—iced coffee—is forever associated in my mind with the success of this endeavor.

Our indexing terms were provided by the contributors of each chapter (as were summaries of their chapters included in the introduction), and Sara Winsky and I organized the terms in the index alphabetically. Ashley Bartlet began the process of indexing the terms, and my parents, Barbara and Rudy

Holthuis, kindly finished indexing all of the terms. I thank everyone who worked on the index with me very much, especially my hard-working, detail-oriented parents, who did a very professional job and helped production stay on schedule.

My relationships to my family and friends provide the rich context of my life that makes my work worthwhile. First to you, Mom, I say thank you because you have been an example of faith, learning, and endurance throughout my life. I thank my parents and my whole family, whose love means so much to me. To my brothers and sisters and their children, who have continually been at the center of my love and concern, especially in this season—James and Bricia; Abraham and Heather and their children, Ada, Daniel, and Isaac; Anne and Jeremy and their daughters, Karisse and Katrina; Andrew and Debbie and their son, Elijah; Alice Frances; Terra and Andrew and their daughter, Grace; Josh and Danielle and their sons, Ethan and Tyler; Dustin and Stephanie and their daughters, Aurora and Avery; Joel and Alise and their children, Averie and Barrett; Erin and Jon and their sons, Ryan and Liam; David and Taylor; Isaiah Israel; Anthony and Skye; and Glory and Aaron—I embrace all of you in my heart.

This book is dedicated to my brother, Abraham, who passed away during the coronavirus pandemic. Abraham, I love you so much, and I miss you more than words can express. Your life is worthy of honor, and I honor you for who you were in this life and who you are now in eternity. I look forward to the day when I will see you again.

Finally, I thank three dear friends of mine, Stacey, Jean-Pierre, and Jesus. You have been with me through the hardships of this journey. I treasure you.

Jane Beal, PhD
University of La Verne

Introduction

Becoming the Pearl-Poet

Jane Beal

The poems attributed to our poet—*Pearl, Cleanness, Patience, Sir Gawain and the Green Knight*, and (sometimes) *St. Erkenwald*—are being widely read, taught, studied, and celebrated now more than ever. This can be seen from a number of recent publications on the poet, including Piotyr Spyra's monograph (Ashgate, 2014), Cecelia Hatt's monograph (Boydell & Brewer, 2015), the Folio Society's facsimile edition (2016), Simon Armitage's translations of *Pearl* (Faber & Faber, 2008) and *Sir Gawain and the Green Knight* (W. W. Norton, 2016), Jane Beal's monograph on *Pearl* (Routledge, 2017), edited collection of pedagogical essays on *Pearl* (MLA, 2018), and edition-translation of *Pearl* (Broadview, 2020), Ethan Campbell's monograph (Western Michigan University Press, 2018), and David Coley's monograph (The Ohio State University Press, 2019). The scholarly scope of these books is enlarged by work done in many shorter studies published in academic journals as well as several dissertations and theses produced at colleges and universities. Yet no new collection of scholarly essays on the poet has appeared as a published book since the *Companion to the Gawain-Poet* (Boydell & Brewer, 1999) volume more than twenty years ago. The time for *Becoming the Pearl-Poet: Perceptions, Connections, Receptions* has come.

Becoming the Pearl-Poet contains within its very title an important notion underlying the volume: namely, that since the rediscovery of the Pearl Manuscript (British Library MS Cotton Nero A.x) in the nineteenth century, our understanding of who the anonymous *Pearl*-poet was, and what he did, has been gradually developing over time. Emerging biographical considerations of the anonymous poet are only a part of this development. Scholars have delved into new critical and theoretical territories in considering the five poems attributed to the poet. This volume addresses key developments in three major sections: Perceptions, Connections, and Receptions.

PART I: PERCEPTIONS

In Part I, "Perceptions," five scholars provide introductions and new analyses of the five poems probably written by the poet: *Pearl* (Jane Beal), *Cleanness* (Corey Own), *Patience* (Matthew Brumit), *Sir Gawain and the Green Knight* (Mickey Sweeney), and *St. Erkenwald* (Michael Drout, et al.).

In my chapter, I explore the genre of medieval *mappaemundi*, in its dual manifestation—cartographic forms and narrative descriptions—and how it constitutes an important context for interpreting the themes of *Pearl*. It appears that the poet crafted the landscapes and geography underlying the Dreamer's dream-vision pilgrimage so as to suggest that the Dreamer travels imaginatively across the face of a world-map from an earthly garden in England (on the margins), to the Earthly Paradise (Eden at the top), to the earthly Jerusalem (in the middle), to the threshold of the heavenly Jerusalem (as he looks beyond the borders of a *mappamundi* into the lunar sphere), and back to an "erber grene" in England in August. Medieval people looked at maps in order to claim territory, become educated, and, most important of all, make spiritual progress through the steps of humility, purgation, and illumination to become unified with God. The Dreamer does, too.

In his chapter, Corey Owen uses ancient and medieval conceptualizations of temperance, the virtue associated with the concupiscible faculty of the soul, to chart the poet's depiction of the progression of concupiscible vice in *Cleanness*. After investigating the various taxonomies of temperance, which can be reduced to the desire for sex, food, and finery, he situates the virtue according to its relationship to prudence, fortitude, and, ultimately, justice. Owen contends that the poet uses the traditional parts of temperance to expand incrementally the range of *clannesse* through the poem's three biblical episodes, and to explore the connection between the vices within the concupiscible faculty, and between those of the concupiscible faculty and the other faculties of the soul.

In his chapter, Matthew Brumit considers how the Middle English poem *Patience* asserts the unity of Virtue and, via nautical metaphor, encourages the members of its audience to let themselves be conformed to Providence. According to the platonic tradition, though we commonly use multiple words to describe its various facets, Virtue is a simple unity. The clearest evidence that this poet understands virtue platonically comes in his emendation of the final Beatitude from Jesus' Sermon on the Mount, recounted in Matthew 5:3–10, which the poet translates from the Vulgate. Coming after a prologue in which the poet emends the Beatitudes to assert that "[þ]ay ar happen also þat con her hert stere" ("they are happy who can steer their heart," l. 27), the exemplum not only indicates that Jonah lacks Virtue, the ability to steer his heart, but also recalls the motif of Christ the helmsman by suggesting that Providence ultimately directs Jonah's course. For this poet, Virtue does not involve steering or controlling things beyond oneself (like a boat) but rather steering that which is most deeply interior to a person: the heart. Given the freedom of the human heart, which does not naturally conform to Providence, humans must receive some manner of moral education if they are to be happy. By the time he reaches Nineveh, then, Jonah's education in Virtue has been sensory, rational, even intellectual, but it has not been imaginative—and Jonah's lack of imagination causes him to fall short of his promise to remain true to Providence even as the Ninevites learn patience from his story in spite of him. By making his "poynt" ("point," l. 1) about patience by means of a story rather than a treatise, using words predicated upon images rather than syllogisms, the poet offers a vicarious experience of patience, Virtue, and Providence that he surely hopes will have a tropological effect on his audience.

In her chapter, Mickey Sweeney notes that *Sir Gawain and the Green Knight* is perhaps the best known of the *Pearl*-poet's poems. It has garnered so much attention from the critics that it is often difficult to keep pace with not only what is written about the poem, or the *Pearl*-poet, but how critical trends in general influence our interpretations. In the last decade alone, work on authorship, nationalism, post-colonialism, and linguistics as well as the advances in technology have provided new platforms for historians, theorists, linguists, and experts in manuscript work. Her chapter, while focusing on a reading of the poem that inspires a questioning of authority and perfection in the romance genre, also attempts to highlight where we are in our critical conversations about select critical points in the poem.

In their chapter, Michael Drout, Scott Kleinman, and Jonathan Gerkin consider a fifth poem sometimes attributed to the *Pearl*-poet. *St. Erkenwald* is a relatively short, Middle English poem in unrhymed alliterative long lines that tells the story of how a single tear from Bishop Erkenwald of London (675–693 AD) serves to baptize an uncorrupted corpse. The poem's sole witness is found in MS Harley 2250, a manuscript of the late fifteenth century, but the poem is usually dated to the late fourteenth century and has long been linked with the *Pearl, Cleanness, Patience,* and *Sir Gawain and the Green Knight*. Because the manuscript containing these poems, Cotton Nero A.x, was copied by a different scribe than *St. Erkenwald*, it has proven difficult to determine how much of the apparent influence of the Cheshire dialect is due to the scribe of Harley 2250 and how much may be evidence that the poem's author spoke a different dialect than that of the Cotton Nero A.x poems.

Statistical and computer-assisted approaches to the authorship problem have generally indicated that *St. Erkenwald* is somewhat more like *Cleanness*, *Patience*, and *Sir Gawain and the Green Knight* than is *Pearl*, so if *Pearl* is accepted as being by the same author as the rest of the Cotton Nero A.x poems, *St. Erkenwald* probably should be as well.

PART II: CONNECTIONS

In Part II, "Connections," six scholars consider subjects that connect the poems to one another: authorship (Ethan Campbell), ecology (Elizabeth Allen), material culture (Jonathan Quick), adornment (Kimberly Jack), shields (Kristin Bovaird-Abbo), and theology (Grace Hamman).

In his chapter, Ethan Campbell's consideration of the *Pearl*-poet's authorship begins with the question of whether a single poet or two or more wrote the works attributed to him. Most contemporary scholars view the four poems in the Cotton Nero A.x manuscript as products of a single author, if only for convenience, but the question has a long and, so far, unresolved history, which also involves the poem *St. Erkenwald* from a separate manuscript. The chapter asks what we can learn about the author from these manuscripts and their texts alone, with a focus on those questions that have a direct bearing on interpretation. For example, was the poet from the rural county Cheshire, home of several place names in *Sir Gawain and the Green Knight*, or from London, where *St. Erkenwald* takes place, or might he have called both places home? Was he a priest, as the themes and sermon structure of *Cleanness* and *Patience* would suggest, or a devout layman, as *Pearl* seems to indicate? Did he have connections with the court of King Richard II? Even if no definitive answers to these questions are possible, the very existence of these five poems along with works such as *Piers Plowman* and *The Siege of Jerusalem* points to a popular tradition of alliterative poetry in the Midlands, which Chaucer comments on with his "southren" Parson. This connection raises the question that ends the chapter: to what extent might the *Pearl*-poet have been known to his poetic contemporaries such as Langland and Chaucer? The conclusion contends that a proper appreciation of the *Pearl* poems involves taking each unique narrator's self-identification at his word, expecting that such a masterful and varied group of poetry will feature multiple voices.

In her chapter, Elizabeth Allen investigates how the *Pearl*-poet's remarkable attention to the material world entails an ecological awareness of non-human forces, from animals and plants to landscapes and weather, even to castles and graves. Even as *Sir Gawain and the Green Knight* and *Pearl* explore human moral limitations, both poems also undercut the assumption of human centrality and hierarchical superiority. Seen through an ecocritical lens, the poems suggest networks of resemblance and dependency among humans, animals, minerals, weather, and time. At the same time, they depict uncanny and alien ecologies that refuse assimilation into either a nature-culture binary or a unified ecological mesh. By examining indeterminate symbols and repeated metaphors, this chapter explores poetry as a resource for pointing beyond itself, toward a complex range of ecological relationships.

In his chapter, Jonathan Quick explores how the *Pearl*-poet describes a number of material objects in his poems. The chapter examines the poet's utilization of these material objects as both descriptive embellishments and didactic symbols conveying divine and moral messages to the poems' audiences. The pearl is an exceptionally vibrant symbol in his poem of the same name. While the Dreamer in *Pearl* calls himself a jeweler and is largely treated as such in critical readings of the poem, the exact definition of a jeweler in Middle English was not clear. Highlighting one sense of the *MED*'s definition of this term, Quick examines *Pearl* and the poet's works in light of this less common interpretation. Objects like Lord Bertilak's axe (*Sir Gawain and the Green Knight*), the Pearl-Maiden's clothes and crown (*Pearl*), and the vessels at Belshazzar's feast (*Cleanness*) serve both as invitations to an imaginative sensory participation with the poem but also represent or point to immaterial concepts like judgment, purity, and pride. These "things" within the poems themselves stretch beyond and throughout the culture in which the poems were written, and yet, despite their symbolic or abstract force, the poet continues to imbue them with a material weightiness. The chapter elucidates the *Pearl*-poet's particular style and the tendency for depicting a varied and vibrant material world—a world continually in contact with immaterial concepts—thereby enriching our understanding of the poems and their contexts.

In her chapter, Kimberly Jack asks: why does the *Pearl*-Poet spend so much time dressing and undressing his characters? The *Pearl*-poet's works include extensive descriptions of bodily adornment in the form of clothing and accessories. While the poet's descriptive verses have been lauded by many critics, the purpose of these descriptions has rarely been addressed except in piecemeal fashion, focusing on isolated details such as the green girdle or the pearls adorning the Pearl-Maiden's robes. This chapter examines these passages as a concerted response to contemporary sumptuary statues and moralist critiques. These and other texts articulated a stable sartorial sign system in which outer attire clearly signified identity, occupation, social status, affiliation in diverse organizations, and the state of one's soul. The *Pearl*-poet acknowledges the sartorial system theorized in these texts in passages such as the parable of the wedding in *Cleanness*, the explication of Gawain's pentangle, the Pearl-Maiden's attire, and the uncorrupted robes of the Judge in *St. Erkenwald*. However, the *Pearl*-poet ultimately critiques the assumption that sartorial signs might be stable identifiers. Instead, the

Pearl-poet dresses and undresses his characters to challenge how agency and interpretation muddle the theoretically clear waters of sartorial signification.

In her chapter, Kristin Bovaird-Abbo explores how, in the anonymous fourteenth-century alliterative poem *Sir Gawain and the Green Knight*, the titular character enters the scene bearing a unique heraldic device: a pentangle. While many scholars discuss the symbolism and meaning of Gawain's shield, focusing on either the outward pentangle or the inner portrait of the Virgin Mary, or both, her focus is not on the shield that Gawain bears in *Sir Gawain and the Green Knight*. Rather, her interests lie in the shields that he bears in other literary texts, and what it means that this poet has assigned a completely new device to this most renowned knight of the Round Table. That is, in the context of fourteenth-century Middle English romance, Gawain is associated with the heraldic device of a griffin; it is only in *Sir Gawain and the Green Knight* that he is given the pentangle, and no later Arthurian romances repeat this detail. What might a griffin represent to a fourteenth-century audience, and what does its absence in this alliterative poem reveal?

In her chapter, Grace Hamman explores the poet's theology. The disparate theological interests of the poet are teleologically oriented toward portraying and provoking recognition and acknowledgment of human weakness. This weakness includes both that caused by sin as well as the natural created weakness of humanity. While many critics have explored the poet's thematic interest in human limitation, her chapter specifically contextualizes this key theme within contemporary, cross-generic pastoral writing. Penitential, didactic, and contemplative materials of the fourteenth century encouraged self-reflexive consideration of human limitation as the foundation of spiritual growth and of the sacrament of penance. The poems share this concern. Each of the poems in its own way pastorally probes human limitation, making space for readers to reflect on their own weaknesses and God's responses to them. In *Cleanness* and *Patience*, these inquiries are centered upon the sacrament of penance and developing a penitential response to sin. *St. Erkenwald*, *Pearl*, and *Sir Gawain and the Green Knight* focus more on the impediments to and methods of fostering self-knowledge itself. These commitments to generate recognition of as well as questions about the shape, appropriateness, and form of human limitation unite the generically and theologically diverse corpus of the *Pearl*-poet.

PART III: RECEPTIONS

In Part III, "Receptions," five more scholars explore the reception and contexts of these poems in chapters on the manuscript illustrations (Joel Fredell), cultural contexts (David Coley), religious contexts (Nancy Ciccione), translations (Kenna Olsen), and audiences, both medieval and modern (John Bowers).

In his chapter, Joel Fredell considers the illustrations of the manuscript, the first formal indicator of the poem's "reception" at the beginning of the fifteenth century. Although we cannot be certain that the decorators who illustrated Cotton Nero A.x worked with the manuscript's scribe, or even produced these miniatures at the same time or place, their sheer number and complexity provide the fullest contemporary response we could hope to have for Cotton Nero A.x's masterful poems. Recent studies in Cotton Nero A.x's dialect, illustrations, and decoration shift the manuscript's provenance from an unknown center in Cheshire to Yorkshire and, in the case of the decorations and illustrations, possibly the city of York. Although the manuscript hand cannot be precisely dated (but is likely to be no earlier than the late fourteenth century), the illustrations can be assigned to the first decade of the fifteenth century based on costume detail. Illustrations in Cotton Nero A.x share a number of resemblances to illustrations in contemporary northern devotional manuscripts that argue for a York provenance for the decorations at least. The illustrations also reveal consistent devotional concerns in visual narratives that communicate the physical and psychological stages of their protagonists' journeys and the struggles for spiritual life in the fallen world.

In his chapter, David Coley observes that, until recently, most scholars took as fact that the poems contained in MS Cotton Nero A.x, as well as MS Harley 2250's London-focused *St. Erkenwald*, were the work of a writer from the Northwest Midlands, one very likely based in Cheshire and, more specifically still, one attached to the royal court of Richard II. The foundational historical study in this regard, Michael Bennett's *Community, Class and Careerism: Cheshire and Lancashire Society in the Age of "Sir Gawain and the Green Knight,"* seemed to support earlier dialectical indicators of such a provenance, and later works, such as John Bowers's *The Politics of Pearl*, built powerfully on Bennett's scholarship to develop an understanding of the four poems within a political and cultural environment marked by both provincial and national concerns. In 2014, however, a path-breaking article by Joel Fredell, "The *Pearl*-Poet Manuscript in York," argued that the unique manuscript containing *Pearl*, *Cleanness*, *Patience*, and *Sir Gawain and the Green Knight* was very likely produced in York during the reign of Henry IV. While Fredell is careful to confine his arguments to the physical artifact of the manuscript itself, the implications of his findings are nonetheless very clear: we can no longer in good conscience take for granted either the Ricardian or the Cheshire provenance of *Pearl* or its companion poems. Rather, we must be attentive to the possibilities arising when we remove *Pearl* from its traditional Northwest Midlands setting and consider alternative regional and temporal possibilities.

In her chapter, Nancy Ciccione explores the religious references, images, and symbols that permeate the *Pearl*-poet's works. Editors provide extensive notes, but these notes frequently fail to elaborate on the complex milieu surrounding the poet. Rather than exhaustive, this chapter offers a glimpse into some of the religious issues in the fourteenth century. Although active pre-Christian, Judaic, and other belief systems coexisted, the Catholic Church continued to hold authority in England from the countryside to urban centers. Religion impacted social, economic, and political communities. Yet theological controversies, such as that regarding the translation of the Bible from Latin into English, mark the period. Factions formed with labels such as the Lollard, Nominalist, and Orthodox, each with subtle distinctions within such categories, and arguments ensued. Some learned scholastics, for example, disparaged friars and wanted to revoke their right to shrive; friars, in their turn, appealed to the Roman Curia, which issued bulls allowing them to continue to perform the sacrament of confession. Such arguments affected the average Christian. Annual confession had been mandated since 1215, but complaints against corrupt clergy occur in various discourses and raise serious questions. How, for example, is forgiveness affected if a sinful priest pardons sins? What effect does debasement have on ministering the Eucharist? What are the steps to salvation? The European Great Western Schism (1378–1417) complicates some of the challenges to orthodoxy because it allowed Richard II greater reign in the appointment of his favorites as bishops. Inviting further investigations, the religious context in the late fourteenth century provides fertile ground for interpreting the *Pearl*-poet's narratives.

In her chapter, Kenna Olsen provides a brief evaluative history of the translations from Middle English to Modern English published of *Pearl, Sir Gawain and the Green Knight, Patience, Cleanness,* and *St. Erkenwald* since the poems were first edited. The translation history and approach to each of the poems are varied, and this chapter offers critical summaries and insights into the most significant Modern English translations of each poem and the approach taken by translators. The chapter identifies omnibus translations, dual-language translation-editions, and singular translations, where only one of the five poems is translated into Modern English. Significant adaptations (text, stage, television, and film) of *Sir Gawain and the Green Knight* are also briefly discussed.

In his chapter, John Bowers considers that questions of audience, whether medieval or modern, inevitably begin with an admission of unknowns. Since we know almost nothing about the author, we can guess few things about his original audiences beyond the contents of his works and the evidence of the

Cotton Nero A.x collection plus the single copy of *Erkenwald* in a Harley manuscript. There is scant evidence of ownership during the fifteenth century, one simplified adaptation, *The Grene Knight*, and no definite readership until the nineteenth century when *Gawain* was first edited in a collection of Arthurian works (1839) and the other three poems were published in the inaugural volume of the Early English Text Society (1864). As *Gawain* and *Pearl* found their ways onto the university syllabus, textbooks were required, and the standard edition of *Gawain* by J. R. R. Tolkien and E. V. Gordon was followed by translations such as Marie Borroff's verse rendering in the *Norton Anthology of English Literature*—with *Gawain* now in the *Norton Anthology of World Literature*—reaching a global audience in the twenty-first century with the translation of *Gawain* and *Pearl* by England's Poet Laureate Simon Armitage.

CONCLUSION: A RESOURCE FOR READERS

This volume is intended as a resource for undergraduate and graduate students, and it will be useful to professors of medieval literature who teach the *Pearl*-poet in their classes. Indeed, the five poems considered here are now being widely studied at the university level. *Sir Gawain and the Green Knight* and *Pearl* have become canonical standards in English literature survey courses. They are frequently taught in a variety of other courses as well: author courses focused on the poet, genre courses on medieval dream visions and spiritual autobiography, and thematic courses on English mystics and Arthurian legend. Thus, *Becoming the Pearl-Poet* can serve as a useful resource for professors and their students in university courses focused on the *Pearl*-poet as well as a reference text for medievalists undertaking new work on the poems. Medieval literary scholars focused on the *Pearl*-poet in particular and late medieval English literature in general will find this book interesting and worthwhile.

The chapters of this book are unified by their focus on a single poet and the poems attributed to him. Their themes overlap and interrelate in ways that the tripartite division of the book, "Perceptions," "Connections," and "Receptions," does not deny. Anyone generally familiar with the poet and his works can read the book straight through, from beginning to end, but chapters can also be read (or assigned) together for purposes of comparison or contrast. In a course on the *Pearl*-poet, an instructor might reasonably begin with Campbell's chapter on authorship, Fredell's on the Pearl Manuscript and its illustration, and Coley's on the Northwest Midlands and the Ricardian court. The syllabus of such a course might proceed to pair a reading of *Pearl* with chapters by Beal and Quick on material cultural influences on the poet's imagery and themes; of *Cleanness* with chapters by Owen on temperance and Ciccione on religious contexts; of *Patience* with chapters by Brumit on virtue and Hamman on the poet's pastoral theology; of *Sir Gawain and the Green Knight* with chapters by Sweeney on the failure of perfection, Jack and Bovaird-Abbo on the significance of sartorial adornment and shield devices respectively, and Allen on ecology; and of *St. Erkenwald* with the chapter by Drout, Kleinman, and Gerkin on the poem's place in the poet's canon. The class could conclude with due consideration of the reception of the poems, as traced through their editorial and translation history as well as audience response, which is explored by Olsen and Bowers. Certainly, this volume can be used as a handbook to the *Pearl*-poet because it balances known scholarship about his poems with new insights, sharing a wide variety of references and resources in the bibliographies of each chapter, which can be consulted by students and scholars alike who wish to pursue further research and deeper understanding of the poet, his poems, and his cultural context in late medieval England.

All the contributions to this book are informed by a spirit of inquiry, freely considering the possibilities of interpretation in light of the extant literary and cultural evidence. The writers aim to open a door, through which readers may step into the *Pearl*-poet's world, to experience and understand more about it than ever before. An open door is an invitation to exploration. So like the teachers we are, we present this book to our readers in hopes that they will learn from it, enjoy it, and respond to it by undertaking new investigations of the *Pearl*-poet.

PART I

Perceptions

Chapter One

The Dreamer's Contemplative Experience of the *Mappamundi* in *Pearl*[1]

Jane Beal

When the Dreamer of the exquisitely beautiful, fourteenth-century, Middle English dream-vision called *Pearl* falls asleep in a garden in August mourning his lost *margarita*, and his "spyryt þer sprang in space,"[2] the Dreamer finds himself in a landscape entirely unlike medieval England. The trees have silver trunks, with blue leaves—as "blew as ble of Ynde"[3]—and the gravel under his feet is made of pearls. He comes to a stream, the bed of which is inlaid with gems, across which he spies cliffs made of crystal. This bejeweled environment is certainly appropriate to a jeweler's imagination, but as the dream is further enriched by a vision of the New Jerusalem, it becomes apparent that the Dreamer has been on a journey—indeed, a pilgrimage—toward a heavenly revelation. Whereas the beginning of the poem suggests that the Dreamer's grief over his lost pearl prompts his dream, the ending of the poem suggests that the Dreamer's dream-vision pilgrimage may have been prompted by the poet's meditation on another material-cultural object as well: the *mappamundi*.

Literary scholars intent upon interpreting *Pearl* have carefully situated the poem in multiple relevant, medieval contexts. Among these contexts are biblical ones, especially the Song of Songs, the New Testament parables of Jesus, and the Apocalypse;[4] liturgical ones, including the Mass and the Eucharistic feast within the Mass, the specific Mass of Holy Innocents, the medieval liturgical Common of Virgins, Septuagesima Sunday (in the season of Epiphany but anticipating Lent), and the Paschal liturgy;[5] and broader literary ones, including sources and analogues, such as Ovidian mythological stories, Boethius' *Consolation of Philosophy*, the Old French *Roman de la Rose*, Dante's *Divine Comedy*, Boccaccio's *Olympia*, and late medieval English sacred and secular song lyrics and even plague treatises,[6] and contemporary, late medieval contemplative and visionary writing.[7] The poem has been considered in the contexts of hagiographical writing and *artes praedicandi* as well as courtesy books, anticlerical polemics, lapidaries, and other scientific treatises.[8] Material culture has been examined for parallels, and structures both great and small—from cathedrals to chantry chapels to saint's reliquaries,[9] from rose windows and rosaries to ecclesiastical chandeliers and royal crowns,[10] from the microcosm of the human body with the heart at its center to the symbol of the pearl itself[11]—have been considered alongside the poem as a means of better understanding it.

Yet at least one important context for *Pearl* has been neglected amid this plethora of excellent approaches. In a single sentence in *Medieval Allegory and the Building of the New Jerusalem*, drawing on insight gained from the *Poetria nova* of Geoffrey of Vinsauf, Ann Meyer insightfully notes that the medieval *mappamundi* is "a particularly intriguing parallel to *Pearl*."[12] She does not develop this line of literary analysis in her book, which is focused on parallels between the structure of *Pearl* and chantry chapels, both of which are informed by medieval beliefs about the New Jerusalem.[13] But her hint deserves development.

The genre of medieval *mappaemundi*, in its dual manifestation—cartographic forms and narrative descriptions—constitutes an important context for interpreting the themes of *Pearl*. For it appears that the poet crafted the landscapes and geography underlying the Dreamer's dream-vision pilgrimage to suggest that the Dreamer travels imaginatively across the face of a world-map from an earthly garden in England (on the margins), to the Earthly Paradise (Eden at the top), to the earthly Jerusalem (in the middle), to the threshold of the heavenly Jerusalem (as he looks beyond the borders of a *mappamundi* into the lunar sphere), and back to an "erber grene" in England in August. To understand how relevant this concept is to the themes of *Pearl*, it is important to consider the genre of the *mappamundi* and the ways medieval people looked at these maps to claim territory, become educated, and, most important of all, make spiritual progress through the steps of humility, purgation, and illumination to become unified with God.

MAPPAEMUNDI: WHAT MIGHT THE *PEARL*-POET HAVE KNOWN?

It appears that the *Pearl*-poet was familiar with world-maps in the late fourteenth century and perhaps even with specific *mappaemundi* that were made in his era, or before, and found in manuscripts of the *Polychronicon*, a fourteenth-century universal history of the world compiled by Ranulf Higden in Chester, and in cathedrals like that of Hereford, which held both books containing world-maps in its chained library as well as a large wall-map, the famous Hereford Mappa Mundi. Both Chester to the west and Hereford to the south were certainly within horse-riding distance of the poet's native Northwest Midlands. For a poet who probably traveled much farther distances between his home and London in the southeast of England, and probably to York in the northeast as well, journeys to closer shires are not inconceivable.[14]

Certainly the poet's contemporary, Chaucer, knew world-maps well enough to allude to them in his lyric, "To Rosamounde," in which he Englished the familiar and commonly used Latin word *mappamundi* as "mappemounde."[15] Chaucer makes ready use of the term in an English poem, a lover's lament that turns into a satiric complaint, for an English-speaking audience—probably an educated, courtly one that would find the punning on "rose of the world" (the translation of the lady's name) and "map of the world" (the translation of the Latin word) amusing. Chaucer's use of the term presumes that the reference to the "mappemounde" will be recognized and understood easily enough by his intended audience.

The *Pearl*-poet's use of the *mappamundi*, however, is different from Chaucer's. First, the poet does not use the word itself, either in Latin or English. Nor does he directly allude to specific world-maps he might have known, such as the *Polychronicon* maps or the Hereford Mappa Mundi. Instead, he demonstrates his familiarity with the genre of the *mappamundi* through his incorporation of it into the Dreamer's journey. The nature of the dream-vision pilgrimage is such that it suggests the poet's knowledge not only of the genre of world-maps, but of the use of those maps for political, educational, and contemplative purposes.[16]

The three landscapes of the poem—the garden, Earthly Paradise, and New Jerusalem—all correspond to specific places in medieval world-maps.[17] The stream that separates the two main speakers of the poem, the Dreamer and the Maiden, functions like the encircling *oceanus mare* in medieval *mappae-mundi* while the central image of the poem, the pearl, is thrice associated with the Orient or the East.[18] The east was a literal and spiritual direction on world-maps: the maps were frequently oriented toward the East, with the east at the top (not the north). Images of Eden in the east, at the top of the map, sometimes with Christ pictured above it, enthroned over the world, can be seen in multiple extant examples. A version of the *Polychronicon* map, contained in an autograph manuscript of the Latin *Polychronicon*, pictures Adam and Eve at the Tree of the Knowledge of Good and Evil in Eden, while the Psalter Map pictures Christ enthroned over the world. A metaphoric comparison between the color of the tree trunks in *Pearl*'s paradisial dreamscape to the "ble of Ynde"[19] associates the poem with an entire realm of medieval English thinking about the East. These details may be meant to draw the attention of reflective readers into a deeper realm of contemplation of *Pearl*, in which the Dreamer's journey is imagined as transpiring across the face of a world-map.

The role world-maps played in medieval culture in fostering the contradictory impulses of political rule, intellectual learning, and spiritual contemplation are significant for the interpretation of *Pearl*. *Pearl* foregrounds a conflict between epistemologies. The Dreamer and the Maiden have very different ways of knowing the world, and the poem stages a debate between their perspectives, one which is exacerbated by the Dreamer's experience of loss and suffering. As the poem begins, the Dreamer is willfully oriented—in a strikingly proprietorial way—toward the East, motivated by a desire to possess (or regain possession of) a beautiful pearl that he knows comes from that direction. He does not yet perceive that which is of greatest value in the East, the Pearl of Great Price, nor what it will cost him. He becomes intellectually disoriented as the poem continues because of his reliance on an Aristotelian worldview in the face of a neo-Platonic form: the Maiden. But by the poem's end, the awakened Dreamer is spiritually reoriented to the *Agnus Dei*, the Lamb in the New Jerusalem.

ORIENTATION: A MAP OF THE WORLD AND THE DREAMER'S POSSESSIVENESS

In a sense, the landscapes of *Pearl* are contextualized by the generic conventions of medieval *mappaemundi*. Jerusalem is the *umbilicus terrae* of the world map genre, and in *Pearl*, the work of salvation accomplished in Jerusalem is reimagined in the Pearl-Maiden's sermon on the Parable of the Workers in the Vineyard, beginning in section IX, continuing in section X, and concluding with the Maiden's personal application of the message in section XI—and her sermon is at the center of the poem.[20] The parable allegorically anticipates the bleeding Lamb, Jesus, whose Crucifixion in the earthly Jerusalem is described by the Maiden (section XIV) and whose iconic form is beheld in the vision of the heavenly Jerusalem by the Dreamer (section XIX). The Lamb is not only the center of the New Jerusalem but becomes the center of the Dreamer's soul, between his *ratio* (reason) and his *voluntas* (will) in his *memoria* (memory). This, of course, is accomplished over time and through a poetic, memorial, spiritual process that, at first, the Dreamer resists. His desire to possess "his" pearl, the Maiden, is a hindrance to his ability to receive the gift of the true pearl: the Pearl of Great Price.

The opening stanza of the poem clearly reveals the speaker's possessive preoccupation with a desirable pearl, set in gold, drawn "oute of orient."[21]

Pearl, ll. 1–12.

Perle plesaunte to prynces paye	Pearl! Desirable to a prince's pleasure,
To clanly clos in golde so clere	purely enclosed in gold so bright:
Oute of oryent, I hardyly saye	out of Orient, I firmly avow,
Ne proved I neuer her precios pere	never found I her precious peer—
So rounde so reken in uche araye	so round, so worthy in every setting!
So small so smoþe her syde3 were	So small, so smooth her sides were,
Queresoever I jugged gemme3 gaye	that wherever I judged bright jewels,
I sette hyr sengely in synglure	I valued her uniquely for uniqueness.
Allas I leste hyr in on erbere	Alas! I lost her in a garden!
Þur3 gresse to ground hit fro me yot	Through grass to ground it fell from me.
I dewyne, fordolked of luf-daungere	I languish, deeply wounded by love's fear
Of þat pryuy perle wythouten spot	because of that secret pearl without a spot.

The speaker is oriented toward this pearl from the beginning, finding "her" peerless, round, worthy, small, smooth, bright, valuable, and unique. But he admits in distress ("allas!") that he lost her in a garden, that she went from him through the grass into the ground,[22] which has caused him to languish because he is deeply wounded by "luf-daungere."[23] He sees his "pryuy" ("secret") pearl as the source of his wound.

As others have discussed, the poet's language here (and elsewhere in the poem) is that of courtly love tradition.[24] A reader encountering the language of the first stanza could easily imagine that the "pearl" being described is a beautiful woman, the garden is in a cloister courtyard or enclosed bower, and the loss and the "luf-daungere" the speaker experiences are part of the suffering and love-sickness of a true lover when separated from his beloved.[25] This particular garden appears to be set in England, in the high liturgical season of August,[26] a garden depicted winsomely in the first of four illustrations that preface the poem in the Pearl Manuscript (British Library MS Cotton Nero A.x).[27] It is planted with plants common to England in the Middle Ages: gillyflower, ginger, and gromwell[28] as well as peonies.[29] However, further contemplation of the poem, with the *mappamundi* in mind, suggests another layer of meaning in the opening lines.

The speaker is oriented toward the Orient, the East, where his pearl comes from. In most extant medieval maps, the topmost portion is not the north, as in our modern-day maps, but the east. In that topmost position in Asia is a garden, the Garden of Eden, often aligned more or less directly with the city of Jerusalem below it. Adam and Eve are often depicted in Eden on either side of the Tree of the Knowledge of Good and Evil.[30] To speak of losing a pearl in a garden, then, could be a way of speaking allegorically about losing salvation in Eden, and the pearl going from the speaker "through the grass into the ground" could be a way of alluding to the Fall, the reality of death, and Christian cultural practice of burying dead bodies in the ground. This layer of meaning need not have been present in the consciousness of the speaker himself when he experienced his own primal loss—the loss of the pearl that he desires to possess—but in these lines, the poet (who presents himself as the speaker remembering his experience at a later time) is not beyond making a subtle allusion to the garden of Eden, the Fall, death, and burial. For this is where we, the readers, might imagine the speaker on the map at the beginning of the poem: first in a garden in England (on the margins of the map), but also, once he falls asleep and enters his dream vision, in the garden of Eden (at the top of the *mappamundi*).

At the beginning of the second section of the poem, the speaker's spirit springs into space[31] while his body remains on the ground: "gon in Godez grace / in auenture ther meruaylez meuen."[32] He admits that he does not know where in the "worlde" he was.[33] He sees cliffs, a forest, and rich rocks "glemande glory" ("gleaming glory"); he sees cliffs of crystal and "bollez as blew as ble of Ynde" ("tree-trunks as blue as indigo from India").[34] Indeed, the Dreamer finds himself walking in a lush, paradisial dreamscape in which the tree-trunks are blue; the tree leaves, silver; the gravel under his feet, "perlez of oryente."[35] With these descriptions, the poet is apparently telling readers that the Dreamer is in the marvelous East.[36]

The Dreamer comes to the banks of a stream; the banks are of bright beryl. When he looks into the streambed, he sees that it is lined with jewels: each pebble in the pool is an emerald, sapphire, or another fair gem.[37] At this sight, the Dreamer himself will wonder if he has reached the limits of Paradise:

Pearl, ll. 137–40.

Forþy I þo3t þat Paradyse	Therefore I thought that Paradise
Wat3 þer ouer gayn þo bonke3 brade	was over there against the broad banks.
I hoped þe water were a deuyse	I hoped the water were a division
Bytwene myrþe3 by mere3 made	made by pools, between pleasant delights.

In terms of the *mappamundi*, the Dreamer seems to have reached not only Paradise, but perhaps the edge of the *oceanus mare*: the encircling sea that forms a division between the world and that which is now beyond the world. In extant examples of *mappaemundi*, sometimes Paradise is shown being firmly in the world, south of the *oceanus mare* (the Psalter Map), or sometimes encircled within the sea (the Hereford Mappa Mundi), so that the water creates a natural barrier between the earth proper and the Earthly Paradise. Beyond the encircling sea, medieval people believed there was the lunar sphere, and though this was not depicted in medieval world-maps, the harmony of all the spheres was depicted in other medieval and early Renaissance drawings.[38] In *Pearl*, the Maiden is positioned beyond the stream, where the Dreamer perceives her to be "vnstrayned" by strife because she is in "paradise erde"[39]—the Earthly Paradise.[40] This suggests the poet may have been meditating on a type of medieval world-map more like the Hereford Mappa Mundi than the Psalter Map. Significantly, the Maiden is not only beyond the stream, but between it and a cliff of crystal:[41] the crystal cliff may be the poet's way of visually alluding to the lunar sphere beyond Paradise and the *oceanus mare.*

At the boundary demarcated by the stream, the Dreamer sees the Maiden for the first time, and cries out, "O perle!"[42] She is crowned in gold, dressed in white, adorned with pearls, and there is a large, luminescent pearl on her breast, which he calls a "wonder perle."[43] The Dreamer asks the Maiden if she is *his* pearl,[44] and so begins their long conversation. In it, he expresses his deep sorrow over her loss, and she attempts to console him with Christian truth. In this series of exchanges, the Maiden, like Lady Philosophy or proverbial Wisdom, is trying to educate the Dreamer.[45] She attempts to lead him out of the possessive desire for her, which has deceived him and trapped him in excessive grief, into an illuminating awareness of the true pearl: the Pearl of Great Price.

DISORIENTATION: THE GIRL WITH THE
PEARL AND THE DREAMER'S EDUCATION

From the moment the Dreamer first sees the Maiden, she is instructing him, not only by what she says, but by her appearance. He sees the "wonder perle" in the midst of her breast; later, she will speak of the "perle of prys,"[46] and he will address her as the one who bears the "pearl of prys."[47] That pearl is meant to remind readers of the one that Jesus spoke of in a parable, a parable that the Maiden retells to the Dreamer, of a merchant who was seeking fine pearls, and finding a matchless one, sold all he had to buy that one.[48] As Jesus did, so too does the Maiden explain that the pearl is like the kingdom of heaven: "lyke þe reme of heuenesse clere."[49] All the Maiden's Christian counsel is directed toward getting the Dreamer to think about heaven. However, not all the Dreamer's questions necessarily tend in that direction.

The dialogue between the Dreamer and the Maiden consists of his relatively simple questions and the Maiden's much more complicated answers. Her answers are usually given in two stages, the first stage (more often than not) being a correction of the Dreamer's perception and the second stage being a longer explanation of a point of Christian doctrine. The tone of the Dreamer's questions seems to vary from sincere to almost sarcastic, and some of his questions imply that the Dreamer thinks that he already knows the answer to what he asks. Yet it is clear that the Dreamer is thinking hard, that he wants to learn, and that his intellect is engaged with the emotional and spiritual problems he is discussing with the Maiden.[50]

The Maiden's answers are surprising, not only to the Dreamer, but also, by extension, to the readers who identify with him in his experience of grief and distress. The Dreamer's focus is on the Maiden, but hers is on the Lamb, and so she consistently tries to draw the Dreamer's focus closer to her own perspective. His talk is of suffering and loss; hers, of salvation and joy. In the conversation, the Maiden consistently disorients the Dreamer's implied understanding and seeks to reset his expectations. She wants him to see the pearl in the midst of her breast and realize that it is a sign of salvation. The reward for all of the Maiden's instruction is that the Dreamer makes limited spiritual progress—and to be clear, her goal for him is *spiritual* progress: his emotional progress is difficult to gauge, and his "intellectual" approach to the Maiden's loss and sudden reappearance to him in his dream nearly stymies him.[51]

The conversation between the speakers has the characteristics of an unequal *debatio*, in which one speaker is clearly the teacher and the other a learner, and it develops fulsomely some important emotional and theological issues that arise from the Dreamer's questions.[52] Sometimes two questions are spoken close together in the same speech by the Dreamer, so there are nine speeches given by the Dreamer (including one speech of objection in which he asks no question), and nine answers given by the Maiden:

- Are you my pearl?: *Art þou my perle þat I haf playned?*[53]
- Am I going to have to suffer again? Am I going to lose you again?: *Deme3 þou me quod I my swete / To dol agayn?*[54] . . . *Now haf I fonte þat I forlete / Schal I efte forgo hit er euer I fine / Why schal I hit boþe mysse and mete?*[55]
- What is your life like now? *I wolde bysech, wythouten debate / 3e wolde me say in sobre asente / What lyf 3e lede erly and late?*[56]
- Are you the Queen of Heaven?: *Blysful quod I may þys be trwe / Dysplese3 not if I speke errour / Art þou þe quene l of heuene3 blwe, / Þat al þys worlde schal do honour?*[57]
- What does one have to do to be crowned in heaven?

What more honour mo3te he acheue
Þat hade endured in worlde stronge,
And lyued in penaunce hys lyue3 longe
Wyth bodyly bale hym blysse to byye
What more worschyp mo3t he fonge
Þen corounde be kyng by cortaysé?[58]

- It is unreasonable and unscriptural that God would reward people equally when they have such different merits. *Me þynk þy tale vnresounable / Godde3 ry3t is redy and euermore rert / Oþer Holy Wryt is bot a fable*[59]
- Who formed your fair figure? What kind of office (status) do you hold?: *O maskele3 perle in perle3 pure / Þat bere3 quod I þe perle of prys / Quo formed þe þy fayre figure*[60] . . . *Breue me, bry3t, quat kyn offys / Bere3 þe perle so maskelle3?*[61]
- What kind of thing is that Lamb that he married you?: *Quat kyn þyng may be þat Lambe / Þat þe wolde wedde vnto hys vyf?*[62]
- Where do you live now? Can you meet other people there?: *Haf 3e no wone3 in castel-walle / Ne maner þer 3e may mete and won?*[63]

The Dreamer's initial questions are about his relationship with the Maiden, and his next few are about the Maiden's life in paradise. A turning point comes when he asks how to receive a heavenly reward—how to be crowned in heaven—his fifth question.

Up to this point, the Dreamer is making spiritual progress. He goes from thinking about himself and his loss, to thinking about the Maiden and her divine experience, to wondering about how to be crowned in heaven as a king as she has been crowned as a queen. But then he states his objection to the "unreasonable" and, in his view, unscriptural nature of the Maiden's description of the equal reward in heaven for everyone. He has already wondered about her youthfulness in comparison to her reward and about whether her status as queen competes with the Virgin Mary. But with this strong objection, which is not paired with a humble question, the Dreamer's spiritual progress is interrupted.

The Maiden answers him with the Parable of the Workers in the Vineyard: a homily in the middle of *Pearl*, taken from the Gospel of Matthew, in which the master pays the servants the same denarius whether they began working early or late in the day.[64] She uses the parable as a basis for explaining that God can reward people as he wishes when they come to heaven, making each one a king or a queen, because all rewards come from him. God's gift of salvation, and his elevation of the status of people to royalty in heaven, is not contingent on how long or hard people work throughout the day of their life.

Yet when the Maiden finishes speaking, the Dreamer asks, "Who formed your fair figure?" Apparently, he hasn't been listening to her with attention; he has been looking at her with desire. He then makes a reference to Pygmalion and another to Aristotle,[65] but he doesn't seem to recognize that this "figure," the Maiden, is better understood as a neo-Platonic form: an ideal, in the mind of God and in heaven, whose temporary manifestation on earth has passed away but which he is encountering now in truth.

The Dreamer next questions the Maiden's office (or status) and then the identity of the Lamb. Without realizing it, the Dreamer is now asking questions about the *sponsa Christi* and her Bridegroom, Christ, which are the questions that would lead to the ultimate spiritual progress for a medieval Christian—if only these questions were sincerely about Jesus and not about the Dreamer's continued desire to possess the Maiden. His possessiveness, however, is gaining the upper hand despite the Maiden's efforts to educate him—that is, to lead him out of his spiritual disorientation.

The Dreamer's final question is about the possibility of getting closer to her, in the castle-wall or in a manor-house where she might be able to meet other people. To this, the Maiden replies, "Þat, God wyl schylde."[66] Instead of agreeing to the Dreamer's request, she tells him that she has asked the Lamb that a vision of the outside of the New Jerusalem be granted to him, though he is not permitted to cross the stream between them or enter the heavenly city.

Looking back over this conversation, it is interesting to note that the Maiden makes comments throughout it that direct the Dreamer (and thus the readers) to question where in the world he is. At the beginning of their exchange, the Dreamer expresses his belief that he has found his pearl again, his intention to go with her through the bright shining woods, and to love the Lord who has brought his bliss near. He says he will be a "joyful jeweler" once he has crossed the waves of the stream to be with her.[67] The Maiden immediately challenges the Dreamer's perception of where he is and where she is—and what he may do as a result.

Pearl, ll. 293–300.

Þou ne woste in worlde quat on dot3 mene	You do not know what in the world you mean;
Þy worde byfore þy wytte con fle	your words fly out before you use your wits.
Þou says þou trawe3 me in þis dene	You say that you believe me to be in this vale
Bycawse þou may wyth y3en me se	because you see me with your eyes.
Anoþer þou says in þys countré	Next, you say in this country
Þyself schal won wyth me ry3t here	you shall wend with me—right here.
Þe þrydde, to passe þys water fre	Third, you plan to cross this water freely.
Þat may no ioyfol jueler	But that may no joyful jeweler do.

The Maiden clarifies that his sight of her in the valley does not correspond to material reality. She echoes back to him his own words, his plan to "wend" with her and cross the water freely, but she denies him permission to fulfill his plan. His hope of reunion with her is misplaced, and crossing the water is forbidden.

The Maiden's words may prompt readers, as well as the Dreamer, to wonder where she is if not in the valley by the stream facing the Dreamer. It seems that she is actually in different places at once: her body, enclosed in a coffer, buried in the ground where the Dreamer fell asleep in the garden on earth; her spirit, not in the Earthly Paradise as the Dreamer supposes, but on a journey (like Dante's Beatrice) from the Emperyean to the utmost edge of the lunar sphere whence, on the other side of the *oceanus mare*, she speaks to the Dreamer. Later, as the Dreamer's vision-within-his-dream will show, the Maiden apparently returns to the New Jerusalem in procession with other saints following the Lamb—if, indeed, she ever actually left. Her appearance to the Dreamer is, after all, in the context of his dream-vision. The metaphysical possibilities of the Maiden's personhood, when associated with her body or spirit or an image ("fygure") in the Dreamer's dream vision, and thus the metaphysical possibilities of her location, given that her post-mortem location(s) are spiritual places, not material ones, remain open as a result of the Maiden's reframing of the Dreamer's assumptions.

As they go on talking, the Maiden makes an allusion to scripture, speaking of how all of us are members of the body of Jesus Christ.[68]

Pearl, ll. 457–62.

Of courtaysye as sayt3 Saynt Poule	Because of courtesy, as says St. Paul,
Al arn we membre3 of Jesu Kryst	all of us are members of Jesus Christ:
As heued and arme and legg and naule	just as the head and arm and leg and navel
Temen to hys body ful trwe and tryste	belong fully to his body, true and trustworthy,
Ry3t so is vch a Krysten sawle	right so is each Christian soul
A longande lym to þe Mayster of myste	belonging to him, the Master of Mystery.

Is this, then, where the Dreamer and the Maiden are—in Christ's body? As Christians, the Dreamer and the Maiden are also both part of Christ's body. This is more than a metaphor: for them and the medieval audience of *Pearl*, it is spiritual reality reinforced by taking the Eucharist, the body and blood of Christ, and by being part of the Church, which is also called the body of Christ, of which Christ is the head.[69]

Significantly, it is a spiritual reality tied to *mappaemundi*, which sometimes depicted Christ's body as part of the map. This can be seen from known examples, such as the Ebstorf Map (ca. 1300). In that map, Christ's head appears at the top (with the garden of Eden and a quintessential depiction of the Fall to the left of his head, and, notably, the Earthly Paradise is inside the

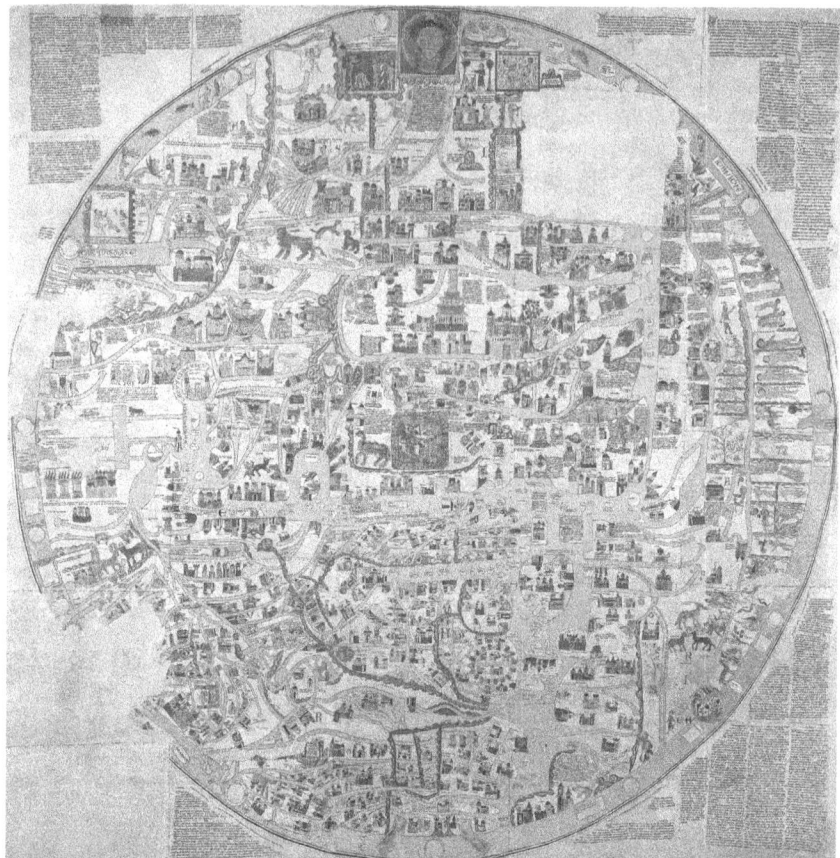

Figure 1.1. Ebstorf Map. By Unknown. https://warnke.web.leuphana.de/hyperimage/
EbsKart/index.html#O9999/. Public Domain.

oceanus mare, like the Psalter Map, not surrounded by it, like the Hereford
Mappa Mundi). Christ has a hand on either side of the map that extends into
the *oceanus mare*, and two feet that protrude at the bottom (also into the
encircling sea).

This, then, is an important context for understanding the Maiden's allu-
sion. Her allusion may not be only to scripture but also to the *mappamundi*.
While the Pauline Epistles of the New Testament do speak of the members
of that body of Christ, and names parts of it (e.g., the foot, hand, eye, ear,
head, and indirectly by reference to the sense of smell, the nose, as well as
unspecified parts called "weaker" and "less honorable"),[70] he never mentions
the navel directly. The Maiden does, and this may be in part because of the
identification of Jerusalem as the *umbilicus terrae* in prose descriptions of the

world. Indeed, the Maiden will speak extensively of the earthly Jerusalem in section XIV.[71]

As readers, we have been lingering where these two speakers, the Dreamer on one side of the stream (in the marvelous East looking over the *oceanus mare* into the Earthly Paradise) and the Maiden (appearing as if in the Earthly Paradise itself on the edge of the lunar sphere with a crystal cliff shining behind her), are talking. But when the Maiden begins retelling the story of the Crucifixion, frequently repeating the word "Jerusalem" (which is the concatenation word in the stanzas of section XIV), our gaze is drawn downward imaginatively across the face of the *mappamundi* from the Earthly Paradise at the top to the center where Jerusalem is. The movement is not only geographical but temporal. It is as if we are traveling back in time to meditate with the Maiden on the Crucifixion. For the *mappamundi* genre is not only about the depiction of places in the world, but also about the representation of the passage of time and key events in the history of the world, as the Hereford Mappa Mundi demonstrably shows.

Pearl, ll. 805–16.

In Jerusalem wat3 my lemman slayn	In Jerusalem was my Love slain
And rent on rode wyth boye3 bolde	and torn on the cross by bold boys;
Al oure bale3 to bere ful bayn	to bear all our sorrows willingly,
He toke on hymself oure care3 colde	he took on himself our cold cares.
Wyth boffete3 wat3 hys face flayn	With buffets was his face laid open
Þat wat3 so fayr on to byholde	that had been so fair to behold.
For synne he set hymself in vayn	Because of sin he made himself empty,
Þat neuer hade non hymself to wolde	Who never had none himself to will.
For vus he lette hym fly3e and folde	For us he let himself be scourged and bowed
And brede vpon a bostwys bem	and stretched upon a cruel beam.
As meke as lomp þat no playnt tolde	As meek as a lamb that utters no complaint,
For vus he swalt in Jerusalem	for us he perished in Jerusalem.

The Maiden's act of meditating on Christ's Passion is in keeping with the general practices of affective piety in the late medieval period,[72] but also with the specific practice of meditating on the *mappamundi* like an icon for what it could reveal to the devoted Christian about God's work in Creation, naturally and historically.[73] Indeed, the Hereford Mappa Mundi places Jerusalem at the center and includes above it a depiction of Christ Crucified, thus connecting historical place and historical event in its extraordinary picture of the world.

Jerusalem was often depicted at or near the center of the *mappamundi*. For medieval Christian contemplatives, the earthly Jerusalem was always spiritually central, corresponding to the heavenly Jerusalem described in Revelation and Augustine's *De Civitate Dei*. This was, in a sense, a reality found in translation: Ezekiel 38:12 calls Jerusalem "tabûr" (Hebrew for "center"), which in the Latin Vulgate is rendered "umbilicus terrae" ("navel of the lands"). The idea that the earth has an "umbilicus," just as the human body does, drew a closer connection between the macrocosm (of the world / cosmos / universe) and the microcosm (of the human body / the body of Christ / even the individual human body of the contemplative identifying with Christ).

Near the end of the conversation, the Dreamer seems to begin to accept that he is not where he thought he was, experiencing "reality" the way he originally perceived it:

Pearl, ll. 919–24.

Þou telle3 me of Jerusalem þe ryche ryalle	You tell me of Jerusalem, the royal kingdom,
Þer Dauid dere wat3 dy3t on trone	where dear David was ordained on the throne,
Bot by þyse holte3 hit con not hone	but by these woods it cannot be situated
Bot in Judee hit is þat noble note	for it is in Judea, that noble state.
As 3e ar maskele3 vnder mone	As you are spotless under the moon,
Your wone3 schulde be wythouten mote	your dwelling place should be without spot.

The Dreamer has heard the Maiden's remembrance of Jerusalem, and the death of Jesus that took place there, but he is also convinced that the woods he is in cannot be situated near it—for it is physically in Judea. Yet if the Dreamer could have entered more fully into imagining the time and place of the suffering and Crucifixion of Jesus, as the Maiden apparently intended, then he could have moved intellectually and even affectively to Jerusalem—and so been in Judea spiritually, as it were. The woods of his dream-vision might fade to a single focus on the Rood-tree on which Christ died, a vision within his vision, made possible by the Maiden's love for Jesus.

When the Dreamer notices at the conclusion of this passage that the Maiden is herself spotless "under the moon," this suggests that he may think she is in a "sub-lunar" sphere of earth as he is. But her "spotlessness"—only possible through the cleansing blood of Jesus in a realm beyond the earthly world—may suggest that she has actually moved somewhere beyond the realm of earth and the lunar sphere, even if some part of her person has temporarily returned, like Beatrice, to try to guide the Dreamer. Indeed, if we continue to follow the idea that the *Pearl*-poet created a parallel between the landscapes of his poem and the *mappamundi*, it is worth noting that in at least one extant example, the Hereford Mappa Mundi, the Latin word "MORS," meaning "death," is written in large, red letters in the four handles projecting from the map, which separates earth from direct contact with Christ enthroned in majesty above the earth at the top of the map. When this is considered alongside the Maiden's particular place beyond the stream, which may symbolize the *oceanus mare*, her position suggests that she has died; the fact that she says that the Dreamer cannot set so much as a foot in the stream without divine permission suggests that it would be his death if he did. Indeed, he awakens when he tries.

As the poem nears its end, the Maiden is clearly not as preoccupied with her location as the Dreamer is. She wants him to look through her and see beyond her. She wants him to behold a vision of the New Jerusalem, the city of heaven descending toward him, in which dwells the bleeding Lamb. She asks for this, and her request is granted.

REORIENTATION: THE *AGNUS DEI* AND THE DREAMER'S SPIRITUAL PROGRESS

Pearl began with the poem's speaker in a garden, remembering and greatly desiring the beauty of "his" pearl. Once he began to dream, it was as if he moved from the insular margins of a *mappamundi* to the wonders of the East to look across the *oceanus mare* into the Earthly Paradise. He made his way to the very edge, to the stream that separated him from the Maiden, who appeared to be standing in Paradise with the ocean surrounding her and the crystal cliff of the lunar sphere behind her. Now, as the Dreamer's vision-within-a-dream unfolds, the New Jerusalem appears to descend from the Emperyean (where medieval people believed heaven to be), through the singing spheres of the universe, to be revealed to his sight.

As *Pearl* itself makes clear, the primary context for this vision is the Apocalypse of St. John. Yet, it is worthwhile to recall that the *mappaemundi* also depict the themes of the Apocalypse.[74] *Pearl* develops an ideal picture of the New Jerusalem thoroughly, calling it a "frech fygure."[75] Within it, the Dreamer perceives the *agnus Dei*, the Lamb of God, and that representation of the Lamb is particularly iconic: an icon of the Lamb within the icon of Jerusalem, a parallel with depictions of the Apocalypse that appear in some *mappaemundi*.

In the dream-vision, the Lamb is strikingly described in terms of pearl-like qualities: "praysed perlez his wedez wasse."[76] The Dreamer cannot help but see the Lamb as a "Juelle."[77] The Dreamer is amazed by the Lamb, and his gaze narrows to focus on the bleeding wound the Lamb bears within his side:

Pearl, II. 1129–40.

Delit þe Lombe for to deuise	To devise such delight the Lamb
Wyth much meruayle in mynde went	went with much marvel in mind.
Best wat3 he blyþest and moste to pryse	Best was he, happiest, and most to praise,
Þat euer I herde of speche spent	that ever I heard of in speech that was spent.
So worþly whyt wern wede3 hys	So worthily white were his clothes—
His loke3 symple, hymself so gent	his looks simple, himself so noble.
Bot a wounde ful wyde and weete con wyse	But a very wide and wet wound could be seen
Anende hys hert þur3 hyde torente	near his heart, torn through his skin.
Of his quyte syde his blod outsprent	From his white side his blood sprayed out.
Alas, þo3t I, who did þat spyt	Alas, I thought, who did that spiteful deed?
Ani breste for bale a3t haf forbrent	Any breast for sorrow ought to have broken
Er he þerto hade had delyt	before he had any delight from that.

For perhaps the first time, the Dreamer realizes that "any breast for sorrow ought to have broken"—including his own—at the sight of the suffering Lamb of God. This is a significant shift in awareness, for he has been almost entirely preoccupied with his own feelings of sorrow over his loss of the Maiden, whom he considers "his" pearl. Yet with this shift, made possible in an instant of beholding the iconic Lamb, his spiritual progress is made possible again. Empathy for the suffering of Jesus elevates his contemplation from his own suffering.

The word "wound," which occurs in this stanza, connects with the Maiden's earlier meditation on the suffering of Jesus in the earthly Jerusalem, where she too sees the wound in Christ's side (albeit in memory) and meditates on its meaning.

Pearl, II. 649–60.

Innoghe þer wax out of þat welle	Enough waxed out of that well—
Blod and water of brode wounde	blood and water from a broad wound.
Þe blod vus bo3t fro bale of helle	The blood bought us from the suffering of hell
And delyuered vus of þe deth secounde	and delivered us from the second death.
Þe water is baptem þe soþe to telle	The water is baptism, truth to tell,
Þat fol3ed þe glayue so grymly grounde	that followed the spear so fiercely sharpened
Þat wasche3 away þe gylte3 felle	and washes away the deadly guilt
Þat Adam wyth inne deth vus drounde	with which Adam drowned us in death.
Now is þer no3t in þe worlde rounde	Now is there nothing in the round world
Bytwene vus and blysse bot þat he wythdro3	between us and bliss except what he withdrew,
And þat is restored in sely stounde	and that is restored in a blessed hour—
And þe grace of God is gret innogh	and the grace of God is great enough.

Thus, the Dreamer, without realizing it when he sees it in his vision, nevertheless has heard from the Maiden what the wound in the Lamb's side means: the water and blood that poured from it "bought us" back from hell (redemption); the water itself is "baptism" that washes away original sin with which Adam "drowned us in death" (hence, salvation). Like the pearl, the wound, then, is an image of grace and salvation.[78] Because of it, nothing in the "round world" stands "between us and bliss"—that is, between us and heaven. In a way, the Dreamer's role in the Earthly Paradise of his dream parallels that of Adam in Eden.

Like Adam, the Dreamer's focus does not remain on God. His concentration does not stay on the *agnus Dei* or the wide, wet, bleeding wound in his side.[79] As much as he marvels at the contrast between the obvious pain caused by that wound and the expression of joy on the Lamb's countenance, it does not command his unwavering attention. Instead, he looks to the procession following the Lamb, where he sees his "lyttel queen."[80] This begins to drive him mad with desire, with "luf-longyng,"[81] and he wants to cross the stream, not to be with Jesus, but to be with her "by3onde þe water."[82] Whether the Dreamer has the self-awareness to realize that this is a suicidal move is not clear. What is clear is that his desire to be with the Maiden overwhelms his desire to stay on his side of the stream. As soon as his intention hardens, and he moves in the forbidden direction, he awakens.

He awakens back in the English garden where he left his body when his spirit sprang into space: the "erber wlonk."[83] He has come full circle—back to the margins of the *mappamundi*, where England is. He knows that the decision he made within his dream-vision to attempt to cross the forbidden stream was "not at my Prynce3 paye."[84] This phrase is striking because he here speaks of "my Prince"—not "his" pearl. His awareness is of Jesus at last, and of what matters to the Lord, not to himself or the Maiden. He will go farther than this and, sighing, say, "Now al be to þat Prynces paye" ("Now let all be to that Prince's pleasure"). He finally acknowledges:

Pearl, ll. 1189–93.

To þat Prynce3 paye hade I ay bente	If to that Prince's pleasure had I always surrendered,
And 3erned no more þen wat3 me gyuen	and yearned for no more than what was given to me,
And halden me þer in trwe entent	and held myself there in true intent,
As þe perle me prayed þat wat3 so þryuen	as the Pearl, who was so thriving, asked me to,
As helde drawen to Godde3 present	as one held, drawn to God's gift,
To mo of his mysterys I hade ben dryuen	to more of his mysteries I would have been driven.

His soul has made spiritual progress. In Augustinian terms, the soul consists of *ratio*, *voluntas*, and *memoria*; in all three, the Dreamer has grown. Whereas before his *ratio* (reason) resisted God's will regarding his loss, now he recognizes what his *voluntas* (will) could have done and should do in the future: surrender. It is not necessary to yearn for more than is given. Accepting God's gift of the vision of the New Jerusalem, as the Maiden asked him to do, would have allowed him to see more of God's heavenly mysteries. It is clear, given what he can recall in his *memoria* (memory) from his dream-vision, that these mysteries are drawing the Dreamer now. His confession is completely humble, and that humility is the beginning of a deeper journey into God. He has undergone purgation and illumination, and he has stood (and perhaps still stands intellectually and affectively through the process of rehearsing his experience in the poem) very near to the possibility of divine unification with the Lamb, whom he beheld in the New Jerusalem. Like the Maiden who instructed him, he is now reoriented to the Lamb of God.

CONCLUSIONS

It appears that *Pearl*-poet was familiar with the genre of *mappamundi* and with three of its major functions in medieval England: political, educational, and contemplative. The movement of the Dreamer from the garden to the dreamscape seems to be like a journey from the insular English margins of a world map to the marvels of the East within visualizing distance of the Earthly Paradise, where the Maiden is. The poet's word choice ("ble of Inde") clearly associates the Dreamer's experience as he moves through a marvelous landscape with medieval English conceptions of India and the marvels of the East. The Dreamer's initial description of "his" pearl from the Orient, and his desire to re-obtain this beautiful treasure when he encounters her at the stream, reveals his possessive orientation.

Yet in his conversation with the Maiden, a neo-Platonic figure, his Aristotelian imagination and conception of the world are challenged. He becomes disoriented in his Edenic setting, asking questions of the Maiden's wisdom and posing challenges to her authority. These intellectual moves, though perhaps emotionally overcharged, appear to reflect the Dreamer's genuine desire to learn and to understand. Thus his disorientation becomes his chance to grow, not only intellectually and emotionally, but spiritually. He receives a true education. His disorientation becomes a chance for his soul to make progress.

When the Maiden describes the Crucifixion of Jesus in section XIV of the poem, a connection is made between Eden, and the Dreamer's Adamic role in the dreamscape, to the earthly Jerusalem, the *umbilicus terrae*, which is so often centrally placed in prose and cartographic *mappaemundi*, and to Christ's role as the Second Adam (cf. the Ebstorf Map). The Maiden is modeling affective piety and contemplative devotion.[85] Her example, like that of a saintly preacher, invites the Dreamer into a new way of being and perceiving.

When the Dreamer is granted a vision of the New Jerusalem, it is as if his eyes are being raised to the top of an eastward-oriented world map, with Christ enthroned in majesty above Eden and the whole world. But instead of a human figure of Jesus (cf. the Psalter Map and the Hereford Mappa Mundi), the Dreamer perceives a Lamb, the *angus Dei*. It is worth noting that in the scriptures, the figure of the Lamb, especially the Paschal Lamb, is repeatedly associated with Christ's Crucifixion, Resurrection, and Second Coming.[86] In his vision-within-his-dream, the Dreamer focuses in a kind of shock on the iconic image of the Lamb with a wide, wet, bleeding wound in his side, and he asks: "Who did that spiteful deed?"

Unfortunately for his spiritual progress, the Dreamer, like a contemplative in the early stages of learning to contemplate divine things, is easily distracted. He takes his eyes off of the Lamb and looks to the Maiden in glorious procession following Jesus, and so feels as if he is going mad with desire. He impulsively decides to try to cross the stream that he was told not to cross, and thus wakes. Still, the Dreamer has moved away from a "possessive" and "intellectual" approach to the world map he is in and significantly closer to a contemplative, devotional orientation. Now when he looks to the East, it is not so that he can take what he wants, but receive what he is given: the Pearl of Great Price, which stands for salvation and redemption and the kingdom of heaven, granted by Jesus, the *agnus Dei*. It is this Christ, the suffering Jesus, that the Dreamer has come to see at the conclusion of the poem as his "Lord" and his "friend."[87]

As this chapter has shown, the Dreamer begins his journey with an initial, proprietorial orientation toward "his" pearl: an attitude of willful possessiveness and a desire to control that which he would possess. This orientation parallels the political attitude evidently fostered among elite medieval nobility who owned and viewed world-maps that contained depictions of their realms and realms that might become theirs through territorial warfare. However, in his dream vision, where he is represented like a figure in a *mappamundi*, the Dreamer becomes disoriented in the intellectually and emotionally challenging conversation that he has with the Maiden who appears to him. This disorientation reflects another purpose that medieval world-maps served: education. The Dreamer does in fact learn new things in his dream-vision and discussion with the Maiden, but this is not the only kind of progress his interlocutor wants him to make.

The Maiden wants him to understand the world-map he is in spiritually. For medieval *mappaemundi* were also icons that medieval contemplatives viewed prayerfully as they sought to go deeper into the mysteries of union with the Divine. In fact, the Dreamer does make spiritual progress, becoming reoriented in the vision of the New Jerusalem and, upon reflection after awakening, to the Lamb of God whom he beheld there. This opens his eyes to a world beyond the map.

NOTES

1. I would like to express my gratitude to the provost of my university, who approved a research grant for me so that I could travel to England to study the Hereford Mappa Mundi *in situ*, and to Michael Tavinor, the Dean of Hereford Cathedral, who discussed the history of the map with me at length; to the staff of the Huntington Library (San Marino, California), who brought to me the autograph manuscript of Ranulf Higden's Latin *Polychronicon* to examine and later provided me a photographic copy of the cartographic *mappamundi* included in its prefatory pages for personal study, which I have had multiple occasions to consult; and to the staff of the British Library, especially Julian Harrison, the Curator of Pre-1600 Historical Manuscripts, who graciously agreed to take the Pearl Manuscript, BL MS Cotton Nero A.x, off display and examine it with me and discuss various interpretative possibilities. I am also thankful for the digitizers of many medieval *mappaemundi*, including the Hereford Mappa Mundi, Psalter Map, and Ebstorf Map (among others), which appear online, because digital copies have allowed me to perform further analysis of medieval world-maps by means of digital humanities methods. All these learning experiences have contributed to the development of the ideas in this academic article.

2. *Pearl*, l. 61. All Middle English quotations and translations in this chapter are taken from *Pearl: A Middle English Edition and Modern English Translation*, ed. and trans. Jane Beal (Peterborough: Broadview, 2020).

3. *Pearl*, l. 76.

4. Ann Astell, *The Song of Songs in the Middle Ages* (Ithaca, NY: Cornell University Press, 1990), chap. 5 "Mourning and Marriage in Saint Bernard's *Sermones* and *Pearl*"; Mary Raschko, *Rendering the Word: Vernacular Accounts of Parables in Late-Medieval England* (Chapel Hill: University of North Carolina, diss., 2009); Cynthia Kraman, "Body and Soul: *Pearl* and Apocalyptic Literature," in *Time and Eternity: The Medieval Discourse*, eds. Gerhard Jaritz and Gerson Moreno-Riaño (Turnhout: Brepols, 2003), 355–62; and Muriel A. Whitaker, "*Pearl* and Some Illustrated Apocalypse Manuscripts," *Viator* 12 (1981): 183–96. For a general overview of scriptural sources of the *Pearl*-poet, see Richard Newhauser, "Sources II: Scriptural and Devotional Sources," in *A Companion to the Gawain-Poet*, ed. Derek Brewer and Jonathan Gibson (Woodbridge: D.S. Brewer, 1997), 257–76. See also Lawrence Clopper, "*Pearl* and the Consolation of Scripture," *Viator* 25 (1992): 231–46.

5. Ian Bishop discusses the Mass of Holy Innocents in his book, *The Pearl in Its Setting* (Oxford: Blackwell, 1968). On the "Common of Virgins," see Santha Bhattacharji *"Pearl* and the Liturgical 'Common of Virgins,'" *Medium Aevum* 64 (1995): 37–51; on Septuagesima Sunday and Paschal liturgies, see Jane Beal, *The Signifying Power of Pearl: Medieval Literary and Cultural Contexts for the Transformation of Genre* (New York: Routledge, 2017), 55–60.

6. For a very brief introduction to the literary sources and analogues, see Marie Borroff, "The Literary Background" in *The Gawain Poet: Complete Works*, ed. Marie Borroff (New York: W.W. Norton, 2011), 118–19; for further detail, see Mark Bradshaw Busbee, "Teaching *Pearl* with Its Sources and Analogues," *Approaches to Teaching the Middle English Pearl*, ed. Jane Beal and Mark Bradshaw Busbee (New York: MLA, 2018), 139–47. On lyrical contexts and Ovidian influence specifically, see Beal, *Signifying Power of Pearl*, chap. 1 and 2. On *Pearl* and Boccaccio's *Olympia*, see W. H. Schofield, "The Source of *Pearl*," PMLA XII (1904), 203–15; and Alistair Minnis, *From Eden to Eternity: Creations of Paradise in the Later Middle Ages* (Philadelphia: University of Pennsylvania Press, 2015), chap. 3. See also Herbert Pilch, "The Middle English *Pearl*: Its Relation to the *Roman de la Rose*," *Neuphilologische Mitteilungen* 65 (1964): 427–46 or as translated by Heide Hyprath in *The Middle English Pearl: Critical Essays*, ed. John Conley (Notre Dame, IN: Notre Dame University Press, 1970), 163–84. On plague treatises and other texts about the Black Plague and their influence on the works of the *Pearl*-poet, see David K. Coley, *Death and the Pearl-Maiden: Plague, Poetry, England* (Columbus: The Ohio State University Press, 2019).

7. On contemplative (or "mystical") writings and *Pearl*, see Sister Mary Madeleva, *Pearl: A Study in Spiritual Dryness* (New York: D. Appleton and Co., 1925) and Annika Sylén Lagerholm, *Pearl and Contemplative Writing*, Lund Studies in English (Stockholm: Almqvist and Wiksell International, 2005). On visionary writings and *Pearl*, see Barbara Newman, "The Artifice of Eternity: Speaking of Heaven in Three Medieval Poems," *Religion and Literature* 37 (2005): 1–24, and Josephine Bloomfield, "Aristotelian Luminescence, Thomistic Charity: Vision, Reflection, and Self-Love in *Pearl*," *Studies in Philology* 108 (2011): 165–88. On seeing in general in the works of the *Pearl*-poet, through a feminist lens, see Sarah Stanbury, *Seeing the Gawain-Poet: Description and the Art of Perception* (Philadelphia: University of Pennsylvania, 1991) and "Feminist Masterplots: The Gaze on the Body of the *Pearl*'s Dead Girl," in *Feminist Approaches to the Body in Medieval Literature*, ed. Sarah Stanbury and Linda Lomperis (Philadelphia: University of Pennsylvania Press, 1993), 96–115. See also Anke Bernau, "Feeling Thinking: *Pearl*'s Ekphrastic Imagination," in *The Art of Vision: Ekphrasis in Medieval Literature and Culture*, ed. Andrew James Johnston, Ethan Knapp, and Margitta Rouse (Columbus: The Ohio State University Press, 2015), 100–123.

8. See James Earl, "Saint Margaret and the Pearl-Maiden," *Modern Philology* 70 (1972): 1–8; Jane Chance, "Allegory and Structure in *Pearl*: The Four Senses of the *Ars praedicandi* and Fourteenth-Century Homiletic Poetry," in *Text and Matter: New Critical Perspectives of the Pearl-Poet*, ed. Robert J. Blanch, Miriam Youngerman Miller, and Julian N. Wasserman (Troy, NY: Whiston, 1991), 31–59; Jonathan

Nicholls, *The Matter of Courtesy: Medieval Courtesy Books and the Gawain-Poet* (Woodbridge: D.S. Brewer, 1985); Ethan Campbell, *The Gawain-Poet and the Fourteenth-Century English Anticlerical Tradition* (Kalamazoo: Medieval Institute Publications/Western Michigan University, 2018); and Robert Blanch, "Precious Metal and Gem Symbolism in *Pearl*," in *Sir Gawain and Pearl: Critical Essays*, ed. Robert J. Blanch (Bloomington: Indiana University Press, 1966), 86–97.

9. On *Pearl* as cathedral, a connection first suggested by Elizabeth Salter, see Barbara Nolan, *The Gothic Visionary Perspective* (Princeton: Princeton University Press, 1977, repr. 2016) and Ann Meyer, *Medieval Allegory and the Building of the New Jerusalem* (Woodbridge: D.S. Brewer, 2003), who also observed the connection to chantry chapels. See, too, Lucy Anderson, *The Architecture of Light: Color and Cathedral as Rhetorical Ductus in the Middle English Pearl* (Diss., New York University, 2009). On *Pearl* and reliquaries, see Seeta Chagnati, *The Medieval Poetics of the Reliquary: Enshrinement, Inscription, Performance* (New York: Palgrave Macmillan, 2008).

10. Bishop made the comparison between the poem's form and a rosary, ecclesiastical chandelier, and royal crown in *Pearl in Its Setting*, 30–31; the comparison to a crown is further developed in John Bowers, *The Politics of Pearl: Court Poetry in the Age of Richard II* (London: Boydell and Brewer, 2001), 108, 234; and John Gatta, "Transformation Symbolism and the Liturgy of the Mass in *Pearl*," *Modern Philology* 71 (1974): 243–56.

11. Kevin Marti, *Body, Heart, and Text in the Pearl-Poet* (Lewiston, NY: Mellen, 1991) and A. C. Spearing, "Symbolic and Dramatic Development in *Pearl*," *Modern Philology* 60 (1962–1963): 1–12.

12. Meyer, *Medieval Allegory and the Building of the New Jerusalem*, 179. Geoffrey of Vinsauf conceived the creation of poetry as a work of building "with a circular structure in mind, a common shape, often subclassified as a 'rose' or other sort of wheel, or . . . *mappa mundi*" (qtd. in Meyer, 179).

13. See Rosalind Field, "The Heavenly Jerusalem in *Pearl*," *Modern Language Review* 81 (1986): 7–17; cf. Elizabeth Alvilda Petroff, "Landscape in *Pearl*: The Transformation of Nature," *The Chaucer Review* 16 (1981): 181–93.

14. On the poet's London connections, see Bowers, *The Politics of Pearl*. See also David Coley's chapter and, on the Yorkshire connections, Joel Fredell's chapter in this volume.

15. For discussion of Chaucer's knowledge of medieval world-maps, see Jane Beal, "Mapping Desire in Chaucer's 'To Rosemounde,' Shakespeare's 'Rape of Lucrece,' and Donne's 'A Valediction: Of Weeping,'" *Peregrinations* 6:3 (Spring 2018): 105–129. Available at: http://digital.kenyon.edu/cgi/viewcontent.cgi?article=1334 &context=perejournal.

16. These three uses of medieval *mappaemundi* are clear from a variety of studies. On the political uses, see Daniel Birkholz, *The King's Two Maps: Cartography and Culture in Thirteenth-Century England* (New York: Routledge, 2004), which analyzes the Psalter Maps. On the educational uses, see Mary Carruthers, *The Craft of Thought: Meditation, Rhetoric, and the Making of Images, 400–1200* (Cambridge: Cambridge University Press, 1998), 213–20, which discusses the *mappamundi* imagined in a

poem of Baudi of Bourgueil, "To Adela." Carruthers demonstrates that the Countess Adela commissioned the poem for the educational benefit of her politically ambitious sons, one of whom was William the Conqueror. On this poem, see also Monika Otter, "Baudri of Bourgueil, 'To Countess Adela,'" *The Journal of Medieval Latin: A Publication of the North American Association of Medieval Latin* 1 (2001), 60 (of pp. 60–141). For the standard Latin edition, see *Baldricus Burgulianus [Baudri of Bourgueil], Carmina*, ed. Karlheinz Hilbert (Heidelberg: Carl Winter, 1979). For a Latin and French dual-language, edition-translation, see Jean-Yves Tilliette, ed. and tr., "Rhétorique et poétique chez les poètes latins médiévaux: Recherches sur Baudrí de Bourgueil" (Univ. de Paris IV, diss., 1991). On the contemplative uses, see J. B. Harley and David Woodard, *The History of Cartography, Vol. 1: Cartography in Pre-historic, Ancient, and Medieval Europe and the Mediterranean* (Chicago: University of Chicago Press, 1987), esp. chap. 18, "Medieval *Mappaemundi*," and in Evelyn Edson, *Mapping Time and Space: How Medieval Mapmakers Viewed Their World* (London: British Library, 1999). See also Hugh of St. Victor, "A Little Book about Constructing Noah's Ark," tr. Jessica Weiss, in Mary Carruthers and Jan Ziolkowski, eds., *The Medieval Craft of Memory: An Anthology of Texts and Pictures* (Philadelphia: University of Pennsylvania Press, 2002), 67ff.

17. This chapter does not seek to prove that the *Pearl*-poet knew a specific *mappamundi*, but rather suggests that he was generally familiar with the genre and uses of it. Of the extant examples of cartographic maps that he could have known are the large Hereford Map that hung in Hereford Cathedral, the T-O maps included in manuscripts of the *Etymologies* of Isidore of Seville, and the much more complex world-maps included in manuscripts of Ranulf Higden's fourteenth-century Latin *Polychronicon*, all of which were present in the West Midlands of England where he was most likely from. Many more world-maps existed that are no longer extant. More significantly, the poet might have been familiar with ideas that we know circulated, from the "Little Book of Constructing Noah's Ark" of Hugh of St. Victor and the *Poetria nova* of Geoffrey of Vinsauf, about the contemplative and poetic practices *mappamundi* inspired. This chapter suggests he participated in these practices and that they informed his writing of *Pearl*. Certainly, the concept of enthroning Christ over the *mappamundi*, as pictured in the Psalter Map, was likely familiar to him from contemplative practices or manuscript traditions as well as ecclesiastical and liturgical ones and scriptural interpretation.

18. *Pearl*, ll. 3, 82, 254.

19. *Pearl*, l. 76.

20. The Maiden's discourse on the Parable of the Workers in the Vineyard has been compared to a sermon by Jane Chance, J. J. Anderson, and Davis Aers. See Chance, "Allegory and Structure in Pearl: The Four Senses of the *Ars Praedicandi* and Fourteenth-Century Homiletic Poetry," in *Text and Matter: New Critical Perspectives of the Pearl-Poet*, ed. Robert J. Blanch, Miriam Youngerman Miller, and Julian N. Wasserman (Troy, NY: Whitson, 1991), 31–60. J. J. Anderson, *Language and Imagination in the Gawain-poems* (Manchester: Manchester University Press, 2005), 31, 35; and David Aers, "The Self Mourning: Reflections on *Pearl*," *Speculum* 68, no. 1 (1993): 54–73.

21. *Pearl*, l. 3.

22. *Pearl*, l. 10.

23. *Pearl*, l. 11.

24. Charlotte Gross, "Courtly Language in *Pearl*," in *Text and Matter: New Critical Perspectives of the Pearl-Poet*, ed. Robert Blanch, Mirriam Youngerman Miller, and Julian Wasserman (Troy, NY: Whiston, 1991), 79–91; Jane Beal, "The Pearl-Maiden's Two Lovers," *Studies in Philology* 100 (2003): 1–21.

25. On courtly love, see C. S. Lewis, *The Allegory of Love: A Study of Medieval Tradition* (Oxford: Oxford at the Clarendon Press, 1936), which remains an insightful study. See also C. Stephen Jaeger, *Ennobling Love: In Search of a Lost Sensibility* (Philadelphia: University of Pennsylvania Press, 1999).

26. *Pearl*, l. 39.

27. The "high season" mentioned by the poet apparently alludes to three major liturgical days in the Church celebrating Lammas (August 1), the Transfiguration of Christ (August 6), and the Assumption of the Virgin (August 15).

28. *Pearl*, l. 43.

29. *Pearl*, l. 44. Gillyflowers were associated with the tears of the Virgin Mary over the Passion of Jesus; ginger was common in England by the eleventh century (imported from India); gromwell bears a pearl-like, white fruit. Peony is named for Paeon, a Greek physician and the student of Aesculepius, the Greek god of medicine; Christians in the Middle Ages associated the flower with healing. Thus these flowers are not only common plants in England, but thematically relevant to *Pearl*, as we would expect.

30. For just a few examples, see the Psalter Map, the Ebstorf Map, and the map of the world in the Huntington Library autograph manuscript of Ranulf Higden's Latin *Polychronicon*. Many of these images are reproduced online; to view them in color, search by their name. See especially http://cartographic-images.net/Cartographic _Images/232_Hidgen.html. The image of Adam and Eve in the Garden of Eden occurs repeatedly in the eastern-oriented, cartographic *mappaemundi* associated with the *Polychronicon*.

31. *Pearl*, l. 61.

32. *Pearl*, ll. 62–63.

33. *Pearl*, l. 65. "Worlde" is a key word that the poet apparently employs to enable his readers to imagine the Dreamer as if he is in a *mappamundi*. It occurs ten times: see lines 65, 293, 424, 476, 537, 579, 657, 743, 761, and 824.

34. *Pearl*, l. 76. On the rhetorical significance of the color blue in *Pearl*, see Mary Carruthers, "Invention, Mnemonics, and Stylistic Ornament in *Psychomachia* and *Pearl*," in *The Endless Knot: Essays on Old and Middle English in Honor of Marie Borroff*, ed. M. Teresa Tavormina and R. F. Yeager (Cambridge: D.S. Brewer, 1995), 201–14.

35. *Pearl*, l. 82.

36. The marvelous East is evoked in medieval English chronicles contemporaneous with the life of the *Pearl*-poet, such as Ranulf Higden's Latin *Polychronicon*, later translated into Middle English by John Trevisa; the *Polychronicon* draws on earlier traditions of representation of India found in the *Etymologies* of Isidore of Seville and

elsewhere. To put medieval English perceptions of the East, and particularly India, in broader context, with appropriate critique, see Thomas Hahn, "The Indian Tradition in Western Medieval Intellectual History," *Viator* 9 (1978): 213–34; Jacques Le Goff, "The Marvelous in the Medieval West," in *The Medieval Imagination*, trans. Arthur Goldhammer (Chicago: University of Chicago Press, 1985), 27–44; and Edward Said, *Orientalism* (New York: Vintage Books, 1979) and his "Orientalism Reconsidered," in *Europe and Its Others*, ed. Francis Barker, Peter Hulme, Margaret Iversen, and Diana Loxley (Colchester: University of Essex, 1985), 14–27. See also Brenda Deen Schildegen, *Dante and the Orient* (Champaign: University of Illinois Press, 2002). Cf. Michelle Karnes, *Medieval Marvels and Fictions in the Latin West and Islamic World* (Chicago: University of Chicago, 2022).

37. *Pearl*, l. 118.

38. In order to comprehend the broad influence of the idea of the "harmony of the spheres," and to show its commonplace nature in the history of ideas, it is useful to consult Joscelyn Godwin, ed., *The Harmony of the Spheres: The Pythagorean Tradition in Music* (Rochester, VT: Inner Traditions, 1992), esp. parts I and II on the classical and medieval periods respectively. Note that the lunar sphere is not depicted on medieval *mappaemundi*, but it was part of the medieval, Copernican conception of the cosmos. In the *Purgatorio*, Dante places the "earthly paradise," which he finds at the top of the purgatorial mountain, *above* the sublunary sphere, and thus, beyond change.

39. *Pearl*, l. 248.

40. The Dreamer's perception of her presence near him in the Earthly Paradise will be called into question by the Maiden.

41. *Pearl*, l. 159.

42. *Pearl*, l. 241.

43. *Pearl*, l. 221. On the Maiden's clothing, see Kimberly Jack's chapter in this volume.

44. *Pearl*, l. 242.

45. On the Maiden as a figure of Wisdom, see Barbara Newman, "The Artifice of Eternity: Speaking of Heaven in Three Medieval Poems," *Religion and Literature* 37, no. 1 (2005): 1–24.

46. *Pearl*, l. 272.

47. *Pearl*, l. 746.

48. Matt. 13:45–46.

49. *Pearl*, l. 735.

50. Worth considering alongside this point is the first illustration of *Pearl* in Cotton Nero A.x. As Kimberly Jack and Jane Beal have observed, the illustrator depicts the Dreamer as a scholar, with his blue scholar's hood sliding off of his head when his "spirit springs into space." See Jane Beal, "Illustrations," *Medieval Pearl*, available at https://medievalpearl.wordpress.com/illustrations/. The first illustration is the nearest contemporary medieval "commentary" that we have on the poem, and as such, it is notable that the illustrator depicts the Dreamer as a scholar. The Dreamer wears no scholar's hood in the next three illustrations, suggesting he lost it when he entered his dream, which may be a comment on how the Dreamer's intellectual, even Aristotelean approach (cf. l. 751) to his loss is going to shift as he enters a realm of spiritual

revelation. See also 1.1091 of the poem, in which the Dreamer refers to "clerkez," a group to which he may belong.

51. Many studies of *Pearl* have engaged in the argument over whether the Dreamer is consoled emotionally by the end of the poem. Most influential in this debate has been Nicolas Watson in his chapter, "The *Gawain*-poet as Vernacular Theologian," in *A Companion to the Gawain-Poet*, eds. Derek Brewer and Jonathan Gibson (Woodbridge: D.S. Brewer, 1999), 293–313, where he expresses that he does not believe the Dreamer is consoled at the poem's conclusion. Yet it does not appear that the Maiden is trying to make the Dreamer feel better. Rather, she is trying to remind him of things he knows are true within their shared Christian worldview. Her approach seems to be that if the Dreamer will return to believing what is true, then he will make spiritual progress, and his suffering will contribute to his growth in faith.

52. On types of debate, especially the unequal debate, see W. A. Davenport, "Patterns in Middle English Dialogues," in *Medieval English Studies Presented to George Kane*, ed. E. D. Kennedy, Ronald Waldron, and Joseph S. Wittig (Cambridge: Brewer, 1988), 127–45 and Thomas L. Reed Jr., *Middle English Debate Poetry and the Aesthetics of Irresolution* (Columbia: University of Missouri Press, 1990). For a broader context, see also Catherine Brown, *Contrary Things: Exegesis, Dialectic, and the Poetics of Didacticism* (Stanford, CA: Stanford University Press, 1998); and Georgiana Donavin, Carol Poster, and Richard Utz, eds., *Medieval Forms of Argument: Disputation and Debate*, Disputatio 5 (Eugene, OR: Wipf and Stock, 2002). This mode has early examples preserved in Socratic dialogues.

53. *Pearl*, l. 242.

54. *Pearl*, ll. 325–26.

55. *Pearl*, ll. 327–29.

56. *Pearl*, ll. 390–92.

57. *Pearl*, ll. 421–24.

58. *Pearl*, ll. 475–80.

59. *Pearl*, ll. 590–92.

60. *Pearl*, ll. 745–47.

61. *Pearl*, ll. 755–56.

62. *Pearl*, ll. 771–72.

63. *Pearl*, ll. 917–18.

64. Matt. 20:1–16.

65. *Pearl*, ll. 750–51.

66. *Pearl*, l. 965.

67. *Pearl*, ll. 282–88.

68. Cf. Romans 12:4–5 and 1 Corinthians 12:12–31.

69. On the Church as the body of Christ, as Christ as the head of the Church, see several verses in the Pauline epistles: Eph. 1:22, Eph. 4:2, Eph. 5:23, Col. 1:18 ("he is also head of the body, the church"), Col. 2:10.

70. 1 Cor. 12:12–27. "Now you are the body of Christ, and each one of you is a part of it." (v. 27).

71. For a complete explanation of section XIV, see Jane Beal, "The Jerusalem Lamb of *Pearl*," *Glossator* 9 (2015): 262–83.

72. On such piety in the Middle Ages, see Sarah McNamer, *Affective Meditation and the Invention of Medieval Compassion* (Philadelphia: University of Pennsylvania Press, 2009).

73. Consider the interior, memorial, and devotional practices of the Victories, who, following the advice of Hugh of St. Victor, would recreate *mappaemundi* within images of Noah's Ark. See Hugh of St. Victor, "The Little Book on Constructing Noah's Ark."

74. On this, see Alessandro Scafi, "Mapping the World: The Apocalypse in Medieval Cartography," *Literature and Theology* 26, no. 4 (2012): 400–416. As he sums up, after a survey of many maps: "Medieval cartographic materials disclose in their portrait of the world a clear emphasis on the coming End of the World: mankind has reached the western limits of the earth; the tribes of Gog and Magog, enclosed by Alexander the Great, are impatient to invade the inhabited world; Enoch and Elijah are waiting patiently in paradise, ready to face death and the Last Things. The angels warn us that the Last Judgment is near; Christ is coming to judge the world. The visual imagery offered by cartographic material sheds light on the complex conception of time and space that developed in medieval Christianity and that emerges from contemporary theological texts" (1).

75. *Pearl*, l. 1185. Note that the term "fygure" was previously applied to the Maiden, and in both her case and that of the New Jerusalem in *Pearl*, the word seems to connect to neo-Platonic idealism.

76. *Pearl*, l. 1112. On the pearlescent qualities of the Lamb, see A. C. Spearing, "Symbolic and Dramatic Development in *Pearl*," *Modern Philology* 60 (1962–63): 1–12 and Hugh White, "Blood in *Pearl*," *The Review of English Studies* 38 (1987): 1–13.

77. *Pearl*, l. 1124.

78. It is not insignificant that some medieval, iconic images depicted the building of the Church within the open wound of Christ's side.

79. *Pearl*, l. 1135.

80. *Pearl*, l. 1147.

81. *Pearl*, l. 1152.

82. *Pearl*, l. 1156.

83. *Pearl*, l. 1171.

84. *Pearl*, l. 1164.

85. For discussion, see Jane Beal, *Signifying Power of Pearl*, chap. 4.

86. For a very brief introduction to the symbolism of the Lamb in the medieval period, see Beryl Rowland, *Animals with Human Faces: A Guide to Animal Symbolism* (Knoxville: University of Tennessee Press, 1973), 114–15. As Rowland observes, "There were three main kinds of illustration: the Lamb of the Crucifixion, bearing the Cross and usually depicted as having blood flowing from its breast into a chalice; the Lamb of the Resurrection, carrying a triumphant cross-emblazoned banner; the Apocalyptic Lamb, usually characterized by the Book Sealed with the Seven Seals, symbolic of Christ as the judge at the end of the world" (114).

87. *Pearl*, l. 1204.

BIBLIOGRAPHY

Aers, David. "The Self Mourning: Reflections on *Pearl.*" *Speculum* 68, no. 1 (1993): 54–73.

Anderson, J. J. *Language and Imagination in the Gawain-poems.* Manchester: Manchester University Press, 2005.

Anderson, Lucy. *The Architecture of Light: Color and Cathedral as Rhetorical Ductus in the Middle English Pearl.* Diss., New York University, 2009.

Astell, Ann. *The Song of Songs in the Middle Ages.* Ithaca, NY: Cornell University Press, 1990.

Beal, Jane. *Becoming the Pearl-Poet: Perceptions, Connections, Receptions.* New York: Lexington Books, 2022.

———. ed. and trans. *Pearl: A Middle English Edition and Modern English Translation.* Peterborough: Broadview, 2020.

———. "Mapping Desire in Chaucer's 'To Rosemounde,' Shakespeare's 'Rape of Lucrece,' and Donne's 'A Valediction: Of Weeping.'" *Peregrinations* 6, no. 3 (Spring 2018): 105–29.

———. *The Signifying Power of Pearl: Medieval Literary and Cultural Contexts for the Transformation of Genre.* New York: Routledge, 2017.

———. "The Jerusalem Lamb of *Pearl.*" *Glossator* 9 (2015): 262–83.

———. "The Pearl-Maiden's Two Lovers." *Studies in Philology* 100 (2003): 1–21.

———. "Illustrations." *Medieval Pearl*, available at https://medievalpearl.wordpress.com/illustrations/.

Bernau, Anke. "Feeling Thinking: *Pearl*'s Ekphrastic Imagination." In *The Art of Vision: Ekphrasis in Medieval Literature and Culture*, ed. Andrew James Johnston, Ethan Knapp, and Margitta Rouse, 100–123. Columbus: Ohio State University Press, 2015.

Bhattacharji, Santha. "*Pearl* and the Liturgical 'Common of Virgins.'" *Medium Aevum* 64 (1995): 37–51.

Birkholz, Daniel. *The King's Two Maps: Cartography and Culture in Thirteenth-Century England.* New York: Routledge, 2004.

Bishop, Ian. *The Pearl in its Setting.* Oxford: Blackwell, 1968.

Blanch, Robert. "Precious Metal and Gem Symbolism in *Pearl.*" In *Sir Gawain and Pearl: Critical Essays*, ed. Robert J. Blanch, 86–97. Bloomington: Indiana University Press, 1966.

Bloomfield, Josephine. "Aristotelian Luminescence, Thomistic Charity: Vision, Reflection, and Self-Love in *Pearl.*" *Studies in Philology* 108 (2011): 165–88.

Borroff, Marie. "The Literary Background." In *The Gawain Poet: Complete Works*, ed. Marie Borroff, 118–19. New York: W.W. Norton, 2011.

Bowers, John. *The Politics of Pearl: Court Poetry in the Age of Richard II.* London: Boydell and Brewer, 2001.

Busbee, Mark Bradshaw. "Teaching *Pearl* with its Sources and Analogues." *Approaches to Teaching the Middle English Pearl*, ed. Jane Beal and Mark Bradshaw Busbee, 139–47. New York: MLA, 2018.

Brown, Catherine. *Contrary Things: Exegesis, Dialectic, and the Poetics of Didacticism.* Stanford, CA: Stanford University Press, 1998.

Campbell, Ethan. *The Gawain-Poet and the Fourteenth-Century English Anticlerical Tradition.* Kalamazoo: Medieval Institute Publications of Western Michigan University, 2018.

Carruthers, Mary. *The Craft of Thought: Meditation, Rhetoric, and the Making of Images, 400–1200.* Cambridge: Cambridge University Press, 1998.

————. "Invention, Mnemonics, and Stylistic Ornament in *Psychomachia* and *Pearl.*" In *The Endless Knot: Essays on Old and Middle English in Honor of Marie Borroff*, ed. M. Teresa Tavormina and R. F. Yeager, 201–14. Cambridge: D.S. Brewer, 1995.

Chagnati, Seeta. *The Medieval Poetics of the Reliquary: Enshrinement, Inscription, Performance.* New York: Palgrave Macmillan, 2008.

Chance, Jane. "Allegory and Structure in *Pearl*: The Four Senses of the *Ars praedicandi* and Fourteenth-Century Homiletic Poetry." in *Text and Matter: New Critical Perspectives of the Pearl-Poet*, ed. Robert J. Blanch, Miriam Youngerman Miller, and Julian N. Wasserman, 31–59. Troy, NY: Whiston, 1991.

Clopper, Lawrence. "*Pearl* and the Consolation of Scripture," *Viator* 25 (1992): 231–246.

Coley, David K. *Death and the Pearl-Maiden: Plague, Poetry, England.* Columbus: The Ohio State University Press, 2019.

Davenport, W. A. "Patterns in Middle English Dialogues." In *Medieval English Studies Presented to George Kane*, ed. E. D. Kennedy, Ronald Waldron, and Joseph S. Wittig, 127–45. Cambridge: Brewer, 1988.

Donavin, Georgiana, Carol Poster, and Richard Utz, eds. *Medieval Forms of Argument: Disputation and Debate*, Disputatio 5. Eugene, OR: Wipf and Stock, 2002.

Earl, James. "Saint Margaret and the Pearl-Maiden." *Modern Philology* 70 (1972): 1–8.

Edson, Evelyn. *Mapping Time and Space: How Medieval Mapmakers Viewed Their World.* London: British Library, 1999.

Field, Rosalind. "The Heavenly Jerusalem in *Pearl.*" *Modern Language Review* 81 (1986): 7–17.

Gatta, John. "Transformation Symbolism and the Liturgy of the Mass in *Pearl.*" *Modern Philology* 71 (1974): 243–56.

Godwin, Joscelyn, ed. *The Harmony of the Spheres: The Pythagorean Tradition in Music.* Rochester, VT: Inner Traditions, 1992.

Gross, Charlotte. "Courtly Language in *Pearl.*" In *Text and Matter: New Critical Perspectives of the Pearl-poet*, ed. Robert Blanch, Mirriam Youngerman Miller, and Julian Wasserman, 79–91. Troy, NY: Whiston, 1991.

Hahn, Thomas. "The Indian Tradition in Western Medieval Intellectual History." *Viator* 9 (1978): 213–34.

Harley, J. B., and David Woodard. *The History of Cartography, Vol. 1: Cartography in Prehistoric, Ancient, and Medieval Europe and the Mediterranean.* Chicago: University of Chicago Press, 1987.

Hilbert, Karlheinz, ed. *Baldricus Burgulianus [Baudri of Bourgueil], Carmina.* Heidelberg: Carl Winter, 1979.

Hugh of St. Victor. "A Little Book about Constructing Noah's Ark." Trans. Jessica Weiss, in Mary Carruthers and Jan Ziolkowski, eds. *The Medieval Craft of Memory: An Anthology of Texts and Pictures.* Philadelphia: University of Pennsylvania Press, 2002.

Jaeger, C. Stephen. *Ennobling Love: In Search of a Lost Sensibility.* Philadelphia: University of Pennsylvania Press, 1999.

Karnes, Michelle. *Medieval Marvels and Fictions in the Latin West and Islamic World.* Chicago: University of Chicago, 2022.

Kraman, Cynthia. "Body and Soul: *Pearl* and Apocalyptic Literature." In *Time and Eternity: The Medieval Discourse*, eds. Gerhard Jaritz and Gerson Moreno-Riaño, 355–62. Turnhout: Brepols, 2003.

Lagerholm, Annika Sylén. *Pearl and Contemplative Writing.* Lund Studies in English. Stockholm: Almqvist and Wiksell International, 2005.

Le Goff, Jacques. "The Marvelous in the Medieval West." In *The Medieval Imagination*, trans. Arthur Goldhammer, 27–44. Chicago: University of Chicago Press, 1985.

———. "Orientalism Reconsidered." In *Europe and Its Others*, ed. Francis Barker, Peter Hulme, Margaret Iversen, and Diana Loxley, 14–27. Colchester: University of Essex, 1985.

Lewis, C. S. *The Allegory of Love: A Study of Medieval Tradition.* Oxford: Oxford at the Clarendon Press, 1936.

Madeleva, Sister Mary. *Pearl: A Study in Spiritual Dryness.* New York: D. Appleton and Co., 1925.

Marti, Kevin. *Body, Heart, and Text in the Pearl-Poet.* Lewiston, NY: Edwin Mellen Press, 1991.

McNamer, Sarah. *Affective Meditation and the Invention of Medieval Compassion.* Philadelphia: University of Pennsylvania Press, 2009.

Meyer, Ann. *Medieval Allegory and the Building of the New Jerusalem.* Woodbridge: D.S. Brewer, 2003.

Minnis, Alistair. *From Eden to Eternity: Creations of Paradise in the Later Middle Ages.* Philadelphia: University of Pennsylvania Press, 2015.

Newhauser, Richard. "Sources II: Scriptural and Devotional Sources." In *A Companion to the Gawain-Poet*, ed. Derek Brewer and Jonathan Gibson, 257–76. Woodbridge: D.S. Brewer, 1997.

Newman, Barbara. "The Artifice of Eternity: Speaking of Heaven in Three Medieval Poems." *Religion and Literature* 37 (2005): 1–24.

Nicholls, Jonathan. *The Matter of Courtesy: Medieval Courtesy Books and the Gawain-Poet.* Woodbridge: D.S. Brewer, 1985.

Nolan, Barbara. *The Gothic Visionary Perspective.* Princeton, NJ: Princeton University Press, 1977, repr. 2016.

Otter, Monika. "Baudri of Bourgueil, 'To Countess Adela.'" *Journal of Medieval Latin: A Publication of the North American Association of Medieval Latin* 1 (2001): 60–141.

Petroff, Elizabeth Alvilda. "Landscape in *Pearl*: The Transformation of Nature." *The Chaucer Review* 16 (1981): 181–93.

Pilch, Herbert. Trans. Heide Hyprath. "Das mittelenglische Perlengedicht: Sein Verhältnis zum Rosenroman." *Neuphilologische Mitteilungen* 65 (1964): 427–46; repr. as "The Middle English *Pearl*: Its Relation to the *Roman de la Rose*." In *The Middle English Pearl: Critical Essays*, ed. John Conley, 163–84. Notre Dame: Notre Dame University Press, 1970.

Raschko, Mary. *Rendering the Word: Vernacular Accounts of Parables in Late-Medieval England*. Diss., University of North Carolina, 2009.

Reed, Thomas L., Jr. *Middle English Debate Poetry and the Aesthetics of Irresolution*. Columbia: University of Missouri Press, 1990.

Rowland, Beryl. *Animals with Human Faces: A Guide to Animal Symbolism*. Knoxville: University of Tennessee Press, 1973.

Scafi, Alessandro. "Mapping the World: The Apocalypse in Medieval Cartography." *Literature and Theology* 26, no. 4 (2012): 400–416.

Schildegen, Brenda Deen. *Dante and the Orient*. Champaign: University of Illinois Press, 2002.

Schofield, W. H. "The Source of *Pearl*." PMLA XII (1904): 203–15.

Spearing, A. C. "Symbolic and Dramatic Development in *Pearl*." *Modern Philology* 60 (1962–1963): 1–12.

Stanbury, Sarah. *Seeing the Gawain-Poet: Description and the Art of Perception*. Philadelphia: University of Pennsylvania, 1991.

———. "Feminist Masterplots: The Gaze on the Body of the *Pearl's* Dead Girl." In *Feminist Approaches to the Body in Medieval Literature*, ed. Sarah Stanbury and Linda Lomperis, 96–115. Philadelphia: University of Pennsylvania Press, 1993.

Tilliette, Jean-Yves, ed. and trans. "Rhétorique et poétique chez les poètes latins médiévaux: Recherches sur Baudrí de Bourgueil." Diss., Univ. de Paris IV, 1991.

Watson, Nicolas. "The *Gawain*-poet as Vernacular Theologian." In *A Companion to the Gawain-Poet*, eds. Derek Brewer and Jonathan Gibson, 293–313. Woodbridge: D.S. Brewer, 1999.

Whitaker, Muriel A. "*Pearl* and Some Illustrated Apocalypse Manuscripts." *Viator* 12 (1981): 183–96.

White, Hugh. "Blood in *Pearl*." *The Review of English Studies* 38 (1987): 1–13.

Chapter Two

Temperance and the Evolution of Concupiscible Vice in *Cleanness*

Corey Owen

In his recent survey, "Moral Philosophy and Wisdom Literature," Charles F. Briggs discusses the frequent appearance of the cardinal virtues in Langland, Gower, Chaucer, Hoccleve, and Lydgate.[1] The *Pearl*-poet is conspicuously absent from this list, yet critics such as R. J. Spendal, Elizabeth Kirk, and Theodore Silverstein have found much evidence of the influence of the cardinal virtues on the poet's craft.[2] Nevertheless, little attention has been given to the influence of the virtues on *Cleanness*, perhaps, in part, because *clannesse* seems to exceed the boundaries of *temperantia*.[3] Cecilia Hatt, for example, argues that "[cleanness] is not a virtue like mercy or temperance that can be described in terms of its component parts and the occasions of temptation to be avoided; even to call 'cleanness' a disposition is to over-reify it."[4] While Hatt's nuanced analysis provides valuable insight into the complexity of the concept, a taxonomic approach to the poem nevertheless clarifies the poet's rationale for his choice of narratives to illustrate *clannesse*.[5]

The poem's focus on the desire for sex, sumptuous food, and sensory delights—that is, on concupiscence in general—suggests the influence of *temperantia*, the virtue that governs the appetitive, or concupiscible, faculty of the soul. In each of the three main scriptural passages, an excessive appetite angers God: the prelude to the Flood emphasizes lust, the destruction of Sodom and Gomorrah emphasizes lust and gluttony, and Belshazzar's Feast suggests the first two vices and emphasizes the desire for excessive visual delights, all of which, collectively, seem to drive Belshazzar to the sins of idolatry and desecration.[6] While the narratives focus on particular concupiscible vices, the poet also investigates the etiology of such sins, tracing their birth in the intellectual faculty through the fall of Lucifer and his angels, and the subsequent fall of Adam and Eve, and exploring their contribution to irascible vices and injustice among created beings and, ultimately, toward the Creator. Thus, while the poet's presentation of the three narratives consistently describes concupiscible vices, he carefully examines the birth of such vices in the Fall, and the potential telos of such vices in idolatry and desecration—that is, the worship and debasement of physicality; he thereby dramatizes the genesis and evolution of concupiscible sin. While the poet characterizes illicit sexuality as the source of God's destructive anger in the first two narratives, he ultimately explores such vices not in isolation, but as manifestations of the interconnected nature of the faculties of the soul. One of the dangers of such a taxonomic approach to the *Pearl*-poet is the reduction of poetry to moral philosophy. I do not wish to insist that the poet's conceptualization of virtues and vices is consistently systematic; rather, I hope to show how he has used these taxonomies—which are early attempts at psychology—to create a work of considerable moral and aesthetic complexity.

TEMPERANCE AND THE CONCUPISCIBLE FACULTY

It would be impossible to find a single source for the poet's knowledge of the cardinal virtues, in part because they were commonplace in a variety of genres. Nevertheless, certain recurring themes tend to appear in the classical exemplars and the medieval texts they influence. In general, temperance is described as the virtue that protects the mean or, more specifically, as the virtue that purifies desire, an emotion that characterizes the activity of the concupiscible faculty of the soul.[7] Scholastic philosophers, influenced by the writings of Cicero and Macrobius, relate varying species of the virtue, yet others seem to have recognized the potential for repetition in such an extensive list.[8] For instance, Thomas of Chobham identifies only two species of temperance: continence, which restrains lust, and abstinence, which restrains gluttony.[9] In his immensely popular and influential treatise on the virtues, William Peraldus lists Cicero's *continentia*, *clementia*, and *modestia* and adds *sobrietas*, which governs taste, *continentia*, which regulates touch, as well as *temperantia secundum visum*, *auditum*, and *olfactum*.[10] While affirming that sex and food are the primary objects of temperance, Aquinas, in his *Summa theologiae*, also includes all other sensory pleasures as secondary objects of temperance.[11] At the level of vernacular theology, the anonymous author of the *Book of Vices and Virtues* refers broadly to temperance as the virtue that moderates the potential harm caused by inappropriate or unlawful sensuality: "Attemperaunce [kepeþ a man þat] he ne be bi no wikked loue fordo no broken."[12] In short, temperance governs the concupiscible appetites, that is, the desires for food, sex, and finery, and such desires unite the three scriptural narratives in *Cleanness*.[13]

The main virtue the poet identifies, of course, is *clannesse*, which refers literally to the state of being without spot or blemish,[14] like that of the maiden that the poet describes in line 12 of *Pearl*. However, the virtue also suggests the state of being unobstructed, cleared of restriction. Both of these definitions also suggest the second denotation of cleanness: moral righteousness, purity, or innocence.[15] Vices are obstructions that inhibit the soul's ability to perceive God. In the virtues and vices tradition in particular, cleanness refers specifically to sexual restraint and inexperience. For instance, the anonymous author of the *Summa virtutum de remediis anime* includes cleanness, *munditia*, under a discussion on continence (*continentia*),[16] a virtue that often appears in discussions of temperance, and the *Book of Vices and Virtues* asserts that clergy members must set an example of "alle clennesses" to help the laity avoid lechery.[17] While, as critics have often claimed, the poet's conception of the virtue is more complex than that of the virtue taxonomists, it is difficult to imagine that the poet did not have the conventional understanding of the virtue in mind when he chose the term, even if his application of the virtue ultimately transcends what he regards as sexual vice. First, cleanness, *munditia*, appears often in taxonomies of virtue, and the poet directly refers to his reading of moral treatises; with respect to God's displeasure about sin, he states, "I haue herkned and herde of mony hy3e clerkez, / And als in resounez of ry3t red hit myseluen" ("I have listened to and heard from many excellent scholars, and also read it myself in discourses of morality," 193–94).[18] Second, the instances of *fylþe* he describes primarily suggest concupiscible vices, the sorts of vices that virtues in the conventional taxonomies of *temperantia* typically remedy.

While the poet at times focuses on sexual transgressions, the gradual broadening of the range of the concept of cleanness in the three main narratives the poet refers to in the conclusion, the *þrynne wyses* (1805), or three ways (the Flood, the Destruction of Sodom and Gomorrah, and Belshazzar's Feast), points more generally to the animating presence of temperance, since the narratives focus on the implications of concupiscible vice. The virtue *munditia*, cleanness, refers specifically to sexual purity and is closely related to continence. However, the poet of *Cleanness* ultimately does not apply the concept of the virtue only to sexual morality, even though the first two scriptural passages suggest that sexual immorality in particular enrages God. As Ad Putter contends, the poet instead illustrates the virtue by gradually broadening both its range of meanings, and those associated with *fylþe*.[19] While concupiscible vice, and sexual vice in particular, is the source of God's destructive anger, the poet places such vice in a context of other vices—both those that contribute to concupiscible vice—and sexual vice in particular—and those that potentially proceed from such vices. While, at least in the first two scriptural narratives, the poet focuses on what he regards as unnatural sexual activity, that such activity appears consistently in the context of other concupiscible and irascible vices in all three narratives implies correlation—if not causation—among the vices of the intellectual, concupiscible, and irascible faculties.

THE ROLE OF TEMPERANCE IN HUMAN ACTION

While the poet focuses his investigation of sin on the vices that originate in the concupiscible faculty of the soul, which is perfected through temperance, his representation of vice naturally includes the failure of the irascible and rational faculties, which are perfected through fortitude and prudence respectively, as well as the will, which is perfected through justice, since each faculty has a role in human action.[20] While taxonomists organize the virtues variously, depending on what aspect of the virtues they wish to emphasize, William Peraldus's ordering reflects the role of the virtues in the movement from thought to action:[21] "Prudence chooses what must be done" ("Prudentia eligit quod agendum est");[22] "temperance and fortitude dispose [the soul] to, and prepare it for, justice, just as desire, which temperance restrains, and fear, which fortitude resists, obstruct justice from its duty" ("temperantia & fortitudo ad iustitiam disponunt & praeparant sicut cupiditas quam temperantia refraenat, & timor cui fortitudo resistit, iustitiam à suo officio impediunt").[23] Because avoiding descent is prior to ascent, Peraldus places temperance, which keeps us from descending further, before fortitude, which assists us in our ascent.[24] Peraldus's rationale is rooted ultimately in the platonic psychology that entered Christian ascetic thought, in part, through the monks of fourth-century Egypt. In this tradition, each vice is born from the excess of a previous one; the passions of the concupiscible faculty eventually produce the passions of the irascible faculty, and thus must be treated as prior.[25] While Aquinas does not order the cardinal virtues in the same manner as Peraldus, preferring instead, like Cicero, to cluster them according to intellectual virtues (prudence and justice) and moral virtues (temperance and fortitude),[26] he also observes that irascible passions follow naturally from concupiscible passions that "involve movement towards some good or away from some evil" ("important motum in bonum vel malum"), such as desire (*desiderium*); in such circumstances, "emotions of the spirited orexis find in emotions of the affective . . . their origin" ("passiones irascibilis . . . principium habent a passionibus concupiscibilis").[27] While vice begins in the intellect, as an idea, which the concupiscible faculty translates into desire, there is a natural movement from excessive or inappropriate desire to passions of the irascible faculty, such as anger or fear. That Peraldus's ordering of the virtue appears in both the *Book of Virtues and Vices* and *Piers Plowman* suggests that the *Pearl*-poet was likely aware of this ordering of the virtue as well as its ratio-nale.[28] The poet continually depicts the connection between the faculties of the soul through the terminology he uses to refer to the process of manifesting thought and disposition through action. While, as others have argued, *clannesse* refers generally to the desired state of the soul and, as I hope to prove, to the ideal state of the concupiscible faculty in particular, it begins in pru-dence, which is located in the intellectual faculty, and is ultimately expressed through just acts.[29]

The poet frames his discussion of wicked clergy using terms that illus-trate the relationship between the intellectual and concupiscible faculties, and the expression of these inner dispositions through just, or, in this case, unjust, action:

> If þay in clanness be clos þay cleche gret mede;
> Bot if þay conterfete crafte and cortaysye wont,
> As be honest vtwyth and inwith alle fylþez,
> Þen ar þay synful himself, and sulpen altogeder
> Boþe God and His gere, and Hym to greme cachen.

(If they are enclosed in cleanness, they obtain a great reward; but if they feign wisdom and lack courtesy, by being pure on the outside and all filth within, then they are sinful themselves and altogether defile both God and His utensils and drive Him to wrath.)[30]

Andrew and Waldron translate *crafte* as "wisdom," yet this word does not quite grasp the sense of practical, as opposed to theoretical, knowledge that the noun denotes: the first entry in the *Middle English Dictionary* defines *craft* as "strength," "force," and "power," but also more specifically as "moral strength" or "virtue." The sense of *craft* as both the ability to exercise right action and the knowledge of virtue suggests the cardinal virtue prudence, the virtue that discerns right action.[31] Furthermore, as Theodore Silverstein has shown in "Sir Gawain in a Dilemma, or Keeping Faith with Marcus Tullius Cicero," *cortayse* suggests the cardinal virtue justice, a virtue that has both courtly and religious implications, and thereby unites the secular and the spiritual.[32] Virtuous actions begin with prudence, which identifies the good that is to be sought, and end with justice, which manifests virtue externally, in our interactions with others. In the case of the naughty priests, inner vision and external action attempt to conceal the failure of temperance to moderate the desires of the appetitive soul; they merely appear "honest," which Andrew and Waldron gloss as "pure," but which suggests "virtuous" and "honorable."

While *honestas*, from which *honest* derives, can refer to virtue in general, in the sense of honor or propriety, it frequently appears among the species of temperance. To paraphrase the *Pearl*-poet, priests fail to act justly when they hide their intemperance by pretending to have an understanding of right action. Without temperance, the virtue that is enabled through the perception of the proper end of human life and consists of the submission of the appetitive capacity of the soul to the rational capacity, justice is impossible.

The pairing of prudence and justice, and the implicit role of temperance in expressing thought through action, occurs throughout the poem. After removing his ill-clad guest from the celebration in the Parable of the Wedding Feast, the host diagnoses the root of the problem as a failure of prudence and justice: he orders him to be shut in a dungeon "to teche hym be quoynt" ("to teach him to be respectful," 160). Here, Andrew and Waldron's translation of *quoynt* suggests that the guest has failed to render the respect he owes his host, yet their choice fails to capture the sense of practical knowledge, as well as the clever pun, that is at the root of the term: the primary definition offered by the *MED* is "wise, clever, prudent" (s.v. "queint[e," 1a), and, in the context of appearance, the *MED* suggests "well-dressed, fashionable, elegant" (1f). While decoding the meaning of the ejected guest's clothing, the poet indicates that they refer to one's deeds ("werkez")—that is, the outward manifestations of the will, and that they are lined with the "lykyng þat lyȝe in [one's] hert" ("the inclination that lay in [one's] heart," 171–75), that is, the identification of a desirable object or objective within one's rational faculty combined with the orientation of one's concupiscible faculty.[33] When God describes his plan to Noah, he explains that Noah has been chosen to survive the Flood because he "in reysoun hatz rengned and ryȝtwys ben euer" ("[has] ruled in wisdom and always been righteous," l. 328). The poet's amplification here conspicuously implies that Noah is both prudent and just, while Genesis 7:1, on which the passage is based, refers to Noah only as *iustu[s]*. While Andrew and Waldron translate "reysoun" as wisdom here, they render it as referring to the faculty of reason in *Pearl* 52 (343). "Ryȝtwys," according to the first entry of the *MED*, refers to someone who is "conforming to divine law" (s.v. "right-wīs[e," 1a), but also "just in all dealings" (1c), and thus is a fitting translation *iustu[s]* in Genesis 7:1.[34] God later acknowledges that humans lack an ability to recognize the telos of life because their intellect is oriented toward concupiscible vice: "alle seggez wyttez / To vnþryfte arn alle þrawen with þoȝt of her herttez" ("all people's minds are turned to wickedness by the thought of their hearts," 515–16). As a result, he resolves never to destroy everyone again "for manez dedez" ("because of mankind's deeds," 520).

RATIONAL AND CONCUPISCIBLE
NATURE DURING THE FALL

While the poet consistently refers to the relationship between the rational faculty, which is perfected by prudence, and human action, which is perfected through justice, the three primary scriptural passages emphasize the role of intemperance in unjust behavior. Nevertheless, he begins by locating the genesis of sin in Lucifer's rebellion, as being rooted ultimately in pride, an intellectual vice that prevents one from perceiving one's place in the hierarchy of being, as well as the telos of created beings. Lucifer's act is unjust since he does not render to God that which he owes; however, it is rooted in imprudence, since he does not recognize the telos of his existence: "He seȝ noȝt bot himself how semly he were" (209).[35] Although his inability to see suggests a failure of the rational faculty, the poet characterizes his fall from Heaven in terms that anticipate the vices of the concupiscible faculty of the soul: he fails to manifest what Peraldus regards as *temperantia secundum visum*, temperance with respect to sight.[36] The poet then focuses on Adam's responsibility for humanity's fall, since he "fayled in trawþe" "failed in loyalty" (236), was "inobedyent" (237), and thus acted unjustly.[37] His act is also rooted in imprudence since he decided to eat the fruit "þurȝ þe egging of Eue": "through the urging of Eve" (241). Furthermore, as many early Christian commentators suggest, the initial temptation to eat the fruit points to gluttony, an act of forbidden eating that points to an imbalance in the concupiscible faculty of the soul, the faculty which temperance is responsible for regulating.[38] Although Adam's decision to eat the fruit suggests the failure of his rational faculty, as well as the improper orientation of the concupiscible faculty, God is not driven by anger to punish Adam's behavior: divine irascibility—the perennial paradox—has not yet become a force in the relationship between the creator and creation, at least in the poet's depiction of this complicated history.[39]

LUST AND ANGER AMONG THE
DILUVIAN GENERATION

From the perspective of the cardinal virtues, which appears to have its origin in Plato, any act begins in the intellectual faculty, through a failure to determine right action. In *Cleanness*, Lucifer and Adam fall because of such a failure, yet Adam's fall results more complexly from the interaction between his rational and concupiscible faculties, even though, as Hatt writes in *God and the* Gawain-*Poet*, "It is almost as if [Lucifer's and Adam's] sins, dire though they are, are intellectual ones that therefore may be categorized as less provocative of divine anger than the 'fylþe' that the poem goes on to describe" (p. 81). With the introduction of gluttony—the inappropriate use of food—through the consumption of the forbidden fruit, created beings became prone to the next concupiscible vice: lust, the vice that the poet uses to characterize God's reason for flooding the earth. The narrative logic of the poet's movement from gluttony to lust reflects a commonplace in medieval psychology: as Thomas of Chobham succinctly states, "gula generat luxuriam" ("gluttony produces lust").[40]

In his description of the events precipitating the Flood, the poet not only expands concupiscible vice to include lust, but he also introduces irascible vice, as well as the proper direction of irascible passion, into his account of the evolution of sin. While discussing the fall of Lucifer and the fall of Adam and Eve, he carefully observes that God has acted without anger; in both instances, He punishes "[i]n þe mesure of His mode" ("in the moderation of his nature," 215).[41] In response to the events that precipitate the Flood, however, "watz malys mercyles and mawgré much scheued" ("merciless anger and great displeasure was shown") because of the "fylþe vpon folde þat þe folk vsed" ("uncleanness practiced on earth by the people," 250–51). While God's response to the first two transgressions is measured, His response to the lustful actions of the diluvian generation is implicitly *without measure*.[42] Anger and violence first occur in the scriptural source in the account of Cain and Abel, yet the poet first refers to irascible vices in the context of his discussion of the events that result in the Flood. In his account, God's anger seems to be a response to the violence of the giants, which appears to be connected to lust.

While the term *meþe* frequently refers to mercy and moderation in general, the use of *meþeless* in the description of the giants suggests intemperance in particular.[43] In his explanation of the events leading up to the Flood, the poet relates the behavior of the giants who inspire God's wrath: "Þer watz no law to hem layd bot loke to kynde, / And kepe to hit, and alle hit cors clanly fulfylle. / And þenne founden þay fylþe in fleschlych dedez" ("No law was imposed on them but to look to nature, and keep to it, and chastely fulfill all its course. And then they discovered filth in fleshly deeds," 263–65). The giants first turn to each other, and then to human women for sexual relations. The poet then provides the following transition from a discussion of the giants' sexual practices to their violent behavior, which seems to proceed from their sexuality, which the poet regards as contrary to the laws of nature:

> Þose wern men meþelez and maȝty on vrþe,
> Þat for her lodlych laykez alosed þay were;
> He watz famed for fre þat feȝt loued best,
> And ay þe biggest in bale þe best watz halden.

(Those were intemperate and mighty men upon earth, who were renowned for their loathsome practices; he who loved fighting best was famed for being honorable, and always the one who did the greatest harm was considered the noblest," 273–76).

The unnatural violence—the uncontrolled irascibility and unjust behavior—that the giants perpetrate seems to proceed from their indulgence in what the poet regards as lustful practices. Furthermore, the giants regard those who indulge in such behaviors as being *fre*, a word that denotes "honourable," "gracious," and "liberal" and thereby manifest a perverse notion of justice.[44] The unjust behavior of the giants enrages even God, who later seems to regret his what-must-have-been a rash decision to flood the earth (561–68). In this context, concupiscible vice erupts into irascible vice, resulting in injustice, all of which elicits an irascible response from God, who presumably does not have an irascible faculty.

The flood sequence concludes with a symbolic rebirth of healthy concupiscible desire, which implies the restoration of temperance. As Sarah Horrall and Jane Lecklider suggest, the poet emphasizes the tragic unity of humanity as the Flood destroys the population: the anger and violence preceding the Flood are replaced with fear, after which the narrative focuses on the pathos of friends and lovers embracing each other as they are separated by death (397–402).[45] God's act of cosmic aggression thus cleanses irascibility. After the Flood waters abate, Noah performs an act of piety—a sacrifice—that, as an act technically classified as fulfilling the requirements of the *iustitia*, reestablishes the proper relationship between humans and God (505–11).[46] In response, God establishes a covenant with humanity, and, now that concupiscible vice has been washed away from the earth, blesses procreative intercourse and promises to provide adequate food; the desire for both points to the proper use of concupiscence. Nature, at both the microcosmic and macrocosmic levels, has been restored through the cleansing of the concupiscible faculty.[47]

GLUTTONY, LUST, AND VIOLENCE:
THE DESTRUCTION OF SODOM

Like the giants who inspire the Flood, the citizens of Sodom inspire divine wrath through their violence and lust. However, the poet also returns to gluttony, which occurs through both overindulgences in food and the adornment of an object of our appetites, particularly when such adornment is contrary to the order of reason and, in this case, justice.[48] The biblical narrative begins with a portrayal of the proper direction of the concupiscible appetites:

Abraham and his wife provide a fitting feast for their guests—which the poet amplifies by referring to the variety of foods and the joyful atmosphere of the meal—and thereby manifest their just nature by upholding the law of hospitality. Immediately after the feast, as though in response to the appropriate use of food as a medium of honor and celebration, God declares that Sarah shall conceive a son; her aside, like the scriptural original, highlights the concupiscible dimension of conception: "May þou traw for tykle þat þou teme moȝtez?" ("Can you believe that you may conceive through sexual pleasure?" 655).[49]

After God and His angels visit Abraham, the scene shifts to Sodom, where Lot's hospitality is slightly compromised by his wife's disrespect of the angels' dietary restrictions, and the feast is followed by the threat of sexual violence. As the poet's amplification of the commentary suggests, her refusal to act justly toward her guests is rooted in a failure of intemperance; she reasons, "hit no skyl were, / Þat oþer burne be boute, þaȝ boþe be nyse" ("it would be unreasonable that anyone else should go without, even though both of them are fastidious," 822–24).[50] In addition to concupiscence, Lecklider notes that "Lot's wife act[s] from intentional malice, coupled with disobedience" (136); thus, the poet suggests that her concupiscible disturbs her irascible faculty, and both contribute in concert to her failure to honor their guests.

When the mob, animated by lust, demands that Lot send his guests to be sexually assaulted, Lot responds with "mesurable wordez," "For harlotez with his hendelayk he hoped to chast" ("for he hoped to restrain evil men with his courtesy," 859–60). On the one hand, his strategy aims, alarmingly, to reorient the sexual desire of the mob toward heterosexual intercourse. On the other hand, his speech attempts to defuse the potential violence, toward him and his guests, that has resulted from the irascible faculty of those in the mob having been upset by the disordered—and extreme—desire of the concupiscible faculty. The poet's depiction of the mob amplifies their rage. In Genesis 19:5, the mob surrounds the house and demands the young men. When they arrive at Lot's home in *Cleanness*, however, the mob addresses him "with a schrylle scharp schout" ("with a shrill sharp shout," 840), demanding that he send out the young men, "If [he] louyez [his] lyf, . . . in þyse wones" ("If [he] values [his] life . . . in these lands," 841–42). Whereas in Genesis 19:9, the mob simply threatens to treat Lot worse than his guests, the mob in *Cleanness* shouts, "We kylle of þyn heued!" ("We will strike off your head," 876). Finally, Genesis 19:11 states that the mob simply became weary trying to find Lot's door after the guests blinded them. The *Pearl*-poet, however, relates that the angels "blwe a buffet inblande þat banned peple" ("blew a tempest among that cursed people," 885) that blinded them and rendered them unable to find Lot's house; as a result, they had trouble sleeping when they returned to their homes, implicitly because they were enraged and frustrated sexually: "Þenne vch tolke tyȝt hem, þat hade of tayt fayled, / And vchon roþeled to þe rest þat he reche moȝt" ("Then every man having failed to obtain his pleasure went on his way, and each hurried to what rest he could get," 889–90).[51] Thus, the extreme concupiscible desire experienced by the residents of Sodom upsets the irascible faculty of their soul as well, and reinforces God's decision to destroy the city, presumably because His investigators failed to find ten righteous people.[52]

GLUTTONY, LUST, IDOLATRY, AND DEFILEMENT AND THE DEATH OF BELSHAZZAR

The final way in which the narrator illustrates God's response to uncleanness is through the example of Belshazzar's feast, which, while characterized by idolatry and the climactic defilement of the Temple vessels, depicts gluttony, lust, and other sensory delights as causal factors in Belshazzar's refusal to offer to God what belongs to Him. In this narrative, the telos and symbol of concupiscible sin converge in the sins of idolatry and defilement. While the poet emphasizes God's hatred of backsliding by describing the conquest of Jerusalem that God allowed because of the idolatry of Zedechiah, he nevertheless focuses on Belshazzar's punishment "For he þe vesselles avyled þat vayled in þe temple" "because he profaned the vessels that were formerly used in the temple," 1151). Whereas in *The* Pearl-*Poet Revisited*, Prior regards the poet as introducing "ritual purity" at this point, that is, "the respectful and proper use of sacred forms and objects, which it closely connects with sexual purity,"[53] Hatt rightfully contends, in *God and the* Gawain-*Poet*, that the poet extends the need for ritual purity to one's relationship to materiality in general: the misuse of the vessels symbolizes the misuse of materiality. After observing that the poet's implication that Belshazzar treats the vessels as love-tokens, she writes, "Their status as physical objects, crafted by hand, emphasises the role of particularity in love; just as God created each person to be *this* individual, with *this* nature, so the craftsmen used *this* wood, *this* metal, to make an artefact that would have use for a particular occasion and no other."[54] They are a sign of God's love, a quality Nebuchadnezzar recognized, but Belshazzar trivialized. Thus, the poet uses Belshazzar and the vessels to signify the anger God feels toward not only reformed sinners who have again misused the members of their body in the service of sin but to those who do not relate to materiality in a manner that reflects their awareness of its divine source.

By emphasizing the context of the defilement of the vessels, which takes place in a drunken orgy, the poet continues his examination of the potential role that concupiscible vices play in injustice; in particular, he implies that idolatry is a potential telos of concupiscible vice. In addition to the emphasis on gluttony and lust that characterizes Belshazzar's feast, the poet focuses on the desire aroused by the intense sensory experience of the feast, from the magnificent description of the palace and the festal hall (1377–425) to the detailed description of the sacred vessels (1441–92). While the appropriate restraint of this desire, according to Peraldus, is "temperance of delights according to sight, sound, and smell" ("temperantia delectationum secundum visum, auditum, & olfactum"),[55] immoderate indulgence in food, sex, and other sensory pleasures characterizes Belshazzar's rule: "In þe clerness of his concubines and curious wedez, / In noting of nwe metes and of nice gettes, / Al watz þe mynde of þat man on misschapen þinges" ("The mind of that man was entirely [fixed] on perverse things, on the beauty of his concubines and exquisite clothes, on trying out new foods and foolish fashions," 1353–55). Gluttony played a role in the fall of Adam and Eve, and Lot's wife was turned to salt partly because of her insistence on garnishing her food. The Flood and the destruction of Sodom were inspired, according to the poet, by inordinate and inappropriate lust. While God allows Belshazzar to be killed for his idolatry and defilement of the temple vessels, the poet emphasizes the concupiscible vices—particularly gluttony, lust, and unrestrained sensory pleasures—that lead directly to his injustice toward God:

> So watz derued fele syþe þe sale alle aboute,
> With solace at þe sere course, before þe self lorde,
> Þer þe lede and all his loue lenged at þe table;
> So faste þay weȝed to him wyne hit warmed his hert
> And breyþed vppe into his brayn and blemyst his mynde,
> And al waykned his wyt, and welneȝ he foles.

Thus [people] all around the hall were served many times, with pleasure in the various courses, before the lord himself, where the man and all his paramours were sitting at the table; they brought wine to him so fast it warmed his heart and rose as a vapour to his brain and impaired his mind, and his reason grew feeble, and he almost goes mad. (1417–22)

At this point, the poet seems less interested in the role inappropriate concupiscible behaviors may have played in the wrath of God than in the role such activities had in driving Belshazzar to defile the treasures from the Temple, an act that the poet suggests is both symbolic of, and teleologically connected to, concupiscence. On the one hand, Belshazzar engages in idolatry, by elevating matter to divinity through worshipping his idols; on the other hand, he simultaneously commits desecration, since he fails to recognize that the idols he worships are made of the same sort of matter as that of the temple vessels—matter that, when regarded appropriately, points to its creator.

CONCLUSION

While the poet ultimately treats uncleanness as a general characteristic of sinfulness, what unifies the three narratives is a focus on concupiscible vices. In the platonic tradition of the virtues, such behaviors begin in the intellectual faculty of the soul, and then reach down to the concupiscible and the irascible, and to outward expression through the activity of the will. While the poet suggests that such concupiscible vices are habituated, he also implies that they are rooted in a lack of understanding of the proper nature of reality and telos of human life, which is the vision of God. This lack of understanding inverts the proper order of the soul, so that food, sex, and finery—all of which should ultimately direct our attention to their source—become ends in themselves, as opposed to signs of God's love. The misuse of matter thereby becomes both idolatry and desecration.

The poet aims, at least on one level, to reorient the soul by addressing concupiscible vices in particular, since, according to the tradition he transmits, such vices can lead to anger, violence, and desecration, and they can further impair the intellect's capacity to recognize the soul's proper telos. Because my purpose here is to uncover the activity of taxonomic approaches to virtues and vices in the poet's craft, I have been unable to explore the implications of his use of such taxonomies more thoroughly. As Jim Rhodes observes, "The task of poetry for Chaucer and his fellow poets is not to affirm a truth already determined by theology but to open up a space, a play world, where values are tested, new modes of thought and perception are tried out, and established ideas are transformed."[56] Ultimately, the poet figures taxonomic approaches to virtues and vices in his "play world," using the poems to explore the implications, boundaries, and contradictions of the ethical system the medieval west inherited from Greek and Roman antiquity. In *Cleanness*, as in his other works, the poet's ultimate project is to humanize the virtues, to flesh out their descriptions through narratives that reveal not only their desirability, but also the potential limitations, difficulties, and dangers of such scholastic taxonomies.

NOTES

1. Charles F. Briggs, "Moral Philosophy and Wisdom Literature," in *The Oxford History of Classical Reception in English Literature, Volume 1: 800–1558*, eds. David Hopkins and Charles Martindale (Oxford: Oxford University Press, 2016), 299–321.

2. Studies that investigate the influence of the cardinal virtues on specific poems include R. J. Spendal, "The Fifth Pentad in 'Sir Gawain and the Green Knight,'" *Notes and Queries* 23, no. 4 (1976): 147–48; Theodore Silverstein, "Sir Gawain in a

Dilemma, or Keeping Faith with Marcus Tullius Cicero," *Modern Philology* 75, no. 1 (1977): 1–17; and Elizabeth Kirk, "Who Suffreth More Than God? Narrative Redefinition of Patience in *Patience* and *Piers Plowman*," in *The Triumph of Patience: Medieval and Renaissance Studies*, ed. Gerald J. Schiffhorst (Orlando: University Press of Florida, 1978), 88–106, as well as my "Patient Endurance in Sir Gawain and the Green Knight," *Florilegium* 10 (2010): 177–207 and "The Prudence of *Pearl*," *Chaucer Review* 45, no. 4 (2011): 411–34. On the poet's concept of virtue in *Patience*, see Matthew Brumit's chapter in this volume: "'Þay are happen also þat con her herte stere': Virtue and Nautical Metaphor in *Patience*," *passim*.

3. In *Courtly Desire and Medieval Homophobia: The Legitimation of Sexual Pleasure in Cleanness and its Contexts* (New Haven, CT: Yale University Press, 1997), Elizabeth Keiser explores the poet's use of Aquinas's discussion of *temperantia*. Whereas her analysis focuses on how the virtue "can help illuminate the vision in *Cleanness* of a continuity between the beauty of the created and social orders and the nature of God himself" (p. 29), my analysis focuses on the poet's portrayal of the connection between the concupiscible vices, which are redirected through *temperantia*, and those of the other faculties of the soul, which are purified through *prudentia*, *fortitudo*, and *iustitia*.

4. Cecilia Hatt, *God and the Gawain-Poet: Theology and Genre in Pearl, Cleanness, Patience and Sir Gawain and the Green Knight* (Cambridge: D.S. Brewer, 2015), 79.

5. Ad Putter, in *An Introduction to the Gawain-Poet* (New York: Longman, 1996), observes that clerics "typically define cleanness simply as virginity and chastity" (202n1). Critical response has generally—and understandably—regarded *clannesse* as more general than *temperantia*. For example, in addition to Putter and Hatt, A. C. Spearing, in *The Gawain-Poet: A Critical Study* (Cambridge: Cambridge University Press, 1970), argues that "moral abstractions" such as *clannesse* and *fylþe* have meaning only insomuch as the poet "juxtapos[es] situations to which they can be applied" (p. 51). Edward Wilson, in *The Gawain-Poet* (Leiden: Brill, 1976), argues that the virtue opposes sexual sin in particular, which is meant to typify "the sinful state of man" (p. 88). In *The Voice of the Gawain-Poet* (Madison: University of Wisconsin Press, 1984), Lynn Staley Johnson writes, "The poet, rather than discussing purity and impurity in general terms, organizes his topic by exploring the three classic sins of lust, avarice, and pride" (p. 111). Monica Brzezinski, in "Conscience and Covenant: The Sermon Structure of *Cleanness*," *Journal of English and Germanic Philology* 89, no. 2 (1990): 166–80, argues that the poem offers "a consistent definition of *clannesse* as purity of conscience, conscience being defined as man's rational soul, created in the image of God" (p. 166). In *The* Pearl-*Poet Revisited* (New York: Twayne, 1994), Sandra Pierson Prior concludes that "'clannes' is a metaphor for virtue and obedience and godliness, but it is also to be understood more literally, as the quality of sexual and physical cleanness" (p. 70). Such taxonomies were particularly important for preparation for the sacrament of Confession. For a discussion of medieval Catholicism, see Nancy Ciccone's chapter in this volume: "Religious Contexts for the *Gawain*-Poet," *passim*.

6. Critics such as A. C Spearing, *The Gawain-Poet*, 41–44, and Lynn Staley Johnson, *The Voice of the Gawain-Poet*, 100, have identified the apparent thematic divergence among the three main scriptural passages as a critical crux in the interpretation of the poem. Much of the subsequent critical history aims to illustrate the unity of the three biblical narratives.

7. See for, instance, Peraldus, who, in his *Summa virtutum ac vitiorum* (Lyons: Guillaume Rouillé, 1585) quotes widely circulating definitions of the virtue from Cicero, "Temperantia est dominium rationis in libidinem & in motus alios importunes" (Temperance is the rule of reason over desire and other troublesome emotions), Augustine, "Temperantia est affectio coercens & cohibens appetitum ab his quae turpiter appetuntur" (Temperance is an affect restraining and confining the appetite for those things that are desired basely), and Macrobius, "Temperantia est nihil appetere poenitendum, in nullo moderationis legem excedere, sub iugo rationis cupiditatem" (Temperance is to desire nothing that must punished, to exceed the law of moderation in nothing, [to restrain] desire under the yoke of reason) (1.323–24 [1.3.3.3]; my translation). He also defines it simply as "virtus . . . regens animam circa delectationes sensuum" (the virtue ruling the soul with respect to the delights of the senses) (1.336 [1.3.3.8]; my translation). On the philosophical commonplace of the platonic tripartite soul in the Middle Ages, see, for example, *On the Properties of Things: John Trevisa's Translation of Bartholomaeus Anglicus De Proprietatibus Rerum*, ed. M. C. Seymour et al. (Oxford: Clarendon, 1975), 95–96 (3.5).

8. For instance, following Macrobius, the anonymous author of the *Summa virtutum de remediis anime*, ed. Siegfried Wenzel (Athens: University of Georgia Press, 1984), like the author of the *Dogma moralium philosophorum*, ed. John Holmberg (Cambridge: W. Heffer and Sons, 1929), includes: "modestia (modesty); "verecundia (shamefacedness); abstinentia (abstinence); honestas (propriety); moderantia (moderation); parcitas (sparingness); sobrietas (soberness); and pudicitia (chasteness) (pp. 268–71).

9. *Summa de commendatione virtutum et extirpatione vitiorum*, ed. Franco Morenzoni (Turnholt: Brepols, 1997), 181 (4.2.3).

10. *Summa virtutum ac vitiorum*, 1.327–74 (1.3.3.5–1.3.3.18).

11. See *Summa theologiae*, ed. Thomas Gilby, O.P., 60 vols. (London: Blackfriars, 1974), 43.17–21 (2.2.141.4). On the possibility of Aquinas's influence on the *Pearl*-poet, see Keiser, Courtly Desire, 231n18.

12. *The Book of Vices and Virtues*, ed. W. Nelson Francis (London: Oxford University Press, 1942), 122.

13. Cf. Lynn Staley Johnson who, in *The Voice of the Gawain-Poet*, sees lust, avarice, and pride as standard vices represented in *Cleanness*—lust of flesh, lust of eyes, and pride of life. I however regard the cluster of vices in the poem as either being rooted primarily in the platonic tradition of the concupiscible faculty of the soul, or as consequences of intemperance.

14. *MED*, s.v. "clēnnesse," 1a.

15. *MED*, s.v. "clēnnesse," 2a.

16. *Summa virtutum de remediis anime*, 290.

17. *Book of Vices and Virtues*, 46.

18. All translations, unless otherwise indicated, are taken from Malcolm Andrew and Ronald Waldron, eds., *The Poems of the Pearl Manuscript: Pearl, Cleanness, Patience, and Sir Gawain and the Green Knight*, 5th ed. (Exeter: Exeter University Press, 2007).

19. Putter, *An Introduction*, 203.

20. In short, prudence discerns appropriate action, temperance moderates desire, fortitude controls anger and fear, and justice renders to others what they are due. Thus, the first three virtues are internal, since they ensure the proper ordering of the soul, and the final is external, inasmuch as it governs our relationship with others, including God. On these commonplace definitions of the cardinal virtues, see the *Moralium dogma philosophorum*, passim, Thomas of Chobham's *Summa confessorum*, ed. F. Broomfield (Paris: Béatrice-Nauwelaerts, 1968), 44, and *Summa de commendatione virtutum et extirpatione vitiorum*, 138–202 (4.2), the *Summa virtutum de remediis anime*, 52–60, and the *Book of Vices and Virtues*, 122–23. For a detailed discussion of the cardinal virtues in the later Middle Ages, see István Bejczy, *The Cardinal Virtues in the Middle Ages: A Study in Moral Thought from the Fourth to the Fourteenth Century* (Leiden: Brill, 2011), 135–221.

21. The ultimate rationale for this ordering of the virtues may be found in Plato's *Laws*, ed. R. G. Bury (Cambridge, MA: Harvard University Press, 1961), 25 (1.631C).

22. *Summa virtutum*, 1.283 (1.3.1.2; my translation).

23. *Summa virtutum*, 1.322 (1.3.3.1; my translation).

24. "[Temperance] prevents a spiritual descent of the soul. [Fortitude] advances a spiritual ascent. Indeed the prevention of spiritual descent is prior to spiritual ascent. Therefore temperance is in the concupiscible faculty, [and] fortitude is in the irascible. Indeed the operation of the concupiscible faculty seems to be prior to the operation of the irascible" ("[Temperantia] spiritualem descensum animae cohibet. [Fortitudo] spiritualem ascensum promouet. Cohibitio vero à spirituali descensu est prior ascensu spirituali. Item temperantia est in concupiscibili: fortitudo vero in irascibili. Operatio vero concupiscibilis naturaliter videtur esse prior quam operatio irascibilis," 322 [1.3.3.1]); my translation). See also Albertus Magnus's *Commentary on the Sentences of Peter Lombard*, found in *The Cardinal Virtues: Aquinas, Albert, and Philip the Chancellor*, trans. R. E. Houser (Toronto: Pontifical Institute of Medieval Studies, 2004), in which he offers a similar account for this order, "if virtue is considered according to the order it has in relation to the subject in which it exists"; since "there can be no correct action unless preceded by correct choice, so . . . prudence must be first. Likewise, one cannot be brave in adversity unless resolute in the face of pleasure, so . . . temperance comes before courage" (p. 139).

25. For instance, see John Cassian, *The Conferences*, translated by Boniface Ramsey, O.P. (New York: Newman Press, 1997): "In order to conquer acedia, sadness must first be overcome; in order to drive out sadness, anger must be cast out beforehand; in order to extinguish anger, avarice must be trampled on; in order to eradicate avarice, fornication must be repressed; in order to overthrow fornication, the vice of gluttony must be disciplined" (p. 189 [5.10.1]); (Jean Cassien, *Conférences*, texte Latin par Dom. E. Pichery (Paris: Les Éditions du CERF, 1955 "ut acedia uicantur, ante superanda tristitia est: ut tristitia propelletur, ira prius extrudenda: ut extinguatur

ira, filargyria calcanda est: ut euellatur filargyria, fornicatio conpescenda est: ut fornicatio subruatur, gastrimargiae est uitium castigandum") (p. 198). According to Carol Straw, "Gregory, Cassian and the Cardinal Vices," in *In the Garden of Evil: The Vices and Culture in the Middle Ages* (Toronto: Pontifical Institute of Medieval Studies, 2005), 35–58 at 37, Cassian adopts a "bubble-up" hamartiology, through which unchecked desire begins as gluttony, and potentially ends as pride. As Morton Bloomfield notes in *The Seven Deadly Sins: An Introduction to the History of a Religious Concept, with Special Reference to Medieval English Literature* (East Lansing: Michigan State College Press, 1952), the Cassianic list of vices suggests the influence of the penitential tradition (105). While I am not suggesting that the *Pearl*-poet is drawing directly from the Cassian's hamartiology, I do contend that the implicit connection of concupiscible vices—and their healing through *temperantia*—has informed the poet's choice and framing of the biblical narratives he includes.

26. See, for instance, Cicero's *De inventione*, 327–29 (2.53), in *De inventione, de optimo genere oratorum, topica* (Cambridge, MA: Harvard University Press, 1949).

27. *Summa theologiae* 19.47 (1.2.25.1). Aquinas also observes that "every spirited emotion . . . has as its term one of the affective emotions which involve coming to rest, viz. joy or sadness" "omnis passio irascibilis terminator ad passionem concupuscibilis pertinentem ad quietem, scilicet ad gaudium vel ad tristitiam" (19:46–47 [1.2.25.1]). However, in his discussion of sin, the poet's primary concern is with the problem of desire, which implies motion.

28. See *Book of Vices and Virtues,* 122 and William Langland's *The Vision of Piers Plowman: A Critical Edition of the B-Text Based on Trinity College Cambridge MS B.15.17*, ed. A. V. C. Schmidt (London: J. M. Dent, 1995), 19.277–319.

29. While prudence is responsible for determining action, the intellectual faculty, which it is to govern, is also informed by the behavior of the agent, that is, by the expression of the other faculties of the soul. Thus, the four virtues—and their corresponding vices—develop cyclically.

30. *Pearl*, lines 11–16.

31. On the pervasiveness of prudence in *Pearl*, see Owen, "The Prudence of *Pearl*," passim.

32. On *cortayse* as *humanitas*, one of the parts of *iustitia*, in *Sir Gawain and the Green Knight*, see Silverstein, "Sir Gawain in a Dilemma," 5.

33. *Herte* has a complex range of meanings, especially when it is used in the context of the tripartite soul. While it can refer to the "center or seat of human emotion" (*MED*, 3a), it can also refer to the intellectual faculty (4a). In this case, the rhetorical pairing with actions points ambiguously to both the intellectual and the concupiscible.

34. Also, when Abraham attempts to soften God's judgement against Sodom, he characterizes those who should not be punished as "reʒtful, resounable, and redy [God] to serue" ("righteous, reasonable, and ready to serve," 724); in Genesis 18:23–33, Abraham consistently refers to those not deserving punishment as *iusti*. On *iustitia* as the virtue that ensures the proper relations among created beings and between created beings and God, see, for example, Peraldus's *Summa virtutum*, 1.436–37 (1.3.5.1–1.3.5.2) and Aquinas's *Summa theologiae*, 39.2–9 (2.2.80), both of which describe justice as the virtue that regards what one owes one's superiors, beginning

of course with God; what one owes one's inferiors; what one owes one's equals; and what one owes everyone in general.

35. On this commonplace account of Lucifer's fall, see Jane Lecklider, *Cleanness: Structure and Meaning* (Cambridge: D.S. Brewer, 1997), 62–64; according to Aquinas, she states, Lucifer "disregarded a precept which . . . was implicit in the status of an angel in the order of creation" (63). Such terms clearly suggest that Aquinas sees Lucifer's act as a violation of the demands of justice. Yet, the poet's terminology suggests that his fall is rooted in a failure of perception, one that implies both imprudence and concupiscence.

36. *Summa virtutum*, 1.373–374 (1.3.3.18).

37. On the connection between *trawþe* and justice in *Cleanness*, see, for example, Michael Twomey, "The Sin of Untrawþe in *Cleanness*," in *Text and Matter: New Critical Perspectives of the* Pearl-*Poet*, ed. Robert J. Blanch, Miriam Youngerman Miller, and Julian N. Wasserman (Troy, NY: Whitston, 1991), 117–45, who writes, "*Cleanness* . . . is a poem of divine justice in which sinners are judged according to the requirements of the covenant of faith and obedience—trawþe" (117). On the poet's understanding of the cardinal virtue *iustitia*, see R. J. Spendal, "The Fifth Pentad," 147–48, and Theodore Silverstein, "*Sir Gawain* in a Dilemma," 1–17.

38. On early Christian writers who associate the fall with gluttony, see Shaw, *The Burden of the Flesh: Fasting and Sexuality in Early Christianity* (Minneapolis, MN: Fortress Press, 1998), 171–81. In *Summa theologiae* 44.189–91 (2.2.165.2), Aquinas cites Augustine's *De trinitate* 12.12, in which the latter describes how the fall began in the concupiscible faculty and reached the intellectual faculty through Adam's consent to sin. For this commonplace sentiment in vernacular theology, see the *Book of Vices and Virtues*, in which the author compares the Devil's strategies for provoking gluttony to the serpent's temptation of Eve, "for first he scheweþ hem good wyn and good aale and good metes and delicious, riȝt as he dide to Eue þe appel" (p. 51). The *Pearl*-poet nevertheless emphasizes the intellectual faculty's role in the fall, and the role of the concupiscible faculty is left implicit. For a summary of prominent medieval interpretations of the fall that pertain directly to the development of harmful concupiscence, see Lecklider, *Cleanness: Structure and Meaning*, 80–92.

39. As, for instance, Lecklider notes in *Cleanness: Structure and Meaning*, "references to the 'emotions' of the Lord . . . are not unusual in Christian exegesis," even though patristic writers generally identify God as being without emotions (p. 79). For a profoundly anthropological reading of God's destructive rage, see, for instance, A. C. Spearing, "Purity and Danger," *Essays in Criticism* 30, no. 4 (1980): 293–310, in which he describes the poet's world as "a world in which everything is linked by a strenuous concrete logic—a touch of leaven in food or a misuse of the human body can unleash terrifying destructive forces—but . . . it is one in which the disorder created is only the material for the creation of further order, including the order of his own poetic art" (307). Thus, God's destructiveness is that from which new order emerges.

40. *Summa de commendatione virtutum*, 207 (5.2). On the earlier classical and Christian roots of the connection between gluttony and lust, see Teresa Shaw, *The Burden of the Flesh*, passim, and, especially, 129–60. On medieval connection

between these vices, see Caroline Bynum, *Holy Feast and Holy Fast: The Religious Significance of Food to Medieval Women* (Berkeley: University of California Press, 1987), 208–18.

41. Cf. 247: "Al in mesure and meþe watz mad þe vengiaunce" ("the vengeance was carried out all in moderation and mildness").

42. See Spearing, *The Gawain-Poet*, 45–46.

43. On God's *meþe*, see line 436 and line 535. On *meþe* as the cardinal virtue temperance, see *MED*, s.v. "mēth(e)," 1c.

44. *MED*, 2a and 2b.

45. See Sarah Horrall, "'Cleanness' and 'Cursor Mundi,'" *English Language Notes* 22 (1985): 6–11 at 9–10, and Lecklider, *Cleanness: Structure and Meaning*, 106. According to Grace Hamman's chapter in this volume, such pathos is particularly effective at inspiring repentance (p. 185).

46. On the worship of God as a requirement of the cardinal virtue *iustitia*, see, for example, Peraldus, *Summa virtutum*, 1.442–82 (1.5.5.3–1.5.9), in which he includes a lengthy description of prayer as an act of justice.

47. The poet suggests a connection between the macrocosm and the microcosm through his invocation of the theme of baptism in his description of the Flood; as Lecklider writes, in *Cleanness: Structure and Meaning*, "The imagery of baptism in *Cleanness* extends to the 'cleansing' of the earth itself" (p. 112).

48. See, for instance, Peraldus's *Summa virtutum*: "To prepare food zealously is to sharpen the sword of our enemy. luxurious food is a sword which the flesh uses against the spirit" ("Studiose cibos praepare, est hostis nostri gladium acuere. Cibus . . . delicatus est gladius quo caro vtitur contra spiritum" (1.343 [1.3.3.9]; my translation).

49. Cf. Genesis 18:12. On temperance and sexual pleasure, see Keiser, *Courtly Desire*, 103–12. While Keiser regards the poet's later description of sexual pleasure without reference to procreation as revolutionary, even though he uses it as a foil, Jeremy Citrome contends that the poet's references imply procreation, and that such references to sexual pleasure are commonplace in classical sources and contemporary medical literature; see "Medicine as Metaphor in the Middle English *Cleanness*," *Chaucer Review* 35, no. 3 (2001): 260–80 at 273–75.

50. The poet again emphasizes the reason for her memorable destruction nearly two hundred lines later: "his make watz myst, þat on þe mount lenged / In a stonen statue þat salt sauor habbes, / For two fautes þat þe fol watz founde in mistrauþe" ("his wife was lost, who remained on the mountain, in a stone that tastes of salt, for two misdeeds in which the fool was found unfaithful," p. 994–95). Here, by failing to fulfill the obligations of hospitality, and for looking back to Sodom, both of which acts are rooted in her disordered concupiscible faculty, Lot's wife is guilty of "mistrauþe." See, for instance, Michael Twomey, "The Sin of Untrawþe," 126.

51. As Peraldus writes in *Summa virtutum*, citing Aristotle, "per ablationem boni quod concupiscebat fit perturbatio vel ira in irascibili" ("through the loss of a good thing that one was desiring, a disturbance or anger happens in the irascible faculty" 1.322 [1.3.3.3]; my translation).

52. While the poet does not allude to idolatry in Sodom, Lecklider notes, in *Cleanness: Structure and Meaning*, that "the historical reason for such unanimous condemnation of sodomy was its link with idolatry" (p. 149). Thus, implicit in the poet's depiction of Sodom is judgment of injustice against God, which idolatry symbolizes.

53. Prior, Pearl-*Poet Revisited*, 70.

54. Hatt, *God and the Gawain-Poet*, 102.

55. *Summa virtutum*, 1.373–74 (1.3.3.18).

56. Jim Rhodes, *Poetry Does Theology: Chaucer, Grosseteste, and the Pearl Poet* (Notre Dame, IN: University of Notre Dame Press, 2001), 7. In *Courtly Desire*, Keiser makes good use of Amos Wilder's term *theopoetic*, since "the church's modifications of theological idioms require the imagination's free play in fictional and poetic revisioning" (p. 2). In a similar vein, Hatt writes, "*Cleanness* uses the posture of preaching for a literary end" (p. 85).

BIBLIOGRAPHY

Andrew, Malcolm, and Ronald Waldron, eds. *The Poems of the* Pearl *Manuscript: Pearl, Cleanness, Patience, and Sir Gawain and the Green Knight*. 5th ed. Exeter: Exeter University Press, 2007.

Aquinas, Thomas. *Summa theologiae*. Ed. Thomas Gilby, O.P., 60 vols. London: Blackfriars, 1974.

Bejczy, István. *The Cardinal Virtues in the Middle Ages: A Study in Moral Thought from the Fourth to the Fourteenth Century*. Leiden: Brill, 2011.

Briggs, Charles F. "Moral Philosophy and Wisdom Literature." In *The Oxford History of Classical Reception in English Literature, Volume 1: 800–1558*. Eds. David Hopkins and Charles Martindale, 299–321. Oxford: Oxford University Press, 2016.

Brzezinski, Monica. "Conscience and Covenant: The Sermon Structure of *Cleanness*." *Journal of English and Germanic Philology* 89, no. 2 (1990): 166–80.

Bynum, Caroline Walker. *Holy Feast and Holy Fast: The Religious Significance of Food to Medieval Women*. Berkeley: University of California Press, 1987.

Cassian, John. *The Conferences*. Trans. Boniface Ramsey, O.P. New York: Newman Press, 1997.

———. *Conférences*, texte Latin par Dom. E. Pichery. Paris: Les Éditions du CERF, 1955.

Cicero, Marcus Tullius. *De inventione, de optimo genere oratorum, topica*. Cambridge, MA: Harvard University Press, 1949.

Citrome, Jeremy. "Medicine as Metaphor in the Middle English *Cleanness*," *Chaucer Review* 35, no. 3 (2001): 260–80.

Francis, W. Nelson, ed. *Book of Vices and Virtues: A Fourteenth Century English Translation of the* Somme le Roi *of Lorens D'Orléans*. London: Oxford University Press, 1942.

Hatt, Cecilia. *God and the* Gawain-*Poet: Theology and Genre in* Pearl, Cleanness, Patience *and* Sir Gawain and the Green Knight. Cambridge: D.S. Brewer, 2015.

Holmberg, John, ed. *Moralium dogma philosophorum.* Cambridge: W. Heffer & Sons, 1929.

Horrall, Sarah. "'Cleanness' and 'Cursor Mundi.'" *English Language Notes* 22 (1985): 6–11.

Houser, R. E., trans. *The Cardinal Virtues: Aquinas, Albert, and Philip the Chancellor.* Toronto: Pontifical Institute of Medieval Studies, 2004.

Johnson, Lynn Staley. *The Voice of the* Gawain-*Poet.* Madison: University of Wisconsin Press, 1984.

Keiser, Elizabeth. *Courtly Desire and Medieval Homophobia: The Legitimation of Sexual Pleasure in "Cleanness" and Its Contexts.* New Haven, CT: Yale University Press, 1997.

Kirk, Elizabeth. "Who Suffreth More Than God? Narrative Redefinition of Patience in *Patience* and *Piers Plowman.*" In *The Triumph of Patience: Medieval and Renaissance Studies,* edited by Gerald J. Schiffhorst, 88–106. Orlando: University Press of Florida, 1978.

Langland, William. *The Vision of Piers Plowman: A Critical Edition of the B-Text Based on Trinity College Cambridge MS B.15.17.* Edited by A. V. C. Schmidt. London: J. M. Dent, 1995.

Lecklider, Jane. Cleanness*: Structure and Meaning.* Cambridge: D. S. Brewer, 1997.

Lewis, Robert E. et al. *Middle English Dictionary.* Ann Arbor: University of Michigan Press, 1952–2001.

Owen, Corey. "Patient Endurance in *Sir Gawain and the Green Knight.*" *Florilegium* 10 (2010): 177–207.

———. "The Prudence of *Pearl,*" *The Chaucer Review* 45, no. 4 (2011): 411–34.

Peraldus, William. *Summa virtutum ac vitiorum Guilelmi Peraldi.* Lyons: Guillaume Rouillé, 1585.

Plato. *Laws.* Ed. R. G. Bury. Cambridge, MA: Harvard University Press, 1961.

Prior, Sandra Pierson. *The* Pearl-*Poet Revisited.* New York: Twayne, 1994.

Putter, Ad. *An Introduction to the* Gawain-*Poet.* New York: Longman, 1996.

Rhodes, Jim. *Poetry Does Theology: Chaucer, Grosseteste, and the Pearl Poet.* Notre Dame, IN: University of Notre Dame Press, 2001.

Seymour, M. C. et al., eds. *On the Properties of Things: John Trevisa's Translation of Batholomaeus Anglicus De proprietatibus rerum.* 2 vols. Oxford: Clarendon, 1975.

Silverstein, Theodore. "Sir Gawain in a Dilemma, or Keeping Faith with Marcus Tullius Cicero," *Modern Philology* 75, no. 1 (1977): 1–17.

Spearing, A. C. *The Gawain-Poet A Critical Study.* Cambridge: Cambridge University Press, 1970.

Spendal, R. J. "The Fifth Pentad in 'Sir Gawain and the Green Knight,'" *Notes and Queries* 23, no 4 (1976): 147–48.

Straw, Carol. "Gregory, Cassian and the Cardinal Vices." *In the Garden of Evil: The Vices and Culture in the Middle Ages.* Toronto: Pontifical Institute of Medieval Studies, 2005.

Thomas of Chobham. *Summa confessorum.* Ed. F. Broomfield. Paris: Béatrice-Nauwelaerts, 1968.

————. *Summa de commendatione virtutum et extirpatione vitiorum.* Ed. Franco Morenzoni. Turnhout: Brepols, 1997.

Twomey, Michael. "The Sin of *Untrawþe* in *Cleanness*." *Text and Matter: New Critical Perspectives of the* Pearl-*Poet*. Edited by Robert J. Blanch, Miriam Youngerman Miller, and Julian N. Wasserman. Troy, NY: Whitston, 1991.

Wenzel, Siegfried, ed. *Summa virtutum de remediis anime*. Athens: University of Georgia Press, 1984.

Wilson, Edward. *The* Gawain-*Poet*. Leiden: Brill, 1976.

Chapter Three

"Þay ar happen also þat con her hert stere": Virtue and Nautical Metaphor in *Patience*[1]

M. W. Brumit

Patience, the third poem in Cotton Nero A.x, has often been underappreciated by critics because it is the least original of the poems commonly attributed to the poet we tend to call the *Pearl*-poet or the *Gawain*-poet in homage to his most appreciated works. But *Patience*, however less original and formally intricate than *Pearl* or *Sir Gawain and the Green Knight* (or even *Cleanness*), brings to the collection something its author must have valued quite highly, for the Virtue of patience—understood in its medieval context—is what we find most lacking in the actors of the negative exempla that fill the manuscript, and for this poet, patience is not one Virtue among many, essentially different virtues but rather an accident of unified Virtue.[2] The poet most clearly expresses the platonic understanding of the unity of Virtue in the poem *Patience* by means of an emendation to the Beatitudes in his prologue when he presents ultimate beatitude as steering one's heart. He reveals through that emendation, and then via nautical metaphor throughout the negative exemplum of Jonah, that patience—and indeed the whole of Virtue—is letting Christ be one's helmsman.[3]

   According to the platonic tradition, though we commonly use multiple words to describe its various facets, Virtue is a simple unity. Like H_2O, Virtue appears differently in different situations but remains substantially unchanged. Depending upon accidental atmospheric conditions, we call H_2O ice, water, steam, and so on. Similarly, we use different words for Virtue in different contexts. In the face of danger and potential fear, we call Virtue fortitude or courage, and in the face of abundance and potential excess, we call it temperance or moderation—but fortitude and moderation, and the like, are accidental expressions of a single essence. Contrarily, vices, failures to attain or maintain Virtue, are disparate.[4] This notion of unified Virtue has its basis in some of Plato's short dialogues, wherein the unity of Virtue typically remains a question (these dialogues tending toward *aporia*, an inability to speak further on the matter), but subsequent participants in the platonic tradition seem to assume the unity of Virtue.[5]

The clearest evidence that this poet understands Virtue platonically comes in his emendation of the final Beatitude from Jesus' Sermon on the Mount, recounted in Matthew 5:3–10, which the poet translates from the Vulgate. Whereas the final Beatitude in the Vulgate reads, "[b]eati, qui persecutionem *patiuntur* propter justitiam: quoniam ipsorum est regnum caelorum" (Matt. 5:10) [blessed are they who *suffer* persecution because of righteousness because theirs is the kingdom of heaven (D-R)], the final couplet of the poet's translation reads, "[þ]ay ar happen also þat *con her hert stere*, / For hores is þe heuen-ryche, as I er sayde," [They are happy also who *can steer their hearts*, / For theirs is the heavenly-kingdom, as I said before].[6] Replacing the Vulgate's reference to those who suffer persecution with a description of those who are simply virtuous, the poet quietly argues that patience is not one virtue among many but rather an accident of unified Virtue. Indeed, J. J. Anderson describes steering one's heart as "self-control in all circumstances," and this image may recall Plato's image of Virtue as a charioteer controlling passionate horses or Aristotle's description of virtue as the golden mean between two extremes.[7] I also see indications of the unity of Virtue in the poet's treatment of patience and poverty, which he says share a theme and are "fettled in on forme, þe forme and þe laste" [fettered in one form, the former/first and the last][8]: poverty begins the list of Beatitudes, patience ends it, and they both offer the kingdom of heaven. The poet may have platonic forms in mind with the first instance of "forme" here and be suggesting that poverty and patience follow the same pattern; indeed, they are "of on kynde" [of one kind/nature].[9] Even the second instance in the line of the word "forme," clearly meaning "former" or "first," punningly refers to *forme* as pattern, a beginning that contains an end, demonstrated by the poet's (aforementioned) single substantial change to his text. The poet also seems to express the contrariety of unified Virtue and disparate viciousness by using the word *vertu* only once in the poem and juxtaposing it to an alliterative list of Jonah's vices when from the belly of the whale Jonah prays to God for pity: "Now, Prynce, of Þy prophete pité Þou haue. / Þaȝ I be *fol and fykel and falce* of my hert, / Dewoyde now Þy vengaunce, þurȝ *vertu* of rauthe" [Now, Prince, have pity on your prophet. / Though I am *foolish and fickle and false* in my heart, / Withhold now your vengeance, by *virtue* of mercy].[10] Invoking *vertu* directly only once—in reference to God—implies that Virtue is heavenly and unified, and juxtaposing this singular *vertu* to foolishness, fickleness, and falsity emphasizes the disparateness of vice.[11]

But even as the poet's emendation of the Beatitudes indicates that he appreciates the platonic view of the unity of Virtue, it reveals the distinctively Christian understanding of Virtue outlined therein. In some contrast to Anderson, Eldredge argues that the poet does not exactly present Virtue as self-control, for the virtues of the Beatitudes are all passive, "virtues of resignation and acceptance."[12] But at least a few other critics fear an argument that may lead its audience to conclude the poem promotes passivity. Spyra, for instance, argues that "the virtue of patience has little to do with being passive . . . the most passive character in the tale, Jonah, represents inaction and impatience at its worst."[13] I mostly agree with Spyra here, and Jonah indeed generally serves as a negative exemplum, but we cannot avoid speaking of passivity altogether because "patience" and "passive" share an etymology. *Patientia*, the Latin noun from which the poet gets his Middle English word *pacience*, comes from *patior, passus*, a deponent verb primarily meaning "to suffer" and that, as a deponent, verbalizes something like active passivity. The central event of Christian salvation history is called the Passion, but (as the Old English "Dream of the Rood" demonstrates) Christ actively embraces a certain passivity in that greatest of historical moments for the medieval Christian that becomes an image of the whole Christian life.[14] Significantly (however anachronistically), Jonah himself fears crucifixion,[15] and his unwillingness to suffer makes him a negative or inverted type of Christ.[16]

Throughout the exemplum, the poet antithetically parallels the life of Jonah, who is unwilling to abide divine Providence, with the life of Christ, who St. Thomas argues most excellently exemplifies patience—indeed, all Virtue—in his Passion.[17] The most pertinent example of such antithesis comes when Jonah's sleep in the hull of a boat sailed by others through a storm typologically parallels Christ's similar (in)action before calming a storm on the sea of Galilee. The poet introduces this antithesis by declaiming the paradox that impatience (an unwillingness to suffer) leads Jonah to increased peril: "Lo, þe wytles wrechche! For he wolde noȝt suffer, / Now hatz he put hym in plyt of peril wel more" [Behold the witless wretch! Because he would not suffer, / Now he has put himself in a much more perilous plight].[18] Because he lacks patience, Jonah's physically active flight from God paradoxically leads to his greatest passivity (physically and spiritually) when he sleeps in the belly of a boat steered by pagans in a storm that renders them rudderless: "Þe bur ber to hit baft, þat braste alle her gere, / Þen hurled on a hepe þe *helme* and þe sterne" [The wind blew to the aft and broke all their gear, / Then hurled in a heap the *helm* and the stern].[19] This one of only two instances of the word *helme* in the entire manuscript shows that the boat carrying Jonah can no longer be steered by human hands.[20] Similarly, the other instance, coming in the compound "hande-helme" [hand-helm] in *Cleanness*, refers to the lack of any navigational tools on Noah's ark,[21] rudderless yet providentially directed.[22] Jonah's attempted self-determination leaves him with no control of his situation, and the poet emphasizes at length the inappropriateness of Jonah's sleeping at a time like this.[23]

Coming after a prologue in which the poet emends the Beatitudes to assert that "[þ]ay ar happen also þat con her hert stere" [They are happy also who can steer their hearts],[24] the exemplum not only indicates that Jonah lacks Virtue, the ability to steer his heart, but also recalls the motif of Christ the helmsman by suggesting that Providence ultimately directs Jonah's course. Numerous references to steering and steersmen in this passage reveal that one's external circumstances rest in the hands of Providence rather than in human hands.[25] Without a "hande-helme" by which to steer the ship, "[a] lodesmon"[26] [navigator] searches the ship to bring together all the men so they can cast lots to determine whose sin has brought this storm upon them.[27] When he finds Jonah asleep below deck and brings him topside, the *lodesmon* asks Jonah whether he has "no *gouernour* ne *god* on to calle" [no governor/ guide nor god to call upon].[28] The sailors—particularly this one whose job is to help guide the ship—ask Jonah to pray to any god who might guide their rudderless boat, and Jonah responds by saying he worships the God who wrought "þe wynde and þe sternes" [the wind and the stars],[29] a reference to the wind and stars that punningly reminds the audience of the stern and helm of the ship ruined by the wind and the waves. Even though—or precisely because—the boat carrying Jonah lacks a "sterne" [stern][30] to be guided by human hands, it rests under the guidance not only of "þe sternes" [the stars][31] but also the one who orders those stars.[32]

For this poet, Virtue does not involve steering or controlling things beyond oneself (like a boat) but rather steering that which is most deeply interior to a person: the heart. Indeed, when (as mentioned earlier) Jonah recognizes his viciousness in the belly of the whale, he confesses, "I be fol and fykel and falce *of my hert*" [I am foolish and fickle and false *in my heart*].[33] The poet's emendation of the Beatitudes suggests that Jonah's failure in Virtue can best be discussed in terms of a lack of patience, and we have seen that patience amounts to an active passivity. Jonah's first step toward embracing Providence is therefore difficult to label active or passive, for he actively asks to be thrown overboard and thereby made markedly passive[34]—apparently at the mercy of the waves but actually at the mercy of God who calls forth the waves, God from whom he previously ran. Patience appears passive because its action is internal. Virtue is not the ability to chart one's own bodily course, as Jonah tries to do at the beginning of his story, but rather the ability to move one's heart to trust Providence, Christ the helmsman. Although Jonah generally fails to steer his heart, the whale that saves him from drowning provides a clear example of a creature living in accord with Providence: "A wylde walterande whal, as Wyrde þen schaped" [A wild, wriggly whale that Providence then shaped].[35] However providentially created and directed, the whale travels through his own volition, "þurȝ ronk of his wylle" [through the strength (or, in the fullness) of his will].[36] Thus, we see in this "wylde" whale a perfect congruence of the will of creature and Creator, for it is simultaneously wild and providentially willed. And lest we overlook the significance of this line, the poet reiterates this notion when he recounts the whale's returning Jonah to land at the Lord's bidding: "Þe whal wendez at His wylle and a warþe fyndez, / And þer he brakez vp þe buyrne as bede hym oure Lorde" [The whale travels at His will and a shore finds, / And there he barfs up the man as our Lord bid him].[37] The capitalization of "His" here is editorial, and the line in the manuscript could be parsed such that "his wylle" refers to the will of the Lord, the will of the whale, or the will of the whale conformed to Providence—and this third option seems most consonant with the whole poem.[38] Creatures outside the animal kingdom also naturally conform themselves to Providence, and Eldredge notices such an instance,[39] when "Eurus and Aquilon, the two winds God commands to cause the storm at sea," immediately and happily oblige.[40] Whether we read the winds as inanimate forces of nature or as personalities, the whale and the winds together foreground by juxtaposition not only Jonah's particular impatience but also the uniqueness of human freedom in the created order.[41]

Given the freedom of the human heart, which does not naturally conform to Providence, humans must receive some manner of moral education if they are to be happy. Because the winds and the whale serve as foils to Jonah in terms of their respective accordance with divine Providence, it is fitting that the little progress Jonah makes in Virtue throughout this poem comes first when he is in the winds and then when he is in the whale.[42] As mentioned previously, in the winds he admits his wrongdoing and asks to be thrown overboard; in the whale, his will (however briefly) apparently becomes fully conformed to Providence. To demonstrate the process whereby Jonah's will becomes so conformed, the poet first reminds his audience of Jonah's prior unwillingness to commend himself to Providence and the consequence of his attempt to evade it: "Þer in saym and in sorȝe þat sauoured as helle, / Þer watz bylded his bour þat wyl no bale suffer" [There in grease and in filth that stank as hell, / There became the bedroom of he who would suffer no trouble].[43] At the beginning of his story, Jonah was unwilling to suffer, but suffering increases his understanding of Virtue: "Now he knawez Hym in care þat couþe not in sele" [Now he knows him in pain who could not (know him) in bliss].[44] Even Jonah recognizes during his typological three days in the belly of the whale, wherein he engages in some manner of contemplation,

"þenkande on Dryȝtyn, / His myȝt and His merci, His mesure þenne" [think-
ing about the Lord, / His might and His mercy, and then His moderation],[45]
that his sensory experience of suffering expands his knowledge of Virtue:

> I haf meled with Þy *maystres* mony longe day,
> Bot now I wot *wyterly* þat þose vnwyse ledes
> Þat affyen hym in vanyté and in vayne þynges
> For þink þat mountes to noȝt her mercy forsaken.

> [I have met with Your masters many a long day,
> But now I know viscerally that those unwise lads
> Who put their trust in vanity and in vain things
> Forsake mercy for what amounts to nothing.][46]

Jonah claims to have been taught rationally something not unlike scholastic
theology from "maystres" like those found in a medieval university, so he
already had a reasoned understanding of Providence—but now he knows
"wyterly" [viscerally] (and maybe even intellectually, given his thinking on
the Lord during these three days) that those who attempt to evade Providence
vainly seek vain things and forsake Mercy thereby. This experiential, sensory,
knowledge—coupled with rational and intellectual knowledge—leads Jonah
to promise due sacrifice to God in the future (in words anticipating a similar
oath in *Sir Gawain and the Green Knight*): "haf here my trauthe" [you have
my word (of honor)].[47]

By the time he reaches Nineveh, then, Jonah's education in Virtue has
been sensory, rational, even intellectual, but it has not been imaginative—and
Jonah's lack of imagination causes him to fall short of his promise to remain
true to Providence even as the Ninevites learn patience from his story in spite
of him.[48] In this context, imagination simply means seeing a mental image;
as the mode of knowing proper to irrational animals, it has more to do with
memory than with art. However, as we shall see, Jonah's failure in memory
ramifies into failures of empathy and patience.

By juxtaposition, the Ninevites prove Jonah slow and dense. Immediately
after hearing Jonah preach his "teme" [theme][49] all of the Ninevites—even
the animals—freely follow their king's decree[50] and repent.[51] The poem does
not reveal exactly what Jonah tells them, but if we imagine him arriving there
having not completely rid himself of the filth that clung to him from the belly
of the whale,[52] then we must imagine him explaining his appearance—even
his odor.[53] So the theme to which the Ninevites respond is probably the theme
they discover in that narrative.

Jonah, however, seems unable even to remember, much less understand,
the theme of his own story, and he inexplicably becomes disappointed that

God will not destroy Nineveh: "Muche sorȝe þenne satteled vpon segge Jonas; / He wex as wroth as þe wynde towarde oure Lorde" [Much sorrow then settled upon the man Jonah; / He grew as angry as the wind toward our Lord].[54] Whereas in the beginning of his story Jonah claims that he wants to flee Providence to avoid personal danger,[55] he now claims that he previously wanted to "flowen fer into Tarce" [flee far into Tarshish][56] precisely because he knew God would forgive the Ninevites. He first claims not to trust Providence, then claims he understood the patience of Providence all along but did not want to be its agent: "Wel knew I . . . Þy quoynt soffraunce" [I knew well . . . Your marvelous patience].[57]

By making his "point"[58] about patience by means of a story rather than a treatise, using words predicated upon images rather than syllogisms, the poet offers a vicarious experience of patience, Virtue, and Providence that he surely hopes will have a tropological effect on his audience.[59] Jonah's last words in the poem come in a prayer in which he says inexplicable things such as "neuer þou me sparez" [You never spared me],[60] apparently forgetting his miraculous experience with the whale. Davenport even deems sinful Jonah's "inability to see the parallel between himself and the men of Nineveh,"[61] and in the poem itself God rebukes Jonah for being "malicious" and unmerciful.[62] The last words spoken in the narrative of the poem come from God, and as the poem moves into its conclusion, they speak to the audience as well as to Jonah: "Be preue and be pacient in payne and in joye" [Be brave and be patient in pain and in joy].[63] Actually, as Andrew and Waldron note, editors disagree about where God's speech ends and the closing narration begins, and there is no decisive way to know whether this line should be read as spoken by God to Jonah or as coming from the poet to the audience.[64] Because we never see Jonah's reaction to God's final rebuke, Jonah ends the poem as an impatient character, but the audience can (like the Ninevites) end the poem already having begun to actualize the Virtue of patience by being open to (and having been open to) the transformative power of its poetry. From the belly of the whale, Jonah proclaims the need to learn patience experientially rather than abstractly, for he admits (though not in these exact words) that his abstract knowledge of Providence never steered his heart.

Similarly, we who read or hear this poem will not learn to steer our hearts if we only assess the poem abstractly; we must participate in it.[65] We must let it become part of us. Virtue must become our helm, part of our craft; it cannot remain external to us. By seeing the contrast between Jonah and the Ninevites, by experiencing that contrast vicariously, we become like the Ninevites in their ability to read and respond to the narrative's teaching without having to live that narrative ourselves. Jonah's experience with the whale should have become part of his personal narrative, but he quickly forgets the moral of his own story and ultimately (at least as far as the poem lets us see) denies the benevolence of Providence and the value of patience. As Anderson argues, only a negative exemplum reveals the necessity of its theme.[66] We see the necessity of patience by vicariously experiencing Jonah's vicious struggle against Providence. As the poem asserts in its closing line (echoing its opening line), "pacience is a nobel poynt, þaӡ it displese ofte" [patience is a noble point, though it is often unpleasant].[67] The poem's final words acknowledge that the audience may not be naturally inclined toward patience, but their echoing of the poem's opening words—with the small but significant inclusion of newfound nobility—suggests that a proper reception of this poem will form in the members of its audience the freedom to steer their hearts by conforming them to the will of Christ the helmsman, who for this poet is the only one who can help those who wish to be patient come to the point whereby they "con her hert stere" [can steer their hearts].[68]

NOTES

1. I would like to acknowledge the assistance (in various ways) of Greg Roper, Jane Beal, Amy (Freeman) Gamez, Serena Howe, Tiffany Schubert, Regina Zabinski, Jordan Grant, James Gillis, other friends and colleagues with whom I have discussed this project, and my wife, Amanda.

2. Toward the end of her chapter on "The Pastoral Theology of the *Gawain*-poet" in this volume, Grace Hamman similarly recalls how "we may see parallels between Jonah of *Patience*, Gawain, and the *Pearl*-dreamer" (p. 188).

3. References to Christ as Palinurus, Aeneas' helmsman in Virgil's *Aeneid*, are one particularly striking example of this motif. See William the Breton's "Invocation for Divine Aid": "Oh Christ . . . You are my Palinurus" (Gregory Stringer, trans., "Book I of William the Breton's 'Philippide': A Translation" [MA thesis, University of New Hampshire, Durham, 2010], 75). For a broad consideration of the motif of the rudderless boat in the English romance, see Helen Cooper, "Providence and the Sea: 'No Tackle, Sail, Nor Mast,'" in *The English Romance in Time* (Oxford: Oxford University Press, 2004), 106–36.

4. In his chapter on "Temperance and the Evolution of Concupiscible Vice in *Cleanness*" in this volume, Corey Owen, in a way that complements how I treat virtue and vice in the remainder of this chapter, says that "virtue also suggests the state of being unobstructed, cleared of restriction" and "[v]ices are obstructions that inhibit the soul's ability to perceive God" (p. 47).

5. See Plato's *Charmides, Euthyphro, Laches*, and—especially—the *Protagoras*.

6. Lines 27–28, emphases mine. Quotations of *Cleanness* are from Malcolm Andrew and Ronald Waldron, eds., *The Poems of the Pearl Manuscript: 'Pearl,' 'Cleanness,' 'Patience,' 'Sir Gawain and the Green Knight'Middle English Dictionary (MED)*, the glosses and commentary by Malcom and Waldron, and in one instance the translation by Margaret Williams.

7. J. J. Anderson, "Introduction," in *Patience*, ed. J. J. Anderson (Manchester: University Press, 1969), 7. Even if this poet had no direct knowledge of these notable images from the platonic tradition, he conceivably could have seen such famous and pithy excerpts in a florilegium or encyclopedic text—and his image is like them regardless.

8. *Patience*, l. 38.

9. *Patience*, l. 40.

10. *Patience*, ll. 282–84, emphases mine.

11. If we accept the gloss of *poynt* in the opening line as "virtue" (Anderson, "Introduction," 50), which the MED supports, then we might also see evidence of Virtue as an essential unity referred to accidentally by various words in the contrast between the single occurrence of *vertu* and the repetition of *poynt*, which appears four times and with other primary or secondary meanings (often spatiotemporal).

12. Laurence Eldredge, "Late Medieval Discussions of the Continuum and the Point of the Middle English *Patience*," *Vivarium* 17, no. 2 (1979): 112.

13. Piotr Spyra, *The Epistemological Perspective of the Pearl-Poet* (Surrey: Ashgate Publishing, 2014), 144.

14. Jessica Barr, *Willing to Know God* (Columbus: Ohio State University Press, 2010), esp. 13–19, considers at length the potential complementarity of activity and passivity.

15. *Patience*, ll. 95–96.

16. In her chapter "The Pastoral Theology of the *Gawain*-poet" in this volume, Grace Hamman similarly calls Jonah "an imperfect type of Christ" at the end of her section of *Cleanness* and *Patience* (p. 186).

17. See St. Thomas's *On the Apostle's Creed*.

18. *Patience*, ll. 113–14.

19. *Patience*, ll. 148–49, emphasis mine.

20. In *SGGK*, the word spelled "helm" always refers to a helmet.

21. *Cleanness*, l. 419.

22. In *Cleanness*, the poet describes God as the navigator of Noah's ark: "Nyf oure Lorde hade ben her lodezmon hem had lumpen harde" [If our Lord had not been their navigator they would have fared ill] (l. 424). Also see Cooper, "English Romance," 119. Cooper mentions this example from *Cleanness* and considers Jonah's whale a rudderless boat, but she never cites *Patience*.

23. *Patience*, ll. 183–92.

24. *Patience*, l. 27.

25. The poet uses the image of hands to make this point throughout this passage. First, in rousing the storm, God "calde on þat ilk crafte He carf with His *hondes*" [summoned that same power He shaped with his *hands*] (l. 131); then, after Jonah tells the sailors to throw him overboard, they try to use their oars to evade the storm and avoid doing so, but their oars break and "[þ]enne hade þay noȝt in her *honde* þat hem help myȝt" [then they no longer had in *hand* what might help them] (l. 222); finally, before they throw Jonah overboard, the sailors pray to (Jonah's) God that he not hold against them the innocent blood they will soon have on "her *handez*" [their *hands*] (l. 227, emphases mine).

26. *Patience*, l. 181.

27. *Patience*, ll. 170–80.

28. *Patience*, l. 199, emphases mine.

29. *Patience*, l. 207.

30. *Patience*, l. 149.

31. *Patience*, l. 207.

32. The poet may have deduced an etymological connection between the word for the stern (here rudder, direction-setter) of a ship and the stars (direction-finders). The *MED* suggests *stern(e)* can mean "guidance, direction" at least by the fifteenth century, citing an example from one version of *The Romance of Guy of Warwick* that apparently refers to Providence: "goddis sterne" [God's guidance]. Although absent from this manuscript, the contemporary compound *lodesterre* [lodestar or north star] (of which the *MED* cites examples from Chaucer), in light of the aforementioned "lodesmon" [navigator], demonstrates the strong connection—even etymologically— between navigators and the stars.

33. *Patience*, l. 283, emphasis mine.

34. *Patience*, l. 211.

35. *Patience*, l. 247.

36. *Patience*, l. 298. Relevant entries in the *MED* suggest an etymological relationship between *will* and *wild* (in various forms) and that the form "willed" would have been familiar to the poet. The "wylde flod" [wild flood] in *Cleanness* (l. 415) may be a similar instance of this pun (and see also *Cleanness*, l. 948).

37. *Patience*, ll. 339–40. Eldredge, "Late," 113–14, similarly considers how "the whale only vomits Jonah onto the beach when God commands him to do so," but Eldredge does not make any claims about the potential pun on "wyld" [wild/willed].

38. Indeed, the aforementioned "þurʒ ronk of his wylle" [through the strength (or, in the fullness) of his will] in line 298 could similarly be parsed as referring ambiguously to the will of the whale, the will of God, or their wills in concert.

39. *Patience*, ll. 135–36.

40. Eldredge, 114. The poet may even punningly suggest a similarity between the whale and the winds, for the whale "*wendez* at His wylle" [travels at His will] (l. 339, emphasis mine).

41. See Boethius, *Consolation of Philosophy* (b. 1, m. 5, esp. ll. 26–27). See also the introductory paragraph in Elizabeth Allen's "Ecology in the *Pearl*-poet" in this volume.

42. Ordell G. Hill, "The Audience of *Patience*," *Modern Philology* 66, no. 2 (1968): 107, quoting Philip of Harveng's *De silentio clericorum*, similarly argues that Jonah's sin of disobedience is emphasized in a contrast between him and the obedient whale: "Mira res! homo ratione praeditus mandatis coelestibus non timet contraire, et marina bellua diligit obedire. . . . Inobedientem itaque prophetam obediens piscis detinuit" [What a wonder! The rational man given a celestial mandate does not fear to go against it, and the whale of the sea lovingly obeys. . . . Therefore the obedience of the fish restrains the disobedience of the prophet] (translation my own, with some helpful suggestions from my colleague Chris Collins).

43. *Patience*, ll. 275–76.

44. *Patience*, l. 296.

45. *Patience*, ll. 284–95.

46. *Patience*, ll. 330–32, emphases mine. My translation of line 332 closely follows that of Margaret Williams in her *The Pearl-Poet: His Complete Works*.

47. *Patience*, l. 336. Compare "haf here my trawþe" [you have my word (of honor)] (*SGGK*, l. 2287).

48. I use these terms (wit, imagination, reason, and intellect) with their Boethian references to the hierarchical system related to the chain of Being in which all living organisms have wit or sense, true animals (moving creatures) have both wit and imagination, humans have these and reason, and super-human creatures (i.e., angels) have all these as well as intellect (see the *Consolation*, b. 5, p. 4). Although intellect is not the distinctively human mode of knowing, humans are granted some intellectual knowledge before being embodied (the platonic doctrine of *anamnesis* referring to the remembering of what has been granted to one's intellect), and humans receive divine inspiration intellectually.

49. *Patience*, l. 358.

50. *Patience*, ll. 388–90.

51. *Patience*, ll. 405–407.

52. *Patience*, ll. 341–42.

53. I have not emphasized Jonah's clothing here, but it may similarly contribute to his message; Kimberly Jack's chapter on sartorial adornment in this volume helpfully reminds us that clothing can be a sign of conversion, for, responding to Jonah's message, the Ninevites tear their clothing in what she calls "an immediate sartorial display of repentance" (p. 158). Perhaps clothing can be an occasion for conversion as well.

54. *Patience*, ll. 409–10. The word "segge" (per the *MED*) can refer not only to a man or person but also to a chair or seat, so there seems to be a pun here: Jonah is like a chair upon which sorrow sits.

55. *Patience*, ll. 75–84.

56. *Patience*, l. 424.

57. *Patience*, l. 417.

58. *Patience*, l. 1.

59. This entire paragraph attempts to describe what Grace Hamman calls "The Pastoral Theology of the *Gawain*-poet" in her chapter with that title in this volume. Hamman argues that "the text and others like it aim to promote self-knowledge of human limitation," that "the *Gawain*-poet's interest in human limitation is pastoral," and that the "theological interests in this poem . . . work pastorally in stimulating acknowledgement of need for God and ensuing spiritual transformation." Furthermore, she recognizes that the audience's "identification [with sinful characters] creates disquieting interior examination," describes our poet as "a pastoral poet keenly interested in the development of the life that Christ describes in the Sermon on the Mount," and concludes that "[t]he poet advocates for a humble reader within a humble church, careful to practice recognition of limitations but contained within the secure knowledge of God's love and grace mediated through the sacraments, despite the high potential for human error" (p. 189).

60. *Patience*, l. 484.

61. *Patience*, l. 132.

62. *Patience*, ll. 522–23.

63. *Patience*, l. 525.

64. Andrew and Waldron, *Poems*, 206.

65. In the chapter on *Patience* in his book *Tropologies*, Ryan McDermott suggests that the poet amplifies the biblical text precisely "to allow the writer and readers to participate in the narrative" (99) and particularly notes the ethical aspect of this participation (107, 116).

66. Anderson, "Introduction," 9.

67. *Patience*, l. 531.

68. *Patience*, l. 27.

BIBLIOGRAPHY

Andrew, Malcolm, and Ronald Waldron, eds. *The Poems of the Pearl Manuscript: 'Pearl,' 'Cleanness,' 'Patience,' 'Sir Gawain and the Green Knight.'* Exeter: University of Exeter Press, 2007.

Anderson, J. J. "Introduction." *Patience*. Edited by J. J. Anderson. Manchester: Manchester University Press, 1969.

Barr, Jessica. *Willing to Know God: Dreamers and Visionaries in the Later Middle Ages*. Columbus: Ohio State University Press, 2010.

Beal, Jane, ed. *Becoming the Pearl-Poet: Perceptions, Connections, Receptions.* New York: Lexington Books, 2022.

Boethius. *Theological Tractates, The Consolation of Philosophy*. Loeb Classical Library. Trans. H. F. Stewart, E. K. Rand, and S. J. Tester. Cambridge, MA: Harvard University Press, 1973.

Cooper, Helen. "Providence and the Sea: 'No Tackle, Sail, Nor Mast.'" In *The English Romance in Time: Transforming Motifs from Geoffrey of Monmouth to the Death of Shakespeare*, 106–36. Oxford: Oxford University Press, 2004.

Eldredge, Laurence. "Late Medieval Discussions of the Continuum and the Point of the Middle English *Patience*." *Vivarium* 17, no. 2 (1979): 90–115.

Hill, Ordelle G. "The Audience of *Patience*." *Modern Philology* 66, no. 2 (1968): 103–109.

Kottler, Barnet, and Alan M. Markman. *A Concordance to Five Middle English Poems*. Pittsburgh: University of Pittsburgh Press, 1966.

McDermott, Ryan. "How to Invent History: *Patience*, the *Glossa ordinaria*, and the Ethics of the Literal Sense." In *Tropologies: Ethics and Invention in England, c. 1350–1600*. Notre Dame: University of Notre Dame Press, 2016.

Spyra, Piotr. *The Epistemological Perspective of the Pearl-Poet*. Surrey: Ashgate Publishing, 2014.

William the Breton. *Book 1 of William the Breton's "Philippide": A Translation.* Translated by Gregory Stringer. MA thesis, University of New Hampshire, Durham, 2010.

Williams, Margaret, R.S.C.J., trans. *The Pearl-Poet: His Complete Works.* New York: Random House, 1967.

Chapter Four

The Failure of Perfection in *Sir Gawain and the Green Knight*

Mickey Sweeney

Sir Gawain and the Green Knight is perhaps the best known of the *Pearl*-poet poems and has garnered so much attention from the critics that it is often difficult to keep pace with not only what is written about the poem, or the *Pearl*-poet, but how critical trends in general influence our interpretations. In the last decade alone, work on authorship, nationalism, post-colonialism, and linguistics, as well as the advances in technology, have provided new platforms for historians, theorists, linguists, and experts in manuscript work. This chapter, while focusing on a reading of the poem that inspires a questioning of authority and perfection in the romance genre, will also attempt to highlight where we are in our critical conversations about select critical points in the poem.

THE CHANGING ROLE OF HISTORY IN *GAWAIN* INTERPRETATIONS: THE *PEARL*-POET'S EXAMINATION OF THE APPLICATION OF CHIVALRY

> Still, shame will haunt the poem's vision of what chivalry finally amounts to, not just in its historical vulnerability but *in its inability to give fully to its own professed ideas*. The motto appended to the poem by one anonymous scribe suggests as much in its aggressive displacement of all shame onto those who would dare to think it "*Honi soit qui mal y pense*![1]

The clear and complicated argument that Walter Wadiak sets in motion in *Savage Economy* delves deeply into the theory of gifts and provides his readers with a very provocative insight into the nature of the chivalric economy. Medieval chivalry, more specifically, fourteenth-century English chivalric knighthood, however, is not the only institution unable to live up to its own professed ideals. We could imagine that critics and reformers of the fourteenth-century English Church and the State had much to keep them occupied.[2] The Avignon Papacy of 1309–1376, the selling of indulgences that fired into focus in late fourteenth-century literature, the sheer weight of hostility aimed at Church figures evident in such texts as Chaucer's *Canterbury Tales* and *Piers Plowman*, tells us much about the possibility of cynicism for Church practices.[3] We might also look at the fraught political scene that engulfed a succession of English kings; Richard with his parliamentary struggles, changing economy, and usurpation is perhaps the most dramatic, but his ancestors were complicated monarchs as well. It is difficult for many reasons to date the poem; so, when it comes to drawing detailed connections to historical events and their implications for *Sir Gawain and the Green Knight*, critics might still hesitate to name the actual date and time of the poem's creation. Recently, however, several interesting and provocative arguments for dating the poem/manuscript as late as the first decade of the fifteenth century have surfaced, Joel Fredell's recent article "The *Pearl*-Poet Manuscript in York" being the most persuasive.[4]

Of course, it is by no means new to examine poems in their historical context. Post-colonial research and the impact of a national identity in formation, two themes of critical interest over the last few years, have also impacted criticism of *SGGK* and many have found that fourteenth-century poets are a natural resource for examining the strained relationship between culture and national identity. Andrea Ruddick's "English Identity and Political Structure in the Fourteenth Century" focuses on the "main audience for prophetic material in the fourteenth century [which] consisted of literate, politically aware secular clergy and laity involved in government, for whom prophecy offered a means of political commentary."[5] This is the audience we would anticipate for readers of the *Pearl*-poet.[6] If we might imagine that our poet could be understood, in part, to have an interest in politics through his treatment of kingship, and the way he unpacks chivalric/noble and Catholic culture, then we can also see the rewards for constructing a plot that needed Morgan and her relationship to Merlin.[7] These specific elements, brought together as they are, create a pseudo "anthology" of interests that are inextricably woven into national history, like the very idea of Arthur himself. The evolving status of the romance genre and its connection to the evolving status of chivalry and knighthood creates additional links that can be fruitfully pursued by the methodology that historians such as Ruddick lay out.

For example, the status of the knight was under assault in the fourteenth century. Michael Prestwich in *The Three Edwards* argues as the thirteenth century becomes the fourteenth, few could maintain the expense of knighthood, and the kings began to look for ways to increase the numbers of their knights.[8] Richard Kaeuper's extensive research into chivalry, knighthood, and its relationship to culture and Catholicism, as well as Nigel Saul's work specifically on English chivalry, make clear to us that the daily tension between ideal standards of Christianity and violence was understood, if not often addressed.[9] What is most pertinent for our understanding of the *Gawain* poem is Kaeuper's assertion that the "key trait of knightly prowess wins divine approbation; disloyalty and anything leading to dishonor becomes a sin, a moral and not merely, social blunder."[10] We should note the claim that God would welcome good and brave knights into paradise, a trope seen often in chivalric literature, but also understand that this certainly suggests a harsher reading of Gawain's, and indeed the entire court's, cowardice. Kaeuper outlines for his readers that:

> Through the practice of chivalry, the heroic life and ideals [which the poet goes to such lengths to detail for his audience], which carried such a strong sense of independent moral standards, combined with selected principles of medieval Christianity . . . warriors fused their violent way of life and their dominance in society with the will of God.[11]

This context creates room for readers to question the human authority which "authorizes" such a version of Christianity. It is radically different in the context of *Pearl*, but it is clear that the mourner too wishes for a different, more comforting form of Christianity. Such an interpretation could provide a careful reader with an understanding of how *Pearl* and *SGGK* might share some common interests; both poems tackle the complications that come when individuals (the mourner, or groups of individuals, such as chivalric knights) seek to adapt their own form of faith, while respecting traditional norms. Both texts struggle with the expectations of ideal or, perhaps better said, idealized behavior.

QUESTIONING THE VOICE OF AUTHORITY THAT IS THE ROMANCE GENRE

When thinking about *Sir Gawain and the Green Knight* in such a framework, we instantly move beyond the formulaic, which is built on the patterns that emerge from medieval English Arthurian romance, of magic, Arthurian courts, and quests, to see how the poet stages his narrative in seemingly familiar places, such as bedrooms and forests, quests and temptations, while at the same time, causing them to function in subversive ways. To analyze the *Gawain* poem on the terms of the romance genre, we have to ask the age-old

question that critics have struggled with: what is a romance?[12] The answer
may hinge on what we understand the function of text to be in the fourteenth
century. If we think of *SGGK* as a conventional romance, as so many critics
do, potentially heavily influenced by continental generic formulas, then we
can see that critics such as Carolyne Larrington have skillfully understood
the power of the *Gawain* text in terms of individual growth. She argues for
example in her work *The Enchantress, the Knight, and the Cleric* that:

> Indeed, in a number of texts—the *Lancelot* and *Sir Gawain and the Green
> Knight* in particular—courtly values tend to be promoted in a distinctively
> female-gendered domain, risking accusations of effeminacy. But the clear con-
> nection between women and courtesy translates into the requirement for the
> knight to cultivate civilized values in order to secure romantic love, and thus
> guarantee his "heteronormativity." It is a powerful incentive to the acquisition
> and display of such talents, as embodied in Lancelot, Gauvain, and his English
> counterpart, Gawain; feminized and intellectual values provide a payoff for the
> knight in terms of sexual success and enhanced status within courtly society.[13]

This reading suggests a *Gawain*-poet interested in culture, emotion, and
human dynamics. The interpretation of how the text functions is clearly very
different from the "cultural currency" that historians such as Kaeuper and
Saul see in the poet's use of chivalric norms. Many literary critics, however,
see the psychological or feminist readings of quest and romance characters
as the most powerful.[14]

But there is no denying that the authoritative underpinnings of the social
norms in this poem—Church and State—come under sharp criticism for
what they demand of Gawain as knight. In *Pearl*, we might safely argue that
Christian and cultural norms for grief are under examination, but in *Gawain*
it is clear that while the personal is crucial (Gawain's fear of death under-
pins the plot), the structural issues demand attention. The way chivalry and
Christianity function in the poem seem to leave Gawain with little chance for
a successful outcome: survival and honor intact. If we were to examine this in
purely psychological terms, we might have to confine our analysis to Gawain
finding flaws in himself, but his response to being tricked, plus his anger and
revealed cynicism, shine a light on the flawed nature of the systems that are
the foundations of chivalric knighthood.[15] To build context for this reading,
consider the insights of Rosalind Field, as so much of her research on insular
romance and the "Matter of England" has resulted in a different perspective
being brought to English texts.[16] Field argues that the Norman interest in the
pre-English past, and the Anglo-Norman belief that "history . . . is the cre-
ation of a clerk" set the stage for a different romance formula. It is the belief
about history that:

leads to the development of a romance past which is importantly different from that of the *romans courtois* of Chrétien and his followers: one in which place is precise and important, in which values are outward looking and non-exclusive, and which events relate to the present not as models but as precedents. It is largely non-escapist and persuades not by its truth to personal experience and emotion but *by its resemblance to external encounters with authority*, geography, warfare, or social relationships.[17]

If the *Gawain* romance *models* external fourteenth-century encounters with authority, both secular and spiritual, then much could be explained.

THE VOICES OF FOURTEENTH-CENTURY AUTHORITY: KING, CHURCH, AND THE MIDDLEMEN

Arthur the beardless boy is not much of a king *yet*. He is not criticized, as such, but Gawain, because of Arthur's reckless invitation to wonders, must substitute his body for Arthur's in the beheading game. Arthur's authority as king must be upheld, even if the young Arthur does not fully appreciate the possible outcomes of his use of that authority.[18] The poem's structure, as well as the nobles of Arthur's court, encourage us to step back from the plot line and be critical of the authority that allows for a waste of Gawain's potential. It is clear that they are unhappy that he is to be sacrificed in this careless manner:

> Carade or that comly, Bi Kryst, hit is scathe
> That thous leude, schal be lost, that art of lyf noble!
> To fynde hys fere upon folde, in faith, is not ethe.
> Warloker to haf wroght had more wyt bene,
> And haf dyght yonder dere a duk to have worthed;
> A lowande leder of ledez in londe hym wel semesz,
> And so better haf ben then britned to noght,
> Hadet with an alvisch mon, for angardez pryde
> Who knew ever any king such counsel to take
> As kynghtez in cavelaciounz in Crystmasse gomnez![19]

[And together they whispered to one another, / Distressed for that handsome one, 'What a pity, by Christ, indeed / That your life must be squandered, noble as you are! / To find his equal on earth is not easy, in faith. / To have acted more cautiously would have been much wiser, / And have appointed that dear man to become a duke: / To be a brilliant leader of men, as he is so well suited, / And would better have been so than battered to nothing, / Beheaded by an ogrish man out of excessive pride. / Who knew a king to take such foolish advice / As knights offer in arguments about Christmas games?'][20]

As support for seeing this romance as critical of how a king uses his voice of authority, I would argue that the poet is not the only poet to use a romance in this way. If we look to Chaucer's knight, if only for a moment, we can see some very similar things happening in the prologue to the *Knight's Tale* and the tale itself. In Chaucer's *Canterbury Tales*, the voices of authority are undermined at every turn. The Knight in his own prologue is made suspect by the controversial nature of the battles that are listed as his source of "worthynesse." The use of historical battles suggests a very real political impact on the literary knight.[21] The other authorities in the poem, such as the gods, are depicted are squabbling children. Theseus, the human face of authority, has acquired it by conquering the Amazons, women, which suggests that he at least has done better against the female challenge than Gawain, but his right to rule seems still somehow unsavory, given knightly duties to cherish women.[22]

In returning to the *Gawain* poem, it becomes clear that not even the love of a woman, although the temptress' temptations do not really compare to the love of Emelye, can dissuade Gawain from following his chivalric duty. It is only the love of his life that proves powerful enough to crack his resolve to remain chivalric. Yet it is his faith that should be his steely guide here. His prayers, his confession, and his belief in Mary should preserve him from harm. But the nature by which faith and chivalry are intertwined in this poem, and in historical terms, creates complexity for Gawain which catches him, but perhaps not the audience, by surprise.

CRITICAL QUESTIONS REGARDING CONFESSION AND THE "WOMAN PROBLEM"

Catholicism and chivalry are often framed by the expectations of perfection in romance: the most handsome knight, the strongest faith, the purest love, and so on. When looking at the work of Elspeth Kennedy, we see that our poet may have built upon the tension between pride and ego, topics that were well-known to knights such as Raymod Llull and Geoffroi de Charny.[23] We should also note that as the fourteenth century progressed, writers such as Gower and Chaucer began to focus on "the falseness of knights, lambasting them for their self-indulgence . . . and their quest for worldly glory."[24] In stark contrast to these concerns, we see the poet deliberately, and in intimate detail, describe Gawain as the "*fautlez*" knight:

> For ay faythful in fyue and sere fyue syþez
> Gawan watz for gode knawen, and as golde pured,
> Voyded of vche vylany, wyth vertuez ennourned in mote;

Fyrst he watz funden fautlez in his fyue wyttez,
And efte fayled neuer þe freke in his fyue fyngres,
And alle his afyaunce vpon folde watz in þe fyue woundez
Þat Cryst kaȝt on þe croys, as þe crede tellez;
That alle his forsnese he feng at the five joyez
The fyft fyve that I fynde that the frek used
Watz fraunchyse and felaghschyp forbe al thyng
His clannes and his cortaysye croked were never
And pite, that passez all poyntez: thyse pure five
Were harder happed on that hathel then on any other.
Now alle these five sythez, for sothe, were fetled on this kynight
And fyched upon five poyntez, that fayld never[25]

[For always faithful in five ways, and five times in each case / Gawain was reputed as virtuous, like refined gold, / Devoid of all vice, and with all courtly virtues adorned. . . . First he was judged perfect in his five senses, / And next his five fingers never lost their dexterity; / And all his earthly faith was in the five wounds / That Christ suffered on the cross, as the Creed declares. . . . All his fortitude should come from the five joys. . . . The fifth group of the five the men respect, I hear / Was generosity and the love of fellow-men above all; / His purity and courtesy were never lacking, / And surpassing all others in compassion: these noble five / Were more deeply implanted in that man than any other. / Now truly, all these five groups were embodied in that knight, / Based upon five points that never failed][26]

Pearl-poet critics have often explored how human nature is framed in his poems, but perfection was a problem that many historical knights grappled with as well. Geoffroi de Charny in *A Knight's Own Book of Chivalry*, as translated by Elspeth Kennedy, says: "Honorable knights must take the risk of losing it all: life, honor, and possessions" and there of course we can see a reflection of Gawain's actions. Geoffroi however *does not expect* perfection; indeed, he warns against it. Kaeuper in his introduction to *Book of Chivalry of Geoffroi de Charny* summarizes:

He expects knights to aspire to greatness, but he never demands that they achieve perfection. A fascinating list of historical examples makes just this point. Even the greatest men from biblical and classical times revealed flaws. Charny's highly personal choices include Samson, Absalom, St. Peter, and Julius Caesar. All failed in at least one aspect of what he considers their good chivalry. Yet he also wants a single great example to remind men to aspire for perfection. He cites that "holy knight" Judas Maccabeus from the Hebrew scriptures. . . . Above all, Charny reminds his contemporaries, such perfection can never be attributed to human effort alone, but rather to God's wonderful grace.[27]

Geoffroi's use of biblical models as flawed knights provides a very useful context and model for the *Gawain* poem. It creates a bridge between Gawain's use of biblical figures and the final bedroom scene, in which Gawain makes the cross and prays to Mary against the allure of the Temptress. This is the most crucial moment in text, even if Gawain does not realize it. It is clear, however, that in Gawain's understanding of temptation as sins of sexuality, female-driven as it were, Gawain has failed to understand the complexity of the nature of sin. Because he has not given in sexually to the Temptress, he believes that he has found the moral path forward. His taking of the girdle is not a moral moment for him, and even with his confession, he is still none the wiser. We are told he confessed "himself honestly and admitted his sins, both great and small, and begs forgiveness; he calls on the priest for absolution. And the priest absolved him completely and made him as clean as if the Judgement were appointed for the next day [*as domezday schulde haf ben dight on the morn*.]"[28] These words and this moment in the poem have troubled critics and audiences most likely from first reading.[29] It is difficult to convince the audience of the confession's efficacy because this confession did not result in Gawain giving up the green girdle.[30] In fact, he proudly displays it on the journey to the Green Chapel. That Gawain feels his confession should have saved him from sin is clear in his enjoyment of his last few hours at Hautedesert, but also in his furious reaction to the discovery that he was tricked. He is angry at both the Church and the courtly game that placed him in such a vulnerable position. The Church's failure to alert him to the complex nature of sin may well deserve to be considered as complicit in the downfall of Gawain, although he and the poet focus his complaints on women.

The poet demonstrates that neither faith nor maintaining strict chivalric standards protects knights from reality, which for Gawain means the potential of an ignominious death or further manipulation and trickery. Gawain's bitterness at having been tricked into acting the coward despite being trained as the best of knights, having the best family connections, and having been given the gift of faith (he is the best of believers, as being Mary's knight suggests), demonstrate that this code of chivalry and church are found wanting. Kaeuper, as quoted earlier, suggested that chivalric knights often focused on "independent moral standards, [and] selected principles of medieval Christianity,"[31] which we may see as an intriguing reading of just how Gawain arrived at this situation. The emphasis on Gawain's body and spirit (note that his body is currently acting as the king's body), his five levels of perfection that the poet emphasizes so strongly, coalesce at this moment to lead the audience's imagination to the very source of that weakness: human nature, but as Gawain sees it, women. It is fascinating to think how desire, temptation, and knowledge were intermingled in the symbolism of the weaker body, that of Eve, and how the poet's pattern of forcing Gawain into the feminized position, makes it possible to rewrite that paradigm. Gawain's bitterness can be understood in such a framework as can his rant against women in the Bible. It is only after he can rationalize his failure in biblical terms that he can see himself as the new Adam, in the company of Solomon, Sampson, and other such betrayed heroes. Church and state are aligned by this diatribe. Arthur, we know, will be betrayed by a woman, and the state will collapse; so too, Adam was betrayed by Eve and man sent from the garden. The Church and State—male patriarchal identities—will always be vulnerable to the tricks and the subversion of what is represented here as female, or at least that is what Gawain is identifying the problem as, though we know it to be human nature.[32]

AUTHORITY AND HUMAN NATURE: COMPLICATED CONCLUSIONS

Gawain had to offer up his life, his body, to restore the pride upon which Arthur's authority rested in the poem, even if it was Arthur's childish whims that brought the need for such a sacrifice. Gawain's return is celebrated, but I would argue the news he brings is bleak. Several critics in recent articles would disagree; Evelyn Reynolds, for one, suggests the poet's use of "kynde" requires a rereading. She argues:

> The court sets aside Gawain's personal shame, his personal outcry at his sin, and takes his sin as success. . . . When Camelot does so, the poem hints that the community can help the individual see his own overlapping affinities. Gawain's actions have betrayed—in both senses of the word—his nature; his actions are both false to his identity and reveal his identity. Although he fails, Camelot as a whole rises to the challenge as it practices its re-creative bent, turning fault into honor, wrenching Gawain's individual misery into communal triumph.[33]

Like so many of the knights who experienced the battles listed in the *Knight's Prologue* in Chaucer, or like historical knights in the fourteenth century, Gawain has had to suffer humiliation to execute his duty. The court seeks to reinvest the feminized "luf token" that represents the sacrifice of Gawain's pride with a new meaning, but that meaning remains vague. It is to honor Gawain, and anyone who wore it after was honored, but for what? Being alive? And even before we have a minute to ask that question, the narrator reminds of us Troy and the great betrayal of honor, and then leaps to the greatest story of sacrifice not for a king, but for all men: "the thorn-crowned" who sacrificed his life for mankind.

In the hands of the poet, the romance genre becomes a subversive tool to critique fourteenth-century foundations of authority—Church and State.[34]

Ironically, the poet manipulates the very genre that was created to reinforce noble, chivalric, Christian, and male superiority, by demonstrating its weak spot: its own insistence on male perfection and resistance to human nature.

NOTES

1. Walter Wadiak, *Savage Economy* (Notre Dame, IN: Notre Dame Press, 2016), 105.

2. See Nancy Ciccione's chapter in the book for a more in-depth reading of religious context and impact.

3. Nigel Saul, *Chivalry in Medieval England* (Cambridge, MA: Harvard University Press), 236. Saul further argues: "Confidence in the papacy was undermined first by the long residence at Avignon and then by the schism between the two obediences" (p. 236).

4. Joel Fredell, "*Pearl*-Poet Manuscript in York," Studies *in the Age of Chaucer* 36 (2014): 1–39. See also the Fredell chapter in this collection for a more current perspective. See Murray McGillivray and Christina Duffy for a fascinating exploration of what information the application of multispectral imaging can provide in regards to the Cotton Nero A.x manuscript. Murray McGillivray and Christina Duffy, "New Light on the *Sir Gawain and the Green Knight* Manuscript: Multispectral Imaging and the Cotton Nero A.x Illustrations," *Speculum* 92:S1 (2017): 110–44. Equally, we are beginning to see critical questioning of the "accepted" fact that the *Gawain* and *Pearl* poems were written by the same poet; see the work of Richard Firth Green.

5. Andrea Ruddick, *English Identity and Political Structure in the Fourteenth Century* (Cambridge: Cambridge University Press, 2013), 42.

6. See David Coley's chapter in this collection for a more in-depth discussion of audience.

7. Ruddick, *English Identity*, 42–43.

8. Michael Prestwich, *The Three Edwards, War and the State in England 1272–1377* (London: Weidenfeld and Nicolson,1980), 139, 140. Extended discussion pages: 138–44. See Saul, *Chivalry*, 86 for a further discussion of why there were so few knights in the fourteenth century; one reason, as given, the cost: "A major disincentive to service were the startup costs which a knight faced in fitting out for war."

9. Saul, *Chivalry*, 348. Saul argues that the decline in chivalry begins at "the first signs of a falling away in mutual respect between knights in war [which] are found in the late thirteenth and fourteenth centuries." "The essence of medieval chivalry was to be found in the set of humane values governing the conduct of war based on the principle of self-preservation among knights." See also pages 159–76 for an expanded discussion of the decline of knighthood. Richard Kaeuper, *Chivalry and Violence in Medieval Europe* (Oxford: Oxford University Press, 1999), 47–48.

10. Kaeuper, *Chivalry*, 48.

11. Kaeuper, *Chivalry*, 50.

12. K. S. Whetter, *Understanding Genre and Medieval Romance* (Aldershot: Ashgate, 2008), 35, 61. Whetter in chapter two of *Understanding* suggested Middle

English romance is defined by "a combination and interaction of love, ladies and adventure, culminating in a happy ending." See also the conclusion: "Romances were not always named as such . . . but the idea and form of the romance genre clearly existed . . . a community of users had a clear conception of the genre and its features" (p. 154).

13. Carolyne Larrington's note cites the phrase "heteronormativity" as Dorsey Armstrong's; see D. Armstrong, *Gender and the Chivalric Community in Malory's Morte d'Arthur* (Gainesville: University Press of Florida, 2003), 17–18. Carolyne Larrington, "The Enchantress, the Knight and the Cleric: Authorial Surrogates in Arthurian Romance," *Arthurian Literature* 25 (2008): 46.

14. There are many critics of this persuasion, but for a general overview of those positions see: Thomas Hahn, "Gawain and Popular Chivalric Romance in Britain" and Sheila Fisher, "Women and Men in Later Medieval English Romance" in *The Cambridge Companion to Medieval Romance*, ed. Roberta L. Krueger (Cambridge: Cambridge University Press, 2000), 218–34, 150–67.

15. Please see Grace Hamman's chapter in this collection for a more in-depth discussion of theology and its focus on human weakness.

16. Rosalind Field, "Romance as History, History as Romance" in *Romance in Medieval England.* eds. Maldwyn Mills, Jennifer Fellows, Carol Meale (Woodbridge: D.S. Brewer: 1991), 168–69.

17. Field, "Romance as History, History as Romance," 169 (my italics).

18. For an interesting discussion of Arthur's status of "without an heir" impacting the response of Gawain and the court, see Joseph Turner, "Lady Bertilak and the Rhetoric of Women in *Sir Gawain and the Green Knight*" in *Later Middle English Literature, Materiality, and Culture*, ed. Brian Castle and Erick Kelemen (Newark: University of Delaware Press, 2018): 57–70.

19. *Sir Gawain and the Green Knight*, ll. 674–83.

20. All translations unless otherwise noted are from *Sir Gawain and the Green Knight*, ed. and trans. James Winny (Peterborough: Broadview Press, 1998).

21. Saul, *Chivalry*, 128–58. See specifically for a discussion of Chaucer's Knight, 231.

22. See Susan Crane, *Gender in Romance in Chaucer's* Canterbury Tales (Princeton, NJ: Princeton University Press, 1994), 169–85, for a much more in-depth discussion of these connections.

23. Elspeth Kennedy from the unpublished "Knight as Reader" as quoted in Kaeuper, *Chivalry*, 31.

24. Saul, *Chivalry*, 129.

25. *Sir Gawain and the Green Knight*, ll. 632–58.

26. This Middle English passage is quoted from the online *Sir Gawain and the Green Knight*, *Corpus of Middle English Prose and Verse*, resource at the University of Michigan source: https://quod.lib.umich.edu/c/cme/Gawain/1:2?rgn=div1;view =fulltext.

27. Geoffroi de Charny, A *Knight's Own Book of Chivalry*, ed. and trans. Elspeth Kennedy, Introduction by Richard W. Kaeuper (Philadelphia: University of Pennsylvania Press, 2005), 39–40. Richard Kaeuper and Elspeth Kennedy, *The Book of*

Chivalry of Geoffroi De Charny: Text, Context, and Translation (Philadelphia: University of Pennsylvania Press, 2005), 58.

28. *Sir Gawain and the Green Knight*, ll. 1880–84. Richard Firth Green's forthcoming work on the poet may offer a very different reading of the priest and Gawain's confession. His research offers some very different and exciting possible readings for the "problem" of the confession. (Richard Firth Green in conversation at ICMS Conference, 2019.) See also Green's *Elf Queens and Holy Friars: Fairy Beliefs and the Medieval Church* (Philadelphia: University of Pennsylvania Press, 2016).

29. Sarah Sprouse reads the exchanges very differently. Unlike Carolyne Larrington, who notes that the poem "relies for much of its literary effect on its audience's knowledge of French Arthurian tradition," Sprouse argues that Gawain "follows the rules of the supposed game until they are superseded by the conventions guiding the Beheading Game in the overarching structure of the poem . . . Anglo-Norman rules of the hunt act as an overlay, obscuring the overtly Welsh character of Morgan La Fay and her domain." Patricia Clare Ingham suggests, as Sprouse includes in her arguments, "that the hybridity of English and French conventions serve to emphasize a postcolonial identity for a 'fractured regnal community.' . . . The poet's use of Morgan as a Welsh trickster allows for the gomen illusion to upset the Anglo-Norman Arthurian court from the margins." See Patricia Clare Ingham, "In Contrayez Straunge": Sovereign Rivals, Fantasies of Gender, and *Sir Gawain and the Green Knight*," *Sovereign Fantasies: Arthurian Romance and the Making of Britain* (Philadelphia: University of Pennsylvania, 2001), 107; Carolyne Larrington, "English Chivalry and *Sir Gawain and the Green Knight*," *A Companion to Arthurian Literature*, ed. Helen Fulton (Oxford: Blackwell Publishing, 2009), 252; and Sarah J. Sprouse, "Two Sets of two Hunters: The Illusion of *Gomen* in *Sir Gawain and the Green Knight*," *Comitatus: A Journal of Medieval and Renaissance Studies* 47 (2016): 163–88. See *Project MUSE*, doi:10.1353/cjm.2016.0045.

30. See Kimberly Jack's chapter in this collection for different perspectives on what the girdle might symbolize.

31. Kaeuper, *Chivalry*, 48.

32. It is not the time or place to argue that Geoffroi's use of biblical models might suggest that literary figures were not the only ones "thinking" this way; further research to follow.

33. Evelyn Reynolds, "*Kynde* in *Sir Gawain and the Green Knight*," *Arthuriana* 28, no. 2 (2018): 45. This article provides an excellent summary of how the *Gawain* poem's conclusion has been treated by the critics. See also Kevin R. West, "Tokens of Sin, Badges of Honor: Julian of Norwich and *Sir Gawain and the Green Knight*," *Renascence: Essays on Values in Literature* 69, no. 1 (2017): 4. West provides a comprehensive summary of critical interpretations of the *SGGK* conclusion.

34. There are several interesting and provocative arguments for dating the poem as late as the first decade of the fifteenth century. See Joel Fredell, "The *Pearl*-Poet Manuscript in York" *Studies in the Age of Chaucer* 36 (2014): 1–39.

BIBLIOGRAPHY

Armstrong, D. *Gender and the Chivalric Community in Malory's Morte d'Arthur*. Gainesville: University Press of Florida, 2003.

Geoffroi de Charny. *A Knight's Own Book of Chivalry*. Translated by Elspeth Kennedy. Philadelphia: University Pennsylvania Press, 2005.

Barber, Richard W. *The Reign of Chivalry*. Woodbridge: Boydell Press, 1980. Reprint 2005.

———. *The Knight and Chivalry*. Woodbridge: Boydell Press, 2000.

Beal, Jane, ed. *Becoming the Pearl-Poet: Perceptions, Connections, Receptions.* New York: Lexington Books, 2022.

Blanch, Robert J., and Julian N. Wasserman. "Judging Camelot: Changing Critical Perspectives in *Sir Gawain and the Green Knight*." *New Directions in Arthurian Studies*, ed. Alan Lupack, 69–82. Cambridge: D.S. Brewer, 2002.

Crane, Susan. *Gender in Romance in Chaucer's Canterbury Tales*. Princeton, NJ: Princeton University Press, 1994.

Field, Rosalind. "The King over the Water: Exile-and-Return Revisited." In *Cultural Encounters in the Romance of Medieval England*, ed. Corinne Saunders, 41–53. *Studies in Medieval Romance*. Woodbridge: D.S. Brewer, 2005.

———. "Romance as History, History as Romance." In *Romance in Medieval England*, ed. Maldwyn Mills, Jennifer Fellows, and Carol Meale, 163–174. Woodbridge: D.S. Brewer, 1991.

———. The Heavenly Jerusalem in *Pearl.*" *The Modern Language Review* 81, no. 1 (1986): 7–17.

Fisher, Sheila. "Women and Men in Later Medieval English Romance." In *The Cambridge Companion to Medieval Romance*, ed. Roberta L. Krueger, 150–56. Cambridge: Cambridge University Press, 2000.

———. "Taken Men and Token Women in *Sir Gawain and the Green Knight*." In *Seeking the Woman in Late Medieval and Renaissance Writings: Essays in Feminist Contextual Criticism*, ed. Sheila Fisher and Janet E. Halley, 71–105. Knoxville: University of Tennessee Press, 1989.

Fredell, Joel. "*Pearl*-Poet Manuscript in York." *Studies in the Age of Chaucer* 36 (2014): 1–39.

Geeraert, Dustin. "'Etaynez þat Hym Anelede of þe Heʒe Felle': Ghosts of Giants in *Sir Gawain and the Green Knight*." *Comitatus: A Journal of Medieval and Renaissance Studies* 49 (2018): 71–101.

Hahn, Thomas. "Gawain and Popular Chivalric Romance in Britain." In *The Cambridge Companion to Medieval Romance*, ed. Roberta L. Krueger, 218–34. Cambridge: Cambridge University Press, 2000.

Heng, Geraldine. *Empire of Magic: Medieval Romance and the Politics of Cultural Fantasy*. New York: Columbia University Press, 2003.

Kaeuper, Richard. *Medieval Chivalry*. Cambridge: Cambridge University Press, 2016.

Kaeuper, Richard, and Elspeth Kennedy. *The Book of Chivalry of Geoffroi De Charny: Text, Context, and Translation*. Philadelphia: University of Pennsylvania Press, 2005.

Kaeuper, Richard, and Elspeth Kennedy. *Chivalry and Violence in Medieval Europe.* Oxford: Oxford University Press, 1999.

Larrington, Carolyne. "The Enchantress, the Knight and the Cleric: Authorial Surrogates in Arthurian Romance." *Arthurian Literature* 25 (2008): 43–65.

Llull, Ramon. *The Book of the Order of Chivalry.* Ed. and trans. by Noel Fallows. Woodbridge: Boydell Press, 2013.

Prior, Sandra Pierson. *The* Pearl-*Poet Revisited.* Twayne's English Authors Series. New York: Twayne's Publishers, 1994.

McGillivray, Murray, and Christina Duff. "New Light on the *Sir Gawain and the Green Knight* Manuscript: Multispectral Imaging and the Cotton Nero A.x. Illustrations." *Speculum* 92:S1 (2017): 110–44. https://www-journals-uchicago -edu.dom.idm.oclc.org/doi/abs/10.1086/693361.

Morgan, Gerald. *Sir Gawain and the Green Knight and the Idea of Righteousness.* Dublin: Irish Academic Press, 1991.

Ralph, I. "An Animal Studies and Ecocritical Reading of *Sir Gawain and the Green Knight.*" *Neohelicon* 44 (2017): 431–44. https://doi-org.dom.idm.oclc.org/10.1007 /s11059-017-0405-x.

Reynolds, Evelyn. "*Kynde* in *Sir Gawain and the Green Knight.*" *Arthuriana* 28, no. 2 (2018): 28–52. *Project MUSE*, doi:10.1353/art.2018.0013.

Ruddick, Andrea. *English Identity and Political Structure in the Fourteenth Century.* Cambridge: Cambridge University Press, 2013.

Saul, Nigel. *Chivalry in Medieval England.* Cambridge, MA: Harvard University Press, 2011.

Sprouse, Sarah J. "Two Sets of two Hunters: The Illusion of *Gomen* in *Sir Gawain and the Green Knight.*" *Comitatus: A Journal of Medieval and Renaissance Studies* 47 (2016): 163–88. *Project MUSE*, doi:10.1353/cjm.2016.0045.

Tolkien, J. R. R., and E. V. Gordon, eds. *Sir Gawain and the Green Knight.* In *Corpus of Middle English Prose and Verse.* Resource at the University of Michigan: https: //quod.lib.umich.edu/c/cme/Gawain/1:2?rgn=div1;view=fulltext.

Turner, Joseph. "Lady Bertilak and the Rhetoric of Women in *Sir Gawain and the Green Knight.*" In *Later Middle English Literature, Materiality, and Culture,* ed. Brian Castle and Erick Kelemen, 57–70. Newark: University of Delaware Press, 2018.

Wadiak, Walter. *Savage Economy.* Notre Dame, IN: Notre Dame Press, 2016.

West, Kevin R. "Tokens of Sin, Badges of Honor: Julian of Norwich and *Sir Gawain and the Green Knight.*" *Renascence: Essays on Values in Literature* 69, no. 1 (2017): 3–16.

Whetter, K. S.. "Subverting, Containing and Upholding Christianity in Medieval Romance." In *Christianity and Romance in Medieval England,* ed. Rosalind Field, Phillipa Hardman, and Michelle Sweeney, 102–18. Woodbridge: Boydell and Brewer, 2010. http://www.jstor.org/stable/10.7722/j.ctt9qdj7h.13.

———. *Understanding Genre and Medieval Romance.* Aldershot: Ashgate, 2008.

Winny, James, ed. and trans.. *Sir Gawain and the Green Knight: Middle English Text with Facing Translation.* Peterborough: Broadview Press, 1992.

Chapter Five

St. Erkenwald

Michael D. C. Drout, Jonathan B. Gerkin, and Scott Kleinman

St. Erkenwald is a relatively short Middle English poem in unrhymed alliterative long lines that tells the story of how a single tear from Bishop Erkenwald of London[1] serves to baptize an uncorrupted corpse discovered in an excavation under St. Paul's Cathedral, sending the spirit of a particularly moral pre-Christian judge to heaven. Surviving in a manuscript of the late fifteenth century, but dated by most scholars to the late fourteenth, the poem has been linked with *Pearl*, *Cleanness*, *Patience*, and *Sir Gawain and the Green Knight* since 1882 when Mauritz Trautmann argued that similarities in vocabulary and poetics indicated that *St. Erkenwald* had been written by the same author as the four poems of British Library MS Cotton Nero A.x.[2] Trautmann's hypothesis has dominated subsequent scholarship on *St. Erkenwald*, the majority of which has focused on this authorship problem—which has not been definitively resolved.

Like *Sir Gawain and the Green Knight*, *St. Erkenwald* begins by setting the poem's action in context of the history of Britain. But while the story in *Gawain* begins with the Fall of Troy and the founding of Britain by the legendary Brutus, the background given at the beginning of *Erkenwald* is that of Anglo-Saxon England: Hengest's leading the Saxons to drive the Britons into Wales, followed by St. Augustine of Canterbury's conversion of the English. At this time, writes the poet, pagan temples were turned into churches (an idea similar to that presented in Gregory the Great's *Libellus Responsionum* as quoted by Bede). Christianity replaced the worship of Satan in London, which was called New Troy.

When, during the subsequent episcopacy of Erkenwald, the "New Werke" is being built at St. Paul's, the workers digging below the foundations of the cathedral find a marble sarcophagus. Upon opening it, they discover an uncorrupted body dressed in rich clothes, wearing a crown and holding a scepter.[3] Bishop Erkenwald is sent for, and when he arrives, the corpse speaks, telling the bishop that it is the body of a pagan judge who had lived in New Troy nearly five hundred years before Christ. The judge, who is never given a name, was buried in kingly attire because the people so appreciated his honesty, virtue, and sense of justice; but, as Erkenwald suspects, the body was not embalmed but has been miraculously preserved. The spirit of the man has presumably been in Limbo, since, he says, he was not among those redeemed from hell by Christ in the Harrowing. The plight of this good soul so moves Erkenwald that the bishop weeps, and one of his tears falls upon the corpse, which tells him that "þe wordes þat þou werpe and þe water þat þou sheddes . . . my bapteme is worthyn."[4] Now baptized, the judge is able to enter heaven, and so the body in the tomb suddenly decays into dust. The people who had gathered around the tomb process joyfully out of the cathedral, and all the bells in the city ring at once.

Although simple in structure and lacking the ethical and moral complexity of *Gawain* or the formal sophistication of *Pearl*, the poem tells an effective story, which is not drawn from any of the surviving Lives of St. Erkenwald but instead appears to be a somewhat original adaptation of a variety of tales relating to Pope Gregory the Great and the Roman Emperor Trajan. The particular combination of the noble judge, uncorrupted corpse, and the deliverance of the condemned soul through the baptism of tears is not found in any known antecedent, and the poet's synthesis makes a more compelling tale than any of the parallels that have been identified. The author of the poem also effectively synthesizes historico-literary material in his treatment of Hengest, Augustine, and, later, a quarrel between Sir Belin and his brother. It is not possible to determine if the poet's historical source was the *Chronica Majora*, Geoffrey of Monmouth's *Historia Regum Britanniae*, or another similar text.[5] The poet's treatment of this material, especially the way that originally pagan entities are replaced by Christian figures whose names often alliterate with theirs—Mohammed by Saint Margaret or Mary Magdalen, Jupiter and Juno by Jesus or James—is both original and aesthetically accomplished.

MANUSCRIPT

St. Erkenwald uniquely survives on folios 72v–75v of British Library MS Harley 2250, a manuscript of the late fifteenth century usually associated with Cheshire.[6] A plain and rough manuscript decorated only with occasional red lettering and highlighting, Harley 2250 gives the impression of having been created for personal use.[7] The manuscript begins with forty-seven folios of the Middle English stanzaic *Life of Christ*, which is followed by a short version of the *Life of St Martin* that is found in the *South English Legendary*, also in English. An abridged version of the *Speculum Christiani* in Latin with interspersed English verses appears on folios 50r–64v, followed by the *Themata Dominicalia* and several short Latin texts.[8] *St. Erkenwald*, the first of a group of saints' lives in Middle English, is the only one of these poems that does not appear in the *South English Legendary*. Each page of the poem is labeled *De Erkenwaldo/De Sancto Erkenwaldo* in red in the same hand as the main text. Minor corrections are also made by the main hand. In the margin next to line 95 of the poem is written "We redyn in a boke" in a sixteenth-century hand. The concluding folios of the manuscript (85r to 87v), contain primarily prose texts from John Mirk's *Festial* and *Instructions for Parish Priests*, collections of vernacular sermons, and other texts useful for preaching. The inclusion of this material, along with the general appearance of the manuscript[9]—for example, the ruled lines are inconsistent and the text regularly bows upwards in the middle of lines, suggesting that the book was copied while bound[10]—has suggested to scholars that Harley 2250 was a commonplace book of a parish priest or other churchman.[11] Various marginal inscriptions in later hands suggest that this compiler lived in Cheshire (perhaps near the Northwich hundred) in 1477.[12] *St Erkenwald*'s position as the first of the group of the saints' lives in verse, and the absence of an Erkenwald poem in the *South English Legendary*, imply that the poem has a different antecedent than its neighbors in Harley 2250 and hence a different transmission and compositional history.

DATE AND DIALECT

Although Harley 2250 was created in the late fifteenth century, most scholars date *St Erkenwald* a century earlier, toward the end of the fourteenth and thus contemporary with the *Gawain*-poet and Chaucer.[13] The establishment of two feast-days in Erkenwald's honor by Robert de Braybroke—concurrent Bishop of London—in 1386[14] is often used as a *terminus a quo* for that poem,[15] but public processions and restorations of Erkenwald's shrine are recorded as late as 1407, and several events could have provided the occasion for commemoration if indeed the poem was occasional in nature.[16] However, there is nothing specific in the poem that indicates that it was written to celebrate the feast-day, or even that its creation was motivated by the establishment of the feast; the poem's dialect forms, and its use of alliterative long lines are much better evidence for *St. Erkenwald* having been written about one hundred years earlier than Harley 2250 was copied.

In his *editio princeps* of 1881, Carl Horstmann recognized that *St. Erkenwald* shared dialect forms with the four poems in Cotton Nero A.x and that these linguistic features could indicate that the poems were composed in the north or northwest of England in the later fourteenth century.[17] This general localization and dating have only occasionally been disputed, with the scholarly consensus never departing very far from Horstmann's original determination.[18] Attempts to locate the poems in time and space with greater precision have been controversial. Richard Morris first described *Pearl*, *Patience*, and *Cleanness* (but not *Sir Gawain and the Green Knight*) as "alliterative poems in the West-Midland dialect" as early as 1864.[19] J. P. Oakden determined that the dialect of *St. Erkenwald* could be localized to near the Ribble and was somewhat more Northern than that of the Cotton Nero A.x poems, but he also saw similarities between *Erkenwald* and the poems of the Cotton Nero A.x manuscript and admitted they could share a collective origin.[20] Several decades later, Clifford Peterson, following a suggestion made in 1927 by Mary S. Serjeantson and by Oakden's own willingness to "accept Cheshire as the manuscript's locale except for the consistent use of *qu-* for OE *hw-*," concluded that the original poet of *St. Erkenwald* wrote with a Cheshire dialect.[21] This view was further supported by more modern scholarship, and in fact, "Erkenwald's language defined the Cheshire dialect for compilers of the *Middle English Dictionary*."[22] Angus McIntosh and the *Linguistic Atlas of Late Mediaeval English* (LALME) similarly locate *St. Erkenwald* in the Cheshire area.[23] Having the poem's forms define the Cheshire dialect and then using their consistency with that dialect to localize the poem creates the potential for circular reasoning and also complicates statistical comparison between *St. Erkenwald* and other poems, but a date in the late fourteenth century and a localization in the northwest seems to be the most parsimonious explanation of the linguistic data.

AUTHORSHIP QUESTION

Basing his conclusion on both overlapping vocabulary and shared alliterative practice, Trautmann argued that the similarities he identified could only be explained by common authorship, not merely participation in fourteenth-century northwest alliterative poetic tradition.[24] Although subsequent scholars have employed a variety of methods in their efforts to substantiate or refute Trautmann's claim, no single analysis has proven to be definitive, in great part because any conclusion depends not only on the evidence itself but how each piece of it is weighted. The possibility that the poem was written to celebrate the establishment of a feast day for the saint, that it is set in London, and that it states that this city was called "New Troy," have all been taken as both support for and evidence against Trautmann's single-author hypothesis, as have studies of syntax, style, theme, and tone.

Additionally, the problem of the authorship of *St. Erkenwald* is inextricably bound up with that of the authorship of all of the Cotton Nero A.x. poems.[25] Although a critical consensus does exist with regard to this question, elements of special pleading in the arguments, the inertia of scholarly tradition, and the desires of critics to have multiple texts by the same author all combine to put the conclusion of shared authorship on less firm ground than is implied by the near-universal assertion that the Cotton Nero A.x poems are by a single author. Because Harley 2250 was copied by a different scribe and up to seventy-five years after Cotton Nero A.x, it is even more difficult to determine if many of the linguistic differences between *St. Erkenwald* and *Pearl, Cleanness, Patience,* and *Sir Gawain and the Green Knight* are authorial or scribal.

The Cotton Nero A.x poems, generally not thought to be occasional in nature,[26] have been dated, based on linguistic forms, as early as the 1360s and as late as the 1400s, but "it is a fair assumption that the *Gawain*-poet was alive in the middle of this period, say the mid-1370s to mid-1380s."[27] Close coincidence in time and space is a necessary but not sufficient condition for the determination of common authorship. In fact, the very similarity of date and localization that allows for a single-author hypothesis makes it more difficult to differentiate between similarities due to a shared dialect and poetic tradition and those caused by the poems sharing an author.[28] Furthermore, as R. W. Chambers and C. F. Brown (among others) have noted, the specific features scholars use to associate *St. Erkenwald* with the Cotton Nero A.x texts are not evenly distributed among these latter poems.[29] *Pearl,* in particular, differs from its manuscript companions in many ways, most obviously in its complex and unique formal structure and use of iambic tetrameters instead of alliterative long lines. If the variations in dialect and presence or absence of formal features between *St. Erkenwald* and these poems are to be used as evidence for or against common authorship of all five poems, the common authorship of the four Cotton Nero A.x texts cannot be assumed solely from their shared manuscript context.[30]

However, although the seemingly inescapable problem of one scholarly generation's conjecture being taken as a proven fact by the next generation does at times recur in the critical history, the current scholarly acceptance of a single author for the Cotton Nero A.x poems should not be summarily dismissed, as it is not based on any single piece of evidence but is rather the culmination of a century's worth of research. Scholars have noted many similarities in formal features among the poems. Drawing upon Robert J. Menner's work on technical vocabulary, alliteration, and phraseology,

Oakden concluded that when this evidence was taken as a whole, "the theory of common authorship becomes unquestionable. . . . The points of vocabulary, alliteration, phraseology and style shared by the four poems are so astonishing in their actual details that mere imitation of one poet's work by another is ruled out."[31]

In addition to sharing dialectal and formal features, the Cotton Nero A.x poems have been seen by many critics as sharing "common themes, attitudes, values, and features." Three of the poems "end with lines which echo their openings, and all four poems involve a confrontation between a human protagonist and a superhuman figure."[32] In all four poems, "some passionate selfish desire is met and controlled," and the texts are characterized by both a generally comical and "enjoying spirit" and a contrasting recognition of the "grim and negative and disagreeable aspects of experience."[33] The critical consensus since at least the middle of the 1960s seems to be that "the thoughtful and inventive use of verse forms and narrative framing, a propensity for balance and symmetry in the shaping of narrative, the highly skilled handling of viewpoint and perspective, a penchant for original and often startling imagery, and the recurrence of key images and themes" are indicative of the four poems being produced by the same mind.[34]

But despite this stable and persistent consensus, several scholars have identified various difficulties in connecting *Pearl* to the other three poems in Cotton Nero A.x.[35] Basing his analysis on differences in lexical frequency, clause length, sentence length, clause type, conjunction use, subordinator type, use of passive forms, and alliterative tendencies, Göran Kjellmer in *Did the "Pearl Poet" Write Pearl?* concluded that *Pearl* does not share authorship with any of the other three Cotton Nero A.x poems or with *St. Erkenwald*. In all of Kjellmer's statistical tests, *Pearl* was a consistent outlier among the poems: even *St. Erkenwald* was more similar to the other Cotton Nero A.x poems than it was.[36] William McColly and Dennis Weier reached somewhat similar conclusions in their statistical analysis of function words in the five poems, but they identify three poets at work: one who wrote *Pearl*, one who wrote *Sir Gawain and the Green Knight*, and a third who wrote *Cleanness*, *Patience*, and *St. Erkenwald*.[37] Although R. A. Cooper and Derek Pearsall argued that *Sir Gawain*, *Patience*, and *Cleanness* are by the same author, they did not include *Pearl* in their analysis because they were convinced that valid statistical analysis was impossible due to the difference between *Pearl*'s tetrameter and the alliterative long lines in the other poems, as well as the presence of refrains in *Pearl* and it being the only one of the four poems to employ the first person point of view.[38]

It is not clear whether Cooper and Pearsall's critique was particularly convincing or whether the majority of scholars were simply uninterested in statistical analysis. Andrew asserts that "the results of these studies are, plainly, inconclusive," but in fact their results are not as inconsistent as he implies. *Cleanness* and *Patience* are identified as products of the same author in all three studies, and in the two investigations which examine it, *Pearl* is an outlier in nearly every measure. Additionally, Kjellmer's various analyses are, for the most part, linguistically independent of each other and so should be weighted as multiple investigations. Nevertheless, these early statistical approaches appear to have done nothing to disrupt the broad if not deep consensus that the Cotton Nero A.x poems are by a single author.

The question of whether or not to include *St. Erkenwald* in that author's canon has been far more contentious. Trautmann's original claim for shared authorship was challenged both early and often. J. R. R. Tolkien and E. V. Gordon in their long-standard edition of *Sir Gawain and the Green Knight* asserted that although all five poems were similar in many ways, *St. Erkenwald* was not as similar to the four Cotton Nero A.x poems as these are to each other.[39] Savage, although he thought common authorship likely, in his 1926 edition of *St. Erkenwald,* rejected much of Trautmann's evidence and, through his use of the *New English Dictionary*, substantially reduced the number of words found exclusively in the five poems. Oakden, in *Alliterative Poetry in Middle English* (1930, 1935), likewise highlighted the differences between the dialect forms in the manuscripts (although he also suggested that many of these variations were due to scribal performance and so did not conclude that common authorship was impossible).[40] Larry Benson's 1965 "The Authorship of 'St. Erkenwald'" further reduced the number of unique shared words among the poems, and Benson dismissed the parallels in phrasing noted by Savage, attributing them to the poetic tradition.[41] Benson's article, like much work from the same period, contributed significantly to an erosion of confidence in the dialectal and formal tests of common authorship. But even if Benson somewhat overemphasized the weaknesses of the linguistic tests,[42] he did demonstrate that the evidence for common authorship was substantially less conclusive than those following Trautmann had originally believed. Furthermore, even those specific parallels that have survived this heightened critical scrutiny are perhaps less persuasive, since there is no consensus as to how they should be interpreted.

Although the lack of confidence in the significance of shared linguistic and formal features engendered by Benson's argument did not entirely eliminate assertions of the poems' common authorship, the scholarly consensus was definitely shifted against seeing *St. Erkenwald* as part of the *Gawain*-poet's canon, to the point where in 1997 Malcolm Andrew could confidently declare that the critical rejection of the common authorship hypothesis was "likely to prove permanent."[43] There were, however, a few exceptions to this scholarly consensus, the most idiosyncratic of which was Clifford Peterson's 1977 contention (never widely accepted) that all five poems were written by a John

Massey of Cotton,[44] thus simultaneously solving both the common-author and the author-identification problems. More significant are two of the statistical analyses discussed earlier: Kjellmer concludes that in a wide variety of linguistic dimensions, *St. Erkenwald* is much more like the other Cotton Nero A.x poems than is *Pearl*, a conclusion partially shared by McColly and Weier (although they argue that a third poet wrote *Sir Gawain and the Green Knight*).

But despite the detail, precision, and judicious manner in which they couch their conclusions, these linguistically focused investigations cannot be credited for the change in thinking that appears to have occurred recently (the reason why the most recent scholarship appears willing to entertain the common-authorship hypothesis is not obvious). This shift is perhaps exemplified by Marie Boroff's arguments that similarities in scene description, character use, and traditional alliterative styling should probably be read as evidence of common authorship. In all five poems, she asserts, the poet draws "us imaginatively into three-dimensional scenes within which we witness predicaments that arouse our capacity to sympathize with moral beings other than ourselves."[45] Boroff, therefore, includes *St. Erkenwald* in her revised 2011 translation, *The Gawain Poet: Complete Works*. John Bowers likewise accepts common authorship in his 2012 *An Introduction to the Gawain Poet*, and the present volume, obviously, includes *St. Erkenwald*. These small shifts in interpretation, however, appear primarily in introductions, translations, and general guides. Among specialists, the debate seems to have settled into a stable consensus that while the Cotton Nero A.x poems are almost certainly by a single author, *St. Erkenwald* was only *possibly* written by that person. As this status quo is convenient both for pedagogy and for the primarily interpretive scholarship now dominant in Middle English studies, it is likely to persist even though few scholars are actively engaged in maintaining it.[46]

In a forthcoming study, the authors of this chapter have employed computer-assisted "Lexomic" methods to compare the overall vocabulary distribution of the poems and used "rolling window analysis" to investigate the possibility that the author(s) may have used Middle English sources for some parts of various poems. Our approach differs from previous statistical analyses (although our conclusions are not incompatible with some of them) in that we divide all the poems into segments rather than only comparing whole poems. We also attempted to control for scribal influence by self-normalizing the spelling of every word in the five-poem corpus, thus allowing us to compare the distribution of lexemes without the false negatives created by scribal variation.

Hierarchical agglomerative clustering[47] performed using the "Lexos" web-based software[48] on all five poems when they are self-normalized[49] and divided into either 2,000- or 3,400-word segments finds that *Erkenwald* is substantially closer in overall vocabulary distribution to *Cleanness, Patience,* and *Sir Gawain and the Green Knight* than is *Pearl.*[50] Even when the repeated words in the refrains are deleted from *Pearl,* that poem clusters separately from the other Cotton Nero A.x texts and *St Erkenwald.* The addition of two other Middle English texts—the *Alliterative Morte Arthure* and the *Wars of Alexander*—to the analysis, however, puts these differences in perspective. *Pearl's* vocabulary is indeed somewhat different from that of *Erkenwald* and the other Cotton Nero A.x poems, but the difference is very small when compared to the differences in vocabulary between these poems and any and all segments of the *Alliterative Morte Arthure* or *Wars of Alexander.* Cluster analysis with self-normalized texts, therefore, is consistent with a conclusion that *St. Erkenwald* is closer in vocabulary distribution than *Pearl* is to the other Cotton Nero A.x poems, but that all five poems are more similar to each other than they are to other Middle English texts.

The evidence derived from the use of Lexomic techniques strongly supports the long-held view that *Cleanness, Patience,* and *Sir Gawain and the Green Knight* were all written by the same author and are not substantially influenced by immediate external sources, and the same can be said for the second half of *Pearl.* Whether this author also wrote the first half of *Pearl* and *St. Erkenwald* is slightly less certain, but both are more similar in vocabulary distribution to the other Cotton Nero A.x poems than they are to any other poems in the Middle English corpus. If we are comfortable concluding that *Pearl* is a single-author poem written by the *Gawain*-poet (and we certainly seem to be), then we should also be comfortable with the inference that *St. Erkenwald* was written by the author of *Cleanness, Patience,* and *Sir Gawain and the Green Knight,* and we are therefore justified in studying the poem not only on its own terms, but also in the context of Cotton Nero A.x.

NOTES

1. Clifford J. Peterson, ed. *Saint Erkenwald* (Philadelphia: University of Pennsylvania Press, 1977), ll. 675–93. All quotations are taken from this edition.

2. Moritz Trautmann, Review of *Altenglische Legenden* by Carl Horstmann, *Anglia* 5 (1882): 21–25.

3. As Kimberly Jack discusses in this volume, the corpse is dressed with clothing that signifies royalty, but in fact, as the spirit explains, this was not the clothing that the judge wore in life. The people who buried him had clothed the body so splendidly in order to indicate his moral excellence.

4. *St. Erkenwald,* ll. 329–330. In this volume, Ethan Campbell notes that the sacrament of baptism also is depicted in *Pearl* and *Cleanness.*

5. That the early British history in the poem seems either to have come from a sophisticated source or to be a synthesis of multiple sources may vitiate the idea of it having been composed in Cheshire (as opposed to by a Cheshire dialect-speaker working in a royal context). As Campbell notes, "Cheshire did not contain an aristocratic culture that could support artistic endeavors like the *Pearl* poems on its own" (p. 114).

6. The date 1477 appears on folio 64v. The poem was first edited by Carl Horstmann, *Altenglische Legenden, Altenglishe Legenden* (Heilbronn: Henninger, 1881).

7. Harley 2250 is in fact a composite manuscript made up of two unrelated manuscripts bound together. The discussion that follows focuses only on the first of these (present folios 1–87). For a discussion of Harley 2250, see Peterson, ed. *Saint Erkenwald*, 1–15.

8. Peterson, *Saint Erkenwald*, 3–6.

9. The manuscript gives the impression of a book used for consultation. Highlights with red ink (usually in the form of rather spidery loops marking out paragraphs or sentences) are not particularly consistent, and the inconsistent number of columns suggests that multiple sources (with varying layouts) were copied into it at various times, implying that the focus of the compilation was the acquisition or preservation of the information rather than any kind of synthesis in either content or appearance.

10. In this volume, Bowers describes the manuscript as "a rather home-made affair, with paper pages devoid of decoration, all reflecting a continued waning in prestige."

11. Peterson notes that the scribe's switching between double and single columns, his practices of scratching out rather than erasing errors, the lack of quire signatures, and the irregular use of catchwords as placeholders for the scribe are consistent with the manuscript having been made for personal use rather than display. Peterson, *Saint Erkenwald*, 7–11.

12. Peterson further concludes that the manuscript was "associated at a relatively early point (probably within fifty years of its creation) with the Lancashire and Cheshire families of Booth and Massey, particularly—but not necessarily exclusively—with the Dunham-Massey and Barton branches of these families," Peterson, *Saint Erkenwald*, 11.

13. Peterson, *Saint Erkenwald*, 11–13.

14. Henry L. Savage, ed., *St. Erkenwald: A Middle English Poem* (Hamden, CT: Archon Press, 1972 [1926]), lxxv.

15. John M. Bowers, *An Introduction to the Gawain Poet* (Gainesville: University Press of Florida, 2012), 87.

16. Peterson, *St. Erkenwald*, 14.

17. Because the manuscripts were copied by two different scribes as much as seventy-five years apart, it is difficult to determine whether differences between them are dialectal or scribal. The preference in the past half-century has been to lean toward scribal variation as a larger factor than dialect difference. See Larry Benson, "The Authorship of 'St. Erkenwald,'" *The Journal of English and Germanic Philology* 64 (1965): 393–405.

18. Some critics, most notably Benson, attribute the poem to a Londoner due to its setting "At London in Englonde noȝt fulle longe sythen," but the majority of scholars appear to accept the northern or northwestern characteristics of the language.

19. Richard Morris, ed. *Sir Gawain and the Green Knight* EETS o.s. 4 (London: Oxford University Press, 1864). Malcolm Andrew and Ronald Waldron, eds. *The Poems of the Pearl Manuscript*, 5th ed. (Exeter: University of Exeter Press, 2007), 14.

20. James P. Oakden, *Alliterative Poetry in Middle English* (Hamden, CT: Archon Books, 1968), 88–89.

21. Peterson, *Saint Erkenwald*, 24.

22. Bowers, *Introduction to the Gawain Poet*, 88.

23. Angus McIntosh, M. L. Samuels, and Michael Benskin, eds. *A Linguistic Atlas of Late Medieaval English*, Vol. 1 (Aberdeen: Aberdeen University Press, 1986).

24. Horstmann was misidentified by Henry Savage as the first scholar to link *St. Erkenwald* to the Cotton Nero A.x poems, but he had in fact only asserted that the poem was part of the same northern alliterative tradition. Savage, *St. Erkenwald: A Middle English Poem*, 1. Clark S. Northup, Review of *St. Erkenwald: A Middle English Poem* by Henry L. Savage, *The Journal of English and Germanic Philology* 27 (1928): 619.

25. See Campbell for a more extensive discussion of the authorship question.

26. Although some scholars have argued that *Sir Gawain and the Green Knight* was written to commemorate the establishment of the Order of the Garter, even if this were the case "it would prove only that the poem was composed after 1345, the probable date of the order's foundation." See J. R. R. Tolkien and E.V. Gordon, eds., *Sir Gawain and The Green Knight* (Oxford: Clarendon, 1930), xx. The motto of the Order of the Garter that appears at the end of *Sir Gawain and the Green Knight* may not be in the hand of the original scribe and thus could be a later addition to the text; Andrew and Waldron, *Poems of the Pearl Manuscript*, 3.

27. Michael Bennett, "The Historical Background," in *A Companion to the Gawain Poet*, ed. Derek Brewer (Cambridge: D.S. Brewer, 1997), 71.

28. Israel Gollancz claimed in 1918 that if the poems did share authorship, *St. Erkenwald* must be a very early or late work of the poet due to its inferior "strength of diction, metre, and other characteristics." Israel Gollancz, ed. and trans., *Pearl; an English Poem of the XIVth Century* (Oxford: Oxford University Press, 1918), xl.

29. Savage, *St. Erkenwald*, liii.

30. Many scholars have asserted that the poems "appear to have been copied as a collection rather than as individual pieces," Andrew and Waldron, *The Poems of the Pearl Manuscript*, 5, but compare Oakden, *Alliterative Poetry*, 261–63.

31. Oakden, *Alliterative Poetry*, 89.

32. Andrew and Waldron, *Poems of the Pearl Manuscript*, 6.

33. D. S. Brewer, "The *Gawain* Poet: A General Appreciation of Four Poems" *Essays in Criticism* 17 (1967): 130–42 at 139.

34. Malcolm Andrew, "Theories of Authorship," in *A Companion to the Gawain Poet*, ed. Derek Brewer (Cambridge: D.S. Brewer, 1997), 23–34 at 32.

35. Andrew, "Theories of Authorship, 23.

36. Göran Kjellmer, *Did the "Pearl Poet" Write Pearl?* (Gothenburg: Acta Universitatis Gothoburgensis, 1975), 96–100.

37. William McColly and Dennis Weier, "Literary Attribution Likelihood Ratio Tests: The Case of the Middle English *Pearl*-Poems," *Computers and the Humanities* 17 (1983): 65–75.

38. R. A. Cooper and D. A. Pearsall, "The *Gawain* Poems: A Statistical Approach to the Question of Common Authorship," *The Review of English Studies* 39 (1988): 365–85.

39. Tolkien and Gordon, *Sir Gawain and The Green Knight*, xviii.

40. Although referring frequently to Oakden's dialectical studies, Benson rejects his conclusion and argues against the poems' sharing thematic paraphrases for God. Benson, "Authorship of 'St. Erkenwald,'" 399.

41. Benson, "Authorship of 'St. Erkenwald,'" 396.

42. There is a parallel here with the effect of Ashley Crandell Amos's *Linguistic Means of Determining the Dates of Old English Literary Texts* on Anglo-Saxon studies in that an important and useful critique of a previous consensus was taken by subsequent scholars to be more of a complete refutation than it really was. See R. D. Fulk, "*Beowulf* and Language History" in *The Dating of Beowulf: A Reassessment*, ed. Leonard Neidorf (Cambridge: D.S. Brewer, 2014), 19–36.

43. Andrew, "Theories of Authorship," 27–28.

44. Peterson argued that *St. Erkenwald* was connected to Massey's home area and that the fleur-de-lis, which can be found "in the upper right-hand corner of f. 39r of Cotton Nero A.x, was a symbol on several branches of the Massey family's coat of arms." Massey was connected to the Cotton Nero A.x poems by the word "oton," found immediately to the left of line 1544 of *Sir Gawain and the Green Knight*, which Peterson takes as "coton" partially destroyed when the edges of the manuscript were trimmed. Peterson, *Saint Erkenwald*, 22.

45. Marie Borroff, ed. and trans. *The Gawain Poet: Complete Works* (New York: W.W. Norton, 2011), 273.

46. For a recent critical assessment of the linguistic and stylistic evidence for common authorship, see Eric Weiskott, *English Alliterative Verse* (Cambridge: Cambridge University Press, 2016), 145–46. For the larger and more abstract problems of linguistic and stylistic dating see also Leonard Neidorf, Introduction to *The Dating of Beowulf: A Reassessment* (Cambridge: D.S. Brewer, 2014), 6–8, and also Patrick Wormald, "*Beowulf*: The Redating Reassessed," in *The Times of Bede: Studies in Early English Christian Society and Its Historian*, ed. Stephen Baxter (Malden: Blackwell, 2006), 71–81, 98–105.

47. For a detailed discussion, see Drout, et al. "Of Dendrogrammatology."

48. All the Lexos software is available for free public use at http://lexos .wheatoncollege.edu. All the code and documentation can be downloaded at https:// github.com/WheatonCS/Lexos.

49. Self-normalization is the process of making the spellings of every lexeme consistent among all five poems (rather than being consistent with some external standard). The point of self-normalization is to try to eliminate variation based solely

on scribal practice in an effort to reveal similarities or differences attributable to composition rather than to transmission history.

50. Rolling Window Analysis (for discussion see Drout and Chauvet) shows that the frequencies of various commonly used words, especially *and*, while slightly lower in *Erkenwald* than in *Cleanness, Patience*, and *Sir Gawain and the Green Knight*, are substantially different in *Pearl*. A particular anomaly in the frequency of *and* in section 17 of *Pearl* could be evidence that the poet was influenced by a text intermediate between this part of the poem and its ultimate source in Revelation. Anomalies in the ratio of <þ> to <th> in the first four sections of *Pearl* may imply that this section of the poem had a somewhat different transmission—or even composition—history than the rest of the text, but none of this evidence is inconsistent with *St. Erkenwald* being by the same author as the other Cotton Nero A.x poems.

BIBLIOGRAPHY

Andrew, Malcolm, and Ronald Waldron, eds. *The Poems of the Pearl Manuscript.* Exeter: University of Exeter Press, 2007.

———. "Theories of Authorship." In *A Companion to the Gawain Poet*, ed. Derek Brewer, 23–34. Cambridge: D.S. Brewer, 1997.

Beal, Jane, ed. *Becoming the Pearl-Poet: Perceptions, Connections, Receptions.* New York, NY: Lexington Books, 2022.

Bennett, Michael. "The Historical Background." In *A Companion to the Gawain Poet*, ed. Derek Brewer, 71–91. Cambridge: D.S. Brewer, 1997.

Benson, Larry. "The Authorship of 'St. Erkenwald.'" *The Journal of English and Germanic Philology* 64 (1965): 393–405.

Borroff, Marie, ed. and trans. *The Gawain Poet: Complete Works.* New York, NY: W.W. Norton, 2011.

Bowers, John M. *An Introduction to the Gawain Poet.* Gainesville: University Press of Florida, 2012.

Brewer, D. S. "The *Gawain* Poet: A General Appreciation of Four Poems." *Essays in Criticism* 17 (1967): 130–142.

Cooper, R. A. and D. A. Pearsall. "The *Gawain* Poems: A Statistical Approach to the Question of Common Authorship." *The Review of English Studies* 39 (1988): 365–385.

Drout, Michael D. C., Michael J. Kahn, Mark D. LeBlanc, and Christina Nelson. "Of Dendrogrammatology: Lexomic Methods for Analyzing the Relationships among Old English Poems." *Journal of English and Germanic Philology* 110: (2011): 301–36.

Drout, Michael D. C. and Elie Chauvet. "Tracking the Moving Ratio of *þ* to *ð* in Anglo-Saxon Texts: A New Method, and Evidence for a Lost Old English Version of the 'Song of the Three Youths.'" *Anglia* 133, no. 2 (2015): 278–319.

Fulk, R. D. "*Beowulf* and Language History." In *The Dating of Beowulf: A Reassessment*, ed. Leonard Neidorf, 19–36. Cambridge: D.S. Brewer, 2014.

Gollancz, Israel, ed. and trans.. *Pearl; an English Poem of the XIVth Century.* Oxford: Oxford University Press, 1918.

Horstmann, Carl. *Altenglische Legenden, Altenglishe Legenden.* Heilbronn: Henninger, 1881.

Kjellmer, Göran. *Did the "Pearl Poet" Write Pearl?* Gothenburg: Acta Universitatis Gothoburgensis, 1975.

McColly, William and Dennis Weier. "Literary Attribution Likelihood Ratio Tests: The Case of the Middle English *Pearl*-Poems." *Computers and the Humanities* 17 (1983): 65–75.

McIntosh, Angus, M. L. Samuels, and Michael Benskin, eds. *A Linguistic Atlas of Late Medieaval English.* Volume 1. Aberdeen: Aberdeen University Press, 1986.

Morris, Richard, ed. *Sir Gawain and the Green Knight* EETS o.s. 4. London: Oxford University Press, 1864.

Neidorf, Leonard. "Introduction." In *The Dating of Beowulf: A Reassessment*, ed. Leonard Neidorf, 1–18. Cambridge: D.S. Brewer, 2014.

Northup, Clark S. Review of *St. Erkenwald: A Middle English Poem* by Henry L. Savage. *The Journal of English and Germanic Philology* 27 (1928): 619.

Oakden, James P. *Alliterative Poetry in Middle English.* Hamden, CT: Archon Books, 1968.

Peterson, Clifford J., ed. *Saint Erkenwald.* Philadelphia: University of Pennsylvania Press, 1977).

Savage, Henry L., ed. *St. Erkenwald: A Middle English Poem.* Hamden, CT: Archon Press, 1972 [1926].

Tolkien, J. R. R., and E. V. Gordon, eds. *Sir Gawain and The Green Knight.* Oxford: Clarendon, 1930.

Trautmann, Moritz. Review of *Altenglische Legenden* by Carl Horstmann. *Anglia* 5 (1882): 21–25.

Weiskott, Eric. *English Alliterative Verse.* Cambridge: Cambridge University Press. 2016.

Wormald, Patrick. "*Beowulf*: The Redating Reassessed" In *The Times of Bede: Studies in Early English Christian Society and its Historian*, ed. Stephen Baxter, 71–81, 98–105. Malden: Blackwell, 2006.

PART II

Connections

Chapter Six

Authorship

What Does the Pearl-Poet Tell Us about Himself?

Ethan Campbell

Contemporary scholarship on the *Pearl*-poet typically begins with a disclaimer: that we know nothing certain about him or her beyond what we can glean from the poems themselves. We cannot even say for certain that this poet is a single person, since the sole extant manuscript containing *Pearl*, *Cleanness*, *Patience*, and *Sir Gawain and the Green Knight* could in theory be a compilation of works by multiple poets with similar alliterative styles. However, nearly all academic articles or books that make this announcement follow it with another—that the scholar will proceed with the assumption that all four poems have a common author.[1] On occasion, another poem from a separate manuscript, *St. Erkenwald*, joins the company. Questions of authorship are mentioned in passing, or relegated to footnotes, on the way to more pressing matters of interpretation.

This shortcut to the issues a critic finds most engaging is understandable—I have done it myself, in a book whose central argument relied on at least two of the *Pearl* poems sharing an author.[2] However, the ritual of brief lip service to authorship questions sidesteps a series of debates that are incredibly varied and complex and may also understate how much we *can* ascertain from the text. Even if we cannot pinpoint the poet's precise identity, a careful reading of his works nevertheless yields clues to his region, vocation, social status, and attitudes toward a variety of religious and political questions dominant in the fourteenth century. Recent groundbreaking work with multispectral imaging by Murray McGillivray and Christina Duffy has also yielded important insights about the physical production of the *Pearl* manuscript itself, British

Library Cotton Nero A.x, and its artwork,[3] though these have not neces-
sarily brought us closer to the poet whose work the manuscript illustrates
and displays. The poems were obviously composed well before the early
fifteenth-century production date, but how much earlier and in which order
remain subjects of speculation. In one sense, we must confess that the *Pearl*-
poet is unknowable; in another sense, he tells us a detailed story about himself
from within each of these texts, if we choose to take them at their word.

The question of whether there is a single *Pearl-Cleanness-Patience-
Gawain-Erkenwald* poet is essentially unanswerable, though scholars have
tried to establish the broad common-author consensus on more solid footing
for decades. Early examples of bringing digital technology to bear on liter-
ary questions involved scholars searching for quantifiable vocabulary and
stylistic links among the *Pearl* poems, starting with the Swedish linguist
Göran Kjellmer in 1975, who used statistical and stylistic analyses to argue
that *Cleanness*, *Patience*, and *Sir Gawain* share a common author, but that
Pearl, the outlier in vocabulary and syntax, does not.[4] In 1978, relying on
syntactical evidence, Matsuji Tajima made a case for dual authorship with
Sir Gawain as the outlier.[5] William McColly and Dennis Weier's 1983 sta-
tistical report on all five poems concludes that "the existence of a so-called
Pearl- or *Gawain*-poet . . . is impossible to demonstrate through a statisti-
cal analysis of internal evidence," and posits three to five separate authors,
although the report concedes that *Cleanness* and *Patience* are the "closest
together" in vocabulary and form.[6] Malcolm Andrew's chapter on "Theories
of Authorship" in *A Companion to the Gawain-Poet* from 1997 summarizes
several more statistical studies, which examine the poet's use of individual
words, clauses, alliteration, meter, line length, and passive verb forms.[7] The
general tendency of these studies, according to Andrew, is to "confirm the
common authorship of the three poems written entirely or predominantly in
the alliterative long line—*Cleanness*, *Patience*, and *SGGK* [*Sir Gawain*],"
while treating *Pearl* more skeptically.[8]

These conclusions might well fit a reader's general experience of the
poems. *Cleanness* and *Patience* are linked structurally by their unrhymed
alliterative long lines, and thematically as sermon-like retellings of biblical
stories. It feels natural to read *Patience* as an extension of *Cleanness*, as if
it were a biblical story of God's judgment the poet simply forgot to include
in his earlier compendium. Both contain shared phrases, such as the unique
honorary titles Marie Borroff calls "periphrases for God,"[9] and even a shared
biblical text in the introductions to their sermons—Psalm 93:9 (94:9 in the
Authorized Version), which appears in *Cleanness* 581–90 and *Patience*
119–24. On the other hand, *Pearl* and *Sir Gawain*, though both alliterative,
feature poetic structures and themes that are significantly different from the
other two poems, and from each other. The rhyming tetrameter stanzas and

precise numerology of *Pearl* tell a story of grief, dream vision, and theological debate, whereas *Gawain*'s unrhymed stanzas of inconsistent length followed by a rhyming trimeter "bob and wheel" form the basis of an Arthurian romance. All four poems are distinctively Christian in outlook, but the intense theological dispute of *Pearl* and the moral dilemma of *Sir Gawain* could hardly be considered in the same genre category as the straightforward sermons of *Cleanness* and *Patience*.

St. Erkenwald is even more of an outlier, both for its blended genre of saint's life and miracle story, which John Bowers calls "a freakishly original episode,"[10] and by virtue of appearing in a different manuscript, although stylistically it has much in common with *Cleanness* and *Patience*, and a shared biblical passage, Psalm 23:3–4 (24:3–4 in AV), quoted in *Pearl* 675–84 and *Erkenwald* 277–78. Support for *Erkenwald*'s inclusion in the *Pearl*-poet's canon was relatively strong in the first half-century after Israel Gollancz made the argument in the poem's first printed edition in 1922.[11] J. R. R. Tolkien and E. V. Gordon, however, called the association "very dubious" in their 1930 edition of *Sir Gawain*,[12] and in the decades that followed, as the publication of the *Middle English Dictionary* began at the University of Michigan in 1956 and as scholars became familiar with the formulaic nature of alliterative poetry, more began to share Tolkien and Gordon's perspective. By 1965, Larry Benson could write that it was "surprising . . . that this theory still survives."[13] Benson's article on *Erkenwald*'s authorship sounded the death knell for the common authorship theory for many years, with his memorable conclusion that "stylistic tests are of only secondary value; on the basis of style alone, no one would conclude that the *Miller's Tale* and the *Parson's Tale* are the work of a single author."[14] Benson could not rule out the possibility of common authorship, but he argued persuasively that evidence beyond stylistic similarities is necessary to make a case for any of the *Pearl* poems.

In recent decades, however, the common authorship theory for *Erkenwald* has made something of a resurgence.[15] Malcolm Andrew and Ronald Waldron do not include *Erkenwald* in their authoritative edition of the *Pearl*-poet's works,[16] but Bowers calls it an "authentic member of his canon" in his 2012 study of the poet, and Marie Borroff includes it among her translations of the poems, as does Casey Finch, who uses Andrew and Waldron's edition for facing-page translations.[17] In an article devoted to a "reconsideration" of the authorship question, Borroff argues that "the poems are linked by particular and profound imaginative affinities, whose presence can be sensed beyond doubt even though it cannot be established by lexigraphical evidence."[18] *Erkenwald*, for example, emphasizes the necessity of baptism (in this case, a miraculous postmortem baptism effected by the saint's tear), a sacrament that also appears in *Pearl* and *Cleanness*, and the efficacy of sacraments in general, like the Eucharist in *Pearl* and *Cleanness* and penance in *Patience* and *Sir Gawain*. Borroff also draws thematic connections between *Erkenwald*'s self-positioning as part of salvation history (as with the Old Testament stories in *Cleanness*) and the history of the British nation (similar to Britain's legendary founding in *Sir Gawain*) as well as its complex numerical structure centered on the number eight (as *Pearl* centers on the number twelve and *Sir Gawain* on five). However, a focus on shared thematic elements could just as easily work against a claim of common authorship for *Erkenwald*, as the British history it relates takes place in a different location geographically (London as opposed to Wales and Cheshire), and the poet's emphasis on the "Holy Goste"[19] as the animating spirit in a story of Christian conversion is unseen in any of the other poems, even *Patience*, which also features a conversion drama.

In the end, without further evidence, no certainty about the number of poets is possible. The most that can be concluded is that common authorship among three poems in the Cotton manuscript is highly likely, *Pearl* is slightly more questionable, and *St. Erkenwald* remains an open question. However, most scholars proceed as though the Cotton poems, at least, share an author, if only for the sake of convenience. Most appear to agree with A. C. Spearing's common-sense conclusion: "It is easier to believe that towards the end of the fourteenth century, within a certain small dialect area, there lived one great poet than to believe that there lived two, or three, or four. For the fact is that the author of each of these poems was a great poet, of a quality rare in any age."[20]

The attempt to attach specific names to the poet is equally a game of pure speculation, which many scholars have played. In his 1891 edition of *Pearl*, Israel Gollancz made an argument for Ralph Strode, the philosopher to whom Chaucer dedicates *Troilus and Criseyde*, as he is noted in a Merton College catalog as having written a "Phantasma," which Gollancz identifies as *Pearl*.[21] Other candidates for the poet or a patron have included Huchoun of the Awle Ryale, John of Erghome, Richard Newton, Hugh Massey, John Massey, and John Stanley.[22] In the 2021 Gollancz Lecture at King's College London, Helen Cooper canvassed a few of these candidates, then drew attention to a group of patrons less commonly considered—the ecclesiastical and episcopal, in particular bishops who frequently came from the gentry, the class most likely to own Middle English manuscripts.[23] Specifically, Cooper identifies a potential patron in Richard Scrope, Bishop of Lichfield in Staffordshire during the likely time of the poems' composition and later Archbishop of York, a close advisor to King Richard II who entertained him twice at Christmas, and a devotee of the Five Wounds of Christ, a major theme in *Sir Gawain*.

So, what exactly *can* we learn about the poet from the texts alone? While conceding that his self-presentation might be fictional, what does the poet tell us about himself? This is more than just an academic question, since interpretations of the poems often rely on information that only a biography can provide—for example, where he lived, what type of occupation he had, his connection to the church or crown, and his social status. We will take these questions in order through the remainder of this chapter and conclude with perhaps the most intriguing and elusive question of all: whether his contemporaries, especially other poets, knew his work.

The first question the poems' language helps us to answer is their native dialect region in England. Angus McIntosh, writing in 1963, traces their origins to county Cheshire and pinpoints the region even more specifically to an area around Holmes Chapel in east Cheshire.[24] Thorlac Turville-Petre replicated McIntosh's work in 1977, locating the dialect in southeast Cheshire or northeast Staffordshire in the northwest Midlands. He warns, however, that in speculating on the poet's origins, "allowance must be made for the possible influence of a literary standard associated with a poetic tradition and differing in some respects from the local dialect, and also for the possibility that the author himself may have migrated from another district, merging his native dialect with that of his new neighbors."[25]

Further evidence for a Cheshire connection comes from within *Sir Gawain*. As Gawain rides north from Camelot in the "ryalme of Logres,"[26] in southern Wales, the knight's geographical location at once becomes highly specific, in a manner unique to the *Pearl* poems:

> Til that he neȝed [reached] ful neghe into the Northe Walez.
> Alle the iles of Anglesay on lyft half he haldez
> And farez ouer the fordez by the forlondez [lowlands];
> Ouer at Holy Hede, til he hade eft bonk [entered]
> In the wyldrenesse of Wyrale.[27]

One excellent way to bring *Sir Gawain* to life tangibly in the classroom is to use the magic of Google Maps to trace Gawain's journey as sketched in this passage, from Camelot's presumed location in southern Wales (for example, Caerleon) to the Wirral Peninsula. The route is about 140 miles north as the crow flies, although as the passage makes clear, Gawain meanders a fair bit. He veers west to see the islands of Anglesey, and he fords the River Dee at "Holy Hede," a name which probably refers to Holywell, a town located where the river is at least two miles wide, meaning Gawain must either cross by boat or backtrack further east, making his overall journey well over two hundred miles.[28]

Of course, the poet could be consulting a map, as we are—his description of Anglesey on Gawain's "left" might indicate as much—but it seems likely that he was also personally familiar with this terrain and expected his readers to know it as well. And if the poet had a personal history with the Wirral in Cheshire, a county that was expanded by King Richard II to become a principality in 1397, this suggests several possible relationships the poet may have had with the crown.[29] The work of Michael Bennett in exploring Richard's attraction to Cheshire in the final decade of his reign has been crucial in establishing the ways an artist from this region might benefit from royal patronage. Richard, who held the title Earl of Chester, spent part of his childhood in Cheshire, and he recruited heavily from the region for his standing army and personal guardsmen.[30] Near the end of his reign, he celebrated the Christmas and New Year holidays in 1397 and 1398 at the aforementioned Bishop of Lichfield's palace in Staffordshire, just to the south,[31] a fact which suggests intriguing possibilities for the *Pearl*-poet's depiction of Christmas festivities at Bertilak's castle. "The Cheshire dialect," Bennett writes, "achieved prominence and even a certain amount of prestige at the end of the fourteenth century when King Richard drew large numbers of Cheshiremen into his household and chatted with his retainers in their provincial language."[32]

Bennett has also observed that Cheshire did not contain an aristocratic culture that could support artistic endeavors like the *Pearl* poems on its own. Bowers notes, "The poll tax returns of 1379 found that Cheshire and south Lancashire had only four university graduates who could have appreciated, never mind written, an intellectually challenging poem like *Pearl*," making the court of Richard II, or the household of his uncle John of Gaunt, Duke of Lancaster, possible candidates for the poet's original audience.[33] These facts have led Bennett, Bowers, and others to argue for *Pearl* and *St. Erkenwald* as explicitly royalist poems.[34] They also suggest that although the poet may have used a Cheshire dialect while writing his poems, the audience who first received them may well have lived elsewhere. Joel Fredell has recently suggested York, one hundred miles northeast of Cheshire and the second-largest city in England at the time, as the site of the manuscript's production and early audience, on the basis of the lack of manuscript production in Cheshire, as well as a reevaluation of the poems' dialect.[35] Fredell also argues for an early fifteenth-century date of composition for *Sir Gawain*, closer to the date of the manuscript; in his reading, it is a Henrician poem addressed to a nation in need of reconciliation after the tumult of civil conflict.

Of course, Cheshire is not the only location where the poet sets his stories. *Pearl*'s earthly scenes take place in an unspecified garden, and *Cleanness* and *Patience* feature biblical locations like the Dead Sea, Babylon, and Nineveh, and *Erkenwald* is set in the heart of London. Though *Erkenwald* shares the same Cheshire dialect region as *Sir Gawain*, the poet clearly has a deep familiarity with the city and its history, particularly St. Paul's Cathedral, which raises the question of whether he lived there. Other Cheshiremen certainly did—in the late fourteenth century, at least two prominent Cheshire nobles lived in London, Sir Robert Grosvenor and Sir John Stanley, who supplied their households with servants and clergy who were Cheshire natives.[36] It is tempting to imagine the *Pearl*-poet filling one of these roles; Andrew Breeze has taken this speculation a step further and argued that the *Pearl*-poet was Sir John Stanley himself.[37]

It would not have been unusual for an artist of the *Pearl*-poet's stature to leave the countryside for a career in the capital, whether that career involved a position at court, in the church, or as part of an aristocratic household. Perhaps in the same way that Shakespeare wrote about the "hempen homespuns" of his Stratford youth for the London stage, the *Pearl*-poet drew from memories of his rural upbringing for inspiration while living in the city. This would help to explain the strong current of nostalgia that runs through *Sir Gawain*, especially noticeable in descriptions of the landscape and seasons.[38] As it happens, it was nostalgia for a natural world that was disappearing. As Bowers observes, "By the 1370s deforestation had come to Wirral, by then the most densely populated and arable district" in the county.[39] The poet sets his romance in the wilderness of his youth, a countryside that is rapidly changing, whether he can see those changes for himself or not.

In all the poems, but particularly *Sir Gawain*, the poet also displays a deep familiarity and appreciation for courtly customs, as well as an awareness of their shortcomings, which might suggest he held a position at court, or at least traveled in royal or aristocratic circles. However, at no point do any of the poems' narrators self-identify as wealthy or aristocratic. In *Pearl*, he styles himself a craftsman, a "joylez juelere"[40] who has lost a precious pearl, though the allegorical nature of this pearl who is actually a young girl may prompt us to view the jeweler's occupation as fictional as well.[41] In *Sir Gawain*, the narrator says little about himself except that he has "herde" the story "in toun,"[42] possibly at court. He says it also appears in written form, "stad [set down] and stoken [fastened, enclosed] / In stori stif and stronge / With lel [true] letteres loken [locked],"[43] and he later refers to a "bok,"[44] "the best boke of romaunce,"[45] and the "Brutus bokez"[46]—apparently both a legendary Arthurian romance and a chronicle history of Brutus's founding of Britain. The poet need not have personal experience with courtly conduct, in other words, since he can hear and read stories about it. In the same way, the *Gawain* narrator is clearly conversant with the technicalities of hunting, a popular pastime for English nobility, as evidenced by the three extended hunting scenes with Bertilak. However, as Ad Putter suggests, these may serve mainly as evidence of his familiarity with courtly literature, which was rife with hunting metaphors, whether he participated in the sport himself or not.[47]

Given that four of the five poems deal primarily with religious themes—and the fifth, *Sir Gawain*, makes significant references to penance, the Virgin Mary, and major holidays of the church calendar—the possibility that the poet worked as a priest or other church official also seems plausible. *Cleanness* and *Patience* in particular function as sermons, with narrators in the position of preachers who read and interpret biblical texts for an audience.[48] Some critics such as Anna Baldwin argue that the poet's intended audience is also clerical, with these poems serving as models of the kind that appeared in preaching manuals.[49] Others such as Nicholas Watson argue that the clerical author may have served as chaplain to a provincial aristocrat, to whom he gave practical spiritual advice.[50] Whatever the poet's real-life vocation, however, he does not ultimately self-identify as a priest, as each of these sermon-like poems also presents its narrator as a listener who attends church services to hear what priests have to say.

The *Cleanness* narrator, for example, notes that he has learned lessons about God's wrath both from listening to clerics and from his own private reading: "Bot I haue herkned and herde of mony hyȝe clerkez, / And als in resounez of ryȝt red hit myseluen."[51] The *Patience* narrator also presents himself as one who reads for himself what "holy wryt tells,"[52] and a congregant who listens to a homily on the Beatitudes on "a halyday, at a hyȝe masse,"[53] perhaps the feast of All Saints, which includes the Beatitudes in its liturgical readings. He later offers "myn vpynyoun"[54] on the text's interpretation, suggesting he is more than a passive reader or listener, although perhaps something short of a priest—he is a devout churchgoer passing along a lesson he has learned.

The *Patience* narrator goes further in distancing himself from the clergy when he mentions his occupation—he serves as a messenger to a "lege lorde" who orders him "to ryde other to renne to Rome in his ernde."[55] The lord's will cannot be denied—the narrator is "made"[56] to follow his command, and resistance can only bring on "grame [trouble]."[57] The narrator is a helpless servant, a state from which he discourses on the theme of unavoidable suffering, and the metaphor of God as an irresistible master. Putter notes that the mention of Rome as the destination for his errand might indicate the narrator is "a cleric in minor orders, employed in some administrative capacity,"[58] and Bowers suggests he "may have become a hanger-on at an episcopal court, doing onerous tasks" such as "Rome-running."[59] If he does work for the church, he occupies the lowest position in its hierarchy. However, he wishes the reader to view him foremost as impoverished and servile, whatever education or religious insight he may have—and regardless of what clerical training or position the poet himself might possess.

This rhetorical trope, in which an obviously well-educated sermonist presents himself as a member of the uneducated lower class, is common in fourteenth-century religious writing, especially among writers who wish to appear independent from the corruptions of the church, as the *Cleanness* narrator does when he rails against hypocrisy of priests who are "inwith alle fylthez."[60] It was a crucial position for the non-conforming followers of John Wyclif to take, for example, despite the irony that Wyclif himself was a priest and highly educated Oxford theologian. In her analysis of Wycliffite rhetoric, Fiona Somerset terms this position "extraclergial"—rhetorically standing outside the clergy while appropriating its spiritual legitimacy.[61] The narrator of *Pearl*, who depicts himself in the closing scene as a congregant viewing the elevated body and blood of Christ which "the preste vus schewez,"[62] and the narrator of *Patience*, who preaches a sermon on suffering that he himself most needs to hear, place themselves at a remove from the priesthood in order to make a personal connection with lay readers through shared experience.

It might appear that the poems cannot tell us much about one of the most interesting questions about the poet—whether any other writers or public figures in the late 14th century knew his work. The mere existence of the Cotton manuscript, however, furnishes at least a partial reception history for the poems inside. It tells us, for example, that someone with the resources to produce a professionally scripted (if not professionally illuminated) manuscript viewed these poems as worthy of inclusion in a stand-alone volume, and also viewed them as linked by authorship, style, or theme, or all three. The Harley manuscript, which dates to 1477 and contains the name Thomas Massey (from the same Massey family that had a long association with the Cotton manuscript),[63] serves as evidence that *Erkenwald* was also regarded highly enough to prompt the production of a copy a century after the poem's composition. The presence of many other great English alliterative poems from the Midlands such as *Piers Plowman*, *Wynnere and Wastoure*, and *The Siege of Jerusalem*, as well as several in the *Piers Plowman* tradition, such as *Piers the Plowman's Crede*, *Richard the Redeless*, and *Mum and the Sothsegger*,[64] demonstrates that the alliterative revival was a popular poetic movement in England which attracted many highly talented writers, a tradition originating in the north which found its way to audiences and manuscript production centers elsewhere, including London.

External evidence for the *Pearl* poems' reception is scant but compelling. For example, the collector Sir John Paston owned a book in the 1470s, now lost, which contained a work titled "The Greene Knyght,"[65] and the sixteenth-century Cheshire poet Humphrey Newton appears to echo *Sir Gawain* in his verses.[66] More intriguingly, a fifteenth-century romance titled *The Grene Knight* parallels the earlier poem's plot—it even includes a kind of sequel, when the Bertilak character, Sir Bredbeddle, returns to Camelot for a feast. The editor Thomas Hahn cautions, however, that this story could be a direct descendant of an ancient folktale which "seems to have been popular before its absorption into *Sir Gawain and the Green Knight*."[67]

Whether his contemporaries were influenced by him or not, the *Pearl*-poet participated in a literary movement, the alliterative revival, whose popularity spread across England. The earliest editors of the *Pearl* poems recognized stylistic similarities to *Piers Plowman*, and considered the two poets linked artistically,[68] though there is little indication that they knew each other's work. Like the *Pearl*-poet, William Langland is largely anonymous, apart from the word puzzle that presumably forms his name ("'I have lyved in londe,' quod I, 'my name is Longe Wille,'" B.XV.152), the date range for his works is similar (c. 1370–1385), and his poetry had widespread popularity beyond its West Midlands origins, so a connection is possible. The two poets do not explicitly reference one another, however, and their subjects overlap in only a broad sense. *Pearl* and *Piers* are both religious dream visions, and *Cleanness* shares Langland's taste for vicious anticlerical critique (5–16),[69] both common themes among fourteenth-century poets, from John Gower to Geoffrey Chaucer.

Chaucer, as far from being anonymous as any writer of this period, offers a tantalizing clue about his awareness of northern-style alliterative poetry. His Parson complains, by way of explaining why he will tell his tale in prose, that he is a "southren man, / I kan nat geeste 'rum, ram, ruff' by lettre, / Ne, God woot, rym holde I but litel bettre" (X.42–44). These lines, along with a reference to "Gawayn, with his olde curteisye . . . comen ayeyn out of Fairye" in the Squire's Tale (V.95–96), were enough to persuade Tolkien that Chaucer knew not only *Sir Gawain* but "probably the author also."[70] Bowers also argues that Chaucer's reference is directed at the *Pearl* poems, on the theory that their survival in only two manuscripts is the result of Lancastrian suppression after Richard II's defeat, not a lack of popularity.[71] In any case, it is a clear indication that Chaucer knew the work of at least a few alliterative poets. Though he seems on the surface to be mocking their style, in truth the Parson, if not Chaucer himself, places it on an equal footing in difficulty with metered rhyme—both require a particular type of poetic talent, neither well suited for the parish priest's plain-spoken sermon.

Whether the *Gawain*-poet was a Cheshireman or Londoner or both, whether a courtier for the king or member of a provincial estate, a priest or layman, well-known or entirely overlooked by his contemporaries, ultimately the best guide for appreciating his work is to follow the lead of his narrators. In one instance, he is a grief-stricken man with sharp theological questions; in another, the preacher of a fiery sermon of God's wrath. He is a lowly servant learning to suffer, a student of romance and courtly manners, a proud Englishman who knows the cathedral of his capital city encloses a miraculous past, as does his nation. He holds many identities and speaks with many voices, as we would expect from the author of such masterful and varied poetry.

NOTES

1. Examples are too numerous to list. One influential reading of the BL Cotton Nero A.x manuscript as a unified whole, Sandra Pierson Prior's *The Fayre Formez of the Pearl Poet* (East Lansing: Michigan State University Press, 1996), reads the four works as following "the basic pattern and variations of providential history," but Prior begins with a disclaimer that the manuscript's unity may be attributable either to "the author, or a perceptive compiler" (15).

2. Ethan Campbell, *The Gawain-Poet and the 14th-Century English Anticlerical Tradition* (Kalamazoo, MI: Medieval Institute, 2018). One of the book's central arguments is that *Cleanness* introduces the theme of anticlerical critique in its opening lines, with the image of hypocritical priests handling the Eucharist with their figuratively dirty hands. This theme continues implicitly into the biblical stories of God's wrath against filth recounted later in *Cleanness*, then into the extended exemplum of the prophet Jonah in *Patience*. See especially Chapter 4, "The Reluctant Priest of *Patience*," 149–92.

3. Murray McGillivray and Christina Duffy, "New Light on the *Sir Gawain and the Green Knight* Manuscript: Multispectral Imaging and the Cotton Nero A.x Illustrations," *Speculum* 92/S1 (October 2017): 110–44.

4. Göran Kjellmer, *Did the "Pearl Poet" Write Pearl?* Gothenburg Studies in English 30 (Gothenburg: Acta Universitatis of Gothoburgensis, 1975).

5. Matsuji Tajima, "Additional Syntactical Evidence against the Common Authorship of MS. Cotton Nero A.X," *English Studies* 59, no. 3 (1978): 198.

6. William McColly and Dennis Weier, "Literary Attribution and Likelihood-Ratio Tests: The Case of the Middle English Pearl-Poems," *Computers and Humanities* 17, no. 2 (1983): 69–70.

7. Malcolm Andrew, "Theories of Authorship," in *A Companion to the Gawain-Poet*, ed. Derek Brewer and Jonathan Gibson (Woodbridge: D.S. Brewer, 1997), 32. In addition to Kjellmer and McColly and Weier, Andrew cites Rene Derolez, "Authorship and Statistics: The Case of the Pearl-Poet and the Gawain-Poet," *Occasional Papers in Linguistics and Language Learning* 8 (1981): 41–51; and R.A. Cooper and Derek A. Pearsall, "The Gawain Poems: A Statistical Approach to the Question of Common Authorship," *Review of English Studies* 39, no. 155 (1988): 365–85.

8. Andrew, "Theories of Authorship," 32.

9. Marie Borroff, "Narrative Artistry in *St. Erkenwald* and the *Gawain*-Group: The Case for Common Authorship Reconsidered," *Studies in the Age of Chaucer* 28 (2006): 43.

10. John M. Bowers, *An Introduction to the* Gawain *Poet* (Gainesville: University Press of Florida, 2012), 90.

11. Israel Gollancz, ed., *St. Erkenwald*, in *Select Early English Poems* vol. 4 (Oxford: Oxford University Press, 1922), lvi–lviii.

12. J. R. R. Tolkien and E. V. Gordon, eds., *Sir Gawain and the Green Knight* (Oxford: Oxford University Press, 1930), xviii.

13. Larry D. Benson, "The Authorship of *Saint Erkenwald*," *Journal of English and Germanic Philology* 64, no. 3 (1965): 393.

14. Benson, "The Authorship of *Saint Erkenwald*," 405.

15. See also Michael D. C. Drout, Jonathan Gerkin, and Scott Kleinman's chapter on *St. Erkenwald* in this volume, whose section on "The Authorship Question" covers these debates as well as the statistical studies noted earlier.

16. Malcolm Andrew and Ronald Waldron, eds., *The Poems of the Pearl Manuscript*, 5th ed. (Exeter: University of Exeter Press, 2007; Reprinted by Liverpool University Press, 2014). All quotes from the Cotton Nero poems are taken from this edition; I have altered the text slightly by replacing all thorns (þ) with "th."

17. Bowers, *Introduction*, xi; Marie Borroff, tr., *The Gawain Poet: Complete Works* (New York: W.W. Norton, 1967, revised ed. 2011); Casey Finch, tr., *The Complete Works of the* Pearl *Poet* (Berkeley: University of California Press, 1993).

18. Borroff, "Narrative Artistry," 46.

19. *St. Erkenwald*, l. 127.

20. A. C. Spearing, *The Gawain-Poet: A Critical Study* (Cambridge: Cambridge University Press, 1970), 37.

21. Israel Gollancz, ed., *Pearl, An English Poem of the 14th Century* (London: D. Nutt, 1891), l–lii.

22. See William Vantuono, ed., *The Pearl Poems: An Omnibus Edition* (New York: Garland, 1984), vol. 1, xxii–xxix; Andrew, "Theories of Authorship," 28–31; and Bowers, *Introduction*, 9. For an extended argument for John Massey as a possible candidate, see Clifford J. Peterson, "The *Pearl*-Poet and John Massey of Cotton, Cheshire," *Review of English Studies* 25:99 (1974): 257–66. See also Bowers's chapter on "Audiences" in this volume, which examines several members of the Massey family as possible "patrons and early readers." For John Stanley, see Andrew Breeze, "Sir John Stanley (c. 1350–1414) and the *Gawain*-Poet," *Arthuriana* 14, no. 1 (2004): 15–30.

23. Helen Cooper, "Five Strokes of the Axe: Patronage and the *Gawain*-poet," King's Gollancz Lecture, Centre for Late Antique and Medieval Studies, King's College London, July 6, 2021, video, 44:54. https://media.kcl.ac.uk/media/Prof .+Helen+Cooper%27s+2021+Israel+Gollancz+Lecture%2C+%22Five+Strokes+of+t he+AxeA+Patronage+and+the+Gawain-poet/1_o0m9570o.

24. Angus McIntosh, "A New Approach to Middle English Dialectology," *English Studies* 44 (1963): 1–11.

25. Thorlac Turville-Petre, *The Alliterative Revival* (Cambridge: D.S. Brewer, 1977), 30.

26. *Sir Gawain and the Green Knight*, l. 691.

27. *Sir Gawain and the Green Knight*, ll. 697–701.

28. Andrew and Waldron, eds., *Poems*, 234. Andrew and Waldron suggest several possible locations for "Holy Hede" and Gawain's crossing, either on horseback or by

boat. The "only real certainty" about the name, they write, "is that it does not refer to Holyhead in Anglesey."

29. For more on the poet's potential connections to Cheshire, and to the readership the poems may have found there, see Bowers's chapter on "Audiences" in this volume. David K. Coley's chapter on "Cultural Contexts," also in this volume, addresses "several recent challenges to the so-called Cheshire hypothesis and . . . the critical possibilities that open when we decenter the poems of Cotton Nero A.x from a region long considered their first textual environment."

30. Michael Bennett, *Community, Class, and Careerism: Cheshire and Lancashire Society in the Age of "Sir Gawain and the Green Knight"* 2 (Cambridge: Cambridge University Press, 1983), 233–34, 246. See also Bennett, *Richard II and the Revolution of 1399* (Stroud: Sutton, 1999).

31. Michael Bennett, "The Historical Background," in *A Companion to the Gawain-Poet*, ed. Derek Brewer and Jonathan Gibson (Woodbridge: D.S. Brewer, 1997), 86–87.

32. Bennett, "The Historical Background," 86–87.

33. Bowers, *Introduction*, 2–3. For the possible connection with John of Gaunt, see Bennett, "Historical Background," 82.

34. See Michael Bennett, "The Court of Richard II and the Promotion of Literature," in *Chaucer's England*, ed. Barbara Hanawalt (Minneapolis: University of Minnesota Press, 1992), 3–20; John Bowers, "*Pearl* in Its Royal Setting: Ricardian Poetry Revisited," *Studies in the Age of Chaucer* 17 (1995): 111–55; and Frank Grady, "*St. Erkenwald* and the Merciless Parliament," *Studies in the Age of Chaucer* 22 (2000): 179–211.

35. Joel Fredell, "The *Pearl* Manuscript in York," *Studies in the Age of Chaucer* 36 (2015), 1–39.

36. Bowers, *Introduction*, 3.

37. Breeze, "Sir John Stanley," 15.

38. *Sir Gawain and the Green Knight*, ll. 500–33 and ll. 713–70.

39. Bowers, *Introduction*, 4.

40. *Pearl*, l. 251.

41. See Tony Davenport, "Jewels and Jewellers in *Pearl*," *Review of English Studies* 59, no. 241 (2008), which dismisses the notion that the poet was a jeweler in part "on the basis of the poem's lack of technical vocabulary" (508).

42. *Sir Gawain and the Green Knight*, l. 31.

43. *Sir Gawain and the Green Knight*, ll. 33–35.

44. *Sir Gawain and the Green Knight*, l. 690.

45. *Sir Gawain and the Green Knight*, l. 2521.

46. *Sir Gawain and the Green Knight*, l. 2523.

47. Ad Putter, "The Ways and Words of the Hunt: Notes on *Sir Gawain and the Green Knight, The Master of Game, Sir Tristram, Pearl*, and *Saint Erkenwald*," *The Chaucer Review* 40, no. 4 (2006): 355.

48. Grace Hamman, in the chapter on "Theology" in this volume, argues that whether the poet was a priest or not, the poems themselves "work pastorally in

stimulating acknowledgment of need for God and ensuing spiritual transformation" (p. 184).

49. Anna Baldwin, "Sacramental Perfection in *Pearl, Patience,* and *Cleanness,*" in *Genres, Themes and Images in English Literature,* Ed. Piero Boitani and Anna Torti (Tübingen, Germany: Gunter Narr Verlag, 1988), 131–33.

50. Nicholas Watson, "The *Gawain*-Poet as a Vernacular Theologian," in *A Companion to the Gawain-Poet,* ed. Derek Brewer and Jonathan Gibson (Woodbridge: D.S. Brewer, 1997), 294–96, 299.

51. *Cleanness,* ll. 193–94.

52. *Patience,* ll. 60.

53. *Patience,* l. 9.

54. *Patience,* l. 40.

55. *Patience,* ll. 51–52.

56. *Patience,* l. 54.

57. *Patience,* l. 53.

58. Putter, *Introduction,* 17.

59. Bowers, *Introduction,* 7.

60. *Cleanness,* l. 13. For more on the anticlerical critiques of the poet and his contemporaries, and the ways the "theological ramifications of corrupt clergy affected the average Christian" in the fourteenth century, see Nancy Ciccone's chapter on "Religious Contexts" in this volume.

61. Fiona Somerset, *Clerical Discourse and Lay Audience* (Cambridge: Cambridge University Press, 1998), 12–14.

62. *Pearl,* l. 1210.

63. Peterson ed., *Saint Erkenwald,* 9–11, 20–23.

64. See Putter, *Introduction,* 29. *The Siege of Jerusalem* shares roughly the same date and dialect region as the *Pearl* poems; *Wynnere and Wastoure* shares the dialect but dates somewhat earlier, to the 1350s; and *Piers Plowman,* which was revised multiple times starting around 1370, originates in the Malvern Hills of the central West Midlands (see the B-text Prologue, line 5).

65. Thomas Hahn, ed., *Sir Gawain: Eleven Romances and Tales* (Kalamazoo, MI: Medieval Institute Publications, 1995), 12.

66. J. A. Burrow, *The* Gawain-*Poet,* Writers and Their Work, series ed. Isabel Armstrong (Horndon, Tavistock, Devon: Northcote House, 2001), 2.

67. Hahn, *Sir Gawain,* 309.

68. A footnote in the first printed excerpt from *Pearl,* in Thomas Warton's *The History of English Poetry* vol. 3 (London, 1781), describes it as "an alliterative poem without rhyme, exactly in the versification of Piers Plowman, of equal or higher antiquity" (107–108, note u).

69. William Langland, *The Vision of Piers Plowman* [B-text]. Ed. A. V. C. Schmidt. (London: Everyman, 1995.)

70. J. R. R. Tolkien, "Sir Gawain and the Green Knight," in *The Monsters and the Critics and Other Essays* (New York: HarperCollins, 2007), 73. See also Christopher Tolkien's note on page 108, note 30.

71. Bowers, *"Pearl,"* 154.

BIBLIOGRAPHY

Andrew, Malcolm. "Theories of Authorship." *A Companion to the Gawain-Poet.* Ed. Derek Brewer and Jonathan Gibson (pp. 23–33). Woodbridge: D.S. Brewer, 1997.

Andrew, Malcolm, and Ronald Waldron, eds. *The Poems of the Pearl Manuscript* 5th ed. Exeter: University of Exeter Press, 2007. Reprinted by Liverpool University Press, 2014.

Baldwin, Anna. "Sacramental Perfection in *Pearl, Patience,* and *Cleanness.*" *Genres, Themes and Images in English Literature.* Ed. Piero Boitani and Anna Torti (pp. 125–40). Tübingen, Germany: Gunter Narr Verlag, 1988.

Beal, Jane, ed. *Becoming the Pearl-Poet: Perceptions, Connections, Receptions.* New York: Lexington Books, 2022.

Bennett, Michael. *Community, Class and Careerism: Cheshire and Lancashire Society in the Age of "Sir Gawain and the Green Knight."* Cambridge: Cambridge University Press, 1983.

———. "The Historical Background." *A Companion to the Gawain-Poet.* Ed. Derek Brewer and Jonathan Gibson (pp. 71–90). Woodbridge: D.S. Brewer, 1997.

———. *Richard II and the Revolution of 1399.* Stroud: Sutton, 1999.

Benson, Larry D. "The Authorship of *Saint Erkenwald.*" *Journal of English and Germanic Philology* 64, no. 3 (1965): 393–405.

Borroff, Marie, tr. *The Gawain Poet: Complete Works.* New York: W.W. Norton, 1967, revised ed. 2011.

———. "Narrative Artistry in *St. Erkenwald* and the *Gawain*-Group: The Case for Common Authorship Reconsidered." *Studies in the Age of Chaucer* 28 (2006): 41–76.

Bowers, John M. *An Introduction to the* Gawain *Poet.* Gainesville: University Press of Florida, 2012.

———. "*Pearl* in Its Royal Setting: Ricardian Poetry Revisited." *Studies in the Age of Chaucer* 17 (1995): 111–55.

Breeze, Andrew. "Sir John Stanley (c. 1350–1414) and the *Gawain*-Poet." *Arthuriana* 14, no. 1 (Spring 2004): 15–30.

Burrow, J.A. *The* Gawain-*Poet.* Writers and Their Work, series ed. Isabel Armstrong. Horndon, Tavistock, Devon: Northcote House, 2001.

Chaucer, Geoffrey. *The Riverside Chaucer,* 3rd ed. Ed. Larry Benson. Boston: Houghton Mifflin, 1987.

Cooper, Helen. "Five Strokes of the Axe: Patronage and the *Gawain*-poet." King's Gollancz Lecture, Centre for Late Antique and Medieval Studies, King's College London, July 5, 2021. Video, 44:54. https://media.kcl.ac.uk/media/Prof .+Helen+Cooper%27s+2021+Israel+Gollancz+Lecture%2C+%22Five+Strokes+o f+the+AxeA+Patronage+and+the+Gawain-poet/1_o0m9570o.

Cooper, R. A., and Derek A. Pearsall. "The Gawain Poems: A Statistical Approach to the Question of Common Authorship." *Review of English Studies* 39, no. 155 (1988): 365–85.

Davenport, Tony. "Jewels and Jewellers in *Pearl.*" *Review of English Studies* 59, no. 241 (2008): 508–20.

Derolez, Rene. "Authorship and Statistics: The Case of the Pearl-Poet and the Gawain-Poet." *Occasional Papers in Linguistics and Language Learning* 8 (1981): 41–51.

Fredell, Joel. "The *Pearl* Manuscript in York." *Studies in the Age of Chaucer* 36 (2015): 1–39.

Gollancz, Israel, ed. *Pearl, An English Poem of the 14th Century.* London: D. Nutt, 1891.

———. *St. Erkenwald.* In *Select Early English Poems* vol. 4. London: Oxford University Press, 1922.

Grady, Frank. "*St. Erkenwald* and the Merciless Parliament." *Studies in the Age of Chaucer* 22 (2000): 179–211.

Hahn, Thomas, ed. *Sir Gawain: Eleven Romances and Tales.* Kalamazoo, MI: Medieval Institute Publications, 1995.

Kjellmer, Göran. *Did the "Pearl-Poet" Write Pearl?* Gothenburg Studies in English 30. Gothenburg, Sweden: Acta Universitatis Gothoburgensis, 1975.

Langland, William. *The Vision of Piers Plowman* [B-text]. Ed. A.V.C. Schmidt. London: Everyman, 1995.

McColly, William, and Dennis Weier. "Literary Attribution and Likelihood-Ratio Tests: The Case of the Middle English Pearl-Poems." *Computers and Humanities* 17, no. 2 (1983): 65–75.

McGillivray, Murray, and Christina Duffy. "New Light on the *Sir Gawain and the Green Knight* Manuscript: Multispectral Imaging and the Cotton Nero A.x Illustrations." *Speculum* 92/S1 (October 2017): 110–44.

McIntosh, Angus. "A New Approach to Middle English Dialectology." *English Studies* 44 (1963): 1–11.

Peterson, Clifford. "The *Pearl*-Poet and John Massey of Cotton, Cheshire." *The Review of English Studies* 25:99 (1974): 257–66.

———, ed. *Saint Erkenwald.* Philadelphia: University of Pennsylvania Press, 1977.

Prior, Sandra Pierson. *The Fayre Formez of the Pearl Poet.* East Lansing: Michigan State University Press, 1996.

Putter, Ad. *An Introduction to the Gawain-Poet.* New York: Longman, 1996.

———. "The Ways and Words of the Hunt: Notes on *Sir Gawain and the Green Knight, The Master of Game, Sir Tristram, Pearl,* and *Saint Erkenwald.*" *The Chaucer Review* 40, no. 4 (2006): 354–85.

Somerset, Fiona. *Clerical Discourse and Lay Audience.* Cambridge: Cambridge University Press, 1998.

Spearing, A.C. *The Gawain-Poet: A Critical Study.* Cambridge: Cambridge University Press, 1970.

Tajima, Matsuji. "Additional Syntactical Evidence Against the Common Authorship of MS. Cotton Nero A.X." *English Studies* 59:3 (1978): 193–98.

Tolkien, J. R. R. "Sir Gawain and the Green Knight." *The Monsters and the Critics and Other Essays* (pp. 72–108). New York: HarperCollins, 2007.

Tolkien, J. R. R., and E. V. Gordon, eds. *Sir Gawain and the Green Knight.* Oxford: Oxford University Press, 1930.

Turville-Petre, Thorlac. *The Alliterative Revival.* Cambridge: D.S. Brewer, 1977.

Warton, Thomas. *The History of English Poetry* 3. London: Vincent Brooks, Day and Son, 1781.

Watson, Nicholas. "The *Gawain*-Poet as a Vernacular Theologian." *A Companion to the Gawain-Poet.* Ed. Derek Brewer and Jonathan Gibson (pp. 293–313). Rochester, NY: D.S. Brewer, 1997.

Chapter Seven

Ecology in the *Pearl*-Poet

Elizabeth Allen

Ecocritical approaches to literature and other cultural productions generally pay attention to non-human systems or ecologies in order to call into question the hierarchy of species in which humans are more valued than other beings.[1] The study of "ecology" thus differs profoundly from the study of "nature," that often-personified supernatural force invoked in medieval and modern contexts to ratify custom and social order as pre-ordained and unchanging realities.[2] Ecology, as the branch of biology that addresses the relations of organisms to one another and to their physical surroundings, has gained metaphorical extension in literary and humanistic studies, so as to map a broad spectrum of relationships between humans and the non-human world. Ecology in this expanded sense describes systems or networks of mutual interaction in the natural environment and in built environments, politics, theology, and literature.[3] Since the 1970s, ecocritical studies have increasingly raised awareness about environmental degradation and global warming, calling into question the ethics of the Anthropocene, the geological age defined by human domination.[4]

Medieval literary studies have taken up a range of ecocritical concerns, paying attention to the ecologies of animals, forests, wildernesses, mineral landscapes, and objects. Many such studies focus on the ways in which literature calls into question anthropocentric modes of action and representation.[5] Humans are only one element in a network of lives and agencies that operate in a complex system; literature can celebrate the encounters and mutual dependencies shared by human and non-human beings.[6] Alternatively, literature can also touch on uncanny or "weird" non-human energies, or expose vast and consequential differences in spatial and temporal scale between humans and the non-human world.[7] Ecological approaches to the *Pearl* poet can help students reflect on problems of environmental loss in the modern day.

The *Pearl*-poet's works reward the full spectrum of ecological approaches. I will begin here with a brief comparison between storms in *Patience* and in *Cleanness*, to show the range of the poet's depictions of ecological systems. I then turn at more length to *Sir Gawain and the Green Knight* and finally *Pearl*, the two poems most likely to find their way onto more general ecology and ecocriticism syllabuses. How do these works complicate the conventional opposition between human culture and the natural world? How do they explore the interrelatedness of the human with the animal, vegetable, and mineral worlds? Both *Pearl* and *Gawain* explore human intimacies with plant and animal life, from the herbs in the *Pearl* dreamer's garden to the hunted animals described with empathy in *Sir Gawain and the Green Knight*. Both poems also explore the implacability of a created world whose agency exceeds purely human ways of knowing, especially in confrontations with death and the grave.

Ecocritical readings can begin by pushing the literary category of setting into the foreground, asking how landscapes and animals and built environments might contribute effects that exceed the human story. Turning students' attention to the setting can point to questions of agency and value. How do non-human beings initiate action in the poems? How do animals, plants, stones, and weather point beyond the human, even as they affect the meaning of human words and actions? Such questions quickly lead beyond "setting" to point out both the power and the limits of human systems, including language itself.[8] What is the place of language, not just as a system of reference but as part of the environment? How do words participate in ecological systems, press beyond the isolation of human action? Or, how does language also contain the diverse and unpredictable forces of other beings in the world? Does language have an ecology of its own? To attend to ecology in the *Pearl*-poet's works, furthermore, raises questions about ways in which human language might leave space for ecosystems that exceed its referential capacity, pointing toward that which it cannot encompass. In bringing to the surface the workings of the non-human world, ecocriticism puts the human concerns of the *Pearl*-poet in a larger moral context, one that highlights the precarity of earthly survival of all kinds, the limits of human agency, and the vitality of the non-human world.

WIND AND WATER: TWO STORMS

Storms are depicted in two of the *Pearl-poet*'s less often taught poems, *Cleanness* and *Patience*. In the former, the poet emphasizes an ecology in which humans have alienated themselves from God and hence from the natural world, and they appear small, even nugatory, in the face of the flood and God's profound wrath. In the latter, the poet emphasizes instead a network of connections among human, animal, vegetable, and atmospheric forms of life.

Patience retells the biblical story of Jonah, who tries to evade God's command that he prophesy doom at Nineveh. God stirs up a storm that threatens to sink Jonah's vehicle of escape, a ship to Tarshish; unlike the rebellious prophet, the violent winds are depicted as "bayn" (obedient) to God. The anthropomorphized weather resembles, even competes with, Jonah's human disorder. But the winds also far exceed human power: to initiate the storm at sea that will force Jonah overboard into the gullet of the whale, these winds blow their breath upon the waters as God did at the Creation.[9] Ecological chaos attends a human error, overwhelming the vulnerable human, like the storm on the heath in *King Lear*.

Yet the storm's origin in Jonah's error—and indeed, its symbolic link to Creation—also show how profoundly significant the human being remains within the network of forces and forms of life that make up the created world. The ship's denizens are terrified; moreover, the winds make the waves tower and crash so violently that the fish themselves are frightened: "breed fysches / Durst nowhere for ro3 arrest at þe bothem" ("Frightened fishes / Could find no rest from the roughness at the bottom").[10] The fishes' fear links the human world to the animal, as sailors and fishes alike seek refuge from the storm's destruction: "For be monnes lode neuer so luþer, þe lyf is ay swete" ("for be man's way of life ever so wretched, life is still sweet").[11] The link between human and animal suffering emerges again when Jonah sojourns inside the whale, whose discomfort the poem emphasizes. Later, the resonance between human and vegetable need surfaces when Jonah identifies with the beautiful woodbine that keeps him cool in the desert.

By widening Jonah's (and our) perspective beyond the human, the poem uses the resemblance between human and non-human beings to emphasize non-human agency, ultimately to connect different kinds of agency in one ecological system. God created the world, the winds blew over the water, the storm obeyed him, and these forces work together in the ecology of Jonah's prophetic obligations.[12] The bodily pains and pleasures of humans, animals, wind, and plants lie at the heart of the poem's account of the value of creation.[13] In bringing together humans and non-human life in their shared desperation to survive, the poem emphasizes God's care for his creatures, the very care that Jonah repeatedly dismisses.

Unlike the storm in *Patience*, the Flood in *Cleanness* points to profound ecological destruction: the Flood is not only an environmental disaster but a violent rejection of human volition.[14] God misaligns the coherent and sustaining operations of the world—its ecology. Rather than raising forms of life into a ruckus of survival, as in *Patience*, *Cleanness* depicts the Flood as an un-Creation: banks burst, clouds cleave, the flood rises to the sky, "þe water of þe welkin with þe worlde mette" ("the waters of the sky joined with the world").[15] The convergence of sky and earth suggests that the created world reverts to chaos, the biblical darkness over the waters that God first breathed upon during the Creation.[16] This breakdown of distinctions among forms of life figures the destruction of any system of natural inclination or human hierarchical dominance. No creatures can live in such an area. The storm is an ecological disaster in a world whose power eclipses human agency.

Afterward, God reestablishes human ascendancy through his covenant with Noah, in part by reiterating human volition as the cause of disaster. Yet even here, an ecological excess is visible in the actions of the birds sent out to see if the waters have receded. The dove brings an olive branch, signaling a new ecological system in line with human needs. But before the dove goes out, Noah sends the raven, who gorges itself on carrion and never returns, a dark avian echo of the Flood's violent un-creation.

In *Patience*, the desperate fear of fish and men alike blurs the boundary between human and non-human worlds, calling attention to their shared precarity and suffering. In *Cleanness*, on the other hand, the Flood's power not only destroys the whole created world but returns the waters to their chaotic origins, making the environment implacable in the face of human suffering and insisting upon an essential, challenging difference between humanity and the larger, inhuman world. Even at the end, the raven is a dark reminder that the hierarchy of species is not a given. The two storms map two different ecological outcomes: *Patience* undercuts human exceptionality by suggesting that non-human animals and things are connected and even mutually dependent; *Cleanness* shunts human ascendancy aside by depicting an implacable, powerful, and alien world within which humans appear limited and temporary sojourners on earth.

EARTH: GAWAIN AND DEATH

Sir Gawain and the Green Knight has typically been understood as a test of aristocratic ethics: although Gawain keeps his promise to show up at the Green Chapel for his beheading, he breaks his promise to exchange each day's winnings with his lord when he accepts the lady's gift of the green girdle. The breach of this promise has consequences for Gawain: it reveals that his brave confrontation with death is qualified by his hope that the girdle's magic will protect him from the Green Knight's mortal blow. However, the poem remains notoriously ambiguous about the severity and meaning of Gawain's error.[17]

The poem's concerns, however, go well beyond human ethics. The Green Knight's greenness associates him with the natural world, and Gawain's journey through the Wirral places his human struggle in a natural environment. This ecology draws attention to aspects of that environment that Gawain cannot assimilate: the cold; the hard ground; the landscape itself, which becomes increasingly defamiliarized as he travels toward the castle whose test he does not understand, and eventually toward the Green Chapel, a profoundly ambiguous grass-covered cave or barrow. How does this alien ecology complicate Gawain's human heroism?

In one resonant ecocritical account of the poem, Randy Schiff argues that the upshot of Gawain's test may be an "ecopoetic lesson" that humans are part of a world beyond their own making—much as we have seen in *Patience*, where Jonah found connections to sea, whale, fishes, and bower.[18] For Schiff, *Gawain* is designed to celebrate "a larger, throbbing whole."[19] This reading privileges the poem's engagement with a network of non-human forces finally bound together with the languages of law and poetry, in a "natural and cultural ecopoetic unity."[20] Schiff argues that Gawain's embeddedness in the non-human world and the poem's capacity to enact a fusion of human and natural spaces and times, binding them together through the power of poetic linkages—principally, in this account, through puns on keywords for law and poetry that coincide with variations on words for time, space, and voice. As we shall see in discussing *Pearl*, the poet is indeed deeply concerned with what we might call the ecology of language, its capacity to blur semantic distinctions to reveal connections among human and non-human lives.

The knitting of oppositions also lies at the heart of Carolyn Dinshaw's ecocritical approach to *Gawain*, which turns to portrayals of the Green Man to link ecology to the poem's deconstruction of the opposition between nature and culture. The Green Knight's body, she writes, is "ecological . . . not only because of its hue and consequent connection to the vegetable realm but also because it hints at a creaturely way of being that refuses hierarchy": even in the image of the Green Knight's body holding its own severed head, she finds that head and body are "connected to one another horizontally."[21] As the opposing forces of natural and artificial landscapes become entangled with each other, as the poem's plot strands become enmeshed, as host and guest become interdependent, the poem reveals an awareness that apparently opposed forces are inextricable. We might note that they even resemble each other, as Gawain's hard cold armor resembles the frozen landscape. Such "intimacy" between human and non-human ecologies returns us often to resemblances.[22] Jane Bennett has even written that embracing "a touch" of anthropomorphism, seeing human-like characteristics in non-human life, can catalyze the ecocritical perception of "variously composed materialities that form confederacies."[23]

Despite the many ways in which the poem makes evocative use of resemblances between human and non-human forces, it can be difficult for readers of the *Pearl*-poet to jettison fully the distinction between what is traditionally distinguished as nature vs. culture. At one point, Dinshaw worries that her questions, designed to steer readers toward the interconnectedness of all created things, remain "too binary."[24] Indeed, the blurring of distinctions does not simply undo all hierarchies in the poem: far from it. An initial perception of contrast and a profound investment in social hierarchy is perhaps what makes the poem's key symbolic figures—the Green Knight, Morgan le Fay, the girdle, the Green Chapel—so resonantly hard to read, so internally contradictory, and so surprising, precisely because they invoke the very opposition between mortal danger and courtly virtue, nature and culture, that they subsequently undermine. Furthermore, as much as the poem creates intimacy between human and natural phenomena, at the same time it reminds us of the sheer, implacable power of seasons, weather, landscape, and the passing of time. In seeking the return blow, Gawain faces not only his ethical limitations but also the mortal precarity of his own life.[25] His mortality at once makes him resemble the animals hunted by Bertilak and marks the alien and implacable agency of death and decay. How do these images fit into the poem's larger ecological concerns? Might we say that it is through an initial experience of binary opposition—the sheer smallness of humans before the implacable world—that we conceptualize interdependence?

In attending to such questions, readers can explore scenes in which non-human life seems to have independent agency. For example, in charting the seasonal cycle during the year before Gawain sets forth to meet his ostensible doom, the poem projects onto the natural world the court's change in mood from hope to encroaching loss; and at the same time, that seasonal description emphasizes the ineluctable passage of time independent of human volition. During Gawain's journey, the winter landscape and the animals hunted by Bertilak seem to suggest externalized aspects of Gawain's mental world—his misery and vulnerability—while at the same time suggesting alien non-human desires, in the case of the animals, and indifferent non-human spatio-temporal scales. In the end, King Arthur's court celebrates Gawain's sheer physical survival as a sign of its own capacity for ordered and leisured life, safely relegating the non-human world to a space "outside" its castle, even while donning an essential symbol of what lies "outside"—the green of nature and of magic—in the form of the green girdle.

Ecocriticism, that is, can draw attention to the poem's ecological networks of resemblance and dependency among humans, animals, minerals, weather, and time; it can also call attention to what *refuses* assimilation into a naturo-cultural mesh. How does *Gawain* balance these aspects of its ecology? In the hunts, a combination of vigorous engagement with the hunters' violence and subtle description of the prey's perspective seems to unsettle their mutual dependency. This instability is even more evident in the poem's climactic scene, when Gawain arrives to receive the mortal blow. Here he confronts a Chapel that is not so much a built as a ruined place, a cave or barrow that blends so fully into the non-human environment that he scarcely recognizes it as a potential human grave. But the Chapel is also a figure for the world's profound otherness: it evinces an indeterminate significance, even a flat lack of concern with significance.

I want to linger on the Green Chapel, as the poem's most profound challenge to any conception of ecology that only celebrates the encounter between human and non-human agencies.[26] It is here, more than anywhere else in the poem, that we see the power of the poem's uncanny ecological shifts. Arguably, the Chapel shows most saliently the poem's profound interest in non-human space at a non-human temporal scale. There is no refuge in the landscape through which Bertilak's servant leads Gawain to meet the Green Knight: the way is steep, foggy, and cold, a "waste," and they stop on a hilltop before Gawain plunges alone down the steep bank into the rugged valley.[27] Gawain seems to expect the Chapel to be a built enclosure and to half-hope for some form of hospitality or containment: as he descends toward it, "wylde hit hym þoȝt, / And seȝe no syngne of resette bisydez nowhere" ("it seemed a wild place, / And he saw no sign of welcome anywhere near").[28] A "resette" implies the possibility of protection, "a place of refuge, shelter, or accommodation."[29] Though his guide has directed him to look to the left, Gawain has trouble identifying the Chapel, seeing "non suche" except a low mound by the banks of a boiling spring.[30] Gawain walks around the hollow cave and debates within himself about what it might be: "nobot an olde caue, / Or a creuisse of an olde cragge, he couþe hit noȝt deme / with spelle" ("nothing but an old cave, / Or a crevace of an old cliff, he could not tell / which it was").[31] These negations foil judgment or interpretation; they fail to cohere into narrative or "spelle."

Neither built nor grown, neither humanly made nor entirely natural, the Chapel houses nothing determinate. With its holes on the end and on either side, it lacks clear boundaries between inside and outside, sacred and profane: "Þis is a chapel of meschaunce, þat chekke hit bytyde! / Hit is þe corsedest kyrk þat ever I com inne!" ("This is a chapel of disaster, may ill luck befall it! / It is the most damnable church I was ever inside").[32] It blurs the boundaries between past and present, life and death: what Gawain sees resembles the hollowness of an empty shrine, overgrown with grasses, the remnant of a now-dead pagan past, like a barrow or a tomb.[33] It is overgrown with grass, emphasizing its dislocation from the present time, its ruined character. It even seems potentially evil: "Here my3t aboute mydny3t / Þe Dele his matynnes telle!" ("Here might around midnight / The devil say his matins!").[34] Students may find that one or another characteristic becomes more salient or definitive, but they might also see that even the Chapel's "evil" is less a moral certainty than an expression of Gawain's disorientation. The possibility of a midnight ritual within a Chapel implies asynchrony or temporal ambiguity that threatens moral distinctions. These ambiguities are spatial as well. The Chapel is not a cemetery, which one might find near a wayside chapel, but a barrow, suggesting the presence of an unrecognizable past. The Green Chapel does not even clearly commemorate Christian death, raising the question of what kind of death awaits the poem's hero.

In these ways, the Green Chapel marks the limits of human processes of signification. It represents human space and time in the grip of an ecosystem whose lush grasses and cavernous underground foil the human order that Gawain had expected. It is both temporally and spatially indeterminate. Without a clear indication of either the design of the chapel or its etiology, Gawain cannot organize the world around it, and its space is porous, without boundaries or clear human significance. By contrast, when he hears the sharpening of the Green Knight's ax resounding in the hills, Gawain's determinate fear for his own life comes as almost a relief.

Ecocritical readings acknowledge the capacity for non-human life to exceed, even violate, the forms of order available to poetic making. Situating Gawain's quest in relentlessly concrete descriptions of non-human life, the poem asks about the place of the human knight, and the court he represents, in relation to the threatening winter, the possibility of animal death, and the sheer illegibility of the Chapel's reversion to natural growth. Here we see a confrontation with mortality: death at once appears emphatically natural and, at the same time, represents the moment when humans are no longer participants in the earth's living system. In another work associated with the *Pearl*-poet, *St. Erkenwald*, there is another human-made grave with opaque significance: a long-buried sarcophagus inscribed with illegible runes, which holds the incorrupt body of a virtuous pagan who could not be saved; there, the body dissolves (and resolves) into dirt when the soul is miraculously baptized at the poem's end.[35] What does it mean in these poems to transcend the human? How do such ancient graves connect humans to non-human agents? In their intense concern with the question of human involvement with the lives of animals, plants, stones, and landscapes, what happens when the *Pearl*-poet's works depict something uninvolved and opaque, which humans cannot encompass?

GROUND OF BLISS: *PEARL* AND METAPHOR

Pearl shares with *Sir Gawain* and *St. Erkenwald* a sense of what Jeffrey Jerome Cohen identifies as "the incomprehensibilities of the eternal to those who exist in mortal brevity."[36] As in *Erkenwald*, the appearance of a body thought to be dead raises questions about the status of the human body more generally, its earthly limits and its salvation. The Dreamer mourns his maiden, who has died, and who appears to him in his dream as if she were real and alive. Unlike the four other poems possibly in the *Pearl*-poet's oeuvre, *Pearl* approaches heaven and depicts a stringent distinction between divine and human realms.[37] This differentiation leads Gillian Rudd, the poem's principal ecological critic, to argue that the poem "privilege(s) the metaphorical world over the literal one."[38]

For Rudd, metaphor is fundamentally anthropocentric. The Pearl Maiden is no literal child; the New Jerusalem is not made of gems mined from the earth; the Dreamer cannot swim across to it because the river that separates him is not made of literal water. The organic and mineral realities of ecological earth are differentiated from, and subordinated to, the symbolic significance of human salvation, and for Rudd, this implies a hierarchy of value that privileges the human soul. This analysis opens difficult questions. Although poetry is human-made, Rudd is interested in the ways in which language can do more than depict human agency. When does symbolic language nonetheless reinscribe the centrality of human endeavor? When, on the other hand, does metaphor work against, or simply exceed, this basic anthropocentrism?[39] It could be argued that the *Pearl*-poet's language system—alliterative linkages and puns, staged dialogue, description, generic mixture, metaphor— "marshalls poetry as a resource for examining" ecological systems.[40] An ecocritical perspective can encourage students to explore not only the relation between human and non-human life, but also the relation between human language and its environmental reference.

Such explorations can begin, as with *Gawain*, by foregrounding setting. *Pearl* takes place in an organic environment that moves from the grave site where the Dreamer first falls asleep to the artificial landscape of his dream, including the gem-encrusted paradise he sees across the river. The landscape forms a kind of "arch-natural" scene, at once echoing the grave site's garden and departing from it, with its blue tree-trunks and silver leaves.[41] Barbara Newman argues that these scenes, and the conversation between Maiden and Dreamer staged within them, show finally "how little mortals can grasp of heaven's ways."[42] A heaven made visible through the hard gleam of minerals confronts the human Dreamer with an implacable ecology: an uncanny spatial extension and temporal span, wholly alien to human comprehension.

Yet the poem remains deeply concerned with the Dreamer's human capacity to perceive that which lies beyond his comprehension. Heaven can be approached, if not achieved, from its basis in earth. The pearl fell "Þruȝ gresse to grounde" ("through grass to the ground") and lies "clad in clot," ("dressed in earth").[43] As highly wrought as the poem's metaphorical language may be, its story remains embedded in the ecology of death, set in the garden to which the Dreamer, when he awakens, must finally return: the grave where he first lost his pearl, "þat erber wlonk" ("that beautiful refuge").[44] Metaphorically, nonetheless, earth grounds and enables the Dreamer's vision of heaven.[45] Metaphors transcend or point beyond the material elements of tenor and vehicle. Not only can heaven be described via metaphor; but there is also a homology between metaphorical language and spiritual transcendence that gives the poem's landscape its peculiar blend of radical difference and accessibility.

The Dreamer initially assumes that the holy maiden he sees in his dream is literally present, and that he can swim across to reach her; but through her correction, he comes to see her spiritual status. In the process, he comes to understand the way metaphor works; that is, he examines the relation between the concrete world and the meaning that accrues to it. Section VII, for example, begins with his stark sense of loss. He begs her not to rebuke him for it: "Of care and me ȝe made acorde, / Þat er watz grounde of alle my blysse" ("You brought suffering to me, / Who had been the ground of all my bliss").[46] "Grounde" no longer refers to dirt, of course, but the lines describe his earthly sense of the maiden's importance and the pain of losing her. As the section develops, dirt returns: "I am bot mol" ("I am but dust") he says, achieving that humility that comes of devotion to Mary and Jesus.[47] Dirt becomes a metaphor for humility. But more than this: humility (etymologically from Latin *humus*, "ground") is now both the concrete and figural "grounde of alle my blysse." The moment of spiritual growth ties the Dreamer at once to the vehicle of the metaphor, "grounde," and to the tenor, Christian devotion. He cannot make such metaphors without the dirt under his feet and the dirt in which his beloved maiden is buried, nor can he imagine heaven without the ecological materials of the created world.[48]

We might say that the poem's ecology is its very topic: it is concerned with how to connect heaven and embodied life, both organic and crafted. Its ecosystem consists of the Dreamer's questions and the Pearl-Maiden's answers about where she resides, how she came there, and what her presence there signifies for human life: the relation between her current appearance and the body that dies. The function of dialogue in this mode is to integrate the Dreamer's earthly and "dreamed" experiences, not simply to split off human spiritual import from the language and imagery of the concrete world that provide its basis or ground. To be sure, between the Dreamer and the Maiden there remains a gap—Newman writes that "their two minds never truly meet"—but the conversation nonetheless takes place and leaves the Dreamer (perhaps) changed in the concluding stanzas.[49]

Might this attention to metaphor offer purchase on the ecological concerns of this highly abstract poem? Metaphors typically begin with the material. In general, they are based, not to say grounded, in the concrete non-human things of the world—dirt, roses, pearls, the distant stars—while the tenor will often catapult into abstraction—bliss, transience, perfection, paradisal glory.[50] Moreover, the concrete vehicle will often be subordinated to human-oriented abstractions. As Rudd argues, metaphors turn the created world—its animals, plants, minerals, weather—to human use. Sarah Stanbury argues that metaphor can serve to naturalize such human ascendancy. But in the case of Chaucer, she also asserts that metaphor can reveal a "disenchanted skepticism about nature's benevolence" and an awareness of how human institutions use ideas about 'the natural' to justify social hierarchies.[51] To be sure, a metaphor's tenor and vehicle may have various relationships. As anthropocentric as figural language may innately be—inasmuch as human language is a human construct—metaphors can never suppress the concrete world-consciousness that gives them birth. What makes them work, in fact, is their continual oscillation between tenor and vehicle, the unarticulated difference that makes the marriage of tenor and vehicle surprising or, in ancient and medieval rhetoric, strange, puzzling, alien.[52]

Looked at in this way, metaphor is less an assertion of human dominion than a signal of all that escapes the human grasp: metaphor deliberately exceeds its own explicit reference, generating unspoken associations, puzzling us with the ineffable, introducing stray associations, or slipping back to the concrete. The ecology of language cannot easily be reduced to that which values only the human. Metaphor points to heaven but never leaves earth behind, and it points to earth as clot and dust, but also as garden and as grounds for life. In this sense it exhibits the paradox of human existence in the world where, whether non-human life seems metaphorically alien and implacable or intimate and kind, humans remain only one aspect of a complex set of ecological systems whose interrelationships exceed the capacity of language fully to represent the world, much less to control or to contain it all.

NOTES

1. Pioneering in the field is Lawrence Buell, *The Environmental Imagination: Thoreau, Nature Writing, and the Formation of American Culture* (Cambridge, MA: Harvard University Press, 1995).

2. For a recent exploration of complex notions of natural hierarchy based on "inclination," see Kellie Robertson, *Nature Speaks: Medieval Literature and Aristotelian Philosophy* (Philadelphia: University of Pennsylvania Press, 2017).

3. Ecology is the central subject of eco-criticism, the study of humanities disciplines through an environmental lens, a term coined by William Rueckert in "Literature and Ecology: An Experiment in Ecocriticism," in *The Ecocriticism Reader: Landmarks in Literary Ecology*, ed. Cheryll Glotfelty and Harold Fromm (Athens: University of Georgia Press, 1996), 105–23.

4. For introductions to the field, see Timothy Clark, *The Cambridge Introduction to Literature and the Environment* (Cambridge: Cambridge University Press, 2011) and Greg Garrard, *Oxford Handbook of Ecocriticism* (Oxford: Oxford University Press, 2014).

5. Gillian Rudd, *Greenery: Ecocritical Readings of Late Medieval English Literature* (Manchester: Manchester University Press, 2007); see also Alfred K. Siewers, *Strange Beauty: Ecocritical Approaches to Early Medieval Landscape* (New York: Palgrave, 2009).

6. The emphasis on networks of mutual dependency borders on the "vital materialism" of Jane Bennett in *Vibrant Matter: A Political Ecology of Things* (Chapel Hill, NC: Duke University Press, 2010). See the series of collected essays edited by Jeffrey Jerome Cohen and Lowell Duckert: *Prismatic Ecology: Ecotheory Beyond Green*, ed. Cohen; *Elemental Ecocriticism: Thinking with Earth, Air, Water, and Fire*, ed. Cohen and Duckert; and *Veer Ecology: A Companion for Environmental Thinking*, ed. Cohen and Duckert (Minneapolis: University of Minnesota Press, 2013, 2015, and 2017, respectively). The recognition of intimacy between human and non-human creatures also borders on the rich terrain of animal studies, as discussed especially in Susan Crane, *Animal Encounters: Contacts and Concepts in Medieval Britain* (Philadelphia: University of Pennsylvania Press, 2013), and Peggy McCracken, *In the Skin of a Beast: Sovereignty and Animality in Medieval France* (Chicago: University of Chicago Press, 2017).

7. The term "weird" is from Timothy Morton, *Dark Ecology: For a Logic of Future Coexistence* (New York: Columbia University Press, 2016), 5–7, 110; it calls up both the strange and the fatefully patterned (from Old English *wyrd*). For the emphasis on a non-human world marked by its distance or inscrutability to humans, see Cohen, *Stone: An Ecology of the Inhuman* (Minneapolis: University of Minnesota Press, 2015). On the violence of human hierarchical responses to such inscrutability, see Karl Steel, *How to Make a Human: Animals and Violence in the Middle Ages* (Columbus: Ohio State University Press, 2011).

8. For approaches that seek to integrate non-human and human ecologies such as law and property, see the collection edited by Randy Schiff and Joseph Taylor, *The Politics of Ecology: Land, Life, and Law in Medieval Britain* (Columbus: Ohio State University Press, 2016).

9. *Patience*, line 138. All quotations from the poems are from *The Poems of the Pearl Manuscript*, ed. Malcolm Andrew and Ronald Waldron, York Medieval Texts, Second Series (Berkeley: University of California Press, 1978). Translations are my own.

10. *Patience*, 143–144.

11. *Patience*, 156.

12. Gillian Rudd, in *Greenery*, her foundational ecocritical account of medieval literature, contends that the poem forces Jonah to recognize that in the sea, "humankind is not the dominant species" (p. 154) and that it thus becomes a force "outside the realms of human imagination" and a "source of unsettling alternative world-views" (p. 160). See Rudd, *Greenery*. I argue that Jonah's sea is far less unsettling than that of the Flood in *Cleanness*.

13. On the intimacy and even identity between God and "kynde" in *Piers Plowman* to his creation in *Patience*, see my "'As Mot in at a Munster Dor': Sanctuary and Love of This World," *Philological Quarterly* 87 (2008): 105–133.

14. On the poem's complex exploration of human desire, see Elizabeth B. Keiser, *Courtly Desire and Medieval Homophobia: The Legitimation of Sexual Pleasure in "Cleanness" and Its Contexts* (New Haven, CT: Yale University Press, 1997).

15. *Cleanness*, 371.

16. The echo is biblical. Gen. 1:2. See also Gen. 8:1.

17. Many scholars have stressed this ambiguity. See the influential studies of A. C. Spearing, *The Gawain-Poet: A Critical Study* (Cambridge: Cambridge University Press, 1970), 171–236, and Ralph Hanna III, "Unlocking What's Locked: Gawain's Green Girdle," *Viator* 14 (1983): 289–302. See also Mickey Sweeney, "The Failure of Perfection," in this volume.

18. Randy Schiff, "Hybrid Alliterative Green: Ecopoetics in *Sir Gawain and the Green Knight*," in *Ecopoetics and the Global Landscape: Critical Essays*, ed. Isabel Sobral Campos (Lanham, MD: Lexington Books, 2019), 177–201, at 197.

19. Schiff, "Hybrid Alliterative Green: Ecopoetics in *Sir Gawain and the Green Knight*," 188.

20. Schiff, "Hybrid Alliterative Green: Ecopoetics in *Sir Gawain and the Green Knight*," 177. See also Jeanne Provost, "Sovereign Meat: Reassembling the Hunter King from Medieval Forest Law to *The Wedding of Sir Gawain and Dame Ragnelle*," in *Politics of Ecology*, 56–81.

21. Carolyn Dinshaw, "Ecology," in *A Handbook of Middle English Studies*, ed. Marion Turner (Hoboken, NJ: Wiley-Blackwell, 2013), 357.

22. Dinshaw, "Ecology," 355.

23. Bennett, *Vibrant Matter*, 99.

24. Dinshaw, "Ecology," 351.

25. For a different reading of death as "the point of ultimate visceral contact with the world, of maximum exposure to its impact," see Mark Miller, "The Ends of Excitement in *Sir Gawain and the Green Knight*: Teleology, Ethics, and the Death Drive," *Speculum* 32 (2010): 215–56, at 232, and Walter Wadiak, *Savage Economies: The Returns of Middle English Romance* (Notre Dame, IN: University of Notre Dame Press, 2017), 88–118.

26. My reading here is based on the more extended account in Elizabeth Allen, *Uncertain Refuge: Sanctuary in the Literature of Medieval England* (Philadelphia: University of Pennsylvania Press, 2021).

27. *Sir Gawain and the Green Knight*, 2098. On the way in which the concept of "waste" troubles legal boundaries in medieval English poetry, see Eleanor Johnson, "The Poetics of Waste: Medieval English Ecocriticism," *PMLA* 127, no. 3 (2012): 460–476.

28. *Sir Gawain and the Green Knight*, 2163–64.

29. *MED*, s.v. "recette," 1a.

30. *Sir Gawain and the Green Knight*, 2174.

31. *Sir Gawain and the Green Knight*, 2182–84.

32. *Sir Gawain and the Green Knight*, 2195–96.

33. Jeffrey Jerome Cohen also points out the ambiguity of the Chapel's origins (*Stone*, 84). On the way in which graves create continuity between death and life, see Robert Pogue Harrison, *The Dominion of the Dead* (Chicago: Chicago University Press, 2003), 1–36.

34. *Sir Gawain and the Green Knight*, 2187–88.

35. On the link between mystical and ecological excesses, see Anne Schuurman, "Materials of Wonder: Miraculous Objects and Poetic Form in *St. Erkenwald*," *Studies in the Age of Chaucer* 39 (2017): 275–96.

36. Cohen, *Stone*, 37.

37. For further discussion of how the Dreamer approaches the heavenly realm, see Jane Beal, "The Dreamer's Contemplative Experience of a *Mappamundi* in *Pearl*," in this volume.

38. Rudd, *Greenery*, 183.

39. On metaphor and ecocriticism, see most recently Shawn Normandin, *Chaucerian Ecopoetics: Deconstructing Anthropocentrism in The Canterbury Tales* (New York: Palgrave, 2018), 85–121. See also Leslie Kordecki, *Ecofeminist Subjectivities: Chaucer's Talking Birds* (New York: Palgrave, 2011).

40. Johnson, "Poetics of Waste," 473.

41. *Pearl*, ll. 76–77. Barbara Newman writes that Heaven may reflect the natural world but also the City on a Hill: "Heaven can be conceived as either arch-natural or supernatural." See "Artifices of Eternity: Speaking of Heaven in Three Medieval Poems," *Religion and Literature* 37:1 (2005): 1–24, at 4.

42. Newman, "Artifices," 14.

43. *Pearl*, 10, 22.

44. *Pearl*, 1171.

45. R. A. Shoaf writes, "it is useful to keep in sight, what in fact *is* often forgotten, namely that the dreamer *has also seen God*." See "*Purgatorio* and *Pearl*: Transgression and Transcendence," *Texas Studies in Literature and Language* 32, no. 1 (1990): 152–68, at 159.

46. *Pearl*, 371–72.

47. *Pearl*, 382.

48. For a developed exploration of the materiality of death, what he calls "the activity of corpse and worms dwelling together," see Karl Steel, "Food for Worms," on *Social Paper (beta)*, CUNY Academic Commons: https://commons.gc.cuny.edu/papers/chapter-3-food-for-worms/ (accessed 6/12/2019).

49. Newman, "Artifices of Eternity," 11. Translations are my own.

50. One of *Pearl's* most moving metaphoric repetitions falls outside this concrete-abstract pattern: the comparison between the dream's light—as seen first in the gem-encrusted river and later in the New Jerusalem—to the light of stars and moon. Here, concrete is compared to concrete, and the implication is that this is because heaven's sheer incomprehensibility would not bear further abstraction. See my essay "Teaching *Pearl* and Landscape," in *Approaches to Teaching the Middle English* Pearl, ed. Jane Beal and Mark Bradshaw Busbee (New York: Modern Language Association of America, 2018), 188–96, at 194.

51. Sarah Stanbury, "Ecochaucer: Green Ethics and Medieval Nature," *The Chaucer Review* 39, no. 1 (2004): 1–16, at 13.

52. On the strangeness of metaphor, see Aristotle, *Rhetoric* 1405a8; for its puzzling the reader, see e.g., Cicero, *De Oratore*, 3, 159–60. The idea of oscillation derives from Gian Biagio Conte, *The Rhetoric of Imitation: Genre and Poetic Memory in Virgil and Other Latin Poets*, trans. Charles Segal (Ithaca, NY: Cornell University Press, 1986), 37–39.

BIBLIOGRAPHY

Allen, Elizabeth. *Uncertain Refuge: Sanctuary in the Literature of Medieval England.* Philadelphia: University of Pennsylvania Press, 2021.

———. "Teaching *Pearl* and Landscape." *Approaches to Teaching the Middle English* Pearl, ed. Jane Beal and Mark Bradshaw Busbee, 188–96. New York: Modern Language Association of America, 2018.

———. "'As Mot in at a Muster Dor': A Sanctuary and Love of This World." *Philological Quarterly* 87 (2008): 105–133.

Beal, Jane, ed. *Becoming the Pearl-Poet: Perceptions, Connections, Receptions.* New York: Lexington Books, 2022.

Bennett, Jane. *Vibrant Matter: A Political Ecology of Things.* Chapel Hill, NC: Duke University Press, 2010.

Buell, Lawrence. *The Environmental Imagination: Thoreau, Nature Writing, and the Formation of American Culture.* Cambridge, MA: Harvard University Press, 1995.

Clark, Timothy. *The Cambridge Introduction to Literature and the Environment.* Cambridge: Cambridge University Press, 2011.

Cohen, Jeffrey Jerome. *Stone: An Ecology of the Inhuman.* Minneapolis: University of Minnesota Press, 2015.

Cohen, Jeffrey Jerome, ed. *Prismatic Ecology: Ecotheory beyond Green.* Minneapolis: University of Minnesota Press, 2013.

Cohen, Jeffrey Jerome, and Lowell Duckert, eds. *Elemental Ecocriticism: Thinking with Earth, Air, Water, and Fire.* Minneapolis: University of Minnesota Press, 2015.

Cohen, Jeffrey Jerome, and Lowell Duckert, eds. *Veer Ecology: A Companion for Environmental Thinking.* Minneapolis: University of Minnesota Press, 2017.

Conte, Gian Biagio. *The Rhetoric of Imitation: Genre and Poetic Memory in Virgil and Other Latin Poets.* Trans. Charles Segal. Ithaca, NY: Cornell University Press, 1986.

Crane, Susan. *Animal Encounters: Contacts and Concepts in Medieval Britain.* Philadelphia: University of Pennsylvania Press, 2013.

Davis, Rebecca. *Piers Plowman and the Books of Nature.* Oxford: Oxford University Press, 2016.

Dinshaw, Carolyn. "Ecology." In *A Handbook of Middle English Studies.* Ed. Marion Turner, 347–62. Hoboken, NJ: Wiley-Blackwell, 2013.

Garrard, Greg. *Oxford Handbook of Ecocriticism.* Oxford: Oxford University Press, 2014.

Hanna, Ralph III. "Unlocking What's Locked: Gawain's Green Girdle." *Viator* 14 (1983): 289–302.

Harrison, Robert Pogue. *The Dominion of the Dead.* Chicago: Chicago University Press, 2003.

Johnson, Eleanor. "The Poetics of Waste: Medieval English Ecocriticism." *PMLA* 127, no. 3 (2012): 460–76.

Keiser, Elizabeth B. *Courtly Desire and Medieval Homophobia: The Legitimation of Sexual Pleasure in "Cleanness" and Its Contexts.* New Haven, CT: Yale University Press, 1997.

Kordecki, Leslie. *Ecofeminist Subjectivities: Chaucer's Talking Birds.* New York: Palgrave, 2011.

McCracken, Peggy. *In the Skin of a Beast: Sovereignty and Animality in Medieval France.* Chicago: University of Chicago Press, 2017.

Miller, Mark. "The Ends of Excitement in *Sir Gawain and the Green Knight*: Teleology, Ethics, and the Death Drive." *Speculum* 32 (2010): 215–56.

Morton, Timothy. *Dark Ecology: For a Logic of Future Coexistence.* New York: Columbia University Press, 2016.

Newman, Barbara. "Artifices of Eternity: Speaking of Heaven in Three Medieval Poems." *Religion and Literature* 37, no. 1 (2005): 1–24.

Normandin, Shawn. *Chaucerian Ecopoetics: Deconstructing Anthropocentrism in the Canterbury Tales.* New York: Palgrave, 2018.

Provost, Jeanne. "Sovereign Meat: Reassembling the Hunter King from Medieval Forest Law to *The Wedding of Sir Gawain and Dame Ragnelle.*" In *The Politics of Ecology: Land, Life, and Law in Medieval Britain*, ed. Randy Schiff and Joseph Taylor, 56–81. Columbus: Ohio State University Press, 2016.

Robertson, Kellie. *Nature Speaks: Medieval Literature and Aristotelian Philosophy.* Philadelphia: University of Pennsylvania Press, 2017.

Rudd, Gillian. *Greenery: Ecocritical Readings of Late Medieval English Literature.* Manchester: Manchester University Press, 2007.

Rueckert, William. "Literature and Ecology: An Experiment in Ecocriticism." *The Ecocriticism Reader: Landmarks in Literary Ecology*, ed. Cheryll Glotfelty and Harold Fromm, 105–23. Athens: University of Georgia Press, 1996.

Schiff, Randy. "Hybrid Alliterative Green: Ecopoetics in *Sir Gawain and the Green Knight.*" *Ecopoetics and the Global Landscape: Critical Essays.* Ed. Isabel Sobral Campos, 177–201. Lanham, MD: Lexington Books, 2019.

Schiff, Randy, and Joseph Taylor, eds. *The Politics of Ecology: Land, Life, and Law in Medieval Britain.* Columbus: Ohio State University Press, 2016.

Schuurman, Anne. "Materials of Wonder: Miraculous Objects and Poetic Form in *St. Erkenwald.*" *Studies in the Age of Chaucer* 39 (2017): 275–96.

Shoaf, R. A. "*Purgatorio* and *Pearl:* Transgression and Transcendence." *Texas Studies in Literature and Language* 32, no. 1 (1990): 152–68.

Spearing, A. C. *The Gawain-Poet: A Critical Study.* Cambridge: Cambridge University Press, 1970.

Stanbury, Sarah. "Ecochaucer: Green Ethics and Medieval Nature." *The Chaucer Review* 39, no. 1 (2004): 1–16.

Steel, Karl. *How to Make a Human: Animals and Violence in the Middle Ages.* Columbus: Ohio State University Press, 2011.

———. "Food for Worms." *Social Papers (beta).* CUNY Academic Commons. Accessed 6/12/2019. https://commons.gc.cuny.edu/papers/chapter-3-food-for -worms/

Wadiak, Walter. *Savage Economies: The Returns of Middle English Romance.* Notre Dame, IN: University of Notre Dame Press, 2017.

.

Chapter Eight

Material Culture of the *Pearl*-Poet

Jonathan Quick

The poet of the four poems in the British Library, Cotton Nero A.x, and of *St. Erkenwald,* revels in description, especially of the material world. Populating his poems with objects both splendid and ordinary, sacred and secular, the poet creates a rich material fabric within these texts. This chapter examines the poet's presentation and utilization of these material objects as both descriptive embellishments and didactic symbols conveying divine and moral messages to the poems' audiences. I pay particular attention to the pearl in *Pearl,* using a reading of that poem to assess the poet's treatment of material objects to poetic effect. Giving close scrutiny to the material world of the poet in light of the social networks these objects inhabited helps readers better understand the poet's aims and designs.

The Dreamer in *Pearl* identifies himself as a "joylez juelere,"[1] joyless because he has lost, among other things, a precious pearl. In the Middle Ages, pearls were prized for their aesthetic qualities in jewelry, clothing, and decoration,[2] but also, like many other gemstones and crystals, pearls were believed to possess curative and palliative qualities. When swallowed, crushed pearls were thought to aid in the healing of flows of blood or bowel and to assist nursing mothers in producing milk.[3] The qualities and benefits of these precious stones were cataloged in medieval lapidaries and encyclopedias.[4]

However, the Dreamer seems less interested in the medicinal attributes of the pearl within the poem and more concerned with its aesthetic qualities. In Middle English, a jeweler could mean either a craftsman or a merchant working with precious stones, gems, or fine metals.[5] In fact, scholars continue to point out that an exact definition is difficult to pin down. Middle English "jeueler" was sometimes treated synonymously or interchangeably with "goldsmith":[6] both crafts dealt with "jeuels" which were understood to be not only gems and stones but any "highly-wrought art-objects."[7]

Europe produced a number of highly-wrought art objects in the late fourteenth and early fifteenth century. An ornate golden crown set with sapphires, diamonds, rubies, and pearls was sent to Bavaria upon the marriage of Blanche, daughter of King Henry IV of England, to Ludwig III.[8] The Royal Gold Cup of the Kings of England and France, probably made around 1380, contains scenes from the life of St Agnes on enamel as well as a row of pearls along its base.[9] The small brooch known as the Founder's Jewel was given to New College, Oxford by William Wykeham in 1404.[10] It is a silver-gilt brooch in the shape of an "M" with several gems framing a scene of the Annunciation. A cluster of three pearls rises above and between Gabriel and Mary while two more pearls decorate the bottom of the right arch.[11] Finally, the Little Golden Horse reliquary, made before 1404, was a New Year's Gift[12] from Isabel of Bavaria to her husband Charles VI.[13] The upper portion contains an image of the Virgin holding her Child. Her clothing is made using the *en ronde bosse* method of applying white enamel to gold, but on her breast is a pendant with six pearls surrounding a ruby. These and many other artifacts of the later Middle Ages show that jewelry-makers and goldsmiths employed the use of pearls as significant features in their works.

If one considers the Dreamer of the poem to be a jeweler-craftsman, it is helpful to recall that artificers were coming under increased political and commercial scrutiny around the time of the poem's composition. The sumptuary laws passed by the Parliament of 1363 targeted the craft of jewelers and goldsmiths limiting which methods craftsmen could use and who could purchase and wear their products. There was a division of practices: craftsmen who made "White Vessel" could not gild nor *vice versa*. These laws seemed to have been aimed partially at the integrity of the process of production, that these intricate items be made "well and lawfully" to prevent craftsmen from defrauding their customers and patrons.[14]

These laws, however, devote more space and specificity to delineating who could wear what attire and ornament. These laws expressly forbade the wearing of gold and precious stones (including pearls) to certain persons due to lower social class or lesser economic worth.[15] Knights, for instance, with an income below two hundred pounds could wear no clothing embroidered with nor any jewelry containing precious stones. Knights and ladies worth up to a thousand pounds could wear what they wished except for ermine[16] or "Apparel of Pearls and Stone."[17] Thus, in two senses, jewelry could only be set in certain ways: a certain setting in the methods used to create jewelry, and jewelry could only be set upon particular and appropriately worthy persons.

The perceived anxiety underlying these laws indicates that within the context of late fourteenth century England the freedom to acquire and to wear certain types of jewelry translated to a certain social status. This is reflected within *Pearl* when the Dreamer, beholding the Pearl-Maiden, scrutinizes her attire—"that of an aristocratic young woman in the second half of the 14th c."[18]—but deems that she has raised herself "ouer hyȝ,"[19] well beyond her proper station according to his own (flawed) understanding. His estimation is certainly affected by her wearing a "pyȝt coroune . . . Of marjorys and non oþer ston";[20] the freedom to wear such an item was reserved for only the highest in society. Judging someone by their attire is also a fundamental part of the Parable of the Wedding Banquet recounted in *Cleanness*. When one examines the cleanliness or filthiness of one's clothes in this poem, it is not social status that is read but spiritual works.

Many studies on the *Pearl* emphasize the Dreamer-as-jeweler strictly taken in the sense of a goldsmith or craftsperson, but certain features of the poem problematize this seemingly straightforward reading. Tony Davenport, taking a more skeptical view of the meaning of "juelere," points out that the poem is largely devoid of the precise, technical language of the jewelry-making trade.[21] The "jeweler" instead tends to use vocabulary on the pearl's aesthetic and moral qualities: its size, shape, color; its purity and clarity. I would add to Davenport's argument that the Dreamer does not openly display an expert knowledge of precious stones. Upon seeing the Heavenly Jerusalem, the Dreamer catalogs the gemstones in the city's foundations, but says he "con nemme" them, not because of his own authority or experience in working with said stones, but by the "tale" of the Apostle John recorded in Revelation.[22] In his activities of *prouing* and *jugging* the pearl,[23] he shows himself to be more like to a "possessor and connoisseur"[24] than an artificer.

In *Patience* and *Cleanness*, however, the poet does get technical, though not about jewel-making. Both poetic homilies contain episodes of sailing or seafaring, and the poet rifles off a number of nautical terms, which in turn heighten the drama and pace of the passages. *Patience* is, perhaps, the poem in the entire set most devoid of overtly described material objects, but the ship carrying Jonah bound for Tarshish is the exception. The poet is at once his most descriptive and most material in this poem during his treatment of the sailing vessel at two episodes: the embarkation and the storm.[25] William Sayers has determined that the terms used by the poet are technical but not overly specialized, suggesting that the poet is recounting widespread knowledge of ships and sailing practices; Sayers writes that "the poet contents himself with exteriors."[26] His language reflects the technological state of shipbuilding in late medieval Europe.[27] The only other highly descriptive portion of the poem is the description of the gastrointestinal tract of the whale. Perhaps by reading these heightened passages of the ship and the whale together, the poet intends to highlight the tension between the two: the civilized, man-made, and exterior descriptions of the ship's tackle are juxtaposed with the wild, animal, and interior of the whale's body. Jonah is thrown at the whale's mouth like a dust mote at a cathedral door. Though the mouth is likened to the entryway of a place of holy worship, the whale is compared to a devil and stinks like one, too. This is a theme the poet weaves into *Sir Gawain* and *Erkenwald* as well: the Green Chapel, in Gawain's estimation, seems like a place of devil worship despite its being called a chapel; in *Erkenwald*, the old temple being excavated to make way for a new cathedral is devoted to devils. Each of these spaces (the whale, the Green Chapel, the tomb's temple) appears hopeless, devilish, and wholly devoid of God's grace, and yet, within each, hope is restored, and mercy is granted: Gawain is absolved by Bertilak for his fault, Jonah is heard and delivered to shore, and Erkenwald's tears baptize the pagan corpse whose soul is then brought from bale to bliss.

Returning to *Pearl*, if the Dreamer was not a craftsman but instead a jewel-lover and connoisseur, someone more prone to look at and judge jewels than to forge and file fine objects, then I suggest that the poet invites his audience to participate in a similar activity as more passive "jeueleres" while the poem follows the symbol of the pearl through different settings. These different settings—both on a literal level but especially playing with the jeweler's art of setting stones[28]—represent different stages of the Dreamer's journey into knowledge and understanding of divine grace. While the language of the Dreamer may not be the technically precise language of a jewelry-maker, the poems themselves are evidence that the poet was a technically precise verse-maker of the English language. When we examine his poems like a medieval jeweler examining and appreciating fine craftsmanship, we gain further insight into the poet's art.

This reading is, in part, inspired by the poet's own reading practices. Legibility and proper reading are concerns in two of his works: the writing on the wall at the Babylonian feast in *Cleanness* and the "roynyshe" gold writing on the tomb in *Erkenwald*.[29] The initial inscrutability of these written messages is met with a call for capable readers and interpreters. Daniel and the ancient judge fulfill the role of explaining cryptic messages. The poet, too, could be considered an interpreter. He shows himself to be a careful reader and explicator of texts, especially of biblical material. Matthew, Luke, Revelation, Genesis, Jonah, and Psalms feature as sources within his poems; however, what is more interesting than his adaptation of these sources is his mode of reading them. In the opening lines of *Patience*, after the narrating persona lists the Beatitudes, he explains that he has chosen patience as his theme because he is in a condition of poverty. He writes that these two themes or virtues (patience and poverty) are textually bound together: "For in þe tyxte þere þyse two arn in teme layde / Hit arn fettled in on forme, *þe forme and þe laste*."[30] This poet is especially concerned with first ("forme") and last ("laste") things and creating or illuminating a congruence or connection between the two. *Pearl*, *Sir Gawain*, and *Patience* are each ringed compositions, ending where they begin as their closing lines echo those that open the poems. In his exposition upon the Beatitudes, it seems, the poet is following in the tradition of Christ himself: the first and final statements of blessedness both promise the same reward to those who are poor and those who are patient.

> Thay arn happen þat han in hert pouerté
> *For hores is þe heuen-ryche* to holde for euer . . .
> Þay ar happen also þat con her hert stere,
> *For hores is þe heuen-ryche,* as I er sayde.[31]

("They are happy that have poverty in heart / For theirs is the kingdom of heaven to hold forever . . . / They are happy also that can steer their heart, / For theirs I the kingdom of heaven, as I said before.")

The poet shows an awareness of the shape and form of texts, bringing attention to the fact that he reiterated an earlier half-line ("as I er sayde"). He is conscious of the internal repetition in this portion of the Sermon on the Mount and draws his audience's attention to it.

As the poet shows concern for the beginnings, it behooves his readers to examine how he begins his poems, and this is especially pertinent to understanding the didactic purposes of *Pearl*. The poem begins: "Perle plesaunte, to prynces paye / To clanly clos in golde so clere."[32] It is the pleasure of a prince to "clos" a pearl in a rich setting, and Davenport notices a connection in the treatment of princes and jewelers in Lydgate's *Fables*. He indicates that "it is for jewellers (i.e. jewel owners) and princes to flaunt the handsomeness of the gems."[33] Yet, before the audience is brought into an appreciation of this peerless, singular jewel surpassing all others "Oute of oryent,"[34] the Dreamer interjects, "Allas! I leste hyr in on erbere."[35] ("Out of Orient . . . Allas! I lost her in a garden.") The pearl's first setting in the poem is in the earth, marred by dirt and filth: "To þenke hir color so clad in clot! / O moul, þou marrez a myry juele."[36] ("To think of her color so clothed in dirt! / O earth, you mar a merry jewel.")

The pearl's second setting is in the bejeweled dreamscape. Here, however, the pearl is transformed into the Pearl-Maiden. She is not marred by the earth as the Dreamer bemoaned in the earthly garden, but her face is "whyt as playn yuore,"[37] ("white as plain ivory") and her resplendent presence attracts the Dreamer's gaze. She is a truly unexpected sight for the Dreamer; he says "Bot baysement gef myn hert a brunt. / I seȝ hyr in so strange a place—"[38] ("But confusion gave a hurt to my heart / I saw her in so strange a place—"). His memory is questioned as he beholds his pearl in a wholly new setting, a strange place. In the dream encounter, his Pearl sits before his unbodied spirit, unsullied, in a paradise that is itself jewel-like with its crystal cliffs, indigo trees, silver leaves, a beryl-like riverbank, under a golden-gleaming sky and, most intriguingly, where the ground consists of pearls crunching beneath one's feet. These pearls are "precious perlez of oryente,"[39] recalling the image of the pearl from the opening stanza. In this dream paradise, the ground is no mere "moul" marring what treads or falls upon it. Just as the pearl symbol is elevated (from jewel pearl to Pearl-Maiden) so too is its setting (earthly garden to marvelous dreamscape).[40] The beauty of the first pearl symbol is outshone by the multiplicity and splendor of the second setting.

The third setting elevates the symbol and setting once again. After their long dialogue, the Pearl-Maiden assents to show the Dreamer a further vision within the dream. In the New Jerusalem, the focal point is the Wounded Lamb whose wooly coat is described "As praysed perlez."[41] The Lamb is the new pearl set in his city among the multitude of its pearl-adorned inhabitants. Just as the singularity of the physical pearl is diminished in a dream landscape strewn about with pearls, so too does the Pearl-Maiden's splendor become subsumed in the throng of the 144,000 where they all are "Depaynt in perlez and wedez qwyte" ("painted in pearls and white clothing") and each one bears a great pearl upon their breast.[42] Only after a long gaze at the vision does the Dreamer say, "Þen saȝ I þer my lyttel quene"[43] ("then I saw there my little queen"). She who had been his sole focus is now almost an afterthought, absent for thirteen stanzas while the Dreamer marvels at the Lamb and the heavenly city. The Lamb is not only pearly in appearance, but he is called a jewel first by the Maiden ("My Lombe, my Lorde, my dere Juelle")[44] and later recognized as such by the Dreamer: "Al songe to loue þat gay Juelle"[45] ("All sung to praise that joyful Jewel"). It is this sight of the worship of the Lamb in the jeweled city that spurs the Dreamer forward to attempt crossing the river which leads to his waking.

Because scholars have often emphasized the tripartite structure of the poem, this may lead us to read only three scenes of pearls in sequential settings. Yet, once the Dreamer wakes, the poet leaves his audience with one final symbol. The final stanza adjures all believers or all hearers and readers of the poem to be precious pearls unto the pleasure of Christ the Lord and Lamb. The pearl symbol is transferred from physical jewel to dream maiden, to Wounded Lamb, and finally, to the audience. This last move is not an elevation in the way that the previous symbol transformations were but rather an illumination and edification. To be reconciled or "sete saȝte"[46] ("be reconciled") is the final setting—that is, it is God's propitiating grace. As we accept the identity of God's "homly hyne" ("his humble servants"), the Dreamer realizes that we become "precious perlez vnto His pay."[47] The opening line of the poem transformed: the True Prince of Christian belief *clanly closes* or firmly establishes us within his grace.

A reading like this takes Davenport's skepticism to an extreme, and it fully accepts the idea of the Dreamer-as-connoisseur who is a learned but passive observer within the poem. All movements or transitions of setting and *closyng* as described in this reading are (quite literally) out of the Dreamer's hands. When the pearl first becomes lost, it maintains the agency and sets itself in the ground: "Þur3 gresse to grounde *hit fro me yot . . . hit fro me sprange*"[48] ("from grass to ground it from me went . . . it from me sprang"). The pearl is ascribed the agency of its first leap. The Dreamer's imagination fancies a past when he possessed and maintained a sense of control over the pearl; see, for instance, the repeated use of personal pronouns in the stanza from lines 241 to 252. His own agency, less like the active goldsmith crafting jewels, is more like the sense of a jeweler admiring the vision of those jewels. Each subsequent vision brings the Dreamer (and audience) along a journey of revelation. Through these parallel processes of learning and discovery, the poet finally maps the last transformation onto the figure of the Dreamer and the audience of *Pearl*. Like the lesson of the Parable of the Laborers in the Vineyard recounted by the Pearl-Maiden, in considering the "joylez juelere" a passive participant, the audience is reminded once again that it is the Master of the vineyard who maintains control and does and gives as he wishes ("To do wyth myn quatso me lykez?")[49] ("To do with my own whatsoever I prefer?").

Again, our Dreamer may lack the qualities of a jewel-*maker*, instead reflecting the values and functions of a jewel-*lover*, but our poet was certainly a fine craftsman, displaying the highest level of skill in creating his textual masterpieces. The material objects within his poems are used to enrich the descriptions and provide a sense of physical realism to his works, but these items also carry meanings that affect our understanding of the poems and their contents. Especially when reading across the poems, the material culture in the works of the *Pearl*-poet enhances and enriches our readings of this late medieval wordsmith.

NOTES

1. *Pearl*, l. 252. Throughout this chapter, quotations from the poems of the Cotton Nero A.x manuscript are taken from Malcolm Andrew and Waldron Ronald, eds., *The Poems of the Pearl Manuscript: Pearl, Cleanness, Patience, Sir Gawain and the Green Knight*, 5th ed., Exeter Medieval Texts and Studies (Exeter: University of Exeter Press, 2007). Modern English translations are provided by Jane Beal. Cf. her *Pearl: A Middle English Edition and Modern English Translation* (Peterborough: Broadview, 2020).

2. For further discussion of this aspect, see Kimberly Jack's chapter, "Sartorial Adornment in the *Pearl* Poems," in this volume.

3. Paul Freedman, *Out of the East: Spices and the Medieval Imagination* (New Haven, CT: Yale University Press, 2008), 67.

4. Classical and early medieval sources available in the Middle Ages included works by Pliny the Elder, Solinus, and Isidore of Seville. In the eleventh century, Marbode of Rennes composed a widely known lapidary. In England, lapidaries were quite popular in the late Middle Ages. For brief surveys of the tradition, see Joan Evans and Mary S. Serjeantson, eds., *English Mediaeval Lapidaries*, Early English Text Society, Original Series 190 (London: Early English Text Society, 1933), and Peter Kitson, "Lapidary Traditions in Anglo-Saxon England: Part I, the Background; the Old English Lapidary," *Anglo-Saxon England* 7 (1978): 9–60, esp. 10–11.

5. *Middle English Dictionary*, "jeueler": 1(a): A worker or dealer in jewelry, gem setter; (b) fig. one who owns or loves jewels.

6. On the terms' interchangeability, compare, for example, Jeremiah 24:1 between the early and later versions of the Wycliffite Bible where "iueler" is replaced by "goldsmith." Other Middle English words sharing a definition of "jeweler" include *enclosere, perirer,* and *gemmarye.*

7. Felicity Riddy, "Jewels in *Pearl*," in *A Companion to the* Gawain-*Poet,* ed. Derek Brewer and Jonathan Gibson, Arthurian Studies, 38 (Cambridge: D.S. Brewer, 1997), 147.

8. John F. Cherry, *Goldsmiths*, Medieval Craftsmen (Toronto: University of Toronto Press, 1992), 48–9, with image.

9. Cherry, *Goldsmiths*, 47, with image.

10. Tony Davenport, "Jewels and Jewellers in *Pearl*," *Review of English Studies* 59, no. 241 (2008): 508–20, 511.

11. John F. Cherry, *Goldsmiths*, 20, with image.

12. Recall the "ʒeres ʒiftes" ("year's gifts") from *Sir Gawain,* l. 67.

13. Cherry, *Goldsmiths*, 51, with image. Also, Riddy, "Jewels in *Pearl*," 148.

14. *Statutes of the Realm* (London, 1810–28), vol. I, 378–82. 37° Edward III, c. 1, 3–15. See c. 7.

15. *Statutes of the Realm,* c. 8–14.

16. Cf. *Sir Gawain,* l. 881.

17. *Statutes of the Realm,* c. 12.

18. Andrew and Ronald, *The Poems of the Pearl Manuscript,* 63.

19. *Pearl,* l. 473.

20. *Pearl,* ll. 205–206.

21. Davenport, "Jewels and Jewellers in *Pearl*," esp. at 510.

22. *Pearl,* ll. 997–98.

23. *Pearl,* see ll. 4 and 6.

24. Davenport, "Jewels and Jewellers in *Pearl*," 513. Davenport also labels this vocabulary as that of an "informed observer" (511).

25. *Patience,* ll. 97–108 and ll. 137–62.

26. William Sayers, "Sailing Scenes in the Works of the *Pearl* Poet (*Cleanness* and *Patience*)," *Amsterdamer Beiträge Zur Älteren Germanistik* 63, no. 1 (2007): 129–55, at 152.

27. For images and terms, see Gillian Hutchinson, *Medieval Ships and Shipping* (London: Leicester University Press, 1994); and Ian Friel, *The Good Ship: Ships, Shipbuilding and Technology in England, 1200–1520* (London: British Museum Press, 1995).

28. *MED*, "setten": 12(a) To mount (a gemstone in a setting, ring, etc.); (b) to ornament (sth. with mounted jewels, precious stones, etc.) . . . (c) . . . to adorn (sb.) with (jewelry), bedeck with . . .

29. *St. Erkenwald*, l. 52.

30. *Patience*, ll. 37–38, emphasis added.

31. *Patience*, ll. 13–124, 27–8, emphasis added

32. *Pearl*, ll. 1–2.

33. Davenport, "Jewels and Jewellers in *Pearl*," 516–17.

34. *Pearl*, l. 3.

35. *Pearl*, l. 9.2

36. *Pearl*, ll. 22–3.

37. *Pearl*, l. 178.

38. *Pearl*, ll. 174–75.

39. *Pearl*, l. 82.

40. For discussion of the depiction of the "marvelous East," see Jane Beal's chapter, "The Dreamer's Contemplative Experience of a Mappamundi in *Pearl*," in this volume.

41. *Pearl*, l. 1112.

42. *Pearl*, ll. 1102–3.

43. *Pearl*, l. 1147.

44. *Pearl*, l. 795.

45. *Pearl*, l. 1124.

46. *Pearl*, l. 1201.

47. *Pearl*, ll. 1211–12.

48. *Pearl*, ll. 10, 13, emphasis added.

49. *Pearl*, l. 566.

BIBLIOGRAPHY

Andrew, Malcolm, and Waldron Ronald, eds. *The Poems of the Pearl Manuscript: Pearl, Cleanness, Patience, Sir Gawain and the Green Knight.* 5th ed. Exeter Medieval Texts and Studies. Exeter: University of Exeter Press, 2007.

Beal, Jane, ed. *Becoming the Pearl-Poet: Perceptions, Connections, Receptions.* New York: Lexington Books, 2022.

———, ed. and trans. *Pearl: A Middle English Edition and Modern English Translation.* Peterborough: Broadview, 2020.

Blanch, Robert J. "The Current State of *Pearl* Criticism." *Chaucer Yearbook* 3 (1996): 21–33.

Cherry, John F. *Goldsmiths.* Medieval Craftsmen. Toronto: University of Toronto Press, 1992.

Davenport, Tony. "Jewels and Jewellers in *Pearl.*" *Review of English Studies* 59, no. 241 (2008): 508–20.

Eldredge, Lawrence. "The State of *Pearl* Studies since 1933." *Viator* (1975): 171–94.

Evans, Joan, and Mary S. Serjeantson, eds. *English Mediaeval Lapidaries.* Early English Text Society, Original Series 190. London: Early English Text Society, 1933.

Freedman, Paul. *Out of the East: Spices and the Medieval Imagination.* New Haven, CT: Yale University Press, 2008.

Friel, Ian. *The Good Ship: Ships, Shipbuilding and Technology in England, 1200–1520.* London: British Museum Press, 1995.

The Holy Bible, Containing the Old and New Testaments, with the Apocryphal books, in the Earliest English Versions Made from the Latin Vulgate by John Wycliffe and His Followers. Edited by Rev. Josiah Forshall and Sir Frederic Madden. 4 volumes. Oxford: Oxford University Press, 1850.

Hutchinson, Gillian. *Medieval Ships and Shipping.* London: Leicester University Press, 1994.

Kitson, Peter. "Lapidary Traditions in Anglo-Saxon England: Part I, the Background; the Old English Lapidary." Anglo-Saxon England 7 (1978): 9–60.

Lydgate, John. *The Minor Poems of John Lydgate, Part II.* Edited by H. N. MacCracken. Early English Text Society, Extra Series 107. London: Early English Text Society, 1934.

Middle English Dictionary [*MED*]. Edited by Robert E. Lewis, et al. Ann Arbor: University of Michigan Press, 1952–2001. Online edition in *Middle English Compendium.* Edited by Frances McSparran, et al. Ann Arbor: University of Michigan Library, 2000–2018. http://quod.lib.umich.edu/m/middle-english-dictionary/. Accessed July 1, 2019.

Peck, Russell A. "Number Structure in *St. Erkenwald.*" *Annuale Mediaevale* 14 (1973): 9–21.

Riddy, Felicity. "Jewels in *Pearl.*" In *A Companion to the* Gawain-*Poet,* edited by Derek Brewer and Jonathan Gibson, 143–55. Arthurian Studies, 38. Cambridge: D.S. Brewer, 1997.

Sayers, William. "Sailing Scenes in the Works of the *Pearl* Poet (*Cleanness* and *Patience*)." *Amsterdamer Beiträge Zur Älteren Germanistik* 63, no. 1 (2007): 129–55.

Statutes of the Realm. London, 1810–28. Reprint, 1963.

Chapter Nine

Sartorial Adornment in the *Pearl* Poems

Kimberly Jack

In 1992, Walter Phelan asserted that "it is one of the great mysteries of [*Sir Gawain and the Green Knight*] why the poet spends so much time dressing and undressing the characters."[1] Scholarship on the *Pearl*-poet has lauded the poems' intense descriptive language, examining the accounts of architecture, landscape, feasts, boat operations, and other passages. Charles Moorman declared that "[nearly] all the commentators have singled out this use of detail as the poet's most accomplished poetic technique."[2] Robert Blanch and Julian Wasserman acknowledged the extensive scholarship "done on the wealth of decoration permeating the work."[3] However, descriptions of sartorial adornment in the poems have rarely received thorough critical attention.[4] Commentary focuses on isolated articles such as the green girdle or the Pearl-Maiden's pearl, or on details such as color.[5] Increasing publication of cross-disciplinary scholarship on medieval clothing, textiles, and sartorial display provide resources and insights that may just help us answer Phelan's "great mystery."[6] Why does the *Pearl*-poet dedicate countless lines to often intricate or obscure descriptions of sartorial adornment?

SARTORIAL SIGNS

Analyses of sumptuary legislation, sermons, wardrobe records, sculptural programs, literary representations, and wills illustrate how clothing and accessories functioned as a readable semiotic system in late medieval and early modern Europe. In the cultural milieu of the *Pearl*-poet, "people were read by, and learned to 'read' the value of textiles and cut of clothing as fixed

155

signs of profession, wealth, social status, and geographical provenance."[7] In theory, "dress proclaimed hierarchy; the quantity of fabric granted for the clothing and the choice of fur used to trim it made obvious the relative status of each person."[8] As early as the eleventh century, rulers utilized sartorial adornment as propaganda within orchestrated public spectacles.[9] Early English sumptuary legislation, dated between 1337 and 1363, iterates a "hierarchical vision of society," articulated through dress and under threat from "clothing oneself above one's station."[10] Moralist criticism condemned "excessive visual display," dress inappropriate to one's estate or occupation, as producing a "confusion of social boundaries" and undermining the body politic.[11] These sources document both the ideal of a fixed sartorial sign system and anxiety over the instability of this system and the social hierarchy it communicated and validated.

The *Pearl*-poet's descriptive passages on clothing, whether extensive or minimalistic, interrogate this contemporary system of sartorial signs. In the ideal manifestation of the system, bodily adornment in the form of clothing, fur, and jewelry clearly signifies collective and individual identity, reinforces social boundaries, and provides an external reflection of the internal state of one's soul. Just as sumptuary legislation reflects anxiety over this system, the *Pearl*-poet complicates the straightforward signification of sartorial signs.[12] The *Pearl*-poet continually "dresses and undresses his characters" because, in so doing, he acknowledges how power dynamics and the ongoing negotiation of meaning challenge the stability of what is signified sartorially.

The parable of the wedding feast in *Cleanness* articulates the ideal operation of the sartorial sign system. Once the invitation is opened to all comers, seating at the feast is determined by attire. As lines 114–17 indicate: "Ay þe best byfore and bryȝtest atyred,/ Þe derrest at þe hyȝe dese, þat dubbed wer fayrest . . . ay as segges serly semed by her wedez" ("aye, the best before and brightest attired, the dearest at the high dais, that dubbed were fairest . . . aye as men individually seemed by their clothes").[13] Those wearing the *bryȝtest* ("brightest") and *fayrest* ("fairest") garments are deemed *derrest* or "most worthy," and are therefore seated in the position of highest honor at the dais. The seating reflects a key assumption behind English sumptuary law: "that people will dress according to their perceived social standing, that is, in a way that accords with and makes visible their status."[14] The marshal, in determining hierarchical relationships of unknown guests, assumes that sartorial adornment accurately reflects social status.

In adapting the parable of the wedding feast from Matthew 22 and Luke 14, the *Pearl*-poet further articulates the moralist's assumption that outward attire (and the violation of hierarchical standards) reflects a spiritual state. In the first iteration of the parable (lines 33–50), the ill-dressed guest wears *rent cokrez at þe kne* ("pants torn at the knee"), *clutte traschez* ("worn shoes"), a *tabarde totorne* ("torn tabard" or outer garment), with *his totez oute* ("his toes showing").[15] The poet elaborates significantly on Matthew 22:11, where the guest offends by "not wearing wedding clothes." *Cleanness* not only expands on the detail but also explicitly connects violations of terrestrial sartorial standards to heavenly judgment. The audience is warned "hyȝ not to heuen in haterez totorne,/ Ne in þe harlatez hod, and handez vnwaschen./ For what vrþly haþel þat hyȝ honour haldez/ Wolde lyke if a ladde com lyþerly attyred,/ When he were sette solempnely in a sete ryche,/ Abof dukez on dece" ("don't hasten to heaven in torn clothing,/ nor in the beggar's hood, and unwashed hands./ For what earthly man that holds high honor/ would like if a man came wretchedly attired,/ when he were set solemnly in a rich seat,/ above a duke at the dais").[16] The ill-dressed guest offends courtly courtesy with his torn clothes and unwashed hands, and he offends heavenly standards with his tattered, uncleansed soul.

Specifically, he threatens hierarchical class distinctions with the possibility that he might be seated "above a duke at the dais." The passage concludes by declaring that "if vnwelcum he were to a wordlych prynce,/ ȝet hym is þe hyȝe Kyng harder in heuen" ("if he were unwelcome to an earthly prince,/ yet to him is the high King [God] harder in heaven").[17] This passage unambiguously articulates the assumption that terrestrial norms of sartorial display and class difference will be echoed more harshly in heaven.

The poet reinforces these associations by expanding significantly in a second iteration of the parable (lines 51–160) and explication (161–204). The offensive guest is "not for a halyday honestly arrayed" ("not honestly dressed for a holiday"), but is "vnþryuandely cloþed/ Ne no festiual frok, but fyled with werkkez" ("meanly clothed not in a festival frock, but one soiled with works").[18] Not only is his attire inappropriate for the "holiday" and "festival," but it is "soiled with works." The poet explicitly declares: "Thus comparisunez Kryst þe kyndom of heuen/ To þis frelych feste" ("Thus Christ's kingdom of heaven/ is comparable to this noble feast").[19] All guests are welcome who "euer wern fulȝed in font" ("ever were baptized in the font"), "Bot war þe wel, if þou wylt, þy wedez ben clene/ And honest for þe holyday" ("but beware, if you will, your clothes be clean and honest for the holiday"), because Christ "hates helle no more þen hem þat ar sowlé" ("Christ hates hell no more than those who are soiled") with sin.[20] Courtly norms for cleanliness and dress are explicitly equated with heavenly judgment, asserting a divine mandate for sumptuary statues and moralist complaints. In addition, this explication authorizes the essential mediation of the Church in cleansing one's spiritual *wedez* ("clothes") through baptism and good *werkez* ("works").[21]

While *Cleanness* presents the clearest articulation of the idealized correla-
tions between dress, social identity, and spiritual state, elements of this social
construct appear in other works within the corpus. In *Patience*, the Ninevites
respond to Jonah's dire prophecy with an immediate sartorial display of
repentance. The people "Heter hayrez þay hent þat asperly bited,/ And þose
þay bounden to her bak and to her bare sydez,/ Dropped dust on her hede"
("suffered rough hair shirts that sorely bit, and those they bound to their backs
and to their bare sides, dropped dust on their heads").[22] The king of Nineveh,
following biblical precedent, "His ryche robe he torof his rigge naked,/ And
of a hep of askes he hitte in þe myddez./ He askez heterly a hayre and hasped
hym vmbe,/ Sewed a sekke þerabof, and syked ful colde" ("tore his rich robe
off his naked back,/ and sat in the midst of a heap of ashes./ He commanded
a hair shirt and fastened it around himself,/ Sewed a sack above it, and sighed
very coldly").[23] By tearing their clothes, donning hair shirts, and covering
themselves with dirt or ash, the king and his subjects initiate the penitential
process, using familiar, outward sartorial signs to signify inner repentance.[24]

Gawain's pentangle in *Sir Gawain and the Green Knight* is introduced
within a courtly context of the romance genre as an idealized synthesis of
chivalric and spiritual sartorial signifiers. Through it, the court at Camelot
asserts Gawain's social status, his exemplary chivalric qualities, and his spiri-
tual purity. The pentangle, described in detail on the shield in lines 619–65,
is worked into his *cote* or "surcoat" in lines 637 and as "þe conysaunce of
þe clere werkez/ Ennurned vpon veluet" in 2025–26, and is likely the *deuys*
("device") on the gold and diamond circlet surmounting Gawain's helmet.[25]
The poet explicates the five fives of the endless knot as representing the
fyue wyttes ("five wits"), *fyue fyngres* ("five fingers"), *fyue woundez* ("five
wounds" of Christ), *fyue joyez* ("five joys" of Mary), and five virtues of
chivalry comprised of *fraunchyse and felaȝschyp* ("franchise and fellow-
ship"), *clannes* ("cleanness"), *cortaysye* ("courtesy") and *pité* (translated
variously as "piety" or "pity").[26] These represent qualities which "acordez to
þis knyȝt" ("correspond to this knight") because "ay faythful in fyue and sere
fyue syþez,/ Gawan watz for gode knawen and, as golde pured,/ Voyded of
vche vylany, wyth vertuez ennourned/ In mote" ("faithful in five and several
five groups,/ Gawain was for good known, and as purified gold,/ devoid of
all villainy, adorned with virtues,/ without blemish").[27] The court at Camelot
assigns the *pentangel nwe* ("pentangle new") to Gawain as a visible sartorial
sign ostensibly proclaiming his identity, exemplary chivalric reputation, and
inner virtue. As I will discuss, the reception of this signifier at Hautdesert
challenges this sartorial assertion.

In *Pearl*, the Pearl-Maiden's attire draws on an iconographic tradition
to announce sartorially her new identity as a bride of Christ and queen of
heaven.[28] Her gleaming white gown is *vpon at sydez* ("open at the sides,"

i.e., a sideless surcoat) with *lappez large* ("wide skirts"), *precios perlez* set *in porfyl* ("precious pearls" set in "fur trim") at the *hemme/ At honde, at sydez, at ouerture* ("hem," "hands," open "sides," and "neckline"), and a singular *wonder perle withouten wemme* set *In myddez hyr brest* ("wondrous pearl without equal" set "in the midst of her breast," i.e., on the front panel of the gown).[29] This description accords with the sideless surcoat, a garment that extant artworks indicate was restricted to royalty after the mid-fourteenth century.[30] By the fifteenth century, this garment appears only as robes of state for royal weddings, and in funerary effigies depicting women, both common and noble, who were depicted as transcending their terrestrial social status to take their places as brides of Christ and queens of heaven.[31] To fourteenth-century readers, the manner in which the Pearl-Maiden and her companions in the New Jerusalem procession are adorned clearly identifies them with this iconographic tradition.[32]

Whether or not we consider *St. Erkenwald* to be part of the *Pearl*-Poet's corpus,[33] the Londoners' reaction to the uncorrupted body and clothing unearthed during construction reflects the assumption that specific sartorial adornments signify regal social standing. The Judge's *gowne* ("gown" or outer robe) is *hemmyd* ("hemmed") with *glisnande golde* ("glistening gold"), adorned with *a precious perle* ("a precious pearl"), and belted with *a gurdille of golde* ("a girdle/belt of gold"), his *mantel* ("mantle" or cape) trimmed with *menyuer* ("minever"), and he is buried with *a coron* ("crown") and *septure* ("scepter").[34] The Londoners' conclusion that "He has ben kynge of þis kythe" ("he has been king of this country") is understandable, given the seemingly clear sartorial signifiers of crown and scepter, and the minever trim on his mantle, a fur type restricted to royalty and close associates.[35] No records exist to identify the body, yet the sartorial sign system unambiguously indicates royal status.[36]

UNSTABLE SIGNS

Although the *Pearl*-poet plays on the hierarchical and spiritual associations with sartorial signs in these examples, the corpus as a whole challenges, rather than validates, the stability of this system. Throughout the corpus, signifiers undergo change and shifts in meaning. Sartorial signs are imposed by others, raising issues of agency in the assigning of identifying markers. Furthermore, what sartorial signs signify is interpreted and reinterpreted repeatedly, complicating the validity of the system.

Gawain's pentangle ultimately fails as a stable, unambiguous signifier of identity or virtue. In courtly circles, the "mottos, heraldic signs, occulted signatures, symbolic colors, and allegorical messages" of a "courtier's dress was a visual manifesto" functioning as a "ritual articulation of identity."[37] The court at Hautdesert grants him guest rights because his armor and horse signify his corporate identity as a knight, yet they cannot identify him as Gawain until he states his name.[38] If the purpose of a knight's device is to provide "a distinctive sign which distinguishes one knight from another, that sign by which he is known," then the pentangle fails.[39] The pentangle is not recognizable outside of Camelot, a detail which corresponds with "thirteenth & fourteenth century rolls of arms describing the fictitious heraldry of Arthurian heroes," in which "Gawain was given a shield: *argent, a canton gules*, i.e., silver, with a red quarter in the upper left."[40]

Instead, the court at Hautdesert utilizes an alternative sign system, his name, to identify Gawain with a somewhat different reputation. When he arrives at Hautdesert, Gawain is *dispoyled* ("stripped") of his armor, surcoat, and horse, separating him from his sartorial signifiers.[41] The court judges him a *prynce withouten pere* ("prince without peer")[42] based on his appearance once he is cleaned and re-clothed, but they articulate their expectations for their visitor once they learn he is *Wawen himself* ("Gawain himself").[43] The name "Gawain," to this court, signifies a knight to whom "alle prys and prowes and pured þewes/ Apendes to hys person" ("all renown and prowess and perfectly courteous manners/ append to his person").[44] While the pentangle includes the virtues of "cleanness" and "courtesy" in line 653, the people at Hautdesert specifically expect examples of *teccheles termes of talking noble* ("faultless expressions of noble speech") and *luf-talkyng* ("love-talk" or seduction).[45] The Lady uses this less virtuous reputation to manipulate Gawain into a kiss the following morning, declaring that he cannot be the man whose name he claims because the name signifies a man who "Couth not lyȝtly haf lenged so long with a lady/ Bot he had craued a cosse bi his courtaysye" ("could not readily have lingered so long with a lady/ but he would have craved a kiss by his courtesy").[46] Not only is the pentangle an insufficient signifier of Gawain's identity once he leaves Camelot, the alternative signifier of his name evokes a less idealized reputation.

Furthermore, Gawain himself heraldically modifies the pentangle with the green girdle. When Gawain leaves Hautdesert, "dressed he his drurye double hym aboute,/ Swyþe sweþled vmbe his swange, swetely, þat knyȝt;/ Þe gordel of þe grene silk þat gay wel bisemed" ("he wrapped the love-token double around himself, earnestly wrapped around his hips, sweetly, that knight, the girdle of green silk that beautifully suited him").[47] He wraps the green *lace* ("lace" or "girdle") twice around his hips above his red surcoat, a color combination complimented by the narrator. The pentangle, *þe conysaunce of þe clere werkez* ("the insignia of the clearly understood works") embroidered upon the red *veluet* ("velvet") of the surcoat, is bisected horizontally by a slash of green.[48] After the encounter at the Green Chapel, Gawain wears "þe blykkande belt . . . Abelef, as a bauderyk, bounden bi his syde,/ Loken vnder his lyfte arme, þe lace, with a knot,/ In tokenyng he watz tane in tech of a faute" ("shining belt diagonally, as a baldric, bound by his side, knotted under his left arm, the lace, with a knot, as a sign that he was caught in stain of a sin").[49] Albert Friedman and Richard Osberg suggest that the diagonal band of the girdle over the pentangle on the surcoat "represents the heraldic differencing of illegitimacy, the bend or bar sinister of nine-teenth-century [sic] novels.[50] As John Plummer notes, "the bar sinister" was developed in heraldry after 1400, but the green diagonal slash still functions as "a 'difference,' in heraldic parlance, specifically a bend," signifying a correspondingly different public identity.[51]

The pentangle's failure as a stable, readable sartorial signifier of Gawain's identity pales in comparison to the complexity and ambiguity of the Green Knight's sartorial message.[52] The Green Knight's tailored *cote* (fitted upper-body garment) is heavily embroidered with *silk werkeʒ* ("silk works") depicting *bryddes and flyʒes* ("birds and butterflies").[53] These peaceful, if not frivolous motifs, combined with his *sholes* ("shoeless" or lacking foot armor) state, and the catalog of other absent armor elements reinforce his statement that he left his armor at home because "I passe as in pes and no plyʒt seche" ("I travel in peace and seek no danger").[54] The explicit listing of armor, though absent, confirms the Green Knight's corporate identity as a knight, and the tailored garments, gold embroidery, and numerous gold and jeweled details indicate wealth and high social status. The adjective comparing his hair to a *kyngeʒ* ("king's") *capados* (possibly "hood") raises speculation of regal standing, yet generic terms such as *blaunner* ("fur") and *pelure pured* ("trimmed fur") for the lining of his mantle, rather than the exclusive *minever pured* ("trimmed minever") or *pured gris* ("trimmed gris" or blue-gray back fur harvested from winter squirrels), thwart hierarchical classification.[55] Combined with his unique and supernatural green complexion, the Green Knight's sartorial display appears contrived to confuse rather than clearly communicate identity, a result Morgan may have intended in contriving his appearance.[56]

Neither Gawain's pentangle nor the Green Knight's attire ultimately adheres to the expectation that sartorial signifiers clearly indicate identity, class, affiliation, or spiritual state. Neither signifies social identity, inner nature, or intention without ambiguity. Sartorial signs are malleable, resulting in the differencing of the pentangle with the green girdle and the declared absence of the Green Knight's armor. These outward signifiers are furthermore open to both imposition by and interpretation by others.

The Judge's identity in *St. Erkenwald* exemplifies the flaws inherent in the system endorsed by sumptuary statutes and moralist critiques. Although the *rialle wedes* ("royal clothes"), crown, scepter, and minever fur mantle are seen as incontrovertible evidence of royal status, the Judge refutes this reading. He states that he was "Neuer kynge ne cayser ne ȝet no knyȝt nothyre,/ Bot a lede of þe laghe" ("never king nor Caesar nor yet no knight neither, but a man of the law").[57] He chose to serve others in life, and in death:

> þus to bounty my body þai burriet in golde,/ Cladden me for þe curtest þat courte couthe þen holde,/ In mantel for þe mekest and monlokest on benche,/ Gurden me for þe gouernour and graythist of Troie,/ Furrid me for þe funest of faithe me wytinne./ For þe honour of myn honesté of heghest enprise/ Þai coronyd me þe kynge of kene iustises/ Þer euer wos tronyd in Troye, oþer trowid euer shulde,/ And for I rewardid euer riȝt þai raght me the septre.[58]

> (In bounty they buried my body in gold,/ And clad me in clothes that were courtly to praise/ The most merciful, moderate man on the bench./ Thus they gave me this governor's garb from respect./ For my faith they put fine, courtly fur in my coat./ And to honor my honesty, equaled by none,/ They crowned me as king, in the courts the most fair, The most honest of arbiters ever to judge./ This scepter you see here, they set in my hand.)[59]

Here, the sartorial signs function solely within a symbolic register. Rather than synthesizing social identity and spiritual state, the Judge's clothing conveys the recognition of his honesty, service, and pursuit of justice by misappropriating the exclusive signifiers of royal state. The posthumous adornment is imposed on the Judge, contrary to his express desires in life. The miraculous preservation of body and attire instigates the circumstances of the Judge's salvation, but his clothes reflect neither his occupation nor his agency.

The Pearl-Maiden's robes likewise raise complications of agency and interpretation. As with the Judge's regal attire, the Pearl-Maiden's heavenly clothes were gifted to her after death. Claiming her as a heavenly bride and queen, "In Hys blod [Christ] wesch my wede on dese,/ And coronde clene in vergynté,/ And pȝt me in perlez maskellez" ("In His blood [Christ] washed my clothes on dais, and crowned [me] clean in virginity, and adorned me in matchless pearls").[60] This investiture ceremonially and sartorially indicates her corporate identity as one of the *hondred and forty þowsande* ("one hundred and forty thousand") virgins who are likewise *Arayed to þe weddyng in þat hyl-coppe* ("arrayed for the wedding on that hill-top").[61] The Pearl-Maiden does not choose these new sartorial signifiers, as Gawain does in differencing the pentangle on his surcoat. She does accept their significance, though, and the authority of her groom to assign her this identity. However, the Dreamer rejects the fundamental change in identity signified by her attire and must be verbally corrected. Whether we interpret the Pearl-Maiden as the

Dreamer's lost daughter or lover,[62] the debate that encompasses the majority of the poem demonstrates the Dreamer's refusal to accept the new identity and authority first signaled by her dress. The culminating vision of the New Jerusalem presents the Dreamer with this corporate identity in the form of a throng of "vergynez in þe same gyse/ Þat watz my blysful anvnder croun./ Depaynt in perlez and wedez qwyte" ("virgins in the same guise that was my blissful [one] under crown, adorned in pearls and white clothes").[63] Yet his fundamental refusal to accept what he sees and hears remains clear in his continuing use of possessive pronouns.

CONCLUSION

The *Pearl*-poet consistently acknowledges and then complicates the sartorial sign system articulated in contemporary sumptuary legislation and moralist complaints. He articulates its ideal functioning in the parable of the wedding feast, the explication of Gawain's pentangle, the Pearl-Maiden's signature attire, the Ninevites' sartorial display of penance, and the regal adornment of the Judge's body. Yet he repeatedly undermines straightforward signification. Gawain's pentangle, as a heraldic insignia, neither identifies the knight unambiguously nor resists change and differencing. The Dreamer repeatedly rejects the Pearl-Maiden's new status, attempting to reassert his terrestrial authority and right to interpret. The Judge's miraculous speech reveals that his regal attire signifies only on the spiritual register and was imposed posthumously. The *Pearl*-poet highlights the instability of sartorial signs, their inability to clearly signify social status, identity, or spiritual state, and the abrogation of agency through the imposition of signs and meaning. In this, the *Pearl*-poet is far from unique.[64] Yet the complexity of the *Pearl*-poet's descriptive language, deployed across the variety of genres present in his corpus, presents an opportunity for analysis of sartorial sign systems in diverse literary contexts. Instead of asking "why" the poet spends so much time "dressing and undressing his characters," therefore, we should delve into these scenes to examine "what" the *Pearl*-poet is doing, "how" adornment can be read in his poems, and "why" this reflects the interrogation of sumptuary signs systems in late medieval literature and art.

NOTES

1. Walter S. Phelan, *The Christmas Hero and the Yuletide Tradition in Sir Gawain and the Green Knight* (Lewiston, NY: Edwin Mellon Press, 1992), 89.
2. Charles Moorman, *The Pearl-Poet* (New York: Twayne Publishers, 1968), 103.

3. Robert J. Blanch and Julian N. Wasserman, *From Pearl to Gawain: Forme to Fynisment* (Gainesville: University Press of Florida, 1995), 23.

4. Some exceptions include chapter three in Nicole D. Smith, *Sartorial Strategies* (Notre Dame, IN: University of Notre Dame Press, 2012), 95–135; Kimberly Jack, "What Is the Pearl-Maiden Wearing, and Why?" *Medieval Clothing and Textiles* 7 (2011), 65–85; Kimberly Jack, "Costume Rhetoric in the Works Attributed to the Pearl-Poet," Dissertation, Loyola University Chicago, 2008.

5. A few examples include William Henry Schofield, "Symbolism, Allegory, and Autobiography in the *Pearl*," *PMLA* 24 (1909): 585–675; Robert Blanch, "Color Symbolism and Mystical Contemplation in *Pearl*," *Nottingham Medieval Studies* 17 (1973): 58–77, and "Games Poets Play: The Ambiguous Use of Color Symbolism in *Sir Gawain and the Green Knight*," *Nottingham Medieval Studies* 20 (1976): 64–85; Derek Brewer, "The Colour Green," *A Companion to the Gawain-Poet*, edited Derek Brewer and Jonathan Gibson (Cambridge: D.S. Brewer, 1997), 181–90.

6. For reviews of this scholarship see Gale R. Owen-Crocker, "Old Rags, New Responses: Medieval Dress and Textiles," *Medieval Clothing and Textiles* 15 (2019): 1–31; and Margaret F. Rosenthal, "Cultures of Clothing in Later Medieval and Early Modern Europe," *Journal of Medieval and Early Modern Studies* 39, no. 3 (2009): 459–81.

7. Rosenthal, "Cultures of Clothing in Later Medieval," 473.

8. Owen-Crocker, "Old Rags, New Responses," 18.

9. Owen-Crocker, "Old Rags, New Responses," 18, citing Stephen Rigby, "Political Thought," *Encyclopedia of Dress and Textiles in the British Isles c. 450–1450*, ed. Gale R. Owen-Crocker, Elizabeth Coatsworth, and Maria Hayward (Leiden: Brill, 2012), 422–26.

10. Frédérique Lachaud, "Dress and Social Status in England Before the Sumptuary Laws," *Heraldry, Pageantry and Social Display in Medieval England*, ed. Peter Coss and Maurice Keen (Woodbridge: Boydell Press, 2002), 105–23.

11. Rosenthal, "Cultures of Clothing in Later Medieval," 465.

12. See Smith for a focused analysis of the green girdle's signification.

13. Unless noted, citations are from *The Poems of the Pearl Manuscript*, 5th ed., ed. Malcolm Andrew and Ronald Waldron (Liverpool: Liverpool University Press, 2007).

14. Claire Sponsler, "Narrating the Social Order: Medieval Clothing Laws," *CLIO* 21, no. 3 (1992): 275.

15. Lines 39–41.

16. Lines 33–38.

17. Lines 49–50.

18. Lines 134–136.

19. Line 160.

20. Lines 161–67.

21. Lines 164, 171. The metaphor of fouled clothing attesting to sin which can only be cleansed through the sacraments is a common one, familiar from Langland's Haukyn and other examples.

22. Lines 373–75.

23. Lines 379–82. Cf. Jonah 3:6: "And the word came to the king of Nineve; and he rose up out of his throne, and cast away his robe from him, and was clothed with sackcloth, and sat in ashes."

24. See Anthony P. Ceresko, "Jonah," *The New Jerome Biblical Commentary*, ed. Raymond E. Brown, Joseph A. Fitzmyer, and Roland E. Murphy (Englewood Cliffs, NJ: Prentice Hall, 1990), 583.

25. See Laura Hodges, "'Syngne,' 'Conysaunce,' 'Deuys': Three Pentangles in *Sir Gawain and the Green Knight*," *Arthuriana* 5, no. 4 (1995): 22–31, and Helmut Nickel, "Arthurian Armings for War and for Love," *Arthuriana* 5, no. 4 (1995): 3–21.

26. Lines 640–54.

27. Lines 631–35.

28. See Jack, "What Is the Pearl-Maiden Wearing, and Why?"

29. Lines 193–222.

30. Robin Netherton, "The Medieval Sideless Surcote: Real and Unreal" (paper presentation, International Congress on Medieval Studies, Kalamazoo, MI, May 1994); Netherton, "Will the Real Sideless Surcote Please Stand Up?" (lecture, Bryn Mawr College, Philadelphia, February 28, 2004).

31. Jack, "What Is the Pearl-Maiden Wearing, and Why?" 81; Netherton, "The Medieval Sideless Surcote."

32. Lines 1095–104.

33. For a current discussion, see Ethan Campbell's "Authorship: What Does the *Pearl*-Poet Tell Us about Himself?" and Drout et al. "St. Erkenwald" in this collection.

34. Lines 75–80. Citations for *Saint Erkenwald* are from Casey Finch, *The Complete Works of the Pearl Poet* (Berkeley: University of California Press, 1993).

35. Line 98; For the "vocabulary of fur," see Reginald Abbott, "What Becomes a Legend Most?: Fur in the Medieval Romance," *Dress* 21, no. 5 (1994); Stella Mary Newton, *Fashion in the Age of the Black Prince* (Woodbridge: Boydell Press, 1980).

36. Line 101–104.

37. Susan Crane, *Performance of Self: Ritual, Clothing, and Identity during the Hundred Years War* (Philadelphia: University of Pennsylvania Press, 2002), 8.

38. Lines 903–906.

39. Hodges, "Syngne," 26.

40. Helmut Nickel, "The Arming of Gawain," *Avalon to Camelot* 1, no. 2 (1983), 18.

41. Lines 822–28, 860–61.

42. Lines 872–74.

43. Lines 904–6.

44. Lines 912–913.

45. Lines 917, 927.

46. Lines 1297–300.

47. Lines 2030–35.

48. Lines 2025–27.

49. Lines 2484–88.

50. Albert B. Friedman and Richard H. Osberg, "Gawain's Girdle as Traditional Symbol," *Journal of American Folklore* 90, no. 357 (1977): 313. See also J. M.

Leighton, "Christian and Pagan Symbolism and Ritual in 'Sir Gawain and the Green Knight,'" *Theoria* 43 (1974): 60.

51. John Plummer, "Signifying the Self: Language and Identity in *Sir Gawain and the Green Knight*," *Text and Matter: New Critical Perspectives of the Pearl-Poet*. Ed. Robert J. Blanch et. al. (Troy, NY: Whitston Publishing, 1991), 205.

52. For a detailed discussion, see Jack, "Costume Rhetoric," chapter 5; this analysis was also presented at the International Congress on Medieval Studies, Kalamazoo in 2004 and 2018.

53. Lines 152, 164, 166–67.

54. Lines 160, 203–205, 266–67.

55. Lines 153–55.

56. Lines 2446–65.

57. Lines 199–200.

58. Lines 248–56.

59. Translation by Casey Finch.

60. Lines 766–68.

61. Lines 786, 791.

62. Jane Beal, "The Pearl-Maiden's Two Lovers," *Studies in Philology* 100, no. 1 (2003): 1–21.

63. Lines 1096–105.

64. See E. Jane Burns, ed., *Medieval Fabrications: Dress, Textiles, Cloth Work, and Other Cultural Imaginings* (New York: Palgrave, 2004); Smith, *Sartorial Strategies*.

BIBLIOGRAPHY

Abbott, Reginald. "What Becomes a Legend Most? Fur in the Medieval Romance." *Dress* 21, no. 5 (1994): 5–14.

Andrew, Malcolm, and Ronald Waldron, ed. *The Poems of the Pearl Manuscript*, 5th ed. Liverpool: Liverpool University Press, 2007.

Beal, Jane, ed. *Becoming the Pearl-Poet: Perceptions, Connections, Receptions.* New York: Lexington Books, 2022.

———. "The Pearl-Maiden's Two Lovers." *Studies in Philology* 100, no. 1 (2003): 1–21.

Blanch, Robert. "Color Symbolism and Mystical Contemplation in *Pearl.*" *Nottingham Medieval Studies* 17 (1973): 58–77.

———. "Games Poets Play: The Ambiguous Use of Color Symbolism in *Sir Gawain and the Green Knight.*" *Nottingham Medieval Studies* 20 (1976): 64–85.

Blanch, Robert J., and Wasserman, Julian W. *From Pearl to Gawain: Forme to Fynisment.* Gainesville: University Press of Florida, 1995.

Brewer, Derek. "The Colour Green." *A Companion to the Gawain-Poet.* Ed. Derek Brewer and Jonathan Gibson. Cambridge: D.S. Brewer, 1997: 181–90.

Burns, E. Jane, ed. *Medieval Fabrications: Dress, Textiles, Cloth Work, and Other Cultural Imaginings.* New York: Palgrave, 2004.

Ceresko, Anthony P. "Jonah." *The New Jerome Biblical Commentary*. Ed. Raymond E. Brown, Joseph A. Fitzmyer, and Roland E. Murphy, 580–84. Englewood Cliffs, NJ: Prentice Hall, 1990.

Crane, Susan. *Performance of Self: Ritual, Clothing, and Identity during the Hundred Years War* (Philadelphia: University of Pennsylvania Press, 2002).

Finch, Casey, ed. and trans. *The Complete Works of the Pearl Poet*. Berkeley: University of California Press, 1993.

Friedman, Albert B., and Osbert, Richard H. "Gawain's Girdle as Traditional Symbol." *Journal of American Folklore* 90, no. 357 (1977): 301–15.

Hodges, Laura. "'Syngne,' 'Conysaunce,' 'Deuys': Three Pentangles in *Sir Gawain and the Green Knight*." *Arthuriana* 5, no. 4 (1995): 22–31.

Jack, Kimberly. *Costume Rhetoric in the Works Attributed to the Pearl-Poet*. Dissertation, Loyola University Chicago, 2008.

———. "What Is the Pearl-Maiden Wearing, and Why?" *Medieval Clothing and Textiles* 7 (2011): 65–85.

Lachaud, Frédérique. "Dress and Social Status in England Before the Sumptuary Laws." In *Heraldry, Pageantry and Social Display in Medieval England*. Ed. Peter Coss and Maurice Keen, 105–23. Woodbridge: Boydell Press, 2002.

Leighton, J. M. "Christian and Pagan Symbolism and Ritual in 'Sir Gawain and the Green Knight.'" *Theoria* 43 (1974): 49–62.

Moorman, Charles. *The Pearl-Poet*. New York: Twayne Publishers, 1968.

Netherton, Robin. "The Medieval Sideless Surcote: Real and Unreal." Paper presentation, International Congress on Medieval Studies, Kalamazoo, MI, May 1994.

———. "Will the Real Sideless Surcote Please Stand Up?" Lecture, Bryn Mawr College, Philadelphia, February 28, 2004.

Newton, Stella Mary. *Fashion in the Age of the Black Prince*. Woodbridge: Boydell Press, 1980.

Nickel, Helmut. "The Arming of Gawain." *Avalon to Camelot* 1, no. 2 (1983): 16–19.

———. "Arthurian Armings for War and for Love." *Arthuriana* 5, no. 4 (1995): 3–21.

Owen-Crocker, Gale R. "Old Rags, New Responses: Medieval Dress and Textiles." *Medieval Clothing and Textiles* 15 (2019): 1–31.

Phelan, Walter S. *The Christmas Hero and the Yuletide Tradition in Sir Gawain and the Green Knight*. Lewiston, NY: Edwin Mellon Press, 1992.

Plummer, John. "Signifying the Self: Language and Identity in *Sir Gawain and the Green Knight*." *Text and Matter: New Critical Perspectives of the Pearl-Poet*. Ed. Robert J. Blanch, Miriam Youngerman Miller, and Julian N. Wasserman, 195–212. Troy, NY: Whitston Publishing Company, 1991.

Rigby, Stephen. "Political Thought." *Encyclopedia of Dress and Textiles in the British Isles c. 450–1450*. Ed. Gale R. Owen-Crocker, Elizabeth Coatsworth, and Maria Hayward, 422–26. Leiden: Brill, 2012.

Rosenthal, Margaret F. "Cultures of Clothing in Later Medieval and Early Modern Europe." *Journal of Medieval and Early Modern Studies* 39, no. 3 (2009): 459–81.

Schofield, William Henry. "Symbolism, Allegory, and Autobiography in the *Pearl*." *PMLA* 24 (1909): 585–675.

Smith, Nicole D. *Sartorial Strategies*. Notre Dame, IN: University of Notre Dame Press, 2012.

Sponsler, Claire. "Narrating the Social Order: Medieval Clothing Laws." *CLIO* 21, no. 3 (1992): 265–83.

Chapter Ten

Switching Shields in *Sir Gawain and the Green Knight*

Kristin Bovaird-Abbo

When Juliet famously asked, "What's in a name?" in William Shakespeare's *Romeo and Juliet*, she was musing on the artificiality of names. Perhaps the anonymous author of the fourteenth-century poem *Sir Gawain and the Green Knight* might have objected to her easy dismissal of the cultural significance of a name, specifically her suggestion that a rose by any other name loses some part of itself. After all, when Sir Gawain, that paragon of Arthurian courtesy, arrives at the isolated castle of Hautdesert during his search for the Green Chapel, his welcome is magnified once the occupants learn his name, and Bertilak's wife repeatedly invokes Gawain's name in her attempts to seduce him. The hero of *Sir Gawain and the Green Knight*, Sir Gawain himself, was already well-known to audiences across medieval Europe thanks to his prominent role in several chronicles and his supporting roles in the romances of Chrétien de Troyes. In late medieval British treatments of the Arthurian legend, Gawain was the most popular character, for as J. R. Osgerby has pointed out, "Gawain is the perfect example of the educated man, the 'complete' gentleman,"[1] and in both French and English medieval romance, Gawain plays a central role by presenting a standard to which other knights may compare themselves.

Keith Busby, in his 1980 *Gauvain in Old French Literature*, argues for a plurality of Gawains in Old French literature, and I would argue that more work on the Middle English Gawain is needed in this vein. As Phillip Boardman notes, the "development of Arthurian romance in England is complex, representing both the growth of English as a literary language and a likely shift in the audience—or audiences—for romance."[2] Not surprising, then, during the fourteenth and fifteenth centuries, Gawain's role in Middle

169

English romances becomes complicated by shifts in authorship and audience, notably affected by the rise of the gentry classes. Due to the effects of the Bubonic Plague, the Hundred Years' War, and the War of the Roses, the tripartite social structure of Britain (namely, the clergy, the aristocracy, and the peasantry) began to deteriorate; labor shortages and constant warfare accelerated the acquisition of power among the lower classes, with the result that, as Philippa Maddern notes, a new social space, occupied by the gentry, emerged between the nobility and the laborers.[3] In their attempts to distance themselves from the lower classes, members of the gentry turned to a traditionally aristocratic genre, the chivalric romance, to educate themselves in the niceties of noble behavior. Scholarship on the distribution of manuscripts, many of which contained Arthurian romances, in English wills reveals the widespread demand for such literature among the gentry.[4]

Yet this social group did not merely consume Arthurian romances; they transformed them. For example, many English redactions of French Arthurian romances, such as the anonymous romances *Ywaine and Gawain*, *Lybeaus Desconus*, and *Sir Perceval of Galles*, along with Thomas Malory's fifteenth-century *Le Morte Darthur*, offer a systematic depreciation of Gawain's noble character. However, the figure of Gawain in *Sir Gawain and the Green Knight* stands apart from the other gentry Gawains. As Boardman notes, "In the English romances . . . Gawain is made the standard by which we judge other 'finished' knights of the Round Table,"[5] and this is certainly the case in the fourteenth-century romances *Ywaine and Gawaine* and *The Avowyng of Arthur*. After all, one of the many unique features of *Sir Gawain and the Green Knight* is that Gawain often is completely alone; earlier romances often pair him with a younger knight, or at the very least, a squire.[6] In this chapter, I intend to shift our focus away from the knights whose true worth Gawain reveals and take advantage of their absence to attend to Gawain himself, centering on the shield that he carries. Perhaps the question we should be asking is not "What's in a name?" but rather "What's in a shield?"

While there are some characteristics of Gawain that remain fairly consistent across medieval time and space—as in previous Arthurian texts, he is King Arthur's nephew, he is accompanied by his faithful steed Gringolet, and he is the paragon of knightly courtesy[7]—there is one notable departure from the poem's antecedents.[8] As Gawain prepares to depart Arthur's court in search of the Green Chapel, he is armed with a shield depicting a pentangle, and the anonymous poet devotes over thirty lines discussing the symbolism behind this device. As Ann Astell notes, the pentangle is "a term unknown in English heraldry,"[9] but she suggests that it is synonymous with "the five-pointed mullet argent found on the first quarter of the quartered shield of gules and or (that is, gold) that distinguished the coat of arms of the de Veres," pointing out as well that the landscape through which Gawain travels is one which would be very familiar to Robert de Vere, the earl of Oxford.[10] J. Stephen Russell echoes Astell's identification, and adds that "the figure evokes the stella maris, star of the sea, an honorific first applied to the Virgin Mary by Isidore of Seville and ubiquitous in the twelfth and thirteenth centuries."[11]

Shields signify, but *what* do they signify? To a fourteenth-century British audience, equally significant to one's identity are the material objects surrounding an individual.[12] We need look no further than the 1389 legal conflict between Richard Scrope and Robert Grosvenor over the use of a specific heraldic device to see the depths to which aristocratic identity was linked to heraldry. Richard Hamilton Green notes that "The heraldic charge which appears on the outside of the shield literally identifies the knight who bears it, but it is also, as the [*Gawain*] poet elaborately makes clear, the symbolic means of identifying his characteristic virtues and aspirations."[13] Many scholars discuss the symbolism and meaning of Gawain's shield, focusing on either the outward pentangle or the inner portrait of the Virgin Mary, or both, but my focus here is not on the shield that Gawain bears in *Sir Gawain and the Green Knight*.[14] Rather, my interests lie in the shields that he carries elsewhere, and what it means that the *Gawain*-poet has assigned a completely new device to this most renowned knight of the Round Table. That is to say, in the context of fourteenth-century Middle English romance, Gawain is associated with the heraldic device of a griffin. It is only in *Sir Gawain and the Green Knight* that he is given the pentangle, and no later Arthurian romances repeat this detail.[15] What might a griffin represent to a fourteenth-century audience, and what does its absence reveal?

I would like to acknowledge some ambiguity in Gawain's heraldry leading up to the fourteenth century. In his 2012 *Introduction to the Gawain-Poet*, John M. Bowers claims that "Prior literature designated Sir Gawain's insignia as a lion or a gryphon, not a pentangle."[16] This, however, is not exactly the case. In some texts, Gawain identifies himself not through a heraldic device but with a red surcoat, as in the late twelfth-century Latin romance *De Ortu Walwanii* ("The Rise of Gawain, Nephew of Arthur").[17] Geoffrey of Monmouth tells us that Gawain received his arms from the Pope, but we are given no description of them in his twelfth-century *Historia regum Britanniae* (The History of the Kings of Britain).[18] The first time that Gawain is connected to a specific animal is in the thirteenth-century *Perlesvaus*, where he bears a red eagle.[19] In Germany, Wolfram von Eschenbach assigns to Gawain a mysterious creature, the *gampilûn*, in his thirteenth-century *Parzival*.[20]

When we turn to Middle English texts contemporary with *Sir Gawain and the Green Knight*, the ambiguity surrounding Gawain's heraldic device remains. In *Ywaine and Gawain, Sir Perceval of Galle*, and the Stanzaic *Morte Arthure*, there is no mention of Gawain's device, although *Ywaine and Gawain* demonstrates an awareness of heraldic devices' power to signify identity; when Gawain fights on behalf of a woman who refuses to share their family inheritance with her younger sister, we are told of Gawain that "The armes he bare war noght his awyn, / For he wald noght in court be knawyn."[21] In the Stanzaic *Morte Arthur*, no explicit mention of Gawain's heraldic device is offered, but Gawain is able to identify Lancelot through seeing his shield. There are, however, two Middle English romances from the fourteenth century that do feature griffins. In the anonymous *Lybeaus Desconus*, Gawain is one of several knights to help arm the titular character. Of the six extant manuscripts containing *Lybeaus Desconus*, one manuscript describes the shield's device as a "chevron," or a v-shaped mark.[22] But in the other five manuscripts of *Lybeaus*, Gawain gives a shield with a griffin to Lybeaus: "He hongid on him a schilde / With grefons overgilde."[23] Given the patrilinear transmission of heraldic devices, this is especially important given the text's later revelation that Lybeaus is Gawain's son. More significant, perhaps, is Gawain's association with griffins in the Alliterative *Morte Arthure*. Following Gawain's death on the battlefield, King Frederick of Frisia asks Mordred if he knows the identity of the knight bearing a gold griffin: "What gome was he, this with the gay armes, / With this griffon of gold, that is on grouf fallen?"[24]

As a variety of medieval sources attest, a griffin is a hybrid creature with the wings and head of an eagle and the body of a lion, and it has a long heraldic history. As John Vinycomb notes,

> This favourite bearing was very early adopted in English armory. So early indeed as 1167 A.D. we find it on a seal of Richard de Redvers, Earl of Exeter, attached to a charter at Newport, Isle of Wight. It also appears on a seal of Simon de Montacute (*temp.* Henry III. and Edward I.). It is one of the principal bearings in heraldry, either charged upon the shield, as the arms, or as the crest placed upon the helm, also as supporters to the shield [149] of arms of many noble and eminent families in this country and the continent.[25]

Vinycomb's last comment about the ubiquity of heraldic griffins is attested by *Glover's Ordinary of Arms*, which devotes three dense pages to listing the various poses that griffins might take on various shields, as well as the specific families to whom these devices belonged.[26]

We can trace the creature even further back to Pliny the Elder's *Natural History* in the first century CE, and beginning in the twelfth century, medieval bestiaries offered allegorical meanings of various animals. As a hybrid creature, the griffin would symbolize characteristics of both the eagle and the lion. Just as heraldic entries revealed great variation of meaning for specific devices,[27] so too do the bestiaries vary in their contents. The entry for "griffin" is very brief in the thirteenth-century MS Bodley 764 bestiary, only offering a physical description without any allegorical commentary.[28] The *Aberdeen Bestiary*,[29] composed in England around 1200 CE, completely lacks an entry for "griffin." The *Aberdeen Bestiary* does offer insight into both the eagle and the lion, however. Although the eagle does have some negative allegorical meanings, it still is a largely positive symbol, representing "the acute understanding of the saints," comparing the vision of the eagle to John, who "on earth, penetrated the mysteries with his acute understanding by reflecting on the word. Likewise, those who still leave behind their earthly mind, seek heavenly things, as the eagle with John, through contemplation."[30] The lion, introduced as the king of beasts and connected to Christ, also is surrounded by positive Christian characteristics.[31]

Although bestiaries were typically composed within monasteries, possibly limiting their dissemination through only homilies and sermons, heraldic interpretations echo much of the bestiary lore. As Vinycomb notes, "The *griffin*, 'sacred to the sun,' combines the bodily attributes of the 'cloud-cleaving eagle' and the 'king of beasts.' . . . It is usually represented with projecting ears, indicating an acute sense of hearing, in addition to its other supposed extraordinary qualities."[32] For medieval heralds, the griffin represented courage, perseverance, and watchfulness.[33] Why then, given the griffin's positive attributes in both medieval bestiaries and heraldry, did the *Gawain*-poet choose to give his hero a heraldic device that had not been used before? Even the word *pentangle* itself was a very recent addition to the language, as the *Oxford English Dictionary* indicates that the first evidence of its usage appears in *Sir Gawain and the Green Knight*. After all, Gawain certainly embodies the traits of the griffin, demonstrating his bravery when he steps forward to accept the challenge, his perseverance on the long, lonely trip to the Green Chapel, and his watchfulness in his (largely successful) avoidance of Lady Bertilak's temptations of pride and lust.

One possible answer for replacing the griffin with a new device may have to do with the frequency of the image in churches, on heraldic charges, and so on. Perhaps by removing all references to the griffin from Gawain, the anonymous poet was preventing any historical figure associated with the griffin from identifying too closely with Gawain.[34] But another possibility exists. As John M. Bowers notes, "The poet certainly knew the French romance tradition and took what he liked, such as the *First Continuation* of Chrétien's *Perceval*, but otherwise he resisted foreign influences including French-derived vocabulary."[35] It may be that the griffin was too foreign. After all, the eagle had close associations with Rome, and readers of the Arthurian chronicle tradition will remember the frequent clashes between Arthur's court and the Romans.

Examining the contexts in which griffins appear in medieval literature also reveals a violent nature that may have dissuaded the poet from perpetuating the association with Gawain. For example, in Book XII of his seventh-century *Etymologies*, Isidore of Seville writes of the griffin that it is "born in the Hyperborean mountains. They are lions in their entire torso, but they are like eagles in their wings and faces. They are violently hostile to horses. They also tear humans apart when they see them."[36] While classical sources vary as regards the actual location of the Hyperborean mountains (Pindar maintained that no one could ever reach its shores), nonetheless it was a distant, exotic place in the British imagination. John de Trevisa echoes this idea of a far away and highly dangerous locale in his translation of the *De Proprietatibus Rerum* of Bartholomeus Anglicus, noting that "It is impossible to come þerto ffor dragouns & gryffouns."[37] *Mandeville's Travels* complicates the figure of the griffin even further, describing the land of Bactria as a place teeming with violent griffins: "Then is the lond of Bakarie wher beth wicked men and felle . . . In this / lond beth many griffons, mo than in other londes . . . he wole bere / fleynge to his neste a gret horse and a man upon hym y-armed . . . / And he hath gret nayles and long on his / feet."[38] Perhaps more importantly, Mandeville's griffins disrupt human activity, destroying the mounts upon which the aristocracy was dependent while also targeting the oxen that made agriculture possible.

As Gawain was a highly popular character in the medieval British imagination, perhaps the *Gawain*-poet felt that Gawain's association with the griffin undermined his position as one of Arthur's premier knights. This is consistent with many Middle English romances, for as Busby argues, "English authors and audiences regarded Gawain as a British hero and [thought] that it was considered unseemly to show such a figure in a poor light."[39] While we can find positive readings of griffins in heraldic texts and bestiaries, we cannot rule out the possibility that by the fourteenth century, the rising gentry classes were less familiar (or perhaps less interested) in the allegorical meanings of such devices, favoring instead the popular associations available to them through travel narratives such as *Mandeville's Travels*.

Regardless of the place that griffins held in the imaginations of the fourteenth century, one thing is clear. The *Gawain*-poet wanted to cut ties with Gawain's chivalric past to create a new chivalric future for him through the pentangle. Yet a cornerstone of many chivalric romances, including ones featuring Gawain, is the battle. Think, perhaps, of the intense combat scenes at the end of *Golagros and Gawain*, or *The Awntyrs of Arthure*. *Sir Gawain and the Green Knight* has been stripped of the violence, mirrored by the stripping of Gawain's heraldic device. It may be that the poet intended to make Gawain great again through the creation of a new past, one grounded in Christian suffering and martyrdom. But the chivalric world, despite its pageantry and ritual, was founded upon violent exchanges, and later adapters of Gawain did not take up this revised narrative past.

NOTES

1. J. R. Osgerby, "Chaucer's *Squire's Tale*," *Use of English* 11 (1959): 105. See also Phillip C. Boardman, "Middle English Arthurian Romance: The Repetition and Reputation of Gawain," in *Gawain: A Casebook*, eds. Raymond H. Thompson, Keith Busby (New York: Routledge, 2006), 255; Maureen Fries, "Teaching *Sir Gawain and the Green Knight* in the Context of Arthurian and Other Romance Traditions," in *Approaches to Teaching Sir Gawain and the Green Knight*, ed. Miriam Youngerman Miller and Jane Chance (New York: Modern Language Association of America, 1986), 69–78; and Tony Davenport, "Sir Gawain and the Green Knight." in *A Companion to Medieval Poetry*, ed. Corinne Saunders (Oxford: Blackwell Publishing, 2010), 385–400 for discussions of Gawain's popular reputation.

2. Boardman, "Middle English Arthurian Romance," 255.

3. Philippa Maddern, "Gentility," in *Gentry Culture in Late Medieval England*, ed. Raluca Radulescu and Alison Truelove (Manchester: Manchester University Press, 2005), 19. See Christine Chism, *Alliterative Revivals* (Philadelphia: University of Pennsylvania Press, 2002) for a discussion of Sir Bertilak as a gentry figure.

4. See, for example, Eileen Power, *Medieval Women*, ed. M. M. Postan (Cambridge: Cambridge University Press, 1975); Edith Rickert, "King Richard II's Books"; Margaret Deanesly, "Vernacular Books in England in the Fourteenth and Fifteenth Centuries," *Modern Language Review* 15 (1920): 350.n.5; Alison Stones, "Secular Manuscript Illumination in France," *Medieval Manuscripts and Textual Criticism*, ed. Christopher Kleinhenz (Chapel Hill: University of North Carolina Department of Romance Languages, 1976): 83–102; Felicity Riddy, "Middle English Romance: Family, Marriage, Intimacy," *The Cambridge Companion to Medieval Romance*, ed. Roberta L. Krueger (Cambridge: Cambridge University Press, 2000): 235–52; and Derek Pearsall, *Arthurian Romance: A Short Introduction* (Malden: Blackwell, 2003).

5. Boardman, "Middle English Arthurian Romance," 262.

6. A number of scholars have briefly discussed some of the ways in which the Gawain of *Sir Gawain and the Green Knight* is unique. John M. Bowers, in *An Introduction to the Gawain Poet* (Gainesville: University Press of Florida, 2012) discusses Gawain's lack of company, including a squire (p. 30). J. A. Burrow, in "The Fourteenth-Century Arthur," considers the ways in which the ending of *Sir Gawain and the Green Knight* varies from other contemporary romances in its lack of a clear moral resolution (p. 81). Several scholars focus on the shift of Gawain's reputation from an eager chivalric lover to a reluctant one: see Maureen Fries, "Teaching *Sir Gawain and the Green Knight* in the Context of Arthurian and Other Romance Traditions"; W. A. Davenport, "*Sir Gawain and the Green Knight*: The Poet's Treatment of the Hero and His Adventure"; Joerg O. Fichte, "Historia and Fabula: Arthurian Traditions and Audience Expectations in *Sir Gawain and the Green Knight*," in *Festschrift Walter Haug and Burghart Wachinger, II*, ed. Johannes Janota (Tübingen: Niemeyer,

1992), 589–602; and Christine Chism, *Alliterative Revivals* (Philadelphia: University of Pennsylvania Press, 2002).

7. As J. R. R. Tolkien and E. V. Gordon note in their critical edition of *Sir Gawain and the Green Knight*, the name "Gringalet" for Gawain's horse can be found as early as in the works of Chrétien de Troyes (Notes, 91, n.597).

8. Mickey Sweeney notes in "The Failure of Perfection" in this volume that "the *Gawain*-poet stages his narrative in seemingly familiar places, such as bedrooms and forests, quests and temptations, while at the same time, causing them to function in subversive ways" (p. 81).

9. Ann W. Astell, *Political Allegory in Late Medieval England* (Ithaca, NY: Cornell University Press, 1999), 125.

10. Astell, *Political Allegory*, 125.

11. J. Stephen Russell, "Sir Gawain and the White Monks: Cistercian Marian Spirituality and *Sir Gawain and the Green Knight*," *Journal of Medieval Religious Cultures* 39, no. 2 (2013): 218.

12. See Susan Crane, *The Performance of Self: Ritual, Clothing, and Identity during the Hundred Years War* (Philadelphia: University of Pennsylvania Press, 2002), as well as Robert W. Barrett Jr., *Against All England: Regional Identity and Cheshire Writing, 1195–1656* (Notre Dame, IN: University of Notre Dame Press, 2009), for discussions of the connections between heraldry and social identities. Barrett also discusses the Scrope-Grosvenor Trial in some detail (133–70).

13. Richard Hamilton Green, "Gawain's Shield and the Quest for Perfection," *English Literary History* 29, no. 2 (1962): 127.

14. For discussions of the possible meanings of Gawain's pentangle shield, see Kimberly Jack's chapter, "Sartorial Adornment in the *Pearl* Poems," in this volume. In addition, see James F. Knapp and Peggy A. Knapp, "The Immense Subtlety of *Sir Gawain and the Green Knight*," in *Medieval Romance: The Aesthetics of Possibility* (Toronto: University of Toronto Press, 2017), 149–75; Susan Crane, *The Performance of Self: Ritual, Clothing, and Identity During the Hundred Years War* (Philadelphia: University of Pennsylvania Press, 2002); Robert W. Barrett, Jr., "Heraldic Devices / Chivalric Divisions: *Sir Gawain and the Green Knight* and the Scrope-Grosvenor Trial," in *Against All England: Regional Identity and Cheshire Writing, 1195–1656* (Notre Dame, IN: University of Notre Dame Press, 2009), 133–70; W. A. Davenport, "*Sir Gawain and the Green Knight*: The Poet's Treatment of the Hero and His Adventure," in *Gawain: A Casebook*, ed. Raymond H. Thompson and Keith Busby (New York: Routledge: 2006), 273–86; Bowers, *An Introduction to the* Gawain *Poet*; Kevin Gustafson, "*Sir Gawain and the Green Knight*," in *A Companion to Medieval English Literature and Culture, c. 1350–c.1500*, ed. Peter Brown (Oxford: Blackwell Publishing, 2009), 619–33; Fichte, "Historia and Fabula," 589–602; J. R. Hulbert, "Syr Gawayn and the Grene Knyzt-(Concluded)," *Modern Philology* 13, no. 12 (1916): 689–730; Russell, "Sir Gawain and the White Monks," 207–226; and Green, "Gawain's Shield and the Quest for Perfection," 121–39.

15. Interestingly, the tail-rhymed *Grene Knight*, which appears in the mid-seventeenth century Percy Folio, devotes an entire stanza to describing Gawain's bridle and stirrups but offers no description of Gawain's heraldic device. We are told only that

Gawain wears "armour bright" and that "His geere glistered as gold." *The Greene Knight*, in *Sir Gawain: Eleven Romances and Tales*, ed. Thomas Hahn, TEAMS (Kalamazoo, MI: Medieval Institute Publications, 1995), ll. 265, 278, https://d.lib .rochester.edu/teams/text/hahn-sir-gawain-greene-knight. Given that this later adaptation of *Sir Gawain and the Green Knight* was generally believed to be intended for a more popular audience, the anonymous poet may have chosen to omit any mention of the pentangle due to its variance with more traditional Gawain narratives. See John M. Bowers, "Audiences, Medieval and Modern," in this volume for a discussion of *The Grene Knight*'s relationship to *Sir Gawain and the Green Knight*.

16. Bowers, *Introduction*, 30.

17. Helmut Nickel, "Notes on Arthurian Heraldry: The Retroactive System in the 'Armagnac' Armorial," *Quondam et Futurus* 3, no. 3 (1993), 8n.6, indicates, "Purpure was originally meant to be a dark crimson red; in the late twelfth century *De Ortu Walwanii*, Gawain was distinguished by his red surcoat; in *Gawain and the Green Knight* his shield with the pentangle is red." For a discussion of the use of the color red in the illustrations accompanying *Sir Gawain and the Green Knight* in its medieval manuscript context, see Joel Fredell's "The Illustrations in London, British Library, MS Cotton Nero A.x (part 2)." As Fredell notes, the Cotton Nero images "do not include crucial visual symbols from the poem such as the pentangle on Gawain's shield," but "red highlights on Gawain's dress, spear, and tack emerge strongly from the austere green background."

18. Nickel, "Notes on Arthurian Heraldry," 2, notes that "In French literary and pictorial sources of the thirteenth and fourteenth centuries Sir Gawain is bearing a white shield with a red canton."

19. Nickel, "Heraldry," in *The New Arthurian Encyclopedia: New Edition*, ed. Norris J. Lacy, Geoffrey Ashe, Sandra Ness Ihle, Marianne E. Kalinke, and Raymond H. Thompson (New York: Routledge, 2013), 231. Nickel notes, "By the fifteenth century, this red eagle has become a double-headed eagle, and on a 'roll of arms attributed to Jacques d'Armagnac," this device is described as being "derived from both the shield of Judas Maccabeus and the emblem of the Holy Roman Empire."

20. Nickel, "Heraldry," 231. Nickel notes that "[t]he *gampilÛn* has escaped zoo-logical classification so far; most likely, it is a Germanic phonetic rendering of the dragon like heraldic *gamelyon*, whose name was later reassigned to the now more familiar chameleon."

21. *Ywain and Gawain*, in *Sir Perceval of Galles and Ywain and Gawain*, ed. Mary Flowers Braswell, TEAMS (Kalamazoo, MI: Medieval Institute Publications, 1995), ll. 3396–402.

22. Lambeth Palace, MS 306.

23. *Lybeaus Desconus* (Naples: Biblioteca Nazionale, MS XIII.B.29). In *Lybeaus Desconus*, eds. Eve Salisbury, James Weldon, TEAMS (Kalamazoo, MI: Medieval Institute Publications, 2013), ll. 94–95. The six manuscripts containing *Lybeaus Desconus* are London, British Library, Cotton, MS Caligula A.ii (C, c. 1400); Naples, Biblioteca Nazionale, MS XIII.B.29 (N, 1457); London, Lambeth Palace, MS 306 (L, c. 1460); Oxford, Bodleian Library, MS 6922, also known as Ashmole 61 (A, c.

1490); London, Lincoln's Inn, MS 150 (LI, c.1400); and London, British Library, MS Additional 27879 (P, the Percy Folio, c. 1650).

24. *The Alliterative Morte Arthure*, in *King Arthur's Death: The Middle English Stanzaic Morte Arthur and Alliterative Morte Arthure*, ed. Larry D. Benson, rev. Edward E. Foster, TEAMS (Kalamazoo, MI: Medieval Institute Publications, 1994), ll. 3868–69. Later Middle English romances, such as *The Awntyrs of Arthur* and *Sir Gawain and the Carle of Carlisle*, consistently represent Gawain as bearing griffons as his heraldic device.

25. John Vinycomb, *Fictitious and Symbolic Creatures in Art with Special Reference to their Use in British Heraldry* (London: Chapman and Hall, 1906), 148–49.

26. *Glover's Ordinary of Arms*, in *A Complete Body of Heraldry*, ed. Joseph Edmonson (London: T. Spilsbury, 1780), 405–407.

27. Crane, *Performance of Self*, 111.

28. *Bestiary: Being an English Version of the Bodleian Library, Oxford M.S. Bodley 764 with all the Original Miniatures Reproduced in Facsimile*, trans. Richard Barber (Woodbridge: Boydell Press, 1999), 39.

29. Aberdeen University Library MS 24.

30. *The Aberdeen Bestiary*, University of Aberdeen, folio 62v, accessed October 3, 2019, https://www.abdn.ac.uk/bestiary/ms24/f62v "subtilis sanctorum \ intelligentia exprimitur," "volando terram deseruit, qui per subtilem intelligentiam in terra misteria verbum videndo pe\ netravit. Similiter qui adhuc [PL, haec] terrena mente deserunt, velut\ aquila cum Johanne per contemplationem petunt celestia."

31. Beal, Jane, "The Life of Christ in Medieval Bestiaries: Imagining the Griffin, Lion, Unicorn, Pelican, and Phoenix," *Imagination and Fantasy in the Middle Ages and Early Modern Time: Projections, Dreams, Monsters, and Illusions*, ed. Albrecht Classen, Fundamentals of Medieval and Early Modern Culture 24 (Berlin: Walter de Gruyter, 2020), 607–36.

32. Vinycomb, *Fictitious and Symbolic Creatures*, 149.

33. Vinycomb, *Fictitious and Symbolic Creatures*, 150.

34. See Gerard J. Brault, "Literary Uses of Heraldry in the Twelfth and Thirteenth Centuries," in *The Court Reconvenes: Courtly Literature Across the Disciplines*, ed. Barbara K. Altmann, Carleton W. Carroll (Woodbridge: Boydell & Brewer and D. S. Brewer, 2003), for a discussion of "heraldic flattery" (18–23), including a possible association, through heraldic devices, between Gawain and a thirteenth-century historical personage.

35. Bowers, *Introduction*, 18.

36. *The Etymologies of Isidore of Seville*, trans. Stephen A. Barney, W. J. Lewis, J. A. Beach, Oliver Berghof, XII.ii.17 (Cambridge: Cambridge University Press, 2006), 252.

37. *On the Properties of Things, John Trevisa's Translation of Bartholomaeus Anglicus De Proprietatibus Rerum, a Critical Text*, eds. M. C. Seymour et al., vols. 1 and 2 (Oxford: Oxford University Press, 1975), 182a.

38. *The Book of John Mandeville*, eds. Tamarah Kohanski and C. David Benson, TEAMS (Kalamazoo, MI: Medieval Institute Publications, 1994), ll. 2383–90.

39. Keith Busby, "Gawain," in *The New Arthurian Encyclopedia: New Edition*, ed. Norris J. Lacy, Geoffrey Ashe, Sandra Ness Ihle, Marianne E. Kalinke, and Raymond H. Thompson (New York: Routledge, 2013), 178. For a discussion of the contemporary audience of *Sir Gawain and the Green Knight*, see David K. Coley, "The Northwest Midlands and the Ricardian Court" in this volume.

BIBLIOGRAPHY

The Aberdeen Bestiary. University of Aberdeen, folio 62v. Accessed October 3, 2019. https://www.abdn.ac.uk/bestiary/ms24/f62v

The Alliterative Morte Arthure. In *King Arthur's Death: The Middle English Stanzaic Morte Arthur and Alliterative Morte Arthure*, ed. Larry D. Benson, revised by Edward E. Foster, TEAMS. Kalamazoo, MI: Medieval Institute Publications, 1994.

Barrett, Robert W. Jr. "Heraldic Devices / Chivalric Divisions: *Sir Gawain and the Green Knight* and the Scrope-Grosvenor Trial." In *Against All England: Regional Identity and Cheshire Writing, 1195–1656*, 133–70. Notre Dame, IN: University of Notre Dame Press, 2009.

Beal, Jane. *Becoming the Pearl-Poet: Perceptions, Connections, Receptions.* New York: Lexington Books, 2022.

———. "The Life of Christ in Medieval Bestiaries: Imagining the Griffin, Lion, Unicorn, Pelican, and Phoenix." In *Imagination and Fantasy in the Middle Ages and Early Modern Time: Projections, Dreams, Monsters, and Illusions*, ed. Albrecht Classen, Fundamentals of Medieval and Early Modern Culture 24, 607–36. Berlin: Walter de Gruyter, 2020.

Bestiary: Being an English Version of the Bodleian Library, Oxford M.S. Bodley 764 with all the Original Miniatures Reproduced in Facsimile. Translated and introduced by Richard Barber. Woodbridge: Boydell Press, 1999.

Boardman, Phillip C. "Middle English Arthurian Romance: The Repetition and Reputation of Gawain." In *Gawain: A Casebook*, ed. Raymond H. Thompson, Keith Busby, 255–72. New York: Routledge, 2006.

The Book of John Mandeville, ed. Tamarah Kohanski, C. David Benson, TEAMS. Kalamazoo, MI: Medieval Institute Publications, 1994.

Bowers, John M. *An Introduction to the Gawain Poet*. Gainesville: University Press of Florida, 2012.

Brault, Gerard J. "Literary Uses of Heraldry in the Twelfth and Thirteenth Centuries." In *The Court Reconvenes: Courtly Literature Across the Disciplines*, ed. Barbara K. Altmann, Carleton W. Carroll, 15–26. Woodbridge: Boydell & Brewer, D. S. Brewer, 2003.

Burrow, J. A. "The Fourteenth-Century Arthur." In *The Cambridge Companion to the Arthurian Legend*, ed. Elizabeth Archibald and Ad Putter, 69–83. Cambridge: Cambridge University Press, 2009.

Busby, Keith. "Gawain." In *The New Arthurian Encyclopedia: New Edition*, ed. Norris J. Lacy, Geoffrey Ashe, Sandra Ness Ihle, Marianne E. Kalinke, and Raymond H. Thompson, 178–79. New York: Routledge, 2013.

Chism, Christine. *Alliterative Revivals*. Philadelphia: University of Pennsylvania Press, 2002.

Crane, Susan. *The Performance of Self: Ritual, Clothing, and Identity during the Hundred Years War*. Philadelphia: University of Pennsylvania Press, 2002.

Davenport, Tony. "Sir Gawain and the Green Knight." In *A Companion to Medieval Poetry*, ed. Corinne Saunders, 385–400. Oxford: Blackwell Publishing, 2010.

Davenport, W. A. "*Sir Gawain and the Green Knight*: The Poet's Treatment of the Hero and His Adventure." In *Gawain: A Casebook*, ed. Raymond H. Thompson and Keith Busby, 273–86. New York: Routledge, 2006.

The Etymologies of Isidore of Seville. Translated by Stephen A. Barney, W. J. Lewis, J. A. Beach, and Oliver Berghof. Cambridge: Cambridge University Press, 2006.

Fichte, Joerg O. "Historia and Fabula: Arthurian Traditions and Audience Expectations in *Sir Gawain and the Green Knight*." In *Festschrift Walter Haug and Burghart Wachinger, II*, ed. Johannes Janota, 589–602. Tübingen: Niemeyer, 1992.

Fries, Maureen. "Teaching *Sir Gawain and the Green Knight* in the Context of Arthurian and Other Romance Traditions." In *Approaches to Teaching Sir Gawain and the Green Knight*, ed. Miriam Youngerman Miller and Jane Chance, 69–78. New York: Modern Language Association of America, 1986.

Glover's Ordinary of Arms. In *A Complete Body of Heraldry*, ed. Joseph Edmonson, 394–502. London: T. Spilsbury, 1780.

Green, Richard Hamilton. "Gawain's Shield and the Quest for Perfection." *English Literary History* 29, no. 2 (1962): 121–39.

Gustafson, Kevin. "*Sir Gawain and the Green Knight*." In *A Companion to Medieval English Literature and Culture, c. 1350–c.1500*. d. Peter Brown, 619–33. Oxford: Blackwell Publishing, 2009.

Hulbert, J. R. "Syr Gawayn and the Grene Knyzt-(Concluded)." *Modern Philology* 13, no. 12 (1916): 689–730.

Knapp, James F., and Peggy A. Knapp. "The Immense Subtlety of *Sir Gawain and the Green Knight*." In *Medieval Romance: The Aesthetics of Possibility*, 149–75. Toronto: University of Toronto Press, 2017.

Lybeaus Desconus (Naples, Biblioteca Nazionale, MS XIII.B.29). In *Lybeaus Desconus*, ed. Eve Salisbury, James Weldon, TEAMS. Kalamazoo, MI: Medieval Institute Publications, 2013.

Maddern, Philippa. "Gentility." In *Gentry Culture in Late Medieval England*, ed. Raluca Radulescu, Alison Truelove, 18–34. Manchester: Manchester University Press, 2005.

Nickel, Helmut. "Heraldry." In *The New Arthurian Encyclopedia: New Edition*, ed. Norris J. Lacy, Geoffrey Ashe, Sandra Ness Ihle, Marianne E. Kalinke, and Raymond H. Thompson, 230–34. New York: Routledge, 2013.

———. "Notes on Arthurian Heraldry: The Retroactive System in the 'Armagnac' Armorial." *Quondam et Futurus* 3, no. 3 (1993): 1–23.

On the Properties of Things, John Trevisa's Translation of Bartholomaeus Anglicus De Proprietatibus Rerum, a Critical Text. Ed. M. C. Seymour, et al, vols. 1 and 2. Oxford: Oxford University Press, 1975.

Osgerby, J. R. "Chaucer's *Squire's Tale*." *Use of English* 11 (1959): 102–107.

Russell, J. Stephen. "Sir Gawain and the White Monks: Cistercian Marian Spirituality and *Sir Gawain and the Green Knight.*" *Journal of Medieval Religious Cultures* 39, no. 2 (2013): 207–26.

Sir Gawain and the Green Knight. Ed. J. R. R. Tolkien, E. V. Gordon, revised by Norman Davis, 2nd ed. Oxford: Oxford University Press, 1967.

The Stanzaic Morte Arthur. In *King Arthur's Death: The Middle English Stanzaic Morte Arthur and Alliterative Morte Arthure*, ed. Larry D. Benson, revised by Edward E. Foster, TEAMS. Kalamazoo, MI: Medieval Institute Publications, 1994.

Vinycomb, John. *Fictitious and Symbolic Creatures in Art with Special Reference to their Use in British Heraldry.* London: Chapman and Hall, 1906.

Ywain and Gawain. In *Sir Perceval of Galles and Ywain and Gawain*, ed. Mary Flowers Braswell, TEAMS. Kalamazoo, MI: Medieval Institute Publications, 1995.

Chapter Eleven

The Pastoral Theology
of the *Pearl*-Poet

Grace Hamman

Feel and perceive your own *vnwitt*, for you can neither understand nor accomplish good on your own, urges the fourteenth-century penitential text, *The Book of Vices and Virtues*.[1] These kinds of exhortations are pastoral in nature: the text and others like it aim to promote self-knowledge of human limitations like a priest counseling a parishioner. For proper confession and penance, each person must self-reflexively consider her unworthiness in sin as well as her powerlessness to achieve good without God's grace. The *Book* connects this self-awareness to humility and the beginning of the life of the Beatitudes. When someone cultivates this feeling that "þat powere of man is nou3t and þat he haþ nou3t and þat he can nou3t and þat he may nou3t" ("the power of humankind is nothing and that he has nothing, understands nothing, and is able to do nothing") then "bigynneþ he to be pore gostliche" ("he begins to become poor in spirit.")[2] Such teachings on human weakness are prominent in penitential texts and other genres; they mark the centrality of acknowledgment of sin and human need in contemporary conceptions of spiritual formation.[3]

Critics, notably A. C. Spearing, have long established human weakness as thematically fundamental in the *Pearl*-poet's corpus.[4] Cecilia Hatt has argued that dual recognitions of the powerlessness of oneself as a created being, and God's love manifested in creation, unite the poems of Cotton Nero A.x.[5] Less explored is that the poet's interest in human limitation is pastoral and shared with sundry contemporary texts, including didactic poems like the *The Prick of Conscience*, contemplative works like Julian of Norwich's *A Revelation of Love*, and, naturally, penitential texts like the *Book*. These texts in their unique ways foster recognition of the self as creaturely, limited, sinful, but ultimately held in the love of God, and they harness other theological inquiries, diverse as they are, into the service of that pastoral, confessional focus.

St. Erkenwald shows us this teleological orientation toward spiritual growth through recognition of limitation. Before Bishop Erkenwald speaks to the mysterious corpse, he preaches to the curious Londoners and by extension, the readers of the poem. The spectacles that follow, Erkenwald contends, reveal the inadequacy of human "might" and "mind": "To seche the soþe at oure selfe 3ee se þer no bote [to seek the truth from ourselves there is no benefit], / Bot glow [rejoice] we alle upon Godde and His grace aske."[6] The bishop senses that the miraculously preserved body prompts onlookers to search for truth within themselves. Upon this examination, a person inevitably finds herself incapable of supplying answers to this phenomenon. This recognition of inherent inability, Erkenwald urges, should initiate rejoicing in God's sufficiency. Thus weakness actually stimulates moral and spiritual growth through its confessional recognition. The coming miracle will "auay" ("inform") the gathered watchers of God's virtue and power, and it will allow those watching to "leue" that God is "my3ty, / And fayne 3our talent to fulfille if 3e Hym frende leues."[7] God is eager to fulfill each person's "talent," a flexible Middle English word that could mean desires, will, or disposition.[8] The ensuing miracles spiritually form the onlookers, not so much through their nature as miracles but through provoking those curious observers to recognize their individual and communal limitations, and the answering, transformative friendship of God.

And they do. At the conclusion of *Erkenwald*, the just pagan's salvation prompts the whole city to remember their own inevitable physical corruption, the grace of salvation in mirth and mourning, and to grow in loving God.[9] The end of the poem follows the pattern of Erkenwald's preaching. Meditations on the sacraments, miracles, human interpretive power, potential attacks on heterodoxy, all pertinent theological interests in this poem, ultimately work pastorally in stimulating acknowledgment of need for God and ensuing spiritual transformation.[10]

In light of that teleology, this chapter does not attempt to consider all of this poet's wide-ranging theological interests but focuses on the poems' diverse commitments to portraying and probing confessions of weakness, sin, or need (or their absence). These pastoral turns are more straightforward in *Erkenwald*, *Cleanness*, and *Patience*; they are examined with greater complexity in *Pearl* and *Sir Gawain and the Green Knight*. Accordingly, I begin with *Cleanness* and *Patience* and end with the latter two.

CLEANNESS AND PATIENCE

In *Cleanness* and *Patience*, recognition of human weakness specifically entails confession of sin. This focus on sin and penance fosters the life of the Beatitudes. These poems proceed along similar narrative lines (i.e., people provoke the wrath of God through sin, and God threatens annihilation); then, these lines deviate. One poem reveals the destruction of those who sinfully engender God's wrath and do not repent, and another displays God's mercy as the repentant faithfully perform penance. Critics, especially in reading *Cleanness*, have tended to focus on the poet's scriptural retellings as emphasizing the limitations of human interpretation of scripture and rationality, and often suggest an influence from the *moderni* theologians and their conceptions of God's power.[11] However, the poet's considerations of God's power do not result in neatly argued conclusions on these questions. *Cleanness* induces more questions than it answers by its portrayal of God's terrifyingly whimsical temperament, intensified by its scriptural sources. *Patience*'s kinder, more patient God provides a provocative counterpoint.[12] The poems' central turn to penance clarifies that in the light of such unanswerable questions both poems creatively direct readers toward self-examination and the sacrament itself.

This guiding interest helps us to understand one of the poet's most theologically risky choices in *Cleanness*: the sympathetic characterization of sinners undergoing divine punishment. David Wallace notes the audience's identification not with Abraham or Noah, but with the poorly prepared wedding guest or those dying in the floodwaters.[13] No longer markedly wicked, ordinary people say final goodbyes to their beloved: "Luf lokez to luf and his leue takez, / For to ende alle at onez and for euer twynne" ("Love looks to love and his leave takes/ For to die at once and be separated forever").[14] This kind of identification creates disquieting interior examination in the reader—I am no different than the sinners with the water lapping around their ankles—and motivates shrift. In this identification, the often disturbing *Cleanness* belongs to a long tradition that justifies instigating fear in order to rouse repentance. Sometimes this tradition is more matter-of-fact: *The Book of Vices and Virtues* counsels that those preparing to confess should scrutinize their conscience, considering "how that he haþ God and his blessed modre and alle the halewen y-wraþed" ("how one has angered God, the blessed mother, and all the saints.")[15] *Cleanness*, in its own more poetically skilled way, is like *The Prick of Conscience*, a text whose primary strategy for promoting the self-examination necessary to penance is raising terror in the hearts of its readers in order to avoid a horrific Doomsday.[16] A far later participant in this resilient, unsettling tradition, the Puritan Jonathan Edwards, justified a frightening sermon with "The use of this awful subject may be for

awakening unconverted persons in this congregation."[17] Substitute "impeni-
tent" for Edwards's "unconverted," and you may hear an echo of *Cleanness.*

However, the late medieval readers of these poems had an outlet for these
fears that the Puritan Edwards did not: penance. The nonviolent center of
Cleanness is the portrayal of Christ's ministry on Earth, where the poet
directly addresses his audience, acknowledging their anxiety: "Nov ar we
sore and sinful . . . / How schulde we se, þen may we say, that Syre vpon
throne?"[18] Perhaps one can become like the scriptural lepers who, identify-
ing their need for healing from uncleanness, flock to Jesus and "claymed His
grace."[19] God is "merciable," for though one may be unclean, there is the
option to "pure þe with penaunce tyl þou a perle worþe" ("purify yourself
with penance until you become pearl-like.")[20]

Patience offers a similar but complete model of fear, repentance, conver-
sion, and then penance in the Ninevites, and a slightly more complicated
version in Jonah himself.[21] The frantic Ninevites muse aloud: "He wyl
wende of His wodschip [anger] and His wraþ leue [leave], / And forgif vus
þis gult, 3if we Hym God leuen."[22] The whole city "leued on His lawe and
laften [left] her synnes, / Parfourmed alle þe penaunce."[23] The repetition of
"leue," or believe, underscores the poet's Augustinian emphasis on faith fol-
lowed by transformative penance. C. David Benson has discussed Jonah and
his recalcitrance in the context of God's repeated mercy as the poet's way
of "forc[ing] his readers to understand the same sin in themselves," a poem
triggering self-examination and confession.[24] Implicitly, Jonah is also an
imperfect type of Christ, in the midst of it all: one who rejects the possibility
of crucifixion rather than embracing it,[25] leaving an echo in readers' minds of
the true savior coming to prompt transformative penitence in sinful people.[26]

SIR GAWAIN AND THE GREEN KNIGHT

In *Gawain*, we are a long way from the clearly delineated sins and repen-
tances of *Cleanness* and *Patience. Gawain* instead portrays the nearly
impossible interpretive challenge of how to know oneself as limited or sinful
within contemporary contexts and competing traditions. The ending of the
oft-described "secular" poem of Cotton Nero A.x hinges on how one reads
Gawain's two confessions and subsequent penitential actions.[27]

Gawain confesses twice. The first is a straightforward and seemingly effec-
tive confession to a priest.[28] The second, in the Green Chapel, is to the Green
Knight, wherein Gawain passionately confesses an impressive laundry list of
sins that include villainy, vice, cowardice, covetise, forsaking his true nature,
falseness, treachery, and untruth.[29] In contrast, the Green Knight characterizes
Gawain's failing as a *natural* failure in that he loved his life, and declares

Gawain "clean," echoing the earlier priestly confession.[30] The critical question usually asked regarding this sequence: was the first confession valid?[31] Closely following is a question that nearly every reader must address—did Gawain actually sin as badly as he says he did? Finally, what do we make of this second, unconventional confession? More questions quickly develop as Gawain assigns himself an unusual penance: wearing the girdle, hardly taught in any penitential manuals. His fierce shame contrasts with the lighter reactions of the Green Knight and Arthur's laughing court. Is Gawain scrupulous, inappropriately reacting to the magnitude of his not very severe sins?

We as readers are strangely adrift, without critical anchors to give us clearly defined answers to such questions. We cannot fully trust the childish court for an adequate response. The Green Knight has oddly been described as a "moral guide" in this moment, but he has been lying through omission throughout the poem.[32] The poet could have opted to show a priest—perhaps Bishop Baldwin—clarifying Gawain's sins or chastising him for penitentially wearing the girdle, but we along with Gawain remain in the dark.

Self-knowledge, how to recognize human error, sin, or weakness, remains a problem. Either Gawain did not know his own sins when he confessed the first time, or he immensely exaggerates them in his shame the second time. However, this is a problem unresolved by Gawain, who accepts neither the Green Knight's judgment nor the court's, *and* it is unresolved by the court, who cannot persuade Gawain otherwise, as far as we see. In effect, girdle-wearing Gawain, his sartorial choice meant to remind him of his limitations and weakness, becomes an object of permanent misinterpretation either to himself or in his community. If we take the girdle as Gawain does—recollecting "þe faut and þe fayntyse of þe flesche" ("the fault and weakness of the body")[33]—it is particularly ironic that the girdle is incorporated into a communal symbol of power.

With multivalence, the poem thus narrates the difficulty of recognizing human limitation whether you agree with Gawain's assessment of his sins or the court's. I agree with David Aers and Nicholas Watson in that the poet here has assimilated penance into chivalric traditions—but unlike Aers or Watson, I believe the poet does it not toward affirming courtly values, but toward subtly examining the contingency of self-knowledge in sin.[34] Formed in chivalric traditions, neither the court nor Gawain is capable of thinking outside of them. When Gawain fails as a knight, he also fails to see his sins clearly, defaulting to blaming women and passionately confessing things that seem tenuous. The court fails in the opposite way, seeing no blame in Gawain's actions, unable to interpret his awkward attempts to practice humility. Both are caught in the traditions in which they have been formed, part of the same "blysse and blunder" that characterized their shared noble forebears.[35]

Readers are finally left with the multiplying questions of the end of *Gawain*, and the inextricability of self-knowledge from tradition.[36]

PEARL

In the fourteenth century, there were ongoing discussions whether in fact this kind of self-knowledge, the confession of one's utter filth in sin, was indeed the best way to begin spiritual transformation. Penitential manuals agreed, citing theologians like Bernard of Clairvaux, that a person must cultivate her awareness of how deeply she has fallen from the glory of God, and that a good way to do that was through enumerating sins. Meanwhile, contemplative writers like Julian of Norwich and the anonymous author of *Cloud of Unknowing*, without denying the importance of seeing one's sin, contended that focusing on humanity's natural dependence on God as loving Creator built a better foundation for loving God and loving one another. *Cloud* confines this method of cultivating humility through meditation on God's colossal love rather than humanity's "wretchedness" to those seeking a contemplative life, but Julian opens up these possibilities to all her fellow Christians.[37] *Pearl*, in a similar vein of contemplation, takes up some of these questions about knowing oneself explored by contemplative texts.[38]

The Dreamer and the Pearl-Maiden embody different types of confessional self-knowledge. "I am bot mol [dirt] and manerez mysse [poor manners]; / Bot Crystes mersy and Mary and Jon, / Thise arn the grounde of alle my blysse," confesses the speaker in acknowledgment of his repeated failure to understand the Pearl-Maiden's teachings in his dream vision.[39] The Dreamer's confession is grounded in the vernacular penitential traditions of self-knowledge (described previously). Defining oneself as dirt refers to the creation of humanity from dust as well as the figurative lowness of human action and understanding. Ironically, however, the Dreamer's awareness of his limitations slips away as the very result of these limitations, as we see time and time again, in his incredulous judgment of the Pearl-Maiden's teachings,[40] and in his rushing into the water to reach "his" pearl.[41] Here we may see parallels between Jonah of *Patience* and Gawain.

In contrast, when the Pearl-Maiden describes herself, however obliquely, she does so in terms that depend on and are shaped by her relationship with the Lamb: she is his *quene*,[42] "holy His,"[43] one of the faithful *hyne*, servants, of the vineyard,[44] and one of the children who come to Jesus.[45] These descriptions are all relational and are meant to disclose the depth of the Maiden's love for Christ and Christ's love for her while also revealing the nature of life in the Kingdom of God. While the Dreamer has acknowledged his suffering and potential sin, the Pearl-Maiden's confessions of her dependence are based not on her own sinfulness but on the natural and loving relationship between God and his mortal creatures, who die and take on a new life.[46]

One might think this model of self-knowledge is only possible because the maiden herself is washed clean through baptism. However, the end of the poem makes it clear that the possibility of being spiritually transformed through confessional acknowledgment of dependence and relationship is open to everyone. The poem begins with the pearl for the pleasure of princes, a symbol of material wealth. The Pearl-Maiden herself opens this image up to include the kingdom of God itself, and individual people in the process of spiritual transformation through penance and recognition of God's love, with herself as model.[47] The final lines of the poem continue to open the image through the prayer for God to transform "us" into "homly hyne" and "precious perlez."[48] Such an expression enfolds readers into the transformative and ultimately pastoral vision of *Pearl*. This poem portrays a particularly poignant and universal form of human limitation in its consideration of death and loss. In this context, over-emphasis on sin as human limitation falls flat. Instead, the "dungeon" of human loss remains, but it is held in tension with the friendship of God. This friendship is hardly understandable but is nevertheless a graced means of continued spiritual transformation accessible to readers.

CONCLUSION

Tracing the *Pearl*-poems' shared orientation toward fostering self-reflexive responses to human limitation suggests a pastoral poet keenly interested in the development of the life that Christ describes in the Sermon on the Mount. The poems' pastorality ultimately takes different forms; this divergence is important to note in order to avoid readings that overly smooth out theological differences between them. However, their teleology is consistent. In their varying ways, the poems gesture toward the places where human strength fails, the places where humility and concomitant transformation can begin. The poet advocates for a humble reader within a humble church, careful to practice recognition of limitations but contained within the secure knowledge of God's love and grace mediated through the sacraments, despite the high potential for human error. Like Augustine, the poet believes that "we needed to be persuaded how much God loves us, and what sort of people he loves; how much in case we despaired, what sort in case we grew proud."[49]

NOTES

1. *The Book of Vices and Virtues; a Fourteenth Century English Translation of the Somme Le Roi of Lorens d'Orléans*, ed. W. Nelson Francis (London: Published for the Early English Text Society by H. Milford, Oxford University Press, 1942), 129. For a helpful overview of penitential texts like the *Book* and their pastoral context, see Nancy Ciccone, "Religious Contexts for the *Pearl*-Poet," in this volume.

2. *Book*, 129. Translations are mine.

3. On self-knowledge and humility in medieval spiritual formation, see Grace Hamman, "Julian of Norwich's Children: Childhood and Meekness in *A Revelation of Love*," *Journal of Medieval and Early Modern Studies* 49, no. 1 (January 2019): 173–75.

4. A small sample: A. C. Spearing, *The Gawain-Poet: A Critical Study* (Cambridge: Cambridge University Press, 1970), on the clash between human and divine power; on human failure, Lynn Staley Johnson, *The Voice of the* Gawain-*Poet* (Madison: University of Wisconsin Press, 1984), xv; the "motif of confounding of reason," in Robert J. Blanch and Julian N. Wasserman, *From Pearl to Gawain: Forme to Fynisment* (Gainesville: University Press of Florida, 1995), 10. Recently, on the poem's interest in the failures of priests specifically as evidence of shared authorship, see Ethan Campbell, *The* Gawain-*Poet and the Fourteenth-Century English Anticlerical Tradition* (Kalamazoo, MI: Medieval Institute Publications, 2018).

5. Cecilia Hatt, *God and the* Gawain-*Poet: Theology and Genre in* Pearl, Cleanness, Patience, *and* Sir Gawain and the Green Knight (Cambridge: D.S. Brewer, 2015), 2. Hatt argues for the poetry as "pastoral endeavor," 13. For an alternative account of the poet's pastorality, see Nicholas Watson, "The *Gawain*-Poet as a Vernacular Theologian," *A Companion to the* Gawain-*Poet*, eds. Derek Brewer and Jonathan Gibson (Cambridge: D.S. Brewer, 1997), 293–313.

6. Clifford Peterson, ed., *Saint Erkenwald* (Philadelphia: University of Pennsylvania Press, 1977), l. 163 and ll. 170–71.

7. Peterson, *Saint Erkenwald*, ll. 173–75.

8. *Middle English Dictionary*, s.v. "talent, n.," https://quod.lib.umich.edu/m/middle-english-dictionary accessed April 2019.

9. Peterson, *Saint Erkenwald*, l. 349. John Bugbee, "Sight and Sound in *St. Erkenwald*: On Theodicy and the Senses," *Medium Aevum* 77, no. 2 (2008), compares the interaction between Erkenwald and the judge and their developing understanding of God's workings to Pope Gregory the Great's gloss on Job and recognizing oneself penitentially, 213.

10. On *Erkenwald*, baptism, and orthodoxy, see William Kamowski, "*Saint Erkenwald* and the Inadvertent Baptism: An Orthodox Response to Heterodox Ecclesiology," *Religion and Literature* 27, no. 3 (1995): 5–27; David Coley, "Baptism as Eucharist: Orthodoxy, Wycliffism, and the Sacramental Utterance in *Saint Erkenwald*," *Journal of English and Germanic Philology* 107, no. 3 (2008): 327–47. On miracles, see Arnold E. Davidson, "Mystery, Miracle, and Meaning in *Saint Erkenwald*," *Papers in Language and Literature* 16, no. 1 (1980): 37–44. T. McAlindon notes how the poet "tease[s] the reader's understanding in order to emphasize its

limitations," "Hagiography into Art: A Study of *St. Erkenwald*," *Studies in Philology* 67, no. 4 (October 1970): 476.

11. David Wallace, "*Cleanness* and the Terms of Terror," *Text and Matter: New Critical Perspectives of the* Pearl-*Poet*, ed. Robert J. Blanch, Miriam Youngerman Miller, Julian N. Wasserman (Troy, NY: Whitston Publishing, 1991), 93–104; Lawrence Clopper, "The God of the *Gawain*-Poet," *Modern Philology* 94, no. 1 (1996): 1–18; Piotr Spyra, "*Simul iustus et peccator: The Theological Significance of Shifts of Perspective in the Middle English* Cleanness *and* Patience," *Parergon* 35, no. 1 (2018): 70–72.

12. See ll. 509–23, where God remembers the elderly, infant, and disabled people of Nineveh in striking contrast to the wholesale wrath of the Flood or Sodom in *Cleanness.*

13. Wallace, *Terror*, 99–100. Allen Frantzen argues the opposite, "The Disclosure of Sodomy in *Cleanness*," *PMLA* 111 (1996): 452; Jim Rhodes sees such arguments for a lack of identification with the sinners of *Cleanness* as underestimating readers and poet, *Poetry Does Theology: Chaucer, Grosseteste, and the* Pearl-*Poet* (Notre Dame, IN: University of Notre Dame Press, 2001), 99–100.

14. *Cleanness*, ll. 399–402.

15. *Vices and Virtues*, 173. Corey Owen, "Temperance and the Evolution of Concupiscible Vice in *Cleanness*," in this volume argues that *Cleanness* "dramatizes the genesis and evolution of concupiscible sin" (p. 46), and that the taxonomy of temperance in influential penitential manuals, such as *The Book of Vices and Virtues*, can help readers better understand the poet's choice of *exempla* in rousing his audience and creating a work of moral complexity.

16. *Richard Morris's Prick of Conscience*, ed. Ralph Hanna and Sarah Wood, Early English Text Society (Oxford: Oxford University Press, 2013), spends a thousand lines reciting the terrors of Hell (ll. 6419–7519).

17. Jonathan Edwards, "Sinners in the Hands of an Angry God," *Jonathan Edwards Reader*, eds. John F. Smith, Harry Stout, and Kenneth P. Minkema (New Haven, CT: Yale University Press, 1995), 95.

18. *Cleanness*, ll. 1111–12. Elizabeth Keiser, *Courtly Desire and Medieval Homophobia* (New Haven, CT: Yale University Press, 1997), criticizes this representation of Christ, 196.

19. *Cleanness*, l. 1093 and l. 1097. See also Sandra Pierson Prior, *The Fayre Formez of the* Pearl-*Poet* (East Lansing: Michigan State Press, 1996), 75–76; Campbell, *Anticlerical*, 140–41.

20. *Cleanness*, l. 1116.

21. On these poems completing each other regarding penance, see J. J. Anderson, *Language and Imagination in the* Gawain-*Poems* (Manchester: Manchester University Press, 2005), 115; Spyra, "*Simul iustus*," 66–68, on the two as a diptych; on penance as a theme throughout the poems, Johnson, *Voice*, 143.

22. *Patience*, ll. 403–404.

23. *Patience*, ll. 405–406.

24. C. David Benson, "The Impatient Reader of *Patience*," *Text and Matter: New Critical Perspectives of the* Pearl-*Poet*, eds. Robert J. Blanch, Miriam Youngerman Miller, and Julian N. Wasserman (Troy, NY: Whitston Publishing, 1991), 147–61.

25. *Patience*, l. 96.

26. On Jonah as type of Christ, see Malcolm Andrew, "Jonah and Christ in *Patience*," *Modern Philology* 70, no. 3 (1973): 230–33.

27. Hatt discusses critical claims of secularity in *Gawain, Theology*, 168–72. Hatt also takes up the relevant critical argument by A. V. C. Schmidt on *Gawain* as against Pelagianism, 210. See Schmidt, "'Latent Content" and the "Testimony in the Text": Symbolic Meaning in *Sir Gawain and the Green Knight*," *Review of English Studies* 38, no. 150 (1987): 145–68.

28. *Sir Gawain and the Green Knight*, ll. 1883–4.

29. *Sir Gawain and the Green Knight*, ll. 2375–85.

30. *Sir Gawain and the Green Knight*, l. 1883 and l. 2391.

31. Israel Gollancz, ed. *Sir Gawain and the Green Knight* (Oxford: Oxford University Press, 1940), 123; John Burrow, "The Two Confession Scenes in *Sir Gawain and the Green Knight*," *Modern Philology* 57, no. 2 (1959): 73–79; Gerald Morgan, "The Validity of Gawain's Confession in *Sir Gawain and the Green Knight*," *Review of English Studies* 36, no. 141 (1985): 1–18. For overviews of this criticism, see David Aers, "Christianity for Courtly Subjects: Reflections on the *Gawain*-Poet," *A Companion to the Gawain-Poet*, ed. Derek Brewer and Jonathan Gibson (Cambridge: D.S. Brewer, 1997), 95–97; and Campbell, *Anticlerical*, 215–16.

32. Recently, see Hatt, *Theology*, 211; David Beauregard, "Moral Theology in *Sir Gawain and the Green Knight*: The Pentangle, the Green Knight, and the Perfection of Virtue," *Renascence* 65, no. 3 (Spring 2013): 146–62; but compare Thomas Aquinas on lying, *Summa Theologiae* trans. Laurence Shapcote, O.P., ed. John Mortensen, Enrique Alarcon (Lander, WY: Aquinas Institute for the Study of Sacred Doctrine, 2012), II–II.110.3.

33. *Sir Gawain and the Green Knight*, ll. 2435.

34. Aers, "Courtly," 95; Watson, "Vernacular," 310–13. Spearing debates Gawain's level of self-knowledge, *Gawain*-Poet, 224–29.

35. *Sir Gawain and the Green Knight*, l. 18.

36. Hatt has commented upon the dialectic, unfinished nature of *Gawain*, which I believe related to these unanswered questions on self-knowledge, 206–209.

37.*The Cloud of Unknowing* ed. Patrick J. Gallacher (Kalamazoo, MI: Medieval Institute Publications, 1997), 15.780–95; Julian of Norwich, *The Writings of Julian of Norwich: A Vision Showed to a Devout Woman and A Revelation of Love*, eds. Nicholas Watson and Jacqueline Jenkins (University Park: Pennsylvania State University Press, 2006), 8.22–36.

38. On contemplative failure, see David Aers, "The Self Mourning: Reflections on *Pearl*," *Speculum* 68, no. 1 (1993): 67; Spearing, Gawain-*Poet*, 114–15.

39. *Pearl*, ll. 382–84.

40. *Pearl*, ll. 481–92 and ll. 590–96.

41. *Pearl*, ll. 1155–64.

42. *Pearl*, l. 415.

43. *Pearl*, l. 418.

44. *Pearl*, l. 632.

45. *Pearl*, ll. 709–28.

46. See Aers, "Reflections," for the Dreamer's rejection of creatureliness and Aers's criticism of readings that focus too heavily on the Dreamer's sin, 58. Gregory Roper argues that the poem is penitential: the "I" of the beginning of the poem is selfish and possessive, *"Pearl*, Penitence, and the Recovery of the Self," *The Chaucer Review* 28, no. 2 (1993): 170. I agree that the poem depicts a "reshaping," to use Roper's language, of the self, but the language of sin is superseded by language of dependence.

47. See also Johnson, *Voice*, 161–78. Jane Beal explores the relationship between the fourfold method of reading and the meanings of the pearl image, *The Signifying Power of* Pearl: *Medieval Literary and Cultural Contexts for the Transformation of Genre* (New York: Routledge, Taylor & Francis Group, 2017). On the relational language of the last stanza, see Laurence Beaston, "The *Pearl*-Poet and the Pelagians," *Religion and Literature* 36, no. 1 (2004): 30.

48. *Pearl*, ll. 1201–202.

49. Augustine, *The Trinity*, trans. Edmund Hill, O.P. (New York: New City Press, 2012), IV.2.

BIBLIOGRAPHY

Aers, David. "Christianity for Courtly Subjects: Reflections on the Gawain-Poet." In *A Companion to the Gawain-Poet.* Ed. Derek Brewer and Jonathan Gibson, 89–104. Cambridge: D.S. Brewer, 1997.

———. "The Self Mourning: Reflections on *Pearl.*" *Speculum* 68, no. 1 (1993): 54–73.

Anderson, J. J. *Language and Imagination in the* Gawain-*Poems.* Manchester: Manchester University Press, 2005.

Andrew, Malcolm. "Jonah and Christ in *Patience*," *Modern Philology* 70, no. 3 (1973): 230–33.

Andrew, Malcolm, and Ronald Waldron, eds. *The Poems of the Pearl Manuscript: Pearl, Cleanness, Patience, Sir Gawain and the Green Knight.* Ed. Rev. 5th ed. Exeter: University of Exeter Press, 2007.

Aquinas, Thomas. *Summa Theologiae.* Translated by Laurence Shapcote, O.P. Ed. John Mortensen, Enrique Alarcon. Lander, WY: Aquinas Institute for the Study of Sacred Doctrine, 2012.

Augustine. *The Trinity.* Translated by Edmund Hill, O.P. 2nd ed. Vol. 5. of *The Works of Saint Augustine: A Translation for the 21st Century.* New York: New City Press, 2012.

Beal, Jane. *Becoming the Pearl-Poet: Perceptions, Connections, Receptions.* New York: Lexington Books, 2022.

———. *The Signifying Power of* Pearl: *Medieval Literary and Cultural Contexts for the Transformation of Genre.* New York: Routledge, Taylor & Francis Group, 2017.

Beaston, Lawrence. "The *Pearl*-Poet and the Pelagians." *Religion and Literature* 36, no. 1 (2004): 15–38.

Beauregard, David. "Moral Theology in *Sir Gawain and the Green Knight*: The Pentangle, the Green Knight, and the Perfection of Virtue." *Renascence* 65, no. 3 (Spring 2013): 146–62.

Benson, C. David. "The Impatient Reader of *Patience*." In *Text and Matter: New Critical Perspectives of the* Pearl-*Poet.* Ed. Robert J. Blanch, Miriam Youngerman Miller, and Julian N. Wasserman, 147–61. Troy, NY: Whitston Publishing, 1991.

Blanch, Robert J., and Julian N. Wasserman, *From Pearl to Gawain: Forme to Fynisment.* Gainesville: University Press of Florida, 1995.

The Book of Vices and Virtues; a Fourteenth Century English Translation of the Somme Le Roi of Lorens d'Orléans. Ed. W. Nelson Francis. London: Published for the Early English Text Society by H. Milford, Oxford University Press, 1942.

Bugbee, John. "Sight and Sound in St. Erkenwald: On Theodicy and the Senses." *Medium Aevum* 77, no. 2 (2008): 202–21.

Burrow, John. "The Two Confession Scenes in *Sir Gawain and the Green Knight.*" *Modern Philology* 57, no. 2 (1959): 73–79.

Campbell, Ethan. *The* Gawain-*Poet and the Fourteenth-Century English Anticlerical Tradition.* Kalamazoo, MI: Medieval Institute Publications, 2018.

Clopper, Lawrence. "The God of the *Gawain*-Poet." *Modern Philology* 94, no. 1 (1996): 1–18.

Coley, David. "Baptism as Eucharist: Orthodoxy, Wycliffism, and the Sacramental Utterance in *Saint Erkenwald.*" *Journal of English and Germanic Philology* 107, no. 3 (2008): 327–47.

Davidson, Arnold E. "Mystery, Miracle, and Meaning in *Saint Erkenwald.*" *Papers in Language and Literature* 16, no. 1 (1980): 37–44.

Edwards, Jonathan. "Sinners in the Hands of an Angry God." In *Jonathan Edwards Reader.* Edited by John F. Smith, Harry Stout, and Kenneth P. Minkema, 89–104. New Haven, CT: Yale University Press, 1995.

Frantzen, Allen. "The Disclosure of Sodomy in *Cleanness.*" *PMLA* 111 (1996): 451–64.

Gallacher, Patrick J., ed. *The Cloud of Unknowing.* Kalamazoo, MI: Medieval Institute Publications, 1997.

Hamman, Grace. "Julian of Norwich's Children: Childhood and Meekness in *A Revelation of Love.*" *Journal of Medieval and Early Modern Studies* 49, no. 1 (2019): 169–91.

Hanna, Ralph, and Sarah Wood, eds. *Richard Morris's The Prick of Conscience.* Oxford: Pub. for the Early English Text Society by Oxford University Press, 2013.

Hatt, Cecilia. *God and the* Gawain-*Poet: Theology and Genre in* Pearl, Cleanness, Patience, *and* Sir Gawain and the Green Knight. Cambridge: D.S. Brewer, 2015.

Johnson, Lynn Staley. *The Voice of the* Gawain-*Poet.* Madison: University of Wisconsin Press, 1984.

Julian of Norwich. *The Writings of Julian of Norwich: A Vision Showed to a Devout Woman and A Revelation of Love.* Ed. Nicholas Watson and Jacqueline Jenkins. University Park: Pennsylvania State University Press, 2006.

Kamowski, William. *"Saint Erkenwald* and the Inadvertent Baptism: An Orthodox Response to Heterodox Ecclesiology." *Religion and Literature* 27, no. 3 (1995): 5–27.

Keiser, Elizabeth. *Courtly Desire and Medieval Homophobia: The Legitimation of Sexual Pleasure in* Cleanness *and Its Contexts.* New Haven, CT: Yale University Press, 1997.

McAlindon, T. "Hagiography into Art: A Study of *St. Erkenwald." Studies in Philology* 67, no. 4 (1970): 472–94.

Morgan, Gerald. "The Validity of Gawain's Confession in *Sir Gawain and the Green Knight." Review of English Studies* 36, no. 141 (1985): 1–18.

Peterson, Clifford, ed. *Saint Erkenwald.* Philadelphia: University of Pennsylvania Press, 1977.

Prior, Sandra Pierson. *The Fayre Formez of the* Pearl-*Poet.* East Lansing: Michigan State Press, 1996.

Rhodes, Jim. *Poetry Does Theology: Chaucer, Grosseteste, and the* Pearl-*Poet.* Notre Dame, IN: University of Notre Dame Press, 2001.

Roper, Gregory. "*Pearl,* Penitence, and the Recovery of the Self." *The Chaucer Review* 28, no. 2 (1993): 164–86.

Schmidt, A. V. C. "'Latent Content" and "The Testimony in the Text": Symbolic Meaning in *Sir Gawain and the Green Knight." Review of English Studies* 38 (1987): 145–68.

Spearing, A. C. *The Gawain-Poet: A Critical Study.* Cambridge: Cambridge University Press, 1970.

Spyra, Piotr. "*Simul iustus et peccator:* The Theological Significance of Shifts of Perspective in the Middle English *Cleanness* and *Patience." Parergon* 35, no. 1 (2018): 61–78.

Wallace, David. "*Cleanness* and the Terms of Terror." *Text and Matter: New Critical Perspectives of the* Pearl-*Poet.* Ed. Robert J. Blanch, Miriam Youngerman Miller, and Julian N. Wasserman, 93–104. Troy, NY: Whitston Publishing, 1991.

Watson, Nicholas. "The *Gawain*-Poet as a Vernacular Theologian." *A Companion to the* Gawain-*Poet.* Ed. Derek Brewer and Jonathan Gibson, 293–313. Cambridge: D.S. Brewer, 1997.

PART III

Receptions

Chapter Twelve

The Illustrations in London, British Library, MS Cotton Nero A.x (Part 2)

Joel Fredell

The poems of Cotton Nero A.x have long been recognized as exceptional works of the highest importance. The same cannot be said about the striking program of miniatures accompanying the poems. Twelve miniatures, all but one of them full-page, illustrate the four poems: four each for *Pearl* and *Sir Gawain and the Green Knight* (hereafter *SGGK*), two each for *Patience* and *Cleanness*.[1] Over many years these miniatures have been given little more than derogatory attention.[2] More recently a consensus has emerged that these illustrations, when understood on their own terms, offer much to the poems' readers and join a tiny cluster of Middle English romance poems given programs of illustrations.[3] Although we cannot be certain that the miniaturist worked with the scribe, or even produced these drawings at the same time or in the same place, their sheer number and complexity provide the fullest contemporary response we could hope to have for these masterful poems.

Cotton Nero A.x's codicology indicates that the illustrations were completed after the scribe's work, probably after the quires had been loosely sewn or even after the book had been bound.[4] The position of the miniatures within the manuscript shows clear signs that they were additions after the completion of the poetic texts. The illustrations for *Pearl* appear before that poem's opening, on a bifolium (a sheet folded to create two folia or four pages) separate from the rest of the manuscript quire structures and so probably inserted later; the remaining illustrations apparently take advantage of blank folios left at the end of each poem.[5] Multispectral imaging has further complicated our understanding of their creation: the drawings under the paint may have been meant to stand alone rather than serve as guidelines for the application of colors. What we can say at this point is that the line drawings visible through the paint present the nuanced response of a single contemporary decorator who has read the poems or at least had them explained, whereas the paint now visible might be the work of one or more later hands.[6]

The most precise dating for Cotton Nero A.x comes from these illustrations nonetheless: the miniatures probably date from the first two decades of the fifteenth century, after the manuscript's text was produced, given costume features such as the women's *houppelande* dresses in the miniatures.[7] Where the miniatures were produced is less clear. The manuscript and the miniatures are undoubtedly from the north of England, based on the scribe's dialect and the style of the illustration. A more precise location for the miniaturist is difficult. The manuscript has long been thought to be connected with, and possibly produced in, the county of Cheshire, though that association has been vigorously disputed in recent years.[8] Another possible connection is with Yorkshire, particularly given the devotional focus that features prominently in the poems. Unlike Cheshire, several illustrated devotional manuscripts have a well-established provenance in the city of York during this period, such as the Bolton hours, a deluxe book produced in York around 1420 for John Bolton, merchant, MP, and Mayor of York.[9] A large body of deluxe liturgical manuscripts firmly given York provenance in this period share many decorative features with Cotton Nero A.x.[10] In terms of illustrations a clutch of figures in York miniatures have a feature called "currant eyes," that occur in these illuminations from the early fifteenth century: black dots for the eyes usually hanging from curved lines indicating the upper eyelid. Although this detail might seem commonplace, the standard mode in this period is to indicate an eye socket and iris. More broadly, Northern figure drawings regularly include elongated bodies and hands, odd plant forms that look like they have been adapted from the abstracted forms of border decoration, and striking greens in their palettes. The figures in the Cotton Nero A.x miniatures exhibit these features consistently (see figure 12.1).[11] A collection of historical texts probably produced in York, including one on the building of the city of York, includes miniatures that share a number of features with Cotton Nero A.x, particularly in figure, gesture, palette, currant eyes, and the peculiar rendering of trees and shrubs (figure 12.2).[12] The Cotton Nero A.x illustrations may be crude by the standards of London and the International Style, but they are nonetheless skilled work much like the miniatures in the Bolton Hours, with skillful drapery, use of space, and coloring among their many virtues. These miniatures survive in concert with elaborate and clearly professional penwork initials throughout Cotton Nero A.x. In the north of England no real contenders for this kind of decoration present themselves outside of Durham, whose house style in the same period is well-documented and quite different from that of Cotton Nero

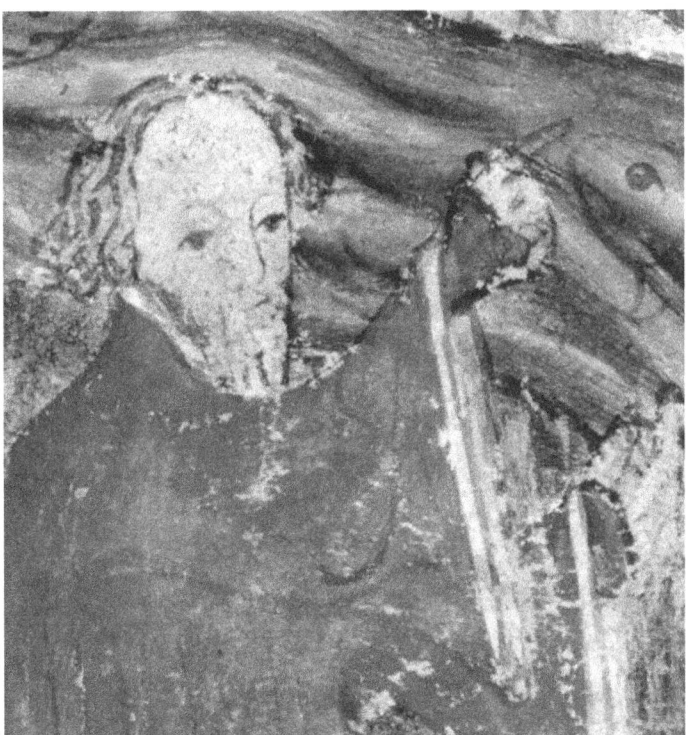

Figure 12.1. London, British Library, MS Cotton Nero A.x, fol. 38/42r detail. © The British Library Board.

A.x.[13] According to the current state of our knowledge, York is the most likely venue for the decoration, at least, of Cotton Nero A.x.

Whatever the provenance of the manuscript or its decorations, most of the interest in Cotton Nero A.x's illustrations comes from their response to the poems. The four miniatures for *Pearl* (fols. 41r–42v) present a coherent sequence of major moments from the poem. The first miniature finds the Dreamer asleep with his hood off in a garden or bower whose meadow of flowers is overspread with water (figure 12.3). Our narrator is firmly planted in a dream-vision landscape that we view at an angle from the right; both the landscape itself and the Dreamer's perspective on that landscape will shift dramatically across the sequence of miniatures, echoing the psychological journey of the grieving Dreamer in the poem. No "crystal klyffes" or "bolles as blwe as ble of Ynde [tree trunks as blue as indigo of India] (*Pearl*, ll. 74, 76) appear to create an exotic atmosphere, but the watery expanse in front of the dreamer is confusing and mysterious. The dark flow over grass and flowers appears to be outlined in the original underdrawing, mimicking the shape of the Dreamer's prone body closely as if to contain that body.[14] Another possibility is that the water indicates Pearl's grave, since the hands of the

Figure 12.2. London, British Library, MS Harley 1808, fol. 45v. © The British Library Board.

Figure 12.3. London, British Library, MS Cotton Nero A.x, fol. 37/41r. © The British Library Board.

prostrate Dreamer reach out toward it.[15] In any case, that grave-like pool
will gradually become a version of the river Jordan, a potent symbol of the
Dreamer's separation from Pearl and the consolations of the New Jerusalem.

The second miniature rotates the image plane about ninety degrees so that
the observer now sees the Dreamer from the left (figure 12.4). Several other
changes are apparent as well: the Dreamer no longer wears his blue hood, the

Figure 12.4. London, British Library, MS Cotton Nero A.x. fol. 37/41v. © The British
Library Board.

undersleeves of his robes have changed from white to blue, but most notably the Dreamer now stands and gestures up (toward Pearl?) and down (toward the river?) with his right and left hands respectively, while the watery expanse has become a stream occupied by a large fish, flowing from the lower left and taking over all the lower right quadrant of the miniature with no other bank to be seen. The Dreamer, who in the poem has been walking alongside the stream, now has arrived where "the water was depe, I dorst not wade" (*Pearl*, l. 143). On the facing recto the third miniature rotates another ninety degrees to reveal Pearl on the opposite side of the river in a garden landscape very similar to the Dreamer's surroundings (figure 12.5).

The river now is crowded with fish, the Dreamer much smaller in the image frame. Stunned, his right hand points directly across at Pearl in the upper right corner. Pearl herself wears a golden crown and white dress, framed by small trees but barely anchored in that landscape, her hands raised in greeting. In the final miniature the Maiden, positioned closer to the center, stands behind a wall before a vision of New Jerusalem, gesturing across the river toward the Dreamer. The Dreamer raises both hands and tilts his head to gaze upward at this vision (figure 12.6).

As will become apparent, the miniatures for all the Cotton Nero A.x poems do not attempt to summarize the texts they illustrate. In *Pearl*, the first three miniatures illustrate only moments up to line 240 in a poem of 1212 lines, and leave out entirely the exemplary parable of the Vineyard that Pearl recounts in the long dialogue with the Dreamer. Yet, the content and the visual design of the scenes represented here emphasize the psychological journey and shifting viewpoint of the narrator quite literally in the spiraling perspectives, the developing boundary between earthly and celestial life, and the final upward tilt of his vision toward Heaven. *Pearl* takes its Dreamer and its reader into a realm of misunderstandings and misinterpretations that finally expel both from a visionary world across a boundary never to be crossed in this life; the miniatures echo those larger movements.[16]

The next two poems, *Cleanness* and *Patience*, are given more limited illustration, but again the thematic strategies contained in these miniatures offer profound readings of their texts.[17] The first miniature in *Cleanness* shows Noah and the ark at the moment when it is being tossed in raging seas.[18] Noah and his family hold on to the mast and the boat as one son holds an oar in the swirling waters, where a large fish swallows a smaller fish and the water resembles closely the stream from the later *Pearl* miniatures. Noah's wife instead holds Noah's shoulder, pointing to the water and possibly the predator fish (figure 12.7).

The second miniature features Daniel kneeling before Belshazzar and his queen, who also rests her hand on the shoulder of her husband. On the banquet table before them are the vessels taken from the Temple of Solomon;

Figure 12.5. London, British Library, MS Cotton Nero A.x. fol. 38/42r. © The British Library Board.

Figure 12.6. London, British Library, MS Cotton Nero A.x. fol. 38/42v. © The British Library Board.

Figure 12.7. London, British Library, MS Cotton Nero A.x. fol.56/60r. © The British Library Board.

Belshazzar points to Daniel and gestures to the writing on the wall, here presented in a scroll running vertically (figure 12.8). The coloring is more selective, highlighting the three figures, the vessels, and the cuff of the writing hand but not the table or scroll. The central story of Sodom and Gomorrah narrated in *Cleanness* is not illustrated. All three exempla in the text examine a long cleansing directed by a vengeful God. What remains after the destruction of Sodom and Gomorrah is a lifeless and unnatural sea, an image that does not fit the thematic patterns of the Cotton Nero A.x illustrator. The other two exempla, which are illustrated, offer a typology of potential salvation within the flow of sacred history, better aligned with the larger themes of the collection of poems in the manuscript.

Patience also includes two miniatures visually linked to earlier illustrations, again selected from early and later incidents in the narrative of Jonah but leaving out the central voyage in the belly of a whale. In the first miniature a sailor feeds Jonah to the whale as a second sailor holds his oar in the water to guide the ship in the storm; in design and execution both the oarsman and the predatory sea creature provide strong parallels with the Noah illustration for *Cleanness*. Also notable is the block of text at the top of the page concluding the poem, the only case in Cotton Nero A.x where the illustrator used a partial page (figure 12.9). The second miniature returns Jonah to land and a walled city reminiscent of *Pearl*'s New Jerusalem, where Jonah prophecies to the people of Nineveh (figure 12.10). As in the diptych for *Cleanness*, the miniatures for *Patience* emphasize a typology of salvation and forgiveness more directly than the text, which ends with Jonah's ongoing defiance and God's withering of Jonah's honeysuckle bower.

The most famous miniatures in Cotton Nero A.x join those of *Pearl* to bookend the manuscript with four images. They do not include crucial visual symbols from the poem such as the pentangle on Gawain's shield or the green belt Gawain wears upon his return to Camelot; they render Gawain in diminishing size as the sequence goes on. However, they do offer well-chosen moments from the poem. The first miniature, serving as a frontispiece for *SGGK*, alone in Cotton Nero A.x includes a narrative sequence: Gawain is shown holding the ax both at the banquet table in the upper left corner before the confrontation and the lower right corner after he has beheaded the Green Knight (figure 12.11). Arthur and another knight have their swords drawn; Guinevere stands slightly behind Arthur; the banquet table itself has two items colored in gold, recalling Belshazzar's feast in *Cleanness*. The striking image at the center of the miniature is the Green Knight's severed head and blond locks, held aloft by the mounted body of the Green Knight and bleeding from the neck.[19] The second miniature, grouped with the remaining two at the

Figure 12.8. London, British Library, MS Cotton Nero A.x. fol. 56/60v. © The British Library Board.

Figure 12.9. London, British Library, MS Cotton Nero A.x. fol. 82/86r. © The British Library Board.

Figure 12.10. London, British Library, MS Cotton Nero A.x. fol. 82/86v. © The British Library Board.

Figure 12.11. London, British Library, MS Cotton Nero A.x. fol. 90/94v. © The British Library Board.

end of the manuscript, jumps to the third section of the poem and also moves from public to private: Gawain, asleep in a curtained bed, is tickled under the chin by the hostess in a polka-dot gown and jeweled hair net (figure 12.12).

Since her robe is modest rather than revealing the miniature may refer to the first encounter. Gawain himself appears to be naked and easily bound by

Figure 12.12. London, British Library, MS Cotton Nero A.x. fol. 125/129r. © The British Library Board.

the bedclothes. A couplet above the miniature, written in a script different from the textura in the main text, may have been added later.[20] In the third miniature Gawain meets the Green Knight at the Green Chapel, a dark hole in the lower left corner whose grave-like qualities recall the dark patch next to the Dreamer in the first *Pearl* miniature (figure 12.13).

Figure 12.13. London, British Library, MS Cotton Nero A.x. fol. 125/129v. © The British Library Board.

The landscape is notably dark, but its plant forms recall the natural world depicted in the *Pearl* sequence. Throughout the *Gawain* sequence reds and greens dominate the illumination, appropriate to the poem's thematic color scheme. In this miniature red highlights on Gawain's dress, spear, and tack emerge strongly from the austere green background. To end the sequence and the program of miniatures as a whole, Gawain's return to Camelot is framed by an archway without other interior detail (figure 12.14).

Both Arthur and Guinevere appear to be holding golden gifts, and the kneeling Gawain accepts one from Arthur's hands. The illustrations of Gawain's public identity at Camelot bookend his private experiences, but

Figure 12.14. London, British Library, MS Cotton Nero A.x. fol. 126/130r. © The British Library Board.

the balance does not extend to the coloring: the private experiences leap off the page thanks to the sheer intensity of the paints in succeeding bright and dark hues.

The *Gawain* miniature sequence taken as a whole equals the success of the *Pearl* sequence in the development of a visual narrative that communicates not just the physical and psychological stages of their journeys, but crucial concerns of the poems about spiritual life in the fallen world. Gawain's return to an earthly home is presented as a more joyful scene than the Dreamer's unreachable New Jerusalem; his series of confrontations form a circle from courtly public to profound privacy to court again, a movement that is both heroic and humbling. Yet Gawain, like *Pearl*'s Dreamer, never crosses any water in text or illustration. The resolution of Gawain's test closes the anthology of poems in Cotton Nero A.x. This final set of miniatures argues that the decorators understood *SGGK* to be more than a romance attached to three devotional texts: *SGGK* is a vital part of the larger program of miniatures and the larger concerns of the anthology itself. All four poems of Cotton Nero A.x examine the loss of perfection and the willingness to return to the conditions of the fallen world despite the shame of individual sin. The illustrations examine spiritual tests and spiritual boundaries in visual terms that echo among all twelve miniatures and offer a penitential reading of these four poems with a perspective close in time and place to the poet (or poets). Whatever we may think about the northern style of illustration in comparison to the elaborate work dominating the book trade in London during the same period, this program of miniatures documents a serious reading of poems whose literary value remains ineffable.

NOTES

1. An ongoing problem for scholars is two different sets of folio numbers on the pages of Cotton Nero A.x: an earlier ink foliation and a later pencil foliation. This study will use the later pencil foliation in the notes below.

2. This tradition begins with the dismissal of the illustrations as "certainly of crude workmanship" in Israel Gollancz's introduction to *Pearl, Cleanness, Patience and Sir Gawain: Reproduced in Facsimile from the Unique Ms. Cotton Nero A.x in the British Museum; With Introduction*, EETS, O.S. 162 (London: Oxford University Press, 1923), 9; this judgment was codified by R. S. and Laura Loomis in *Arthurian Legends in Medieval Art* (New York: MLA, 1938), 138, who proclaim that the Cotton Nero A.x illustrations represent the "nadir of English illustrative art."

3. See Jennifer A. Lee, "The Illuminating Critic: The Illustrator of Cotton Nero A.x," *Studies in Iconography* 3 (1977): 17–46; Sarah Horall, "Notes on British Library, MS Cotton Nero A.x.," *Manuscripta* 30 (1986): 191–98; Kathleen Scott, *Later Gothic Manuscripts: 1390–1490*, 2 vols. (London: Harvey Miller, 1996) 1.10,

2.67; Paul F. Reichardt, "'Several Illuminations, Coarsely Executed': The Illustrations of the Pearl Manuscript," *Studies in Iconography* 18 (1997): 119–42; A. S. G. Edwards, "The Manuscript: British Library Cotton Nero A.x" in *A Companion to the Gawain-Poet*, ed. Derek Brewer and Jonathan Gibson (Cambridge: D.S. Brewer, 1997), 202–19; and four articles by Maidie Hilmo: "The Image Controversies in Late Medieval England and the Visual Prefaces and Epilogues in the Pearl Manuscript: Creating a Meta-Narrative of the Spiritual Journey to the New Jerusalem," *Studies in Medieval and Renaissance History* 3, no. 1 (2001): 1–40; *Medieval Images, Icons, and Illustrated English Literary Texts: From the Ruthwell Cross to the Ellesmere Chaucer* (Aldershot: Ashgate, 2004), 138–59; "The Power of Images in the Auchinleck, Vernon, Pearl, and Two *Piers Plowman* Manuscripts," in *Opening Up Middle English Manuscripts: Literary and Visual Approaches*, ed. Kathryn Kerby-Fulton, Maidie Hilmo, and Linda Olson (Ithaca, NY: Cornell University Press, 2012), 153–205; "Did the Scribe Draw the Miniatures in British Library, MS Cotton Nero A.x (the Pearl-Gawain Manuscript)?," *Journal of the Early Book Society* 20 (2017): 111–36. Only two other Middle English manuscripts containing verse romances survive with miniature programs: the substantially earlier (c. 1340) Auchinleck and c. 1400 Bodley 264 pt. 2 (ff 209–15v); see further Edwards, "The Manuscript," 210.

4. See Horrall, "Notes," 192, for the distinction and an argument for the former.

5. The *Pearl* bifolium (fols. 41r–42v) shows no sign that it was ruled for text or otherwise included before its use for the miniatures. Other folia with illustrations (fols. 60r–v, 82r–v, 94v, 129r–130r) contain evidence of earlier scribal ruling and offsets from wet ink that support a later and separate production of the miniatures, possibly for a new owner. See the discussion by Edwards, "The Manuscript," 213–218.

6. Murray McGillivray and Christina Duffy, "New Light on the *Sir Gawain and the Green Knight* Manuscript: Multispectral Imaging and the Cotton Nero A.x. Illustrations," *Speculum* 92 (2017): 110–44. Also see Hilmo, "Scribe," 111–36; Hilmo, 119, cites without reference the opinion of Jane Roberts that the writing on the scroll in the miniature on f. 60r resembles the display script of the scribe. A forthcoming article by Hilmo will argue that the ink gall underdrawings for the illustrations were in the same ink as that of the text.

7. A. I. Doyle, "The Manuscripts," in *Middle English Alliterative Poetry and Its Literary Background: Seven Essays*, ed. David Lawton (Cambridge: Cambridge University Press, 1982), 92.

8. Ad Putter and Myra Stokes, "The *Linguistic Atlas* and the Dialect of the *Gawain* Poems," *Journal of English and Germanic Philology* (2007): 468–91; their evidence directly contradicts the longstanding assumption that the linguistic evidence for Cotton Nero A.x is a settled question. On the Cheshire identification see also in this volume Ethan Campbell, "Authorship: What Does the *Pearl*-Poet Tell Us about Himself?" On the possibility of a Yorkshire provenance for Cotton Nero A.x based on decoration see Joel Fredell, "The Pearl-Poet Manuscript in York," *Studies in the Age of Chaucer* 36 (2014): 1–36; and, in this volume, David K. Coley, "The Northwest Midlands and the Ricardian Court."

9. On the Bolton Hours (York, Minster Library, MS Add. 2), see most recently Anneke Mulder-Bakke and Jocelyn Wogan-Browne, eds., *The Bolton Hours of York:*

Female Domestic Piety and the Public Sphere (Turnhout: Brepols, 2005); Felicity Riddy and Sarah Rees Jones, "Female Domestic Piety and the Public Sphere: The Bolton Hours of York," in *Women and the Christian Tradition*, ed. Anneke Mulder-Bakke and Jocelyn Wogan-Browne (Turnhout: Brepols, 2006) 215–30; and Sarah Rees Jones, "Richard Scrope, the Bolton Hours and the Church of St Martin in Micklegate: Reconstructing a Holy Neighbourhood in Later Medieval York," in *Richard Scrope, Archbishop and Martyr*, ed. P. J. P. Goldberg (Donington: Shaun Tyas, 2007), 214–36.

10. Scott, *Later Gothic Manuscripts*, 2.119–21, identifies five major illuminated manuscripts ca. 1400 with a definite York provenance and shared decorative features: Boulogne-sur-Mer, Bibliothéque Municipale, MS 93, fols. 1–41v (#7) 2.37–9; Brussels, Bibliothéque Royale MS 4862–4869a (#24), 2.97–8; Cambridge, Trinity College, MS O.3.10 (#32) 2.117–9; Dublin, Trinity College MS 83, 2.38; York, Minster Library, MS Add. 2 (Bolton Hours, #33). John Friedman, *Northern English Books, Owners, and Makers in the Late Middle Ages* (Syracuse, NY: Syracuse University Press, 1995), 108–47, examines a larger but overlapping group of manuscripts using a much broader regional perspective; also see 237–54 for a useful list of northern manuscripts, though details should be treated with caution.

11. See, for example, the Bolton Hours miniature at https://hoaportal.york.ac.uk/hoaportal/yml1414image.jsp?id=46&figure=2. Other examples among the many northern manuscripts which testify to these features are York, Minster Library, MS XVI.K. 6, f. 108v; Cambridge, MA, Harvard University Library, MS Widener 1, f. 67v; Cambridge, Trinity College MS O.3.10 f. 52r; and Oxford, Bodleian Library, MS Gough Liturgies 1, f. 11v.

12. Scott, *Later Gothic Manuscripts*, 2.67, offers a short list of miniatures similar in style to those in Cotton Nero.

13. See Friedman, *Northern English Books, Owners, and Makers*, 208–15, on manuscripts decorated by the Durham master.

14. See McGillivray, "New Light on the *Sir Gawain and the Green Knight* Manuscript," 114 and fig. 2; Hilmo, "Scribe," 113–21.

15. Hilmo, "Visual Narratives," 148; Hilmo, "Power of Images," 173–76.

16. Also see in this volume the discussion on *Pearl*'s large-scale narrative movement by Jane Beal, "'Out of Oryent': The Dreamer's Contemplative Experience of the *Mappamundi* in the Middle English *Pearl*."

17. For a typological reading of these two sets of miniatures see Hilmo, "Power of Images," 179–183.

18. Edwards, "The Manuscript," 210–13, notes two contradictions between text and image in this miniature: *Cleanness* specifies eight figures in Noah's ark, but the miniature contains only seven; *Cleanness* emphasizes the ark's lack of human control by saying it had no tiller or oar, but the miniature features an oar prominently.

19. The Green Knight's blonde locks, which seem to violate the poem's description, are not as distinctive in context: all the figures in the illustrations are given blonde hair, as Hilmo, "Scribe," 124, notes. More importantly, Hilmo points out that the Green Knight's painted hair obscures an original underdrawing that includes a crown of leaves on his head.

20. The text of this display script reads: "Mi minde is mukul on on þ[at] wil me noȝt amende/ Sum time was trewe as ston & fro schame couþe hir defende" [My mind is much on one that will not amende me/ At one time she was as true as stone and could defend me from shame]. Gollancz, *Pearl*, xlvii–xlviii, speculates that these lines are a personal outburst by the *Pearl*-poet. Edwards, "The Manuscript," 213–18, argues that these lines are a later addition since the evidence strongly indicates that the images were added after the text.

BIBLIOGRAPHY

Beal, Jane. *Becoming the Pearl-Poet: Perceptions, Connections, Receptions*. New York: Lexington Books, 2022.

———. "The Dreamer's Contemplative Experience of the *Mappamundi* in Pearl." In *Becoming the Pearl-Poet*, edited by Jean Beal, 13–35. Lanham, MD: Lexington Books.

Campbell, Ethan. "Authorship: What Does the *Pearl*-Poet Tell Us about Himself?" In *Becoming the Pearl-Poet*, edited by Jean Beal, 107–125. Lanham, MD: Lexington Books.

Coley, David K. "The Northwest Midlands and the Ricardian Court." In *Becoming the Pearl-Poet*, edited by Jean Beal, 223–235. Lanham, MD: Lexington Books.

Doyle, A. I. "The Manuscripts." In *Middle English Alliterative Poetry and Its Literary Background: Seven Essays*, ed. David Lawton, 88–100. Cambridge: Cambridge University Press, 1982.

Edwards, A. S. G. "The Manuscript: British Library Cotton Nero A.x." In *A Companion to the Gawain-Poet*, edited by Derek Brewer and Jonathan Gibson, 202–19. Cambridge, UK: Brewer, 1997.

Fredell, Joel. "The Pearl-Poet Manuscript in York." *Studies in the Age of Chaucer* 36 (2014): 1–36.

Friedman, John. *Northern English Books, Owners, and Makers in the Late Middle Ages*. Syracuse, NY: Syracuse University Press, 1995.

Gollancz, Israel. *Pearl, Cleanness, Patience and Sir Gawain: Reproduced in Facsimile from the Unique Ms. Cotton Nero A.X in the British Museum; With Introduction*. EETS, O.S. 162. London: Oxford University Press, 1923.

Hilmo, Maidie. "The Image Controversies in Late Medieval England and the Visual Prefaces and Epilogues in the Pearl Manuscript: Creating a Meta-Narrative of the Spiritual Journey to the New Jerusalem." *Studies in Medieval and Renaissance History* 3 (2001): 1–40.

———. *Medieval Images, Icons, and Illustrated English Literary Texts: From the Ruthwell Cross to the Ellesmere Chaucer*. Aldershot: Ashgate, 2004.

———. "The Power of Images in the Auchinleck, Vernon, Pearl, and Two *Piers Plowman* Manuscripts." In *Opening Up Middle English Manuscripts: Literary and Visual Approaches*, ed. Kathryn Kerby-Fulton, Maidie Hilmo, and Linda Olson. Ithaca, NY: Cornell University Press, 2012.

———. "Did the Scribe Draw the Miniatures in British Library, MS Cotton Nero A.x (the Pearl-Gawain Manuscript)?" *Journal of the Early Book Society* 20 (2017): 111–36.

Horall, Sarah. "Notes on British Library, MS Cotton Nero A x." *Manuscripta* 30 (1986): 191–98.

Jones, Sarah Rees. "Richard Scrope, the Bolton Hours and the Church of St Martin in Micklegate: Reconstructing a Holy Neighbourhood in Later Medieval York." In *Richard Scrope, Archbishop and Martyr*, ed. P. J. P. Goldberg, 214–36. Donington: Shaun Tyas, 2007.

Lee, Jennifer A. "The Illuminating Critic: The Illustrator of Cotton Nero A.x." *Studies in Iconography* 3 (1977): 17–46.

Loomis, R. S., and Laura Loomis. *Arthurian Legends in Medieval Art*. New York: MLA, 1938.

McGillivray, Murray, and Christina Duffy. "New Light on the *Sir Gawain and the Green Knight* Manuscript: Multispectral Imaging and the Cotton Nero A.x. Illustrations." *Speculum* 92 (2017): 110–44.

Mulder-Bakke, Anneke, and Jocelyn Wogan-Browne, eds. *The Bolton Hours of York: Female Domestic Piety and the Public Sphere*. Turnhout: Brepols, 2005.

Putter, Ad, and Myra Stokes. "The *Linguistic Atlas* and the Dialect of the *Gawain* Poems." *Journal of English and Germanic Philology* (2007): 468–91.

Reichardt, Paul F. "'Several Illuminations, Coarsely Executed': The Illustrations of the Pearl Manuscript." *Studies in Iconography* 18 (1997): 119–42.

Riddy, Felicity, and Sarah Rees Jones. "Female Domestic Piety and the Public Sphere: The Bolton Hours of York." In *Women and the Christian Tradition*, ed. Anneke Mulder-Bakke and Jocelyn Wogan-Browne. Turnhout: Brepols, 2006.

Scott, Kathleen. *Later Gothic Manuscripts: 1390–1490*. 2 vols. London: Harvey Miller, 1996.

Chapter Thirteen

The Northwest Midlands
and the Ricardian Court

David K. Coley

Among the many critical puzzles surrounding the four poems of MS Cotton Nero A.x—authorial and poetic identity; composition dates; contemporary reception—the linked issues of geographical and dialectical provenance have long seemed the most solvable, or at least the most settled. Even before considering dialect, Sir Gawain's elliptical peregrination from Arthur's court across "Norþe Walez," past Anglesey, through "þe wyldrenesse of Wyrale" and into southern Yorkshire suggests that *Sir Gawain and the Green Knight* was written by a poet with strong ties to the Northwest Midlands and the northern Welsh borderlands.[1] *Pearl*'s dreamscape, too, with its steep "crystal klyffez" (*Pe*. 74), sweeping river, and "Holtewodez bryȝt"[2] seems to draw from similar landscapes, transforming England's rugged Peak District into the dazzling, jagged liminal space of the Jeweler's vision. The works' regionally inflected landscapes have been reinforced by the poet's dialect, which the authors of *The Linguistic Atlas of Late Medieval English* (*LALME*) suggest is from "a very small area either in SE Cheshire or just over the border in NE Staffordshire," near the uplands of the Southern Pennine Chain.[3] Taken together, such considerations have encouraged Michael Bennett, arguably the most prominent historian of the Northwest Midlands, to describe late-medieval Cheshire and Lancashire as "the little world . . . in which the author of *Sir Gawain and the Green Knight* and his patrons were rooted," an assessment that has gone virtually unquestioned for most of the poems' recent critical history.[4]

This chapter will begin by considering the poems' putative Northwest Midlands provenance, especially *Sir Gawain and the Green Knight* and *Pearl*, the two works most implicated in the region's overlapping spheres of seigneurial power, military careerism, and literary patronage. It will then address several recent challenges to the so-called Cheshire hypothesis and, in so doing, attend to the critical possibilities that open when we decenter the poems of Cotton Nero A.x from a region long considered their first textual environment.[5]

CHESHIRE, RICHARD, AND THE *GAWAIN*-POET

Sir Gawain and the Green Knight

The social and seigneurial mores that are central to *Sir Gawain and the Green Knight* can hardly be in doubt. Its detailed scenes of game and feast, breathless depictions of contemporary aristocratic clothing, nuanced accounts of courtly "luf-talkyng,"[6] and pervasive concern with chivalric behavior suggest that it was composed for a decidedly aristocratic audience, one that might see itself favorably reflected in the glistening halls of Camelot and Hautdesert. In an influential monograph, A. C. Spearing refers to Sir Gawain's Camelot as "an innocent version of the ideal aimed at by any of the great courts of Western Europe in the later Middle Ages,"[7] and the subtle distinctions between Arthur's legendary court and Bertilak's—distinctions that would have been particularly legible to readers steeped in courtly life—have been variously understood as revealing the divisions between royal center and provincial margin,[8] indicating the links between regional identity and imperial aggression,[9] challenging the legitimacy of a nascent British imperialism,[10] and marking a temporal rift between pre- and post-plague socioeconomic patterns.[11] And yet, as Bennett has shown, the Northwest Midlands could not boast the opportunities for landed aristocratic patronage that might be expected for a poem like *Sir Gawain and the Green Knight*, a detail that would initially seem to trouble the assignment of Cotton Nero A.x to the region. The works of the *Gawain*-poet, Bennett concludes, demand "a far more courtly and cosmopolitan milieu than the Northwest alone provided."[12]

What the Northwest Midlands *could* boast in the closing two decades of the fourteenth century—and this was particularly true of Cheshire itself—was an increasingly close relationship with Richard II, one that culminated in 1397 when the still-ascendant king elevated the county palatinate of Chester to the status of principality and styled himself its prince. Richard's affinity for Cheshire, as well as his sustained exploitation of its human and military resources, became one of the defining features of its political economy in the late fourteenth century. Already militarized due to its position near the Welsh border, Cheshire became Richard's favored recruiting ground not only for international military incursions (a habit he seems to have carried forward from his father, the Black Prince)[13] but also for developing his own national power base. Throughout the late 1380s and up to the point of his deposition in 1399, Richard increasingly relied on his Cheshire favorites, drawing heavily from the region during his unsuccessful 1387 attempt to resist the appellants at Radcot Bridge,[14] employing significant numbers of Cheshiremen in his Irish expeditions,[15] and gathering around him a personal retinue of badged loyalists from the region, including his notorious personal bodyguard of Cheshire archers.[16]

For the king's detractors, this relationship with Cheshire was suspect, even damning: the Lancastrian partisan Thomas Walsingham, for one, recounts that Richard's "bestial" entourage of Cheshiremen "regarded only the King as their equal, treating everybody else, however powerful and noble he was, with contempt"; the more sympathetic Dieulacres Chronicler recalls that by wearing the "royal badge of the white hart resplendent," Richard's Cheshire followers caused the king to be "held in fatal odium by his ordinary sub- jects."[17] For Cheshire's regional economy, however, Richard's patronage both crystalized and accelerated patterns of military careerism that had developed during Edward I's colonization of Wales a century earlier. The patronage and political favor that Richard offered to Cheshire, as well as the economic and in-kind benefits that accrued it, amounted to "an unprecedented build up of royal power in one county."[18]

If Cheshire itself was itself unlikely to provide the modes of courtly patronage that would engender a poem like *Sir Gawain and the Green Knight*, could the poet have been one of the many Cheshire transplants who accompanied Richard in Westminster and on his progress around England? This is the hypothesis advanced by Bennett, and it has enabled literary crit- ics to revaluate a poem once viewed as the eccentric production of some isolated northern genius, untroubled by the cosmopolitan concerns evident in other fourteenth-century works. Indeed, the poem's vision of Camelot itself, decked with "tars tapites innoghe / Þat were enbrawded and beten wyth þe best gemmes"[19] and inhabited by "Þe most kyd knyȝtez . . . / And þe loue- lokkest ladies"[20] resonates with a royal court noted for its lavish continental style, sumptuous banquets, and great tournaments.[21] Likewise, the poem's description of a "sumquat childgered"[22] Arthur, flush with "his ȝonge blod and his brayn wylde,"[23] recalls the youthful Richard from paintings like the Wilton Diptych and the Westminster Abbey Portrait: a "fair-haired [king] with a pale complexion and a rounded, feminine face," a ruler "capricious in his behaviour . . . prodigious with gifts, [and] extravagantly ostentatious in his dress and pastimes."[24] Particularly through the retrospective lens of Lancastrian propaganda, it is possible to detect a hint of anti-Ricardian satire in the poem's depiction of the young Arthur;[25] however, if Bennett's hypothesis holds true, it seems more likely that such details, while not entirely uncritical, are a knowing nod to the courtly extravagance deployed by Richard in glorifying his reign.[26]

If Richard's royal court is legible in Arthur's Camelot, then the broader physical and courtly geography of *Sir Gawain and the Green Knight* provides similar glimpses of the poet's regionalized world and the tensions within it. Separated from Arthur's court by a monster-infested wilderness, Bertilak's court of Hautdesert offers a provincial alternative to Camelot's royal nexus, one equally steeped in luxury and ritualized behavior but animated by economic and social systems that diverge from Arthur's centralized feudal realm. As Christine Chism has articulated, the subtle misfits between Camelot and Hautdesert reflect conflicts "between a royal court becoming increasingly alienated from traditional seigneurial modes of chivalry and a conservative and insecure provincial gentry, whose status, livelihoods, and careers were increasingly coming to depend on careers at the royal court."[27] That careerism is precisely what accelerated Richard's increased patronage of Cheshire in the later years of his rule: Gawain's errant progress in both courts suggests, at the very least, the difficulties of navigating the shoals between capital and province, both for the courtier and, perhaps, for the court poet. So too might social differences between the women of the courts—Camelot's passive Guinevere; Hautdesert's agential lady and powerful Morgan le Fay—suggest important regional distinctions. Indeed, within the careerist economy of the Northwest Midlands, where men frequently engaged in military action away from home, women often found themselves in positions of pronounced social and economic power, a situation mirrored in Hautdesert's more fluid gender roles.[28]

Casting a still wider regional net, *Sir Gawain and the Green Knight* may also implicate the English colonial project in Wales, a project with which Cheshire, a militarized border county, was closely associated. With remarkable exactitude, Gawain's "anious uyage"[29] in Fitt 2 takes the knight first into and then seemingly out of North Wales, a route that encompasses several identifiable landmarks and geographic features: Anglesey,[30] the Wirral between the Dee and Mersey rivers,[31] and the coastal areas of Conwy and Clwyd.[32] Wales in the late fourteenth century was outwardly at peace with its colonizing neighbor, enjoying a lull between the thirteenth-century revolts against Edward I and the fifteenth-century Glyn Dŵr rebellion. Nonetheless, tensions between England and Wales simmered throughout the late fourteenth century, and Richard's extensive travel within the country,[33] as well as the occasional financial subsidies that he levied on the Welsh,[34] ensured that English colonial ambitions in Wales were not out of sight during his reign. By sublimating the violence of the Green Knight's beheading into a series of ludic exchanges between a royal emissary and a hinterland demesne, *Sir Gawain and the Green Knight* implies a vision of Anglo-Welsh colonialism wherein, as Patricia Ingham suggests, "colonial union becomes an act of cultural synchronicity," a model of harmonious coexistence and mutually informing contact.[35] Such a vision, however, provides glib poetic cover for the subjugation of Wales and the exploitation of its resources, providing "a self-congratulatory perspective on England" that implicitly promoted England's colonial stance.[36]

Pearl

An enigmatic romance staging the collision of two divergent courts in an identifiably Northwest Midlands landscape, *Sir Gawain and the Green Knight* practically begs to be read against its complex regional and regnal affinities. By contrast, the first of the four poems bound in Cotton Nero A.x, a ravishing meditation on loss and salvation rendered through the visionary experience of a grieving jeweler, initially seems to resist such regionally and politically inflected analyses. Indeed, its intricate formal poetics, aesthetic beauty, and investment in the "eternal" have long made *Pearl* a darling of the New Criticism, while its unvarnished Christian didacticism has endeared it to exegetically minded critics as well.[37] Following Bennett's study however, *Pearl* has found itself situated amidst the same cultural and regional currents as *Sir Gawain and the Green Knight*, emerging neither as a generically "Christian" devotional work nor a generically "medieval" elegy but as the distinct product of a specific cultural and textual environment. In other words, *Pearl* may be a rarified gem of a poem, but it did not spring forth *ex nihilo*. At the end of the day, one cannot have a pearl without an oyster.

No one has done more to flesh out *Pearl*'s cultural oyster than John Bowers, who has painstakingly traced the material, institutional, and economic details that articulate the poem's position in the patronage nexus of the Ricardian court. Bowers shows how key devotional images resonate not only with medieval Christian praxis but with Richard's own personal devotional practices, as well as with the political and personal strife that wracked his kingship in the 1380s and 90s. The lamb of God, for instance, radiant in *Pearl* with its halo of "lombe-ly3t,"[38] reads as a political symbol as much as a spiritual one, "powerfully implicated not only in the English king's personal piety but also in his political dealings with the French, including the arrangements for his marriage to the child-bride Isabelle."[39] Likewise, the central image of the Pearl-Maiden "with precios perlez al vmbepy3t"[40]—a child-woman surrounded by pearls and bearing a pearl upon her breast—articulates not only the dreamer's heartbreaking personal loss and the promise of his redemption but also, if more mundanely, the admixture of bereavement, hope, and political expediency surrounding the death of Richard's first queen, Anne of Bohemia, and the arrival of the seven-year-old Isabelle of France, the king's second bride. Both were "consistently associated with pearl imagery in literary texts."[41] While the specificity of such correlations can certainly be called into question, the sheer weight of material and documentary evidence points to *Pearl*'s conscious instantiation of the intricate symbology of Richard's court.

If the courtly and even royalist dimensions of *Pearl* emerge in its pearly livery badges and imposing "mayden of menske," the simmering tensions between the aristocratic and mercantile classes likewise emerge in the figure of the Jeweler, a visionary dreamer whose social location as a merchant informs his interactions with the "debonere" Pearl-Maiden.[42] Much as *Sir Gawain and the Green Knight* limns economics defined by military careerism, *Pearl* limns the hierarchical dynamic between a restless late-medieval middle class and the entrenched hierarchies of the aristocracy to which they catered. As Helen Barr notes, the jeweler held a particularly complicated position within that hierarchy: at once included in and excluded from aristocratic culture, the jeweler "inscribe[s] a mercantile consciousness which defines the horizons of expectations for the reader/audience."[43] Within a regional center like Cheshire, which traded military and personal service to the royal affinity in exchange for economic prosperity and cultural capital, the intricacies of such relations would have taken on a heightened significance. Such tensions are underscored in the very first moments of the Dreamer's exchange with the Pearl-Maiden—the deference with which he treats her, the hostility she shows to his queries, the awe that he experiences in her presence. Locally, these moments might describe a relationship between jeweler and patron, between merchant and aristocrat; more broadly, they subtly bespeak the relationship between the poet's Northwest Midlands and a Ricardian court that had established an increasingly robust presence within it.

Cleanness, Patience, and *St. Erkenwald*

Cleanness and *Patience*, the two remaining poems in Cotton Nero A.x, and *St. Erkenwald*, which is bound in MS Harley 2250 and may share common authorship,[44] do not articulate the same rich associations with either the Ricardian court or Cheshire as *Sir Gawain and the Green Knight* and *Pearl*. Nonetheless, they too evince courtly identities that comport with those of their two better-known counterparts. *Cleanness*'s opening and closing exempla, embellished retellings of Christ's parable of the wedding feast and of Belshazzar's doomed banquet respectively, offer lavish depictions of contemporary aristocratic society that align with feast scenes in *Sir Gawain and the Green Knight*, while the poem's overbearing emphasis on physical comportment and sexual sin—what the poet calls "fylþe in fleschlych dedez"[45]—renders within the work an "aristocratised theology" that demands not introspective contemplation but rather a rote adherence to a code of outward-facing gestures.[46] Indeed, the poem's unusual embrace of heterosexual pleasure and concomitant rejection of homosexual sex work to reinforce heteronormative sexual behavior within the slippery homosocial structures of the court.[47] *Patience* likewise stages the essential courtliness of Christian devotion, prefacing its retelling of the Book of Jonah with a depiction of Christ's Beatitudes as a group of courtly ladies—"Dame Pouert, Dame Pitée, Dame Penaunce,"[48]—and explicating its titular virtue in terms of a vassal's forbearance of the demands of his "lege lorde."[49] *St. Erkenwald*, a poem that seems to bear few of the court-centered hallmarks of the other four poems discussed here, may speak to the presence of a Cheshire-poet in Richard's peripatetic retinue in different ways. While written in the same dialect as the Cotton Nero A.x poems, *St. Erkenwald* is "emphatically a London poem, written in praise of the capital's patron saint."[50] The possibility of a Northwest Midlands *Gawain*-poet removed from his "fayre regioun"[51] to the courtly circles imagined by Bennett lends credence to the possibility that a Cheshire writer could be engaged with the urban center of London.[52]

BEYOND CHESHIRE, BEYOND RICHARD

Arguments for Cotton Nero A.x's Northwest Midlands provenance have been entrenched for so long that one could be forgiven for thinking the case entirely closed on the matter. It is, thus, particularly important to conclude with some recent scholarship that points away from the "Cheshire hypothesis" and toward alternative regional and global underpinnings for the poems.

One such alternative emerges from the city of York, an important center of book production in the later Middle Ages, about ninety miles to the northeast. Joel Fredell has argued—convincingly in my opinion—that paleographical and decorative elements of the manuscript suggest that it was produced (or at least embellished) in York in the first two decades of the fifteenth century, an argument that puts pressure on the notion that the poems were products of the Northwest Midlands.[53] Fredell also calls into question the accuracy of the *LALME*'s assignment of the Cotton Nero A.x dialect to Cheshire and underscores lingering problems of separating the poet's dialect from the scribe's, concluding that while it remains a possible origin point for the poems, "we cannot with certainty privilege Cheshire as a given home base for the poet or for the scribe founded on dialect evidence."[54]

While Fredell is careful to distinguish the creation of the poems from the creation of the manuscript—Cotton Nero A.x is almost certainly copied from at least one earlier exemplar—his findings trouble decades of critical consensus, decenter more than a little Neo-historicist criticism, and raise important questions about the works and their reception. Paramount among them is the erasure of *Sir Gawain and the Green Knight* and *Pearl*, two works of undisputed genius, from the early literary record. Unlike other canonical works from the later Middle Ages—the *Canterbury Tales*, *Piers Plowman*, *The Showings of Julian of Norwich*, *The Confessio Amantis*—the works of Cotton Nero A.x exist only in a single manuscript, and they reveal little if any trace of an immediate literary afterlife. We do not talk about a *Pearl*-tradition in the same way we talk about a Chaucerian one, and unlike *Piers Plowman*, which was widely read in the Early Modern period, *Sir Gawain and the Green Knight* seems to vanish with little more than a trace. Bowers has suggested that the poems' close alignment with the Ricardian court rendered them unwelcome in the new literary-cultural world promoted by the succeeding Lancastrian kings, in which pseudo-laureate writers like John Lydgate celebrated the poetry (and dialect) of Chaucer and Gower while tactfully eliding the more suspect work of "shadowy provincials such as . . . the nameless Cheshire author of *Pearl*."[55] But, if Cotton Nero A.x was produced in the region of Yorkshire during the reign of Richard's usurper, Henry IV, we must reconsider the political and cultural pressures commonly understood as curtailing alliterative verse in the post-Ricardian period.[56]

Opening the aperture wider still, Su Fang Ng and Kenneth Hodges have recently speculated that the figure of the Green Knight himself, whose greenness is often (if hesitantly) aligned with the natural world or with Anglo-Celtic precursors,[57] may equally derive from a riddling Islamic folk character known as al-Khidr, "The Green One."[58] Often conflated with the prophet Elijah and, more salient still, with Saint George, al-Khidr "was one of the most important figures in Islamic mythology, and stories of him would have been ubiquitous, from Constantinople, through the Near East and North Africa, and into Spain."[59] Those stories offer tantalizing parallels with the Green Knight: not only is al-Khidr frequently green, he at times offers hospitality to travelers, at other times teaches spiritual lessons using surprisingly confrontational methods, and tends to appear and disappear without warning.[60] Like Fredell's consideration of the manuscript's Yorkshire connections, Ng and Hodges's work cannot without new evidence crystalize into hard fact; it does not definitively foreclose the possibility of a Cheshire provenance, nor does it necessarily sever the poet's link to the Ricardian court. (Insofar as both Richard and Cheshire were implicated in the overlapping networks of mercantilism and militarism that defined England's engagement with the Islamicate world, there is good reason to suppose that a Northwest Midlands poet working within the royal affinity might have had access to stories featuring a green-skinned trickster figure.[61]) Nonetheless, what Ng and Hodges show, and what scholars and students alike would do very well to remember, is that what Bennett termed "the little world" of the *Gawain*-Poet is, in fact, a far larger one than has been commonly acknowledged.

NOTES

1. *Sir Gawain and the Green Knight*, ll. 697, 701. All quotations from MS Cotton Nero A.x are from *The Poems of the Pearl Manuscript: Pearl, Cleanness, Patience, Sir Gawain and the Green Knight*, 5th ed., eds., Malcolm Andrew and Ronald Waldron (Exeter: University of Exeter Press, 2007).

2. *Pearl*, l. 75.

3. Angus McIntosh, "A New Approach to Middle English Dialectology," *English Studies* 44 (1963): 1–11, at 5. McIntosh, M. L. Samuels and Michael Benskin, confirm these conclusions in *The Linguistic Atlas of Late Mediaeval English*, 4 vols. (Aberdeen: Aberdeen University Press, 1986), http://www.lel.ed.ac.uk/ihd/elalme/elalme.html. MS Cotton Nero A.x is listed as Linguistic Profile (LP) 26; its provenance is specified as Cheshire.

4. Michael J. Bennett, *Community, Class and Careerism: Cheshire and Lancashire Society in the Age of* Sir Gawain and the Green Knight (Cambridge: Cambridge University Press, 1983), 7. See also Bennett, "The Historical Background," in *A Companion to the Gawain-Poet*, Derek Brewer and Johnathan Gibson, eds. (Cambridge: D.S. Brewer, 1997), 71–90.

5. The phrase "Cheshire hypothesis" is from Joel Fredell, "The *Pearl*-Poet Manuscript in York," *Studies in the Age of Chaucer* 36 (2014): 1–39, at 2.

6. *Sir Gawain and the Green Knight*, l. 927.

7. A. C. Spearing, *The Gawain-Poet: A Critical Study* (Cambridge: Cambridge University Press, 1970), 181.

8. Christine Chism, *Alliterative Revivals* (Philadelphia: University of Pennsylvania Press, 2002), 74–81.

9. Randy P. Schiff, *Revivalist Fantasy: Alliterative Verse and Nationalist Literary History* (Columbus: Ohio State University Press, 2011), 79.

10. Alex Mueller, *Translating Troy: Provincial Politics in Alliterative Romance* (Columbus: Ohio State University Press, 2013), 179.

11. David K. Coley, *Death and the Pearl Maiden: Plague, Poetry, England* (Columbus: Ohio State University Press, 2019), 131.

12. Bennett, *Community, Class and Careerism*, 233. See also in this volume, Ethan Campbell, "Authorship: What Does the Pearl-Poet Tell Us about Himself?" and particularly Campbell's assertion, while "the poet may have used a Cheshire dialect while writing his poems, the audience who first received them may well have lived elsewhere" (p. 114) an assertion that obviously complicates a straightforward alignment of poem with region.

13. See John Bowers, *The Politics of* Pearl: *Court Poetry in the Age of Richard II* (Cambridge: D.S. Brewer, 2001), 70.

14. Nigel Saul, *Richard II* (New Haven, CT: Yale University Press, 1997), 172.

15. *Saul, Richard II*, 274, 289.

16. *Saul, Richard II*, 393.

17. Thomas Walsingham's *Annales Ricardi Secundi* and the *Dieulacres Chronicle* quoted and translated in Chris Given-Wilson, *Chronicles of the Revolution: 1397–1400, the Reign of Richard II* (Manchester: Manchester University Press, 1993), 73 (Walsingham), 154 (Dieulacres).

18. Saul, *Richard II*, 394.

19. *Sir Gawain and the Green Knight*, ll. 78–79.

20. *Sir Gawain and the Green Knight*, ll. 51–52.

21. See Saul, *Richard II*, especially Chapter 14, "The King and His Court."

22. *Sir Gawain and the Green Knight*, l. 86.

23. *Sir Gawain and the Green Knight*, l. 89.

24. *Vita Ricardi Secundi*, quoted and translated in Given-Wilson, *Chronicles of the Revolution*, 241.

25. For one instance, see Bowers, *The Politics of* Pearl, 17–18.

26. For an assenting opinion, see Jill Mann, "Courtly Aesthetics and Courtly Ethics in *Sir Gawain and the Green Knight*," *Studies in the Age of Chaucer* 31 (2009): 231–65, at 235–36.

27. Chism, *Alliterative Revivals*, 66.

28. Randy Schiff addresses the impact of Cheshire's culture of military careerism in *Revivalist Fantasy*, particularly chapter 3, "Destabilizing Arthurian Empire: Gender and Anxiety in Alliterative Texts of the Militarized Midlands."

29. *Sir Gawain and the Green Knight*, l. 535.

30. *Sir Gawain and the Green Knight*, l. 698.

31. *Sir Gawain and the Green Knight*, l. 701.

32. For this last identification, see Andrew and Waldron, *The Poems of the Pearl Manuscript*, 234 n.699. The criticism surrounding Gawain's route is summarized in Robert W. Barrett, *Against All England: Regional Identity and Cheshire Writing, 1195–1656* (Notre Dame, IN: University of Notre Dame Press, 2009), 134–36.

33. Richard traveled throughout Southern Wales in 1394 and in Northeastern Wales in 1397. See Saul, *Richard II*, 291, 392.

34. Saul, *Richard II*, 258.

35. Patricia Clare Ingham, *Sovereign Fantasies: Arthurian Romance and the Making of Britain* (Philadelphia: University of Pennsylvania Press, 2001), 135. See also Rhonda Knight, "All Dressed Up with Someplace to Go: Regional Identity in *Sir Gawain and the Green Knight*," *Studies in the Age of Chaucer* 25 (2003): 259–84.

36. Lynn Arner, "The Ends of Enchantment: Colonialism and *Sir Gawain and the Green Knight*," *Texas Studies in Literature and Language* 48, no. 2 (2006): 79–101, at 94.

37. John Bowers provides an overview of the New Critical approaches to the poem in *The Politics of* Pearl, 1–2. For exegetical criticism on *Pearl*, see D. W. Robertson, "The Pearl as a Symbol," *Modern Language Notes* 65, no. 3 (1950): 155–61; Jane Beal, *The Signifying Power of* Pearl: *Medieval Literary and Cultural Contexts for the Transformation of Genre* (New York: Routledge, 2017).

38. *Pearl*, l. 1046.

39. Bowers, *The Politics of* Pearl, 93.

40. *Pearl*, l. 204.

41. Bowers, *The Politics of* Pearl, 181.

42. *Pearl*, l. 162.

43. Helen Barr, "*Pearl*—or 'The Jeweller's Tale,'" *Medium Ævum* 69 (2000): 59–79, at 61. In this volume, Jonathan Quick raises similar issues concerning the Jeweler's complex social location. See "Material Culture of the Pearl-Poet."

44. Marie Borroff, "Narrative Artistry in *St. Erkenwald* and the *Gawain*-Group: The Case for Common Authorship Reconsidered," *Studies in the Age of Chaucer* 28 (2006): 41–76.

45. *Sir Gawain and the Green Knight*, Cl. 265.

46. Nicholas Watson, "The Gawain-Poet as a Vernacular Theologian," in *A Companion to the Gawain-Poet*, Derek Brewer and Johnathan Gibson, eds. (Cambridge: D.S. Brewer, 1997), 312.

47. Elizabeth B. Kiser, *Courtly Desire and Medieval Homophobia: The Legitimation of Sexual Pleasure in* Cleanness *and Its Contexts* (New Haven, CT: Yale University Press, 1997), 160–64.

48. *Patience, Pat.* 30.

49. *Patience*, l. 51.

50. Malcolm Andrew, "Theories of Authorship," in *A Companion to the Gawain-Poet*, Derek Brewer and Johnathan Gibson, eds. (Cambridge: D.S. Brewer, 1997), 26.

51. *Sir Gawain and the Green Knight, Pe.* 1178.

52. Ruth Nissé *refutes* the theory of common authorship on precisely the theory articulated by Bennett and Bowers, arguing that while the *Pearl*-Poet evinces a consistently Ricardian outlook, the writer of *St. Erkenwald* looks to London to criticize Richard's authoritarianism. See Ruth Nissé, "'A Coroun Ful Riche': The Rule of History in *St. Erkenwald*," *English Literary History* 65 (1998): 277–95.

53. Fredell, "The *Pearl*-Poet Manuscript in York," 37. See also Fredell's chapter in this volume, "The Illustrations in London, British Library, MS Cotton Nero A.x."

54. Fredell, "The *Pearl*-Poet Manuscript in York," 5.

55. Bowers, *The Politics of* Pearl, 195.

56. For Yorkshire's relationship with the Lancastrian affinity in the early 1400s, see Fredell, "The *Pearl*-Poet Manuscript in York," 10–11.

57. See Derek Brewer, "The Colour Green," in *A Companion to the Gawain-Poet*, Derek Brewer and Johnathan Gibson, eds. (Cambridge: D.S. Brewer, 1997), 181–90.

58. Su Fang Ng and Kenneth Hodges, "Saint George, Islam, and Regional Audiences in *Sir Gawain and the Green Knight*," *Studies in the Age of Chaucer* 32 (2010): 257–94.

59. Ng and Hodges, "Regional Audiences," 292.

60. Ng and Hodges, "Regional Audiences," 265–66.

61. Ng and Hodges suggest not only Richard's court as a possible environment for the poet but also that of Richard's Uncle, John of Gaunt. See Ng and Hodges, "Regional Audiences," 281–86.

BIBLIOGRAPHY

Andrew, Malcolm. "Theories of Authorship." In *A Companion to the Gawain-Poet*, eds. Derek Brewer and Johnathan Gibson, 22–33. Cambridge: D.S. Brewer, 1997.

Andrew, Malcolm, and Ronald Waldron, eds. *The Poems of the Pearl Manuscript: Pearl, Cleanness, Patience, Sir Gawain and the Green Knight*. 5th ed. Exeter: University of Exeter Press, 2007.

Arner, Lynn. "The Ends of Enchantment: Colonialism and *Sir Gawain and the Green Knight*." *Texas Studies in Literature and Language* 48 (2006): 79–101.

Barr, Helen. "*Pearl*—or 'The Jeweller's Tale,'" *Medium Ævum* 69 (2000): 59–79.

Barrett, Robert W. *Against All England: Regional Identity and Cheshire Writing, 1195–1656*. Notre Dame, IN: University of Notre Dame Press, 2009.

Beal, Jane. *The Signifying Power of* Pearl*: Medieval Literary and Cultural Contexts for the Transformation of Genre*. New York: Routledge, 2017.

Bennett, Michael J. *Community, Class and Careerism: Cheshire and Lancashire Society in the Age of* Sir Gawain and the Green Knight. Cambridge: Cambridge University Press, 1983.

———. "The Historical Background." In *A Companion to the Gawain-Poet*, eds. Derek Brewer and Johnathan Gibson, 71–90. Cambridge: D.S. Brewer, 1997.

Borroff, Marie. "Narrative Artistry in *St. Erkenwald* and the *Gawain*-Group: The Case for Common Authorship Reconsidered." *Studies in the Age of Chaucer* 28 (2006): 41–76.

Bowers, John. *The Politics of Pearl: Court Poetry in the Age of Richard II*. Cambridge: D.S. Brewer, 2001.

Brewer, Derek. "The Colour Green." In *A Companion to the Gawain-Poet*, eds. Derek Brewer and Johnathan Gibson, 181–90. Cambridge: D.S. Brewer, 1997.

Brewer, Derek, and Jonathan Gibson, eds. *A Companion to the* Gawain-*Poet*. Cambridge: D.S. Brewer, 1997.

Chism, Christine. *Alliterative Revivals*. Philadelphia: University of Pennsylvania Press, 2002.

Coley, David K. *Death and the Pearl Maiden: Plague, Poetry, England*. Columbus: Ohio State University Press, 2019.

Fredell, Joel. "The *Pearl*-Poet Manuscript in York." *Studies in the Age of Chaucer* 36 (2014): 1–39.

Given-Wilson, Chris. *Chronicles of the Revolution: 1397–1400, the Reign of Richard II*. Manchester: Manchester University Press, 1993.

Ingham, Patricia Clare. *Sovereign Fantasies: Arthurian Romance and the Making of Britain*. Philadelphia: University of Pennsylvania Press, 2001.

Knight, Rhonda. "All Dressed Up with Someplace to Go: Regional Identity in *Sir Gawain and the Green Knight*." *Studies in the Age of Chaucer* 25 (2003): 259–84.

Kiser, Elizabeth B. *Courtly Desire and Medieval Homophobia: The Legitimation of Sexual Pleasure in* Cleanness *and Its Contexts*. New Haven, CT: Yale University Press, 1997.

Mann, Jill. "Courtly Aesthetics and Courtly Ethics in *Sir Gawain and the Green Knight*." *Studies in the Age of Chaucer* 31 (2009): 231–65.

McIntosh, Angus. "A New Approach to Middle English Dialectology." *English Studies* 44 (1963): 1–11.

McIntosh, Angus, M. L. Samuels, and Michael Benskin, with Margaret Laing and Keith Williamson. *A Linguistic Atlas of Late Middle English.* 4 vols. Aberdeen: Aberdeen University Press, 1986. http://www.lel.ed.ac.uk/ihd/elalme/elalme.html.

Mueller, Alex. *Translating Troy: Provincial Politics in Alliterative Romance.* Columbus: Ohio State University Press, 2013.

Ng, Su Fang, and Kenneth Hodges. "Saint George, Islam, and Regional Audiences in *Sir Gawain and the Green Knight.*" *Studies in the Age of Chaucer* 32 (2010): 257–94.

Nissé, Ruth. "'A Coroun Ful Riche': The Rule of History in *St. Erkenwald.*" *English Literary History* 65 (1998): 277–95.

Robertson, D. W., Jr. "The *Pearl* as a Symbol." *Modern Language Notes* 65, no. 3 (1950): 155–61.

Saul, Nigel. *Richard II.* New Haven, CT: Yale University Press, 1997.

Schiff, Randy. *Revivalist Fantasy: Alliterative Verse and Nationalist Literary History.* Columbus: Ohio State University Press, 2011.

Spearing, A. C. *The Gawain Poet: A Poetic Study.* Cambridge: Cambridge University Press, 1970.

Watson, Nicholas. "The *Gawain*-Poet as a Vernacular Theologian." In *A Companion to the Gawain-Poet*, eds. Derek Brewer and Johnathan Gibson, 293–313. Cambridge: D.S. Brewer, 1997.

Chapter Fourteen

Religious Contexts for the *Pearl*-Poet

Nancy Ciccone

Numerous literary scholars have attested to the *Pearl*-poet's familiarity with religious discourses, ranging from those of church fathers to those of his contemporaries. The interpretative literature has turned to the writings of Augustine, Hugh of St. Victor, Thomas Aquinas, Wycliffe, and others; it has relied on preachers' handbooks, bulls, treatises, and other documents to elucidate the poems. In this collection of essays, Grace Hamman's "The Pastoral Theology of the *Pearl*-Poet" points out the poet's specific concerns "shared with sundry contemporary texts, including didactic poems like the *The Prick of Conscience*, contemplative works like Julian of Norwich's *A Revelation of Love*, and, naturally, penitential texts like the *Book of Vices and Virtues*. As H.L. Spencer has affirmed, the poet was "vitally engaged with political and theological arguments which were preoccupying others also experimenting with the vernacular in the last two decades of the fourteenth century."[1] The following essay, rather than exhaustive, provides a sample of some of the issues shaping the religious contexts in which the *Pearl*-poet wrote. The issues include the offices of the Church, its social centrality, economic impact, and theological controversies, such as passionate debates about the means to salvation, in order to provide a window into the complex religious milieu of the late fourteenth century.

The institution of the Church was Catholic. It housed bishops, civil servants, scholars, monastics, anchorites, hermits, Roman Curia officials, and clergy. Their offices were in the universities, in parish churches, in monasteries, in cathedrals, on streets in villages and cities. The Church dominated and united social communities. That is not to discount active pre-Christian, Judaic, and other belief systems, but to stress the authority of the Church. In theory, the king answered to the Pope, who appointed bishops and archbishops after considering the king's suggestions.[2] Complicating this process, the European Great Western Schism (1378–1417) saw three popes, each with his own cardinal college and administrative offices, divided by politics rather than by theology. The Schism affected England in that Richard II met with little opposition in the appointment of his favorites to powerful sees, and with that, the exile of those disagreeing with him to remote locations. From aristocrat to peasant, religious practices permeated daily life. Church law, for example, required fasting on certain days and feasting on others. However frugal the feast might be for some, the community shared in the occasion. The tendrils of the institution reached from the countryside to the urban centers, from the cathedral to the hearth.

Participating in the sacraments glued the community together. The Fourth Lateran council (1215) mandated Christians' confession at least once a year to their parish priest (*Omnis utriusque sexus*).[3] Visual representations of the sacrament suggest it occurred face to face. Confessor and penitent most likely knew each other from their community,[4] but there was an understanding of privacy, and sometimes, the clergy shielded his face with a hood. Roughly, the sacrament entailed the penitent's narrative consisting of (1) an analysis of his/her compliance with Christian virtue and secular law, (2) the confession of all sins, (3) request for penance, (4) an act of penance, appropriate restitution, and finally (5) absolution. The analysis (#1) depended in turn on the penitent's disposition, which John Bromyard, a Dominican friar (d. c.1390), spells out in his handbook for preachers: "[The penitent] ought to be sorrowful from the commission of sin . . . ; second, he makes restitution for his sin; third, he promises to stop, and then show better faith in that he flees sinful occasions. . . . [Confession] necessarily works in this way, but unless so disposed, the maximum judgement hangs over [the penitent]."[5] The necessity of confession encouraged Christians to develop a sense of inferiority based on moral behavior and self-examination.

The requirement of confession created a need for guidelines for its ministration. Handbooks flourished in the vernacular and in Latin. Rhyming poems promoted memorization of the ritual and its punishments. John Grimstone (Franciscan friar) compiled a book of lyrics (1372) for preaching and arranged topics alphabetically: "Since I have come and have thee brought/ A blissful boot of bale,/ Undo thy heart, tell me thy thought,/ Thy sins great and small" ("Since I have come and brought to you /A blissful boat of woe/ Unburden your heart, tell me your thought, your sins great and small.")[6] William of Doune's fourteenth-century *Memoriale presbiterorum* prescribes topics according to social station. Issues raised for a knight, for example, differ from those for merchants.[7] Has the knight indulged in pride, in lecherousness, in litigation that rightly belongs under the Church's purview?[8] Has the burgher paid his personal tithe; has he committed usury?[9] The *Memoriale* reminds the clergy to probe not only the interiority of the penitents but also their social responsibility.

For penance, the fourteenth-century preacher's handbook, *Fasciculus Morum*, recommends the trifold action of "prayer, fasting, and almsgiving" to counteract sin committed with "heart, mouth, and deed."[10] Upon absolution, the Christian becomes eligible for the Eucharist, taking the body and blood of Christ into their own bodies through the sanctified elements of bread and wine. As Thomas Tentler has argued, "confession provided a comprehensive and organized system of social control."[11] If so, however, it also fostered civic peace. Confession offered an opportunity for neighbors to air hostilities and wrongdoing. Once intervention quelled aggression, the parties were required to perform the Pax, a social act of salutation and forgiveness.[12] Yet institutional and civic interests need not overwhelm the individual's spirituality.[13] Confession fostered sanctification within Christians and granted them full participation in the community.

The encouragement of self-reflection and prayer was also the focus of the mass. A contemporary of the *Pearl*-poet, Julian of Norwich (1342–c.1416) describes faith as entailing three aspects: God's gift of natural reason, the teachings of Holy Church, and the inward working of the Holy Ghost.[14] Whereas natural reason may entail the practical, it blends with the influence of the Holy Ghost, which inwardly fosters sanctification to solidify faith and direct ethical behavior. Since Mass excluded the laity from participation and the altar was behind a screen, silence and the lack of visual spectacle encouraged internal prayers and self-reflection among all of the attendees. "The late fourteenth-century poem 'How to Hear Mass' suggests that," the laity ought to "priueliche ȝor preyers preye/ To him þat may vn-bynde,/ In saluyng of ȝor synnes seuene/ To þe mihtful kyng of heuene" ("pray your prayers privately/ to Him who may unburden you/ In removing of your manifest sins/ To the mighty king of heaven.")[15] Sermons included didactic *exempla*, stories, and homilies, which were also woven into the liturgy to be easily remembered. One preacher's handbook likens the slothful, for example, to the cuckoo who "does not hatch its own eggs but puts them into the nest of another bird and eats the other bird's eggs."[16] Participation in the communal life of church ritual, however, maintained social stratification. As Garrison has argued, aristocrats frequently attended mass with an expensive book of hours tucked under their arms. They built private pews and chapels, donated stained glass windows that depicted their devotional selves, and shared the purposefully egalitarian Pax only among themselves.[17] Although fundamentally communal, mass was an opportunity to display wealth and to parade finery during processions. That the *Pearl*-poet attended to such spectacle is evidenced by the various artifacts peppering his works. In "Material Culture of the *Pearl*-Poet," Jonathan Quick, for example, notes their significance "as both descriptive embellishments and didactic symbols conveying divine and moral messages to the poems' audiences.[18] Whether in church or in manuscripts, literal and figurative artifacts invite contemplation.

Yet within the institution of the Catholic Church, conflicts characterize the theology of the latter half of the fourteenth century and so impacted social networks. Julian of Norwich's requirements for faith suggest a simplicity transcending political and scholastic debates. For the educated, the Trivium (grammar, rhetoric, dialectic) and the Quadrivium (music, arithmetic, geometry, astronomy) served Theology. Many of the divisive conversations began earlier in the century. Various flavors of heresy also brewed within the Church. For most of the Middle Ages, for example, Latin was the language of the Church. The orthodox Bible was the Latin Vulgate. It fell under the auspices of the learned, ostensibly for fear of misinterpretation by the laity. With many ideas looking forward to the Reformation, Wycliffe (c. 1330–1384), most notably, championed the translation of the Bible into English, making it available to the literate laity whose familiarity with the Bible was mostly limited to popular stories. In addition to the very language of the Church being challenged, conflictual religious ideas entailed political and economic concerns. Wycliffe's followers, known as the Lollards, spread many of his views including those of divesting the Church of its wealth. But the charge of heresy depended on the determination of orthodoxy at any given moment. In 1323, for example, Pope John XXII declared it heresy "to assert that Christ and the Apostles had not owned property" (*Cum inter nonnulos*).[19] As David Aers has pointed out, heresy "became dealt with and classified as sedition (through parliamentary acts and the secular power)"; as a result, "the languages and practices of religion" overlapped with those of governance and politics.[20] Wycliffe escaped the stake during his lifetime partially due to his popularity and his friends in high places, only to have his body exhumed (1427) under Pope Martin V, his remains burned, and his ashes scattered in the river Swift flowing through Lutterworth, where he had died of a stroke (1384).

Among their conflicts, intellectual theologians targeted the issue of salvation: is God's grace a prerequisite for human merit? Roughly two groups emerge—the orthodox and the nominalists—with many variations within each grouping. Modern scholars continue to parse out the individual beliefs of participants in these debates; William Courtney has argued against the term nominalism to designate a school of thought in the fourteenth century due to the disparate views of people associated with that term.[21] Although lacking unity of thought, the debate over salvation essentially depends on the placement of the workings of grace: whether it is a prerequisite for good works or not. Representing the conservative orthodoxy following Augustine

(354–430), Thomas Bradwardine (c. 1290–1349) maintained Christians achieve salvation only by grace. Augustine had argued for man's inability to achieve good works without God's first granting grace because of mankind's innate sinfulness. Once grace is granted, then man is allowed the freedom to choose. Augustine disputed Pelagianism because it denied original sin and upheld man's basic goodness, and the early Church condemned Pelagianism as heresy. In the fourteenth century, Bradwardine's *De causa Dei* labeled those disagreeing with him as guilty as Pelagians in undermining the role of grace in the freedom to choose. Those called nominalists disagreed with Bradwardine's view. They maintained the freedom to choose rightly and the workings of grace as a given with natural reason. Although perhaps not crucial to his theology, William of Ockham (c. 1288–1348) considered mankind to have a natural ability to love God and therefore to choose to do good. His system, however, depended on definitions of God's absolute (*potentia absoluta*) and ordained (*potentia ordinata*) powers, wherein the latter maintains the given order and the former maintains God's omnipotent freedom.[22] For the most part accepting the philosophical positions of Ockham, Robert Holcot (d. 1349) takes practical reasoning in respect to God one step further. Whereas both theologians noted the limits of human reason in its ability to comprehend God, Holcot asserted that pre-Christians still had access to God's grace because they lived according to natural law; even without the texts of Christianity, God could grant them revelation.[23] Although many other scholastic theologians contributed to the conflict, these three examples point to the divisions steering discussions in the second half of the century.

Controversy also brewed around the privileges of those serving the Church. Friars were one of the targets. Although the relationship between them and parish clergy had been established by bulls following the Fourth Lateran Council granting the privilege,[24] the friar's right to shrive the laity became a point of contention as the fourteenth century progressed. The mendicant friar provided a loophole in confession in that Christians might confess mortal sins to a traveler, and then annually confess other sins to their parish priests, a practice condemned by the Church. Richard FitzRalph (c.1300–60) was among those arguing friars exceeded their purview and indulged Christian sinners, offering absolution where it was unwarranted.[25] The problem as FitzRalph and others presented it did not only pertain to a Christian's salvation but to the economy: if a mendicant friar absolved a Christian, then the parish church might stand empty, not receive a tithe, and suffer economically as well as socially. The friars defended their rights; the Popes at various turns supported them despite the insistence that Christians confess to the parish clergy. The universities at Cambridge and Oxford took up the argument to support the clergy against the friars.

The corruption of the clergy was a common complaint. In addition to the priest in *Cleanness* (9–16), other literary examples occur in Gower's *Vox Clamantis*, throughout Langland's *Piers Plowman*, and of course, there is Chaucer's Pardoner. The theological ramifications of corrupt clergy affected the average Christian. Did, for example, the sinfulness of the person hearing confession negate the penitent's absolution? What if the Christian did not know of the confessor's sinfulness? What if he or she did? At stake was not only salvation, but death itself, if sin, for example, caused the Black Death, which Bishop Thomas Brinton implied in his 1375 sermon referring to English faithlessness "tam crudelis pestilencia" ("as a cruel pestilence.")[26] An individual's sin had the power to contaminate the entire community, either if the sin went undisclosed in the sacrament of confession, or if it went without penance and absolution. A debased clergy also affected the validity of the Eucharist. Since Augustine's argument against the Donatists, the Church considered it heresy to assign corruption to the Eucharist no matter the virtue of the ministrator because the qualities of Christ's blood and body inhered in the elements. The charge of Donatism was lobbed against Lollards, followers of Wycliffe. They denied the accusation in articles 34 and 35 of the *Thirty-Seven Conclusions of the Lollards* (1395): "And though [the priest] be of cursid lif, he mai make verrili the sacrament and to his owne harm, though profitabili othere men that knowen not his synne" ("And although [the priest] lives a reprobate life, he may truly minister the sacrament and to his own harm, although he profits other men who do not know of his sin.")[27] Yet while preserving the salvation of the recipient, Article 35 also affirms God's power to deny the miracle of the Eucharist to a corrupt priest: "Netheles a synnere mai be so moche vndisposid bi his owne malice or other vnableness, that the Lord vouchith not saaf to worche with him in sacramentis" ("Nevertheless a sinner may be so much indisposed by his own malice or other inability, that the Lord grants it unsafe to work with him in sacraments.")[28] The affirmation of God's ultimate power seemingly contradicts Augustine's insistence on the inherence of sanctity in the objects to reveal a theological paradox.

Throughout these conflicts, the Bible remained the ultimate authority. Reformers depended on it to support their views with a kind of back-to-basics movement. Biblical passages, for example, provided fuel for complaints against clerics. The preeminence of the Bible figured large in Wycliffe's system of theology, but also for Thomas Netter of Walden (c. 1372–1430), and even FitzRalph is thought to have converted from scholastic argumentation to the power of scripture. Yet, those advocating for the authority of scripture disagreed. Thomas Netter, a Carmelite (White Friar), argued against Lollardy (Wycliffe's followers) and ushered some to the stake. He argued against the translation of the Bible into English, but Netter also wrote and preached in the vernacular.[29] His persistent complaints against Wycliffe assured the latter's name and ideas lived on after his death.

Literary scholars differ on attributing a specific theology to the *Pearl*-poet. Cecilia Hatt has recently argued for his belief in "gifted autonomy": "All four poems are driven toward an acknowledgment of utter indebtedness to God for creation."[30] In this view, the goal of living is to return the gift, however inadequately, until death consummates divine union. Hatt points to the biblical passage Romans 5:5 to support her viewpoint: "spes autem non confundit: quia caritas Dei diffusa est in cordibus nostris per Spiritum Sanctum, qui datus est nobis" (Vulgate) ("And hope maketh not ashamed; because the love of God is shed abroad in our hearts by the Holy Ghost which is given unto us" [*KJV*]). Hatt's study challenges that of Aers, who quotes the same biblical passage to support the poet's nuanced unorthodoxy. Aers has argued that the lack of specific virtues and the vagueness of church practices promotes "a pelagian and courtly vision."[31] His reading cites the Augustinian distrust of materiality, which the poet's narratives indulge. Yet whereas Aers finds *Cleanness* to support orthodoxy,[32] Ethan Campbell reads it in terms of anti-clerical attitudes.[33] The number of viewpoints during this period permits the discourses of Aquinas, which Hatt relies on, and those of Augustine, which Aers relies on in addition to Campbell's investigation into the anti-clerical movement, to be considered in light of the poet's narratives.

If located in the north of England, the *Pearl*-poet found himself in the middle of complex, deeply significant theological discussions.[34] His narratives continue to invite further study of their religious contexts. Some of the controversies, such as that of the Immaculate Conception, were later put to rest. But others, such as the rights belonging to the state and those under church authority remain. Issues of endowments and taxation endure. Yet many of the fourteenth-century theological controversies become somewhat distanced from our present due to the conservatism that followed. As Archbishop of Canterbury and kingmaker of Henry IV, Thomas Arundel (1353–1414) ostensibly aimed to stop Lollardy. His Constitutions (1409) established orthodoxy.[35] Articles in it forbade the translation of the Bible, required licenses for preachers granted only after examination, and many other mandates. The Constitutions deterred, if not censored, vernacular theology—at least until the Reformation.

NOTES

1. H. L. Spencer, "*Pearl*: 'God's Law' and 'Man's Law,'" *Review of English Studies*, n.s. 59, vol. 240 (June 2008): 319.

2. W. A. Patin, *English Church in the Fourteenth Century* (Toronto: University of Toronto Press, 1955, rpt. Medieval Academy of America, 1980), 23.

3. For the representation of confessional concerns within the poems, see Grace Hamman's chapter in this volume.

4. Confessional booths were not in general use until the seventeenth century. See Anthony Low, "Privacy, Community, and Society: Confession as a Cultural Indicator in 'Sir Gawain and the Green Knight,'" *Religion & Literature* 30, no. 2 (Summer 1998): 5.

5. John Bromyard, *Summa prædicantium, Prima Pars* (Italy: Venice, 1586): Cap. VI.119. Haec autem dispositio debet esse quod dole- at commissa . . . ; secundo quod restituat ablata; tertio quod promittat cessare, et ut de hoc pleniorem faciat fidem quod fugiat peccati occasiones . . . In tam necessario opere nisi bene disponatur, maximum imminet periculum." See also John Burrow, "Two Confession Scenes in 'Sir Gawain and the Green Knight,'" *Modern Philology* 57, no. 2 (1959): 74. All translations are mine unless otherwise noted.

6. Patin, *English Church*, 142.

7. Michael Haren, "The Interrogatories for Officials, Lawyers and Secular Estates of the *Memoriale presiberorum*," in *Handling Sin*, eds. Peter Biller and A. J. Minnis (York: York Medieval Press, 1998), 123–63. For an extensive study, see Haren, *Sin and Society in Fourteenth-Century England* (Oxford: Clarendon Press, 2000).

8. Haren, "Interrogatories," 141.

9. Haren, "Interrogatories," 145.

10. Siegfried Wenzel, ed. and trans. *Fasciculus Morum: A Fourteenth-Century Preacher's Handbook* (University Park: Pennsylvania State University Press, 1989): 509.

11. Thomas Tentler, *Sin and Confession on the Eve of the Reformation* (Princeton, NJ: Princeton University Press, 1977), 345; See also Gregory Gross, "Secret Rules: Sex, Confession, and Truth in *Sir Gawain and the Green Knight*," *Arthuriana* 4, no. 2 for a discussion of power relationships, 148–50.

12. Low, "Privacy," 25. See also John Bossy, "Social History of Confession in the Age of Reformation," *Transactions of the Royal Historical Society* 25 (1975): 21–38, 25.

13. Low, "Privacy," 2.

14. "Be three things man stondith in this life, be which three God is worshippid and we be spedid, kept, and savid. The first is use of manys reason naturall. The second is commen teching of Holy Church. The thred is inward, gracious werking of the Holy Gost." Ed. G. R. Crampton, *Showings of Julian of Norwich*, TEAMS (Kalamazoo, MI: Medieval Institute Publications, 1993): chap. 80, ll. 3254–58.

15. Jennifer Garrison, "Liturgy and Loss: *Pearl* and the Ritual Reform of the Aristocratic Subject," *Chaucer Review* 44, no. 3 (2010): 296–97; "How to Hear Mass," occurs in Carl Horstmann and F. J. Furnivall, eds., *The Minor Poems of the Vernon MS*, EETS (London: Paul, Trench, Truebner, 1892–1901): XLVII, ll. 20–21.

16. Wenzel, *Fasciculus Morum*, 401.

17. Garrison, "Liturgy," 297–98.

18. For references to clothing within the poems, see Kimberly Jack's chapter on "Sartorial Adornment" in this volume.

19. Patin, *English Church*, 24.

20. David Aers, *Faith, Ethics and Church: Writing in England, 1360–1409* (Cambridge: D.S. Brewer, 2000), 14.

21. William Courtenay, "Nominalism and Late-Medieval Religion," in *The Pursuit of Holiness in Late Medieval and Renaissance Religion*, ed. Charles Trinkaus with Heiko Oberman (Leiden: Brill, 1974), 52.

22. For additional explanation, see Courtenay, "Nominalism and Late-Medieval Religion," 39–44. Spencer applies the concepts in *"Pearl*: 'God's Law' and Man's Law.'"

23. Hester Gelber and John Slotemaker, "Robert Holkot," *The Stanford Encyclopedia of Philosophy* (Spring 2017 Edition), ed. Edward N. Zalta: "Natural Theology," 3:1, https://plato.stanford.edu/archives/spr2017/entries/holkot/.

24. See for example, *super Cathedram*, bull of Pope Boniface VIII in 1300; Patin, *English Church*, 124.

25. Patin, *English Church*, 156.

26. Mary Aquinas Devlin, ed., *Sermons of Thomas Brinton, Bishop of Rochester*, vol. 1 (London: Royal Historical Society, 1954), 216. See also David Coley, *"Pearl* and the Narrative of Pestilence," *Studies in the Age of Chaucer* 35 (2013): 250.

27. J. Forshall, ed., *Remonstrance against Romish Corruptions in the Church* (London: Longman, 1851), Article 35. See also Ethan Campbell, *The Gawain-Poet and the Fourteenth-Century English Anti-Clerical Tradition* (Kalamazoo, MI: Medieval Institute Publications, 2018), 10.

28. Forshall, *Remonstrance against Romish Corruptions*, 10.

29. Johan Bergström-Allen and Richard Copsey, eds., *Thomas Netter of Walden*, Carmel in Britain, Studies in Early History of the Carmelite Order, vol. 4 (Carmel: St. Albert's Press & Edizioni Carmelitane, 2009), 15–16. See also Patin, *English Church*, 133.

30. Cecilia Hatt, *God and the Gawain-Poet* (Cambridge: D.S. Brewer, 2015), 2.

31. Aers, *Faith, Ethics, and Church*, 100.

32. Aers, "Christianity for Courtly Subjects," in *A Companion to the Gawain-Poet*, eds. Derick Brewer and Jonathan Gibson (Cambridge: D.S. Brewer, 1997), 100.

33. Campbell, *Gawain-Poet*, 91–148.

34. For a discussion of the controversy regarding the *Pearl*-poet's authorial location and "political identity," see David K. Coley's "The Northwest Midlands and the Ricardian Court" in this volume.

35. David Wilkins, *Concila Magnae Britanniae et Hiberniae, from 1850 to 1545.* vol. 3 (London: Gosling, 1737), 314–19. For an analysis, see Nicholas Watson, "Censorship and Cultural Change in Late-Medieval England: Vernacular Theology, the Oxford Translation Debate, and Arundel's Constitutions of 1409," *Speculum* 70, no. 4 (October 1995): 822–64.

BIBLIOGRAPHY

Aers, David. "Christianity for Courtly Subjects: Reflections on the *Gawain*-Poet." In *A Companion to the Gawain-Poet.* Editors, Derick Brewer and Jonathan Gibson, 91–101. Cambridge: D.S. Brewer, 1997.

———. *Faith, Ethics and Church: Writing in England, 1360–1409.* Cambridge: D.S. Brewer, 2000.

Bergström-Allen, Johna, and Richard Copsey, eds. *Thomas Netter of Walden.* Carmel in Britain, Studies in Early History of the Carmelite Order. Vol. 4. Carmel: Saint Albert's Press and Edizioni Carmelitane, 2009.

Borrow, John. "Two Confession Scenes in 'Sir Gawain and the Green Knight.'" *Modern Philology* 57, no. 2 (1959): 73–79.

Bossy, John. "The Social History of Confession in the Age of Reformation." *Transactions of the Royal Historical Society* 25 (1975): 21–38.

Bradwardine, Thomas. *De Causa Dei, contra Pelagium.* Nortoniana, John Bill, 1618.

Bromyard, John. *Summa prædicantium, Prima Pars.* Italy: Venice, 1586.

Campbell, Ethan. *The Gawain-Poet and the Fourteenth-Century English Anti-Clerical Tradition.* Kalamazoo, MI: Medieval Institute Publications, 2018.

Coley, David. "*Pearl* and the Narrative of Pestilence." *Studies in the Age of Chaucer* 35 (2013): 209–62.

Courtney, William J. "Nominalism and Late-Medieval Religion." In *The Pursuit of Holiness in Late Medieval and Renaissance Religion.* Ed. Charles Trinkaus with Heiko Oberman, 26–59. Leiden: Brill, 1974.

Crampton, G. R., ed. *Showings of Julian of Norwich.* TEAMS. Kalamazoo, MI: Medieval Institute Publications, 1993.

Devlin, Mary A., ed. *Sermons of Thomas of Briton, Bishop of Rochester (1373–1389),* Vol.1. London: Royal Historical Society, 1954.

Foreshall, Josiah, Ed. *Remonstrance against Romish Corruptions in the Church.* London: Longman, 1851.

Garrison, Jennifer. "Liturgy and Loss: *Pearl* and the Ritual Reform of the Aristocratic Subject." *Chaucer Review* 44, no. 3 (2010): 294–322.

Gelber, Hester, and John T. Slotemaker. "Robert Holkot." *The Stanford Encyclopedia of Philosophy.* Ed. Edward N. Zalta. Spring 2017 Edition: "Natural Theology," 3, no. 1 https://plato.stanford.edu/archives/spr2017/entries/holkot/.

Gross, Gregory. "Secret Rules: Sex, Confession, and Truth." *Sir Gawain and the Green Knight. Arthuriana* 4, no. 2 (Summer 1994): 146–74.

Haren, Michael. "The Interrogatories for Officials, Lawyers and Secular Estates of the *Memoriale presiberorum.*" In *Handling Sin.* Ed. Peter Biller and A. J. Minnis, 123–63. York: York Medieval Press, 1998.

———. *Sin and Society in Fourteenth-Century England.* Oxford: Clarendon Press, 2000.

Hatt, Cecilia A. *God and the Gawain-Poet.* Cambridge: D.S. Brewer, 2015.

Horstmann, Carl, and F. J. Furnivall, eds. *Minor Poems of the Vernon MS,* EETS. London: Kegan Paul, Trench and Truebner, 1892–1901.

Low, Anthony. "Privacy, Community, and Society: Confession as a Cultural Indicator in 'Sir Gawain and the Green Knight.'" *Religion and Literature* 30, no. 2 (1998): 1–20.

Patin, W. A. *The English Church in the Fourteenth Century.* Toronto: University of Toronto Press, 1955; repr. Medieval Academy of America, 1980.

Schnyder, Hans. *"Sir Gawain and the Green Knight": An Essay in Interpretation,* Cooper Monographs on English and American Literature, No. 6 Bern: Franke, 1961.

Spencer, H. L. *"Pearl:* 'God's Law' and 'Man's Law.'" *Review of English Studies* 59 (2008): 317–41.

Tentler, Thomas. *Sin and Confession on the Eve of the Reformation.* Princeton, NJ: Princeton University Press, 1977.

Trinkaus, Charles with Heiko Oberman, dds. *Pursuit of Holiness in Late Medieval and Renaissance Religion.* Brill: Leiden, 1974.

Watson, Nicholas. "Censorship and Cultural Change in Late-Medieval England: Vernacular Theology, the Oxford Translation Debate, and Arundel's Constitutions of 1409." *Speculum* 70, no. 4 (1995): 822–64.

Wenzel, Siegfried, ed. and trans. *Fasciculus Morum: A Fourteenth-Century Preacher's Handbook.* University Park: Pennsylvania State University Press, 1989.

Wilkins, David. *Concila Magnae Britanniae et Hiberniae, from 1350 to 1545.* Vol. 3, 314–19. London: Gosling, 1737.

Chapter Fifteen

Translations and Paraphrases

Kenna L. Olsen

The scribal dialect of the Cotton Nero A.x poems, *Pearl*, *Cleanness*, *Patience*, and *Sir Gawain and the Green Knight* (*SGGK*), has meant that translations of these four poems have been necessary for students and for a general readership. The poems are copied in a dialect that has been localized to near that of Cheshire in the Northwest Midlands of England,[1] meaning that in their original Middle English dialect, the poems are removed and remote from the Chaucerian dialect that is more recognizable to speakers of Modern English. Even scholars capable of negotiating the Northwest Midlands dialect of the poems, and of *St. Erkenwald*, another late fourteenth-century poem written in the same dialect as the *Pearl*-poems, have relied upon Modern English translations of the poems.[2]

This chapter provides a discussion of the poems' translation history, and in the case of *SGGK*, the most popular and well-known of the poems, it also surveys various adaptations (text, film, and stage).[3] As the translation history and approach to the poems is varied, this chapter offers summaries and insights into the most significant translation for each work, so that current and future readers, scholars, and students of the poems can negotiate the available translation and adaptations available to them effectively, and with ease.

It may seem obvious to claim that the poems' language is crucial to their understanding, yet this articulation is both vital and complex. The Northwest Midlands scribal dialect is the method of delivery and preservation of the poems, but it is also part of the poems' character of description, which is simultaneously subtle, yet rich, and is one of the reasons the poems are often studied and celebrated. Indeed, the poems' language itself often mimics, or serves to localize, the concerns or actions of the poems. For instance, in *SGGK*, Gawain's sincere physical journey, if he has one, is against nature— not against the anticipated fanciful beasts of a knight's quests, nor against the

Green Knight's challenge, which proves to be more pathologically complex than the straight-forward "exchange of winnings" game to which the Green Knight/Bertilak challenges Gawain.[4] The poem's localized vocabulary offers a clear visualization of the rare landscape of Northwest England in which Gawain is placed. Indeed, the poet makes much of Gawain's discomfort in nature while Gawain journeys to find the Green Chapel. The word *raged* (line 745) means "hoarfrosted" and is a Northwest Midlands dialect word unique in Middle English, used to describe the Northwest midland environment Gawain encounters.[5] This unique dialect, vital for understanding and appreciating the poems, makes the job of translation, already challenging, acutely so. Translators must communicate what the poems say, in order to express what the poems truly are, in a language far removed, in terms of time and place, from their origin. Additionally, translators of the poems are faced with issues of poetic form: should a translation be in verse? If so, in the meter of the original? Should alliteration—a poetic device crucial to the *Gawain*-poet—be adhered to? While such concerns are common within the discipline of literary translation, the national and literary importance of the poems has perhaps heightened the interest and import of their treatment in translation and adaptation.

FIRST TRANSLATIONS

Despite not receiving any scholarly attention until the early nineteenth century, the Cotton Nero A.x poems are now considered canonical to the English literary tradition. At least two of them, *SGGK* and *Pearl* have enjoyed immense scholarly attention, and they have solidly gained popular interest over time, making the choice of translation complex and important. As such, some attention to the relationship between the initial editorial treatment and the subsequent translation tradition is worthwhile, as this relationship serves to helpfully categorize translation types across omnibus editions, dual language (facing page) omnibus editions, and verse or prose translations; additionally, the translation history of the poems is partly indicative of their scholarly and public popularity. This interest was only possible after the initial editions broadened the poems' accessibility beyond that of their manuscripts.

Of the five poems, the first to be edited was *SGGK* by Sir Frederic Madden in 1839. In 1864, Richard Morris provided the first edition of *Pearl*, along with *Cleanness* and *Patience*. *St. Erkenwald* was first edited in 1881 by Carl Horstmann. The translation tradition begins with *SGGK*, nearly sixty years after the publication of its initial edition, with Jessie Weston's 1898 *Sir Gawain and the Green Knight: A Middle English Arthurian Romance Retold in Modern Prose*. *Pearl* was first translated by Sir Israel Gollancz in 1891, nearly thirty years after its first published edition. The entirety of *Cleanness* first appears as a translation in 1965 in John Gardner's *The Complete Works of the Gawain-Poet*;[6] this omnibus translation also includes the first translation of *St. Erkenwald*. *Patience* was first published as a translation by Brian Stone in 1964 (alongside *Pearl*) in his *Medieval English Verse*. So while *SGGK* and *Pearl* receive translations still in the nineteenth century, and not significantly long after their first editions, it takes a century to pass before *Cleanness* and *Patience* receive significant interest from translators; *St. Erkenwald*, too, takes substantially longer to be rendered into Modern English (eighty-four years).

ST. ERKENWALD

St. Erkenwald's first Modern English translation, by Gardner in 1965 alongside his translations of all of the *Gawain*-poems, is a close verse translation in quatrains. Gardner's translation includes substantial introductory chapters on poetic form, the *Gawain*-poet's poetic and thematic traditions and interests, and poetic interpretations (though significantly no such interpretation is afforded to *St. Erkenwald*). *St. Erkenwald*'s subsequent translation treatment has been largely dependent on the belief of common authorship between *St. Erkenwald* and the Cotton Nero A.x poems. The poems held in Cotton Nero A.x and *St. Erkenwald* were next translated in another omnibus translation collection by Margaret Williams in 1967; Williams also agreed with the shared-poet theory. Williams provides a close verse translation in quatrains (like Gardner), and the collection is accompanied by substantial supporting materials, including poetic analysis, critical commentary on the poems, and annotated charts for the fourteenth century and each of the poems (though, significantly, *St. Erkenwald* does not receive the same analysis). Still working within the shared author theory, Casey Finch's 1991 facing-page omnibus edition, *The Complete Works of the* Pearl-*Poet* is the most scholarly and poetic translation of *St. Erkenwald* available. Finch's translation edition uses, for the Cotton Nero A.x poems, the highly regarded, and most used, modern omnibus Middle English edition by Andrew and Waldron, and Peterson's 1977 Middle English scholarly edition for *St. Erkenwald*, which is generally considered to be authoritative. In so doing, Finch was first to offer a complete, facing-page Middle English and Modern English translation of all five poems. In 1971, Brian Stone published *St. Erkenwald* in a translation collection with *Cleanness* and *The Owl and the Nightingale*. Stone's translations of *St. Erkenwald* and *Cleanness* were the first to be offered in the poems' original meter.

Marie Borroff's translation of *St. Erkenwald*, in her *The* Gawain-*Poet: Complete Works*, is yet another translation of the poem that accords with the shared-author theory. This translation collection deserves attention for at least two reasons: first, Borroff is one of the scholars who advocate the common author theory most fervently, and her translation of *St. Erkenwald* is accompanied by an essay that firmly and thoroughly argues for common authorship. Second, the publication history of this translation edition is complex, formed through accretions of translations of the individual poems. Borroff, now professor emerita at Yale University, a practicing poet, and a philologist, first translated *SGGK* into verse in 1967, and then *Pearl* in 1977. In 2001, Borroff re-published these, but alongside her new translation of *Patience*. And finally, in 2011 Borroff added *St. Erkenwald* and *Cleanness*, publishing all five poems together. Borroff's translations are often considered to be the most poetic and capable of preserving the linguistic character of the original Middle English, and they have been the most reprinted of the many translation editions that offer translations of more than one poem.

OMNIBUS TRANSLATIONS NOT INCLUDING *ST. ERKENWALD*

William Vantuono's two-volume omnibus facing page translation-edition, *The Pearl Poems*, was published in 1984. Vantuono provides significant and thorough supporting material for his Middle English edition, and he offers editorial commentary on each of the four poems. Disappointingly, his decision to provide a literal facing page Modern English translation is given much less thorough articulation or explanation. Vantuono's translation is perhaps best, and most generously, characterized by Jane Beal as having "infelicities" and "leav[ing] something to be desired."[7]

In 1978 Malcolm Andrew and Ronald Waldron published their omnibus edition, *The Poems of the Pearl Manuscript*. This edition, largely regarded as the best modern edition of more than one of the poems, was revised and reprinted in 1987, 1989, 1994, and 1996. In the 2007 reprint, the editors included a prose translation on CD-ROM, and in 2008 a print copy of the omnibus translation was made available. The translations stay close to the original; like many of the poems' previous translators, Andrew and Waldron articulate their reason for translation as an attempt to encourage understanding of the poems, which they characterize as "superb, but linguistically difficult."[8] They offer a thorough discussion of their methodology and approach to translation, including a discussion of the difficulty of translating alliterative Middle English poetry into Modern English. *SGGK* and *Pearl* are translated according to the stanzaic divisions in the manuscript; *Cleanness* and *Patience* are divided into structural prose paragraphs—the translators do not agree with the argument that the poems are copied in quatrains in the manuscript.

TRANSLATIONS OF MORE THAN ONE POEM, EXCLUDING OMNIBUS TRANSLATION COLLECTIONS

In 1912, Jessie Weston published *Romance Vision and Satire: English Alliterative Poems of the Fourteenth Century.* This collection includes translations of all of the *Gawain*-poems (the entirety of *SGGK* and *Pearl* are translated, with excerpts of *Cleanness* (lines 1357–1812) and *Patience* (lines 61–344)), along with the *Adventures of Arthur at the Tarn Wadeling, Morte Arthure, Vision of Piers Plowman* (A text) and an extract from the B text of the *Vision of Piers Plowman*, in the poems' original meters. Weston's favoring of *Pearl* and *SGGK* became common practice through translations published in the twentieth century and is still noticed today. Tolkien's posthumous 1975 edition features *Pearl* and *SGGK* alongside *Sir Orfeo.* Significantly, Tolkien's translation of *SGGK* was broadcast on the BBC's *Third Programme* in 1953.[9] The translations imitate the poems' original verse form. Finally, Borroff's translation of *Pearl, SGGK,* and *Patience* (noted in the section on *St. Erkenwald* and comprised of reissues of Borroff's 1967 publication of *SGGK,* her 1977 publication of *Pearl,* and the 2001 addition of *Patience*) reveal the continued and established desire for accessible poetic translations of *SGGK* and *Pearl* especially, but also the comparative omission of accessible translations of both *Patience* and *Cleanness* in the translation history of the *Pearl*-poems.

Brian Stone's 1964 translations include *Pearl* but also *Patience.* Stone's 1971 translation of *Cleanness* (including *St. Erkenwald* and *The Owl and the Nightingale*) is a conscious attempt to make the lesser known and less popularized poems of the *Pearl*-poet widely available. Of *St. Erkenwald* and *Cleanness,* Stone comments that the poems, "deserve rescuing from comparative neglect."[10] His translation is in unrhymed alliterative lines in quatrains.

SINGULAR TRANSLATIONS OF THE COTTON NERO A.X POEMS: *CLEANNESS* AND *PATIENCE*

Cleanness's translation history as a singular poem in its own right would not appear to alleviate the "comparative neglect" that impressed Stone. In 1974 Gollancz reprinted his 1921 and 1933 edition and glossary of *Cleanness,* along with a parallel prose translation by D.S. Brewer. *Cleanness* was not translated as a poem in its own right until 2010 with Kevin Gustafson's facing page volume, and it has not been translated since. Gustafson attempts to preserve alliteration, but not at the expense of incorporating archaic diction and vocabulary.

Patience, as a poem in its own right and therefore deserving of translation and editorial attention, has not been better treated than *Cleanness*. In 1964, Ronald Boyd Koertge translated the poem as his MA thesis; to date, this is the only translation of *Patience* available beyond omnibus collections. Additionally, the internet has not had a great influence on Modern English translations of *Cleanness* and *Patience*. Currently, Richard Alan Scott-Robinson on his *eleusinianm* website devoted to medieval romance, offers translations of both, though these may be better categorized as modern paraphrases, as they are loose retellings, in Modern English prose, and entirely without any articulation of translation approach, methodology, or support apparati.

The disparity in translation treatment between the comparatively expeditious translation notice of *SGGK* and *Pearl* and the other three poems is reflective of their continued translation (and scholarly) treatment over time. It is fair to say that *Pearl* and *SGGK* remain the most popular of all the poems, both within and without academia. Moreover, both poems have received and generated a resurgence in popular interest due to their recent translation treatment, which has generally focused on the descriptive poetic fluidity of both poems.

SINGULAR TRANSLATIONS OF THE
COTTON NERO A.X POEMS: *PEARL*[11]

Given the numerous translations of *Pearl* available, and following Jane Beal's useful categorization, it is sensible to divide the discussion of singular translations of *Pearl* into those including dual-language (edition-translations), and those that include Modern English translations of only one of the poems. It is apparent that *Pearl* enjoyed substantial literary interest as a poem in its own right, from very early in the twentieth century. An accentuated interest in the essentiality of the language of the poem, alongside its poetic devices and character, seems to have flourished later in the twentieth century, and has recently experienced some resurgence.

Sophie Jewett's 1908 translation follows the rhyme and meter of the original Middle English—Jane Beal has called it elegant.[12] Other translations that follow the meter and rhyme of the original Middle English poem include

Coulton's (1906) and Chase's (1932) publications. Marian Mead's 1908 translation follows the original meter, as does Ernest Kirtlan's translation, interestingly called *"Pearl": A Poem of Consolation*. *Pearl*'s thematic focus on aspects of consolation may have contributed to the British Red Cross's decision to publish Gollancz's blank verse translation as a fundraiser campaign to support need after World War I in 1918.[13] Gollancz's 1891 translation, the first of the dual-language translation editions, and in blank verse, provided the translation text for the 1918 stand-alone version. Hillman's, de Ford's and Crawford and Hoyem's dual language translations take different translation approaches. Hillman's (out of print) does not preserve rhyme scheme or alliteration; de Ford, in collaboration with her students, aims to preserve rhyme scheme; and Crawford and Hoyem's translation is unrhymed, and interlinear, rather than facing page. Bill Stanton's 1995 non-scholarly translation is available online, on a rather inelegant but usable site. Interestingly, it offers both verse and prose translations. Watts's posthumous dual-language translation includes introductions by Watts, Kathleen Raine, and Corinne Saunders. Significantly, Watts, in his introduction, wrestles with the traditional belief that *Pearl* is rare as a poem, for its poetics of sensitivity in the treatment of loss and consolation, wondering if the poem is "not really a misguided and overwrought failure,"[14] going further to call the poet's style in *Pearl* one of "preciousness and awkwardness," and claiming the poem to be an experiment in poetic form.[15]

David Gould's 2012 translation is an important addition to the incorporation of manuscript study in Middle English literary scholarship that has occurred over recent decades. Gould's translation includes reproduced photographic images of the manuscript text with transcriptions. Giles Watson's 2012 translation (available in print and online) aims to retain alliteration and rhyme scheme. Additionally, Watson has recorded his translation on *YouTube*, and he has made black and white plates that accompany the print translation available in color on *Flickr*. The online contributions have an unfortunate non-scholarly feel—the online translation is without supporting apparati or commentary, and the *Flickr* content appears randomly selected and without appropriate navigational aids.

Two translations, both supported by Andrew and Waldron's editions, are uniquely concerned with communicating the poetry of *Pearl*. Jane Draycott's 2011 version, introduced by Bernard O'Donoghue, is considered noteworthy for its Modern English readability, yet adherence to the original Middle English. Simon Armitage, in his 2016 translation of *Pearl*, consulted Andrew and Waldron, but includes Osgood's Middle English edition for its facing page Middle English text. This translation of *Pearl* was commissioned by Faber and Faber and W.W. Norton, in response to Armitage's extremely successful translation of *SGGK* in 2007. Alliteration is retained, and footnotes focused on biblical sources and allusions are provided by James Simpson. Armitage's translation won the PEN award for poetry in translation in 2017,[16] and received positive reviews in *The New Yorker*[17] and *The London Magazine*.[18] YouTube clips of Armitage reading the poem are available from Faber and Faber.[19] Jane Beal's 2020 facing-page translation is a recent addition to the corpus of dual-language editions of *Pearl*. This edition offers a thorough introduction that places the poem in its literary and cultural context; additionally, and significantly for students and scholars, it includes both biblical and literary sources.[20]

SINGULAR TRANSLATIONS OF THE COTTON NERO A.X POEMS: *SGGK*

SGGK's scholarly and public interest, as a poem in its own right, has been significant since the first edition of the poem in 1839. The substantial and increased interest in *SGGK* through the twentieth and twenty-first centuries is clear.[21] Translators have, in general, adopted two approaches since Jessie Weston's 1898 prose "retelling" and her 1913 omnibus verse translation. Prose translations tend to focus on the importance of the poem's story—in its plot and high level of description. The usefulness of prose translations for modern students and scholars is likely very limited. John Harrington Cox's 1910 prose translation is of some interest for its contribution to the establishment of the poem's popularity, in that it was included with a similarly loose translation of *Beowulf*. James Winny's 1992 facing-page prose translation is often chosen for undergraduate students. Prose translations continued to be published through the mid-twentieth century, but by the last two decades, it is clear that translators favored verse. Notable recent facing-page verse translations include W. S. Merwin's 2002 approach, which retains alliteration, but in general, was not favorably received,[22] and Larry D. Benson's 2012 contribution, which is well-regarded for its fidelity to the original. The Middle English text in Benson's translation is edited by Donoghue, but is nearly entirely reliant on Davis's 1967 revision of Gordon and Tolkien's 1925 edition.

Verse translations of *SGGK* are by far more numerous than prose translations and have been more influential. Theodore Howard Banks's 1929 translation is viewed as an early successful translation that retains both alliteration and stanzaic form. Others have adopted this approach, with some success, including Brian Stone's 1959 translation, but Borroff's 1967 translation, often reprinted, has by far been the preferred translation for multiple audience types. In 2010, Borroff edited the poem with Laura L. Howes, and the accompanying translation, which retains the original's poetic form and alliteration, has been published as the "authoritative translation."

Simon Armitage's hugely successful 2007 translation retains the bob and wheel rhyme scheme, and alliteration, what Armitage calls the "warp and weft" of the poem.[23] The 2007 and 2009 publications by Faber and Faber include one verse paragraph per page; the 2007 facing-page publication by W.W. Norton uses A. C. Cawley and J. J. Anderson's 1976 Middle English edition of the poem for its facing page original text. Armitage's translation is often praised for its deep poetic sensibility and interpretation; as such, it has generated much public attention. Armitage's translation was profiled in *The Guardian*,[24] and very recently (2018), it was included on the British Library's "Discovering Literature" website.[25] Edward Hirsh's review in the *New York Times* (2007)[26] and John Garth's in *The Telegraph*[27] further popularized Armitage's translation. In 2009, the BBC produced a documentary (available via YouTube) that featured Armitage and was designed to follow Gawain's journey as told in the poem.[28] The BBC has also produced recordings of Armitage's translation read by Ian McKellen.

WEB RESOURCES, ADAPTATIONS, AND PARAPHRASES OF *SGGK*

Because *SGGK* has generated substantial popular interest, countless web-pages devoted to general interest in the poem and its poet exist. For this reason, students and scholars will find the vetted selection provided by the *Cotton Nero A.x. Project* particularly helpful. The site provides links to accepted online texts of *SGGK* and its manuscript companion poems, and to resources such as *Luminarium*, which collects a wide array of materials to support the study of popular medieval and early modern texts.

As a medieval text that continues to be translated and popularized, *SGGK*'s adaptation as a modern children's story is of interest. Notable recent children's adaptations include Zach Weinersmith's 2015 *Augie and the Green Knight*, which alters the Gawain story to feature a female protagonist, and Gerald Morris's 2011 adaptation for the popular *Knights' Tales Series, The Adventures of Sir Gawain the True*, which includes illustrations by Aaron Renier. Morris also adapted *SGGK* for a young adult readership in 1997 with his *The Squire, His Knight, and His Lady*. Michael Smith's illustrated translation (2018) with accompanying linocuts is of particular importance for readers interested in book history.

Sir Gawain and the Green Knight has been adapted as an opera three times. Richard Blackford's 1978 adaptation was based on John Emlyn Edwards's adaptation for children; Harrison Birtwistle's 1991 operatic adaptation *Gawain* was considered successful in its fidelity to the original poetic form; Lynne Plowman's 2002 *Gwyneth and the Green Knight* adapted the story to focus on Gawain's female squire. Theater adaptations have, like operatic, been produced since the 1970s. Of particular note is the Tyneside Theatre company's 1971 version, directed by Michael Bogdanov, a version that featured medieval carols and relied upon Brian Stone's translation. Simon Corble has quite regularly adapted and revised *SGGK* for the stage, beginning in 1992. His most recent version was produced in Oxford at the O'Reilly Theatre in 2014.

SGGK was animated for television in 2002 by Tim Fernee. Famously, among film adaptations, Sean Connery played the Green Knight in Stephen Weeks's 1984 adaptation, *Sword of the Valiant: The Legend of Sir Gawain and the Green Knight.* In 2021, A24 released *The Green Knight*, featuring the actor Dev Patel and directed by David Lowery. The movie was announced in 2018 and was highly anticipated until its release in 2021.[29] The film has been largely well received and has been noted for its attempt to, unlike other screen adaptations, maintain fidelity to the original poem. Perhaps *The Green Knight* film will create a resurgence of interest in the poem itself.

NOTES

1. Angus McIntosh, M. L. Samuels, and M. Benskin, *Linguistic Atlas of Late Mediaeval English*, 4 vols. (Aberdeen: Aberdeen University Press, 1986), III 36–54. Ethan Campbell, in "Authorship: What Does the *Pearl*-Poet Tell Us about Himself?" in this volume, notes Angus McIntosh's earlier work (1963) in determining the poems' dialect and Thorlac Turville-Petre's 1977 contribution to locating the dialect to the Northwest Midlands.

2. Michael D. C. Drout, Jonathan Gerkin, and Scott Kleinman, in "St. Erkenwald," note the similarity of the dialect between *St. Erkenwald* and the Cotton Nero A.x poems, reminding that the question of common authorship is still unresolved. Ethan Campbell, in "Authorship" in this volume, deals with questions concerning identity and its nuance, and what might be claimed as character, knowledge, and interests of the author, among a discussion of common authorship. David K. Coley's "The Northwest Midlands and the Ricardian Court," briefly notes the poems' "regionally inflected landscapes," among a thorough consideration of the Northwest Midlands localization against the context of the court of Richard II.

3. See also John Bowers, "Audiences, Medieval and Modern" in this volume, for a discussion of some editorial and translation history of the poems, including a discussion of select recent editions and translations, and their intended or appropriate audiences.

4. For a thorough discussion of ecology in, and ecocritical approaches to, the *Pearl*-poet's works, including *SGGK*, see Elizabeth Allen, "Ecology in the *Pearl*-Poet" in this volume.

5. For further discussion of the localized dialect of the poem and its connection to landscape, see Ralph Elliott, "Landscape and Geography," in *A Companion to the* Gawain-*Poet*, ed Derek Brewer and Jonathan Gibson (Cambridge: D.S. Brewer, 1997), 105–17. See also David K. Coley, "The Northwest Midlands and the Ricardian Court."

6. Translations that offer only excerpts of the poems and those in anthologies are not discussed here. For these, see Malcolm Andrew, *The* Gawain-*Poet: An Annotated Bibliography, 1839–1977* (New York: Garland, 1979). See also Robert J. Blanch, *The* Gawain-*Poems: A Reference Guide, 1978–1993* (Albany, NY: Whitston Publishing, 2000), and Meg Stainsby, *Sir Gawain and the Green Knight: An Annotated Bibliography, 1978–1989* (New York: Garland Publishing, 1992).

7. Jane Beal, "Classroom Texts," in *Approaches to Teaching the Middle English Pearl*, ed. Jane Beal and Mark Bradshaw Busbee (New York: Modern Language Association, 2018), 27.

8. Malcom Andrew and Ronald Waldron, *The Poems of the* Pearl *Manuscript in Modern English Prose Translation. Pearl, Cleanness, Patience, Sir Gawain and the Green Knight.* (Exeter: Exeter Press, 2008), Preface.

9. Christopher Tolkien, "Preface," in *Sir Gawain and the Green Knight, Pearl, and Sir Orfeo*, trans. J. R. R. Tolkien (London: Allen and Unwin, 1975), 7.

10. Brian Stone, in *The Owl and the Nightingale. Cleanness. St. Erkenwald* (Harmondsworth: Penguin, 1971), Foreword.

11. For a more thorough discussion of translations of *Pearl*, see Jane Beal, "Classroom Texts," 26–34.

12. Beal, "Classroom Texts," 32.

13. Beal, "Classroom Texts," 32.

14. Victor Watts, *Pearl: A Modernised Version of the Middle English Poem* (London: Enitharmon Press, 2005), 7.

15. Watts, *Pearl*, 7–8.

16. "2017 Pen America Literary Awards Winners," https://pen.org/2017-pen-literary-awards-winners/.

17. Josephine Livingstone, "The Strange Power of a Medieval Poem about the Death of a Child," *New York Times*, June 16, 2016, https://www.newyorker.com/books/page-turner/the-strange-power-of-a-medieval-poem-about-the-death-of-a-child.

18. Robert Hawkins, "*Pearl* by Simon Armitage," *The London Magazine*, July 18, 2016, https://www.thelondonmagazine.org/pearl-simon-armitage/.

19. "*Pearl* by Simon Armitage," last modified May 6, 2016, https://youtube/PN9pRgel2zk.

20. Beal, ed. and trans., *Pearl: Text and Translation* (Peterborough: Broadview, 2020).

21. Mickey Sweeney's "The Failure of Perfection in *Sir Gawain and the Green Knight*" in this volume, notes the poem's popularity for scholarly study, and in her study of the role and functioning of authority and perfection in the poem itself and the romance genre, provides an examination of recent trends in *SGGK*'s recent scholarly treatment.

22. Jeremy Noel Tod, "To Sleep among Icicles," *The Guardian*, February 21, 2004, https://www.theguardian.com/books/2004/feb/21/featuresreviews .guardianreview15.

23. Simon Armitage, trans., *Sir Gawain and the Green Knight* (London: Faber and Faber, 2007), viii.

24. Nicholas Lezard, "There's Life in the Green Giant Yet," *The Guardian*, March 8, 2008, https://www.theguardian.com/books/2008/mar/08/simonarmitage.

25. Simon Armitage, *Sir Gawain and the Green Knight: An Introduction*, in *Discovering Literature: Medieval*, January 31, 2018, https://www.bl.uk/medieval -literature/articles/sir-gawain-and-the-green-knight-an-introduction.

26. Edward Hirsch, "A Stranger in Camelot," *New York Times*, December 16, 2007, https://www.nytimes.com/2007/12/16/books/review/Hirsch-t.html.

27. John Garth, "Sir Gawain Rides Again," *The Telegraph*, February 4, 2007, https: //www.telegraph.co.uk/culture/books/3662939/Sir-Gawain-rides-again.html.

28. "BBC Documentary: *Sir Gawain and the Green Knight*," YouTube, https:// youtu.be/74glI1lg1CQ.

29. Amanda N'Duka, "The Old Man & The Gun' Director David Lowery, A24 Team On Fantasy Epic 'Green Knight,'" *Deadline*, November 5, 2018, https:// deadline.com/2018/11/the-old-man-the-gun-director-david-lowery-a24-green-knight -1202496454/.

26 Mark Kermode, "The Green Knight Review—A Rich and Wild Fantasy," *The Guardian*, September 26, 2021, https://www.theguardian.com/film/2021/sep/26/the -green-knight-review-david-lowery-dev-patel-gawain.

BIBLIOGRAPHY

Andrew, Malcolm. *The Gawain-Poet: An Annotated Bibliography, 1839–1977*. New York: Garland, 1979.

Andrew, Malcolm, and Ronald Waldron, eds. *The Poems of the Pearl Manuscript: Pearl, Cleanness, Patience, Sir Gawain and the Green Knight*. London: Edward Arnold, 1978. Rev. ed. Exeter: University of Exeter Press, 1987, 1989, 1994, 1996, 2007.

Andrew, Malcolm, and Ronald Waldron. *The Poems of the Pearl Manuscript in Modern English Prose Translation. Pearl, Cleanness, Patience, Sir Gawain and the Green Knight*. Exeter: Exeter Press, 2008.

Armitage, Simon, trans. *Pearl.* New York: W.W. Norton, 2016.

———, trans. *Pearl.* London: Faber and Faber, 2016.

———, trans. *Sir Gawain and the Green Knight*. London: Faber and Faber, 2007.

———, trans. *Sir Gawain and the Green Knight.* New York: W.W. Norton, 2007.

———. *Sir Gawain and the Green Knight: An Introduction.* In *Discovering Literature: Medieval*. Accessed January 31, 2018. https://www.bl.uk/medieval -literature/articles/sir-gawain-and-the-green-knight-an-introduction.

Banks, Theodore Howard Jr., trans. *Sir Gawain and the Green Knight*. New York: Appleton, 1929.

Beal, Jane. "Classroom Texts." In *Approaches to Teaching the Middle English Pearl*, ed. Jane Beal and Mark Bradshaw Busbee. New York: Modern Language Association, 2018.

———, ed. and trans. *Pearl: Text and Translation*. Peterborough: Broadview, 2020.

Benson, Larry D., trans. *Sir Gawain and the Green Knight: A Close Verse Translation*. Morgantown: West Virginia University Press, 2012.

Birtwistle, Harrison. *Sir Gawain*. Libretto by David Harsent. London: Universal, 1991.

Blackford, Richard, composer. *Sir Gawain and the Green Knight*. London: Argo, 1979.

Blanch, Robert J. *The Gawain-Poems: A Reference Guide, 1978–1993*. Albany, NY: Whitston Publishing, 2000.

Bogdanov, Michael, director. *Sir Gawain and the Green Knight*. Newcastle: Tyneside Theatre, 1971.

Borroff, Marie, trans. *The Gawain-Poet: Complete Works. Patience. Cleanness. Pearl. St. Erkenwald*. New York: W.W. Norton, 2011.

———, trans. *Sir Gawain and the Green Knight: A New Verse Translation*. New York: W.W. Norton, 1967.

———, trans. *Sir Gawain and the Green Knight. Patience. Pearl*. New York: W.W. Norton, 2001.

Borroff, Marie, and Laura Howes, eds. Marie Borroff, trans. *Sir Gawain and the Green Knight*. New York: W.W. Norton, 2010.

Cawley, A. C. And J. J. Anderson, eds. *Pearl, Cleanness, Patience, Sir Gawain and the Green Knight*. London: Dent, 1976.

Chase, Stanley Perkins, trans. *The Pearl: The Fourteenth Century English Poem Rendered in Modern Verse*. London: Oxford University Press, 1932.

Corble, Simon, director. *Sir Gawain and the Green Knight*. Oxford: O'Reilly Theatre, 2014.

Cotton Nero A.x. Project. "Web Resources for Pearl-Poet Study: A Vetted Selection." Murray McGillivray, ed. Accessed June 31, 2019. http://people.ucalgary.ca/~scriptor/cotton/blognew.

Coulton, G. G., trans. *Pearl: A Fourteenth-Century Poem, Rendered into Modern English*. 1906. London: Nutt, 1907.

Cox, John Harrington, trans. *Sir Gawain and the Green Knight. Knighthood in Germ and Flower: the Anglo-Saxon Epic, "Beowulf," and the Arthurian Tale "Sir Gawain and the Green Knight."* Boston, MA: Little, 1910.

Crawford, John F., and Andrew Hoyem, trans. *The Pearl*. San Francisco: Grabhorn-Hoyem, 1967.

De Ford, Sara, ed and trans. *The Pearl*. New York: AHM, 1967.

Draycott, Jane, trans. *Pearl*. London: Carcanet Press, 2011.

Elliott, Ralph. "Landscape and Geography." In *A Companion to the Gawain-Poet*, edited by Derek Brewer and Jonathan Gibson, 105–17. Cambridge: D.S. Brewer, 1997.

Firnee, Tim, director. *Sir Gawain and the Green Knight*. Moving Still Productions, 2002.

Finch, Casey, trans. *The Complete Works of the Pearl Poet.* Berkeley: University of California Press, 1993.

Gardner, John, trans. *The Complete Works of the Gawain Poet: In a Modern English Version with a Critical Introduction.* Chicago: University of Chicago Press, 1965.

Garth, John. "Sir Gawain Rides Again." *The Telegraph*, February 4, 2007. https://www.telegraph.co.uk/culture/books/3662939/Sir-Gawain-rides-again.html.

Gollancz, Sir Israel, ed. *Cleanness: An Alliterative Tripartite Poem on the Deluge, the Destruction of Sodom, and the Death of Belshazzar, by the Poet of Pearl.* London: Oxford University Press, 1921.

———, ed. *Cleanness: An Alliterative Tripartite Poem on the Deluge, the Destruction of Sodom, and the Death of Belshazzar, by the Poet of Pearl, with New English Translation by D.S. Brewer.* Cambridge: Brewer, 1974.

———, ed. *Cleanness: Glossary and Illustrative Texts.* London: Oxford University Press, 1933.

———, ed. and trans. *Pearl: An English Poem of the Fourteenth Century with a Modern Rendering.* London: Nutt, 1891.

———, trans. *Pearl: An English Poem of the Fourteenth Century.* Ed. British Red Cross. London: Jones, 1918.

Gould, David, trans. *Pearl of Great Price: A Literary Translation of the Middle English Pearl.* Lanham, MD: University Press of America, 2012.

Gustafson, Kevin, ed and trans. *Cleanness.* Peterborough, ON: Broadview Press, 2010.

Hawkins, Robert. "*Pearl* by Simon Armitage." *The London Magazine*, July 18, 2016. https://www.thelondonmagazine.org/pearl-simon-armitage/.

Hillman, Sr. Mary Vincent, ed and trans. *The Pearl: Mediaeval Text with a Literal Translation and Interpretation.* Morristown, NJ: College of Saint Elizabeth Press, University Publishers, 1961; Notre Dame, IN: University of Notre Dame Press, 1967.

Hirsch, Edward. "A Stranger in Camelot." *New York Times*, December 16, 2007. https://www.nytimes.com/2007/12/16/books/review/Hirsch-t.html.

Horstmann, Carl, ed. *Altenglische Legenden: Neue Folge.* Heibronn: Gr. Henninger, 1881.

Kermode, Mark. "The Green Knight Review—A Rich and Wild Fantasy." *The Guardian.* September 26, 2021. https://www.theguardian.com/film/2021/sep/26/the-green-knight-review-david-lowery-dev-patel-gawain.

Kirkland, Ernest J. B., trans. *Pearl: A Poem of Consolation. Rendered into Modern English Verse.* London: Kelly, 1918.

Koertge, Ronald Boyd. *A Translation of the Middle English Poem Patience.* MA Thesis. University of Arizona, 1964.

Lezard, Nicholas. "There's Life in the Green Giant Yet." *The Guardian*, March 8, 2008. https://www.theguardian.com/books/2008/mar/08/simonarmitage.

Livingstone, Josephine. "The Strange Power of a Medieval Poem about the Death of a Child." *New Yorker Times*, June 16, 2016. https://www.newyorker.com/books/page-turner/the-strange-power-of-a-medieval-poem-about-the-death-of-a-child.

Lowery, David, director. *The Green Knight.* A24, 2021.

Luminarium: Anthology of English Literature. Accessed June 31, 2019. http://www.luminarium.org.

McIntosh, Angus, M. L. Samuels, and M. Benskin. *Linguistic Atlas of Late Mediaeval English.* 4 vols. Aberdeen: Aberdeen University Press, 1986.

McKellen, Ian. "Sir Gawain and the Green Knight." BBC Radio Four. December 21, 2006.

Madden, Frederic. *Syr Gawayn: A Collection of Ancient Romance-Poems, by Scotish and English Authors, Related to That Celebrated Knight of the Round Table.* 1839. New York: AMS, 1971.

Mead, Marian, trans. *The Pearl: An English-Vision Poem of the Fourteenth Century Done into Modern Verse.* Portland, OR: Mosher, 1908.

Merwin, W.S. *Sir Gawain and the Green Knight: A New Verse Translation.* New York: Knopf, 2002.

Morris, Gerald. *The Adventures of Sir Gawain the True.* Boston, MA: Houghton Mifflin Harcourt, 2011.

———. *The Squire, His Knight, and His Lady.* Boston, MA: Houghton Mifflin Harcourt, 1997.

Morris, R[ichard], ed. *Early English Alliterative Poems in the West-Midland Dialect of the Fourteenth Century.* 1864. London: Oxford University Press, 1869.

Amanda N'Duka, "'The Old Man and The Gun' Director David Lowery, A24 Team on Fantasy Epic 'Green Knight.'" *Deadline.* November 5, 2018, https://deadline.com/2018/11/the-old-man-the-gun-director-david-lowery-a24-green-knight-1202496454/.

Osgood, Charles G., Jr., ed. *The Pearl: A Middle English Poem.* London: Heath, 1906.

Pen America. "2017 Pen America Literary Awards Winners" Accessed June 30, 2019. https://pen.org/2017-pen-literary-awards-winners/.

Peterson, Clifford. *St. Erkenwald.* Philadelphia: University of Pennsylvania Press, 1977.

Plowman, Lynne, composer. *Gwyneth and the Green Knight.* Breton: Music Theatre Wales, 2002.

Scott-Robinson, Richard Allen. *Eleusinianm.* Accessed June 30, 2019. http://www.eleusinianm.co.uk/index.html.

Smith, Michael, trans. and illustrator. Sir Gawain and the Green Knight. London: Unbound, 2018.

Stainsby, Meg. *Sir Gawain and the Green Knight: An Annotated Bibliography, 1978–1989.* New York: Garland Publishing, 1992.

Stanton, Bill. trans. "This Being a Translation in Verse of the Middle English poem *Pearl* by an Unknown Poet." Accessed 30 June 2019. http://www.andystanton.co.uk/BillStanton/pearl/menu.htm.

Stone, Brian., trans. *Sir Gawain and the Green Knight.* Harmondsworth: Penguin, 1959.

———, trans. *Medieval English Verse.* Harmondsworth: Penguin, 1964.

———, trans. *The Owl and the Nightingale. Cleanness. St. Erkenwald.* Harmondsworth: Penguin, 1971.

Tod, Jeremy Noel. "To Sleep Among Icicles." *The Guardian*. February 21, 2004. https://www.theguardian.com/books/2004/feb/21/featuresreviews.guardianreview15.

Tolkien, J. R. R., trans., and Christopher Tolkien, ed. *Sir Gawain and the Green Knight, Pearl, and Sir Orfeo*. London: Allen and Unwin, 1975.

Vantuono, William, ed., and trans. *The Pearl Poems: An Omnibus Edition. Vol. 1: Pearl and Cleanness. Vol 2: Patience and Sir Gawain and the Green Knight*. New York: Garland, 1984.

Watson, Giles. *Pearl: A Translation from the Middle English*. Lulu, 2014.

———. *Pearl*. Flickr. Accessed 30 June 2019. https://www.flickr.com/photos/29320962@N07/6927356054.

Watts, Victor, trans. *Pearl: A Modernised Version of the Middle English Poem*. London: Press, 2005.

Weeks, Stephen, director. *Sword of the Valiant: The Legend of Gawain and the Green Knight*. Cannon, 1983.

Weinersmith, Zachary. *Augie and the Green Knight*. New York: Breadpig, 2015.

Weston, Jessie, L., trans. *Sir Gawain and the Green Knight: A Middle English Arthurian Romance Retold in Modern Prose*. 1989. London: Nutt, 1900.

Weston, Jessie L., trans. *Romance Vision and Satire: English Alliterative Poems of the Fourteenth Century*. 1912. Gloucester, MA: Peter Smith, 1965.

Williams, Margaret, trans. *The Pearl-Poet: His Complete Works*. New York: Random House, 1967.

Winny, James, ed. and trans. *Sir Gawain and the Green Knight: Middle English Text with Facing Translation*. New York: Broadview Press, 1992.

YouTube. "*Pearl* Read by Giles Watson." Accessed June 30, 2019. https://youtu.be/xU497BZRyHs.

———. "*Pearl* by Simon Armitage." Accessed June 30, 2019. https://youtu.be/PN9pRgel2zk.

———. "BBC Documentary: Sir Gawain and the Green Knight." Accessed June 30, 2019. https://youtu.be/74glI1lg1CQ. Originally aired via BBC Four, June 4, 2009.

Chapter Sixteen

Audiences, Medieval and Modern

John M. Bowers

The complete anonymity of the *Gawain*-poet requires examining his works themselves along with the two manuscripts in which they survive for evidence of an original fourteenth-century audience more specific than simply a mixed coterie of pious layfolk and courtly clergy.[1] The recovery of these poems in the nineteenth century, after four hundred years of almost total neglect, then led to the emergence of a variety of modern audiences reflected in a series of scholarly editions, critical studies, university textbooks, and poetic translations.

Though the author almost certainly recited his poetry to his original audience, the unknown patron who commissioned the Cotton Nero A.x manuscript is the crucial early reader who valued the works highly enough to hire a scribe to preserve them in a volume of ninety vellum leaves small enough at 5 x 7 inches to be portable for different readers in different places.[2] If Gervase Mathew was correct that the scribe copied from a grand presentation manuscript,[3] another patron had already invested richly in the poet's works. Perhaps selecting from a larger corpus while excluding *St. Erkenwald* (plus other works possibly), Cotton Nero A.x's patron also played a role in starting and ending his collection with the two works still considered the best: *Pearl, Cleanness, Patience,* and *Sir Gawain and the Green Knight.* Some of the approximately four hundred scribal errors may already have entered the textual transmission as evidence of earlier readerships. The primary scribe inserted forty-eight decorated initials that have been judged as reader-responses to structure, symbolism, and meaning.[4] Since his hand has not been identified elsewhere, the copyist may have been a skilled amateur who literally loved what he wrote out.

Sir Israel Gollancz identified two other scribal interventions: "a corrector has here and there tampered with the original, and another hand seems to have gone over some passages which evidently had already become almost illegible."[5] These two correctors must also be counted among early readers who took seriously the texts and respected their precise wordings, even their spellings. In addition to a listening audience, that is, the author had attracted readers who appreciated his literary artistry and craftsmanship, including even the intricate numerical structures which would have been lost upon listeners, specifically the 1212 lines in *Pearl* and the 2,530 lines in *Gawain*.[6]

The Cotton Nero A.x's twelve illustrations, more than survive for any other Middle English romance manuscript, were executed at some time after the copying of the poems, probably during the first two decades of the fifteenth century, and they were inserted wherever they fitted on blank pages.[7] This hiatus between copying and decorating probably resulted from a change in ownership, hence a second early reader who wanted to make his little volume look more impressive. The artist may have been following the directions of this new owner whose reading led to conscientious efforts at highlighting significant moments in the narratives, even though the resulting pictures have been routinely disparaged as crude in execution. The artist himself, to a degree hard to disentangle from whoever hired him, nonetheless represents another early reader who brought independent insights to the poems. Yet as reader-responses, his pictures also show lapses in attentiveness. *Cleanness*, for example, says that Noah's Ark was "withouten mast" (417), but the illuminator went ahead and included a mast.

The poet's original audience readily understood his Cheshire dialect along with his audacious vocabulary reckoned by J. R. R. Tolkien and E. V. Gordon as "a new word in every line."[8] A. C. Spearing expressed the critical consensus that emerged by the second half of the twentieth century that these were "works of high art for aristocratic patrons" that originated "in an area remote from the metropolis and from the cultural influences which, under Richard II, radiated from the royal court."[9] The challenge became locating within the poet's dialect region these aristocratic patrons with an appreciation for the courtly lifestyle of jewelry, luxurious clothing, tapestries, feasts, music, dancing, armor, jousting, hunting, and castles. The historian Michael Bennett's 1983 book on Cheshire society searched for this literary milieu only to conclude that there was an "absence of any major aristocratic court or ecclesiastical establishment" which might have provided patronage or audience for such lavish poetic productions.[10] His subsequent studies have sought these Cheshire-dialect speakers in exactly the place which Spearing had considered too remote—the Ricardian court.[11]

Richard II bestowed especial favor upon leading Cheshiremen such as Sir John Stanley and Sir Richard Cradock as well as scores of Cheshire archers selected to form his personal bodyguard. The Garter motto's insertion into the Cotton Nero A.x manuscript connects all-too-neatly with Sir John Stanley's induction in 1405 as the first Knight of the Garter based in Cheshire.[12] Local clerks such as Thomas Langley and Robert Hallum also found successful careers in Westminster. Cheshireman John Macclesfield enjoyed a series of high-level appointments serving as Richard II's secretary, his privy seal clerk, and finally keeper of the wardrobe.[13] During the final years of Richard II's reign, Bennett concluded, "It is hard to find a single Cheshire family of note who did not have a member in the royal retinue."[14] For the *Gawain*-poet as a participant-observer of this southward migration, his expatriate audience occupied metropolitan niches far more courtly and sophisticated than anything available in his dialect region.[15] The author's intended audience, then, would have been these Cheshire natives whose careers in military service and royal administration had advanced them along patronage networks toward the centers of national power, even the mobile household of Richard II himself.

Already E. V. Gordon's edition of *Pearl* had boldly suggested that the poetry's dialect may localize the author's Cheshire upbringing, but "it is not necessary to assume that he was actually living there when he wrote."[16] Nor was his immediate audience necessarily living there, either. In 1386, Chaucer testified during the Scrope-Grosvenor controversy that he had seen the disputed coat-of-arms hanging from the London townhouse of Sir Robert Grosvenor, a knight of the county of Cheshire. This heraldic dispute played out in miniature the conflict between Londoners and Cheshiremen in which the *Gawain*-poet would naturally have sided with his compatriots.[17] More to the point, Grosvenor's London townhouse is exactly the sort of establishment in which to imagine the author pursuing some clerical career in which poetry-making became a sideline—and in which to imagine, too, a coterie of Cheshiremen who constituted his first audience. Thus Bennett believes that Grosvenor assuredly knew the *Gawain*-poet.[18] Nor did the author labor in isolation from the vibrant literary activities ongoing elsewhere in the metropolis. Tolkien believed that Chaucer knew *Gawain* and probably its author, too.[19] Thus the author of the *Squire's Tale* with its reference to Sir Gawain (in lines 89–97) had become another member of the Cheshire poet's London audience.

The author's original audience would have shared to varying degrees the social, political, and religious values embodied in his writings. For example, *Pearl*'s Parable of the Vineyard implicitly took the side of landowners against laborers in wage disputes, and both *Pearl* and *St. Erkenwald* defended the orthodox doctrine of baptism against assaults by Lollard reformers. Conservative Cheshire was never a hotbed of Wycliffism.[20] The poet's rich imagery and technical expertise aspired not simply to the courtly but to the regal, with a splendor and a savor for lavish details befitting the magnificence of Richard II's court. The poet's audience was near enough to the household to joke about the king and his youthful courtiers as "berdlez chylder"[21] in *Gawain*, and the Kenilworth chronicler recounted how the

Cheshire bodyguard had license to banter with Richard II—and to do so in their regional language.[22] Deep differences nevertheless persisted between the poet and his courtly audience: the clerical against the aristocratic, the Cheshire outsider against the London establishment, the value of religious poverty against the opulence of royal display, and clerical celibacy against arranged aristocratic marriages as well as wide-ranging sexual intrigues.

Evidence put forward for identifying the author as a Massey, now almost universally discredited,[23] nonetheless points to likely candidates for patrons and early readers. The Mascy surname has been spotted in wordplay in *Pearl*;[24] two marginal decorations in *Cleanness* are thought to conceal the name "J Macy";[25] and the name Thomas Masse appears in the *St. Erkenwald* manuscript.[26] Cheshire was plentifully supplied with Masseys. There was John de Massey who served as rector of Stockport until his death in 1376, John de Mascy of Sale who was rector of Ashton-on-Mersey in Cheshire, and John Massey of Cotton who was later retained by Richard II.[27] John de Mascy of Podington fought for Henry IV against John de Mascy of Tatton who supported Henry Percy, both of whom were slain at the battle of Shrewsbury in 1403. Bennett notes that Alliterative poets pursued careers in manor-houses of knightly families much like the Mascys of Tatton.[28] Reduced to provinciality, the Cotton Nero A.x and the Harley 2250 manuscripts reflect the fifteenth-century decline of Cheshire privilege following the deposition of Richard II and the narrowing, even the disappearance, of the author's first audiences.[29]

The Harley 2250 manuscript with its unique copy of *St. Erkenwald* is unusually informative, even dated in a colophon to 1477.[30] It is a rather home-made affair, with paper pages devoid of decoration, all reflecting a continued waning in prestige. The alliterative poem appears in context of thirty-eight other hagiographic items such as excerpts from the Stanzaic *Life of Christ* and *South English Legendary* written in the same Cheshire dialect. Elizabeth Salter reckoned the poem originally had a profile identical to what we imagine for *Gawain*—"written for westerners living and working in London by a poet who was himself an immigrant"[31]—and Marie Borroff has gone further reasserting, convincingly I think, the case for common authorship with the Cotton Nero A.x poems.[32] John Scattergood shrewdly guessed the compilation functioned as private devotional reading for some prominent local clergyman who pursued a career that took him to London where the poem's action is set.[33] Besides Thomas Massey, the manuscript's pages contain the names of other Cheshire natives such as Elizabeth Booth; Laurence Booth was appointed Dean of St. Paul's in 1456. Inclusion of Sir Thomas Bowker's name allows the manuscript's custodians to be traced into the 1530s.[34] The many marginal glosses in a seventeenth-century hand bear witness to an ongoing engagement with *St. Erkenwald*.

The tail-rhyme *Grene Knight*, sounding like Chaucer's jingle-jangle *Sir Thopas*, survives along with ten other Arthurian romances in the Percy Folio compiled in the 1640s by a copyist with antiquarian enthusiasms. It was discovered in the late 1750s by Thomas Percy and included in his landmark *Reliques of Ancient English Poetry* in 1765. Fifteenth-century vocabulary provides an approximate dating, and resemblances in plot and phrasing indicate some relationship to *Sir Gawain and the Green Knight*, though it is not clear what this tells us about this later poet's sense of audience. Did he assume that his listeners already knew *Gawain*'s story well enough that he could streamline it for economy's sake? Or did he fear that the original fourteenth-century narrative had been so audacious and potentially baffling that he needed to simplify and make obvious what had been most intriguing in the original?

George Lyman Kittredge believed that plot similarities and line echoes, forty of which he listed, resulted either because the *Grene Knight* was based upon some common French source, now lost, or more likely because the poet knew *Gawain* and simplified it to popularize the contents of its highly literate antecedent.[35] Diane Speed was impressed that the compiler's language belonged to Cheshire, the dialect region of the original audience, but she too wrestled with the question of influence, wondering if there had been intermediate versions, with some stage of memorial reconstruction, which brought forward the folk-motifs of the beheading game and the lady's temptation without any of the psychological subtleties.[36] Thomas Hahn cast a wide net and concluded that Cotton Nero A.x's sophisticated text exercised little influence upon the popular Gawain tradition of the fifteenth century, and while details of the *Grene Knight*'s plot appear to have been drawn from *Gawain*, this quirky later poem made its appeal mostly as a plot-summary for oral performance.[37]

Gillian Rogers believes that the fifteenth-century redactor did indeed know *Gawain* not merely at several removes, but very directly, with close verbal parallels and clusters of resemblances, although the later writer may have forgotten details over time as his memory compressed and made more swift-moving the original storyline. Landscape descriptions were among the saddest casualties. So too were the dramatically tense moments such as the Green Knight's challenge to Arthur where the *Grene Knight*'s redactor simply misunderstood the episode's purpose. "He introduced three major structural changes into his version which, in effect, reduce the carefully-wrought, finely-detailed architecture of the plot of *Gawain* to rubble."[38]

Generally the storyteller felt that his audience needed more obvious, hence cruder motivations for the action. Modern readers continue to puzzle over Lady Bertilak's role in the plot, for example. Is her brilliant campaign of seduction in the bedroom simply an extension of her husband's participation in Morgan's vindictive plotting? How indeed did Morgan recruit this beautiful, clever lady to tempt Gawain into a sexual trap that could have cost her virtue? Banishing such perplexities, the *Grene Knight* creates an almost fabliau-like directness: "Bredbeddle is sent to court by his mother-in-law, the witch Agostes, to lure Gawain to his castle to satisfy his wife's love-longing."[39] This motivation, however kinky with the husband acting as his wife's pimp, was rendered easy enough to grasp by a listening audience. All in all, the *Grene Knight*'s debasement of a great poetic achievement further attests to the decline of a local Cheshire audience for refined courtly literature.

Rossell Hope Robbins argued that the gentry aficionado Humfrey Newton, who lived at Macclesfield in Cheshire in the early sixteenth century, possessed an intimate acquaintance with *Sir Gawain* because one (but only one) of the twenty poems copied into his commonplace book echoed the romance in four (but only four) of its forty lines.[40] A closer look at the evidence suggests that whoever composed these uneven octosyllabic lines drew upon the same Alliterative tradition and therefore could hardly have avoided approximating a few phrases used in *Sir Gawain*. It is remarkable not that the poem shares some vocabulary but that it does not share more. Who was this versifier? Robbins thought it was Newton himself, though the poem resembles none of the others in his manuscript. The more fanciful conclusion is that an early sixteenth-century versifier tried, like Edmund Spenser later, to write in a self-consciously archaic language but without necessarily reading *Sir Gawain* itself. Another possibility is that the poem survived as an authentic fourteenth-century relic drawing upon the same Alliterative language as *Sir Gawain*.

It would not be surprising if Edmund Spenser himself had taken an interest in the Cotton Nero A.x poems, but C. L. Wrenn does not provide convincing evidence from *The Shepheardes Calendar*. His conjecture that the flower-passage in the April Eclogue bears a close resemblance to the beginning of *Pearl* goes no further than noting both poets described flowers with medicinal properties. The single Spenserian phrase *madding mynd* is then juxtaposed with a single line in *Pearl*—"My manneȝ mynde to madding malte"[41]—before the argument leaps headlong to the conclusion "Spenser may have known something of the work of the *Gawain*-poet."[42] Wrenn seems to have shared everyone's disappointment that a major medieval poet had dropped into oblivion after his lifetime, and engaging in wishful thinking, he was overly eager to insert *Pearl* into England's literary genealogy alongside works, such as *Troilus and Criseyde*, which were actually read by great writers of the Renaissance.

The first hard evidence of the *Pearl*-poet's emergence is a list of manuscripts compiled before 1614 indicating that the unique copy had found its way to the physician Henry Savile of Banke in Yorkshire. This avid collector had secured spoils from suppressed Northern religious houses where this modest volume may have lain unread by the monks for decades. Another possibility is suggested by Joel Fredell who proposes York as a center for book production where Cotton Nero A.x was actually copied.[43] In any case, Savile's catalog identifies the manuscript only by the first line of the first poem: "An owld booke in English verse beginning Perle plesant to Princes pay." This hardly indicates anyone's close reading. Somewhat more effort at examining the manuscript is evident when it was acquired by the great antiquarian Sir Robert Cotton around 1621. His catalog described it as "Gesta Arthuri regis et aliorum versu anglico" as indication that his librarian had delved into the vellum pages far enough to find *Gawain* on folio 95.

If scribes were arguably the first readers of the *Pearl*-poet, nineteenth-century editors provide abundant evidence for modern readers with their own various appreciations and agendas. In 1839, Sir Frederic Madden published the first edition upon which he bestowed the title that stuck: *Syr Gawayn and the Grene Knyȝt*. The subtitle of his omnibus edition announced the patriotic motive for his project: *A Collection of Ancient Romance-Poems by Scotish and English Authors*. Madden tells how Thomas Warton had inspected the manuscript for his *History of English Poetry* (1781) and how he himself had communicated his discovery of the work to Sir Walter Scott, who was eager for its publication as a specimen of "ancient Scottish literature." The famous poet and novelist promoted subscriptions for the collection's publication by the Bannatyne Club which he had founded to print rare works of Scottish interest. As a result of this sponsorship, Madden was quick to follow prior suggestions that the anonymous author was the Scottish writer Huchown of the Awle Ryale. This deluxe edition enjoyed an elite distribution restricted to the Club's one hundred aristocratic members, though in terms of gauging a modern audience, it is doubtful whether *Sir Gawain* was read attentively (if at all) by members such as the Earl of Aberdeen, the Earl of Ashburnham, or the Duke of Bedford.

Madden could say only that the unknown author was Northern, and it would await Richard Morris's *Specimens of Early English* (1867) to distinguish the dialects of Middle English and provide the grounds for disqualifying the *Pearl*-poet as a Scotsman. Morris himself had already become the first editor of *Pearl*, *Patience*, and *Cleanness* in the inaugural edition of the Early English Text Society in 1864 with a title that rebutted Madden's claims for a Scottish author: *Early English Alliterative Poems in the West-Midland Dialect of the Fourteenth Century.*

In 1864, the formidable Frederick J. Furnivall had gathered a small group of scholars from the Philological Society and established the Early English Text Society in order to bring "the mass of unprinted Early English literature within the reach of students and to provide sound texts from which the *New English Dictionary* could quote."[44] Furnivall had democratic as well as philological impulses, and he wanted affordable texts different from the deluxe volumes of printing societies such as the Bannatyne Club. Yet when Morris published his ground-breaking edition, EETS itself had only 145 members who could be reckoned as the first modern readers of Cotton Nero A.x's three religious poems. Since one of these subscribers was Lord Tennyson, however, the edition could be said to have enjoyed, in the words of John Milton, a "fit audience though few."

Morris prefaced his *Alliterative Poems* with remarks anticipating the trajectory of the readership into the twentieth century. His sense that the three poems were "evidently the work of a man of birth and education" and "may claim to stand in the foremost rank of England's early bards"[45] looked forward to securing places for these literary masterpieces on the university syllabus at Oxford and Cambridge. Already, too, he was straddling the academic division between Language and Literature—"Leaving out of consideration their great philological worth, they possess an intrinsic value of their own as literary compositions"[46]—and when he acknowledged the "hardness of the language" and provided extracts with interlinear translations that "give the reader stomach to digest the whole,"[47] he looked forward to the need for modern English translations in order for non-specialist readers, including undergraduates, to negotiate these highly intricate poems written in a non-London dialect which Morris located more precisely in Cheshire or Lancashire.[48]

Sir Israel Gollancz's *Pearl: An English Poem of the Fourteenth Century Edited with a Modern Rendering* (1891) hoped that Tennyson's endorsement would encourage a popular readership: "graced with the imprimatur of his honored name, *Pearl* will, I feel sure, find kindly welcome in many an English home."[49] He was over-optimistic. The Cotton Nero A.x poems established themselves in the canon only with the emergence of the English degree at universities in the early twentieth century when classroom teachers needed affordable editions as well as critical studies aimed at fellow academics as well as their students. At Harvard, Kittredge's *Study of "Gawain and the Green Knight"* (1916) specifically addressed "students of medieval literature."[50] However challenging for a fourteenth-century audience, these works placed even heavier demands upon modern readers, so much so that they became favorites for the "crux-busting" of New Criticism starting with René Wellek's classic 1933 study of *Pearl*.

At Oxford, Kenneth Sisam became instrumental in the move toward inexpensive textbooks for a growing educational market after young men returned from the Great War. His own Clarendon edition *Fourteenth Century Verse & Prose* (1921), which was to enjoy a longevity rare among textbooks, included excerpts from both *Pearl* and *Gawain*. Tolkien's extensive glossary for Sisam's anthology made him an obvious choice to edit these texts for separate Clarendon volumes. His *Sir Gawain and the Green Knight* (1925) co-edited by E. V. Gordon began with a statement about audience: "The first endeavor of this edition has been to provide the student with a text." Meanwhile Gollancz forged ahead with his editions of *Patience* (1913) and *Cleanness* (1921). Tolkien and Gordon were commissioned to produce the Clarendon edition of *Pearl* which, after years of complications including Gordon's death, finally appeared in 1953 with Tolkien's contributions silently included, but without his name on the title page.

Textbooks aimed at the classroom featured the durable edition of all four Cotton Nero A.x works by A. C. Cawley and J. J. Anderson (1962), while the challenge of the language encouraged a number of translations. Tolkien's posthumously published renderings of *Pearl* and *Sir Gawain* (1975), though virtuoso in versification, had been produced in an archaic style neither faithful to the originals nor particularly inviting to modern readers. As a standard classroom anthology, *The Norton Anthology of English Literature* remedied the situation by including Marie Borroff's nimble verse translations of *Sir Gawain* (1967) and *Pearl* (1976); her *Gawain* would later win a coveted place in *The Norton Anthology of World Literature*. Thereafter *Sir Gawain* has remained the translation favorite with well-established poets such as W. S. Merwin (2002) and Simon Armitage (2008). Now Poet Laureate, Armitage followed up with a translation of *Pearl* (2017). *The Complete Works of the "Pearl" Poet* (1993) edited by Malcolm Andrew, Ronald Waldron, and Clifford Peterson with facing-page translations by Casey Finch—now welcoming *St. Erkenwald* into the corpus—provided everything that a classroom audience might require, even if the translations take more freedoms than first-time readers find helpful. Monty Python's Terry Jones recorded Tolkien's translations of *Pearl* and *Sir Gawain* (1997) and thereby closed the circle, so to speak, with a return to listeners, not book-readers, and thus demonstrated the effectiveness of these poems when recited aloud for a modern audience.

NOTES

1. William Vantuono, ed., *The "Pearl" Poems: An Omnibus Editions, Volume I: "Pearl" and "Cleanness"* (London: Garland, 1984), xxii–xxix.

2. A. S. G. Edwards, "The Manuscript: British Library MS Cotton Nero A.x.," in *A Companion to the "Gawain"-Poet*, ed. Derek Brewer and Jonathan Gibson (Cambridge: D.S. Brewer, 1997), 197–219.

3. Gervase Mathew, *The Court of Richard II* (New York: W.W. Norton, 1968), 116–17.

4. Edwards, "The Manuscript," 201–202.

5. Sir Israel Gollancz, "Introduction," in *Pearl, Cleanness, Patience, and Sir Gawain: Reproduced in Facsimile from the Unique MS. Cotton Nero A.x in the British Museum.* EETS o.s. 162, 1923, 8.

6. Edward I. Condren, *The Numerical Universe of the "Gawain" Poet* (Gainesville: University Press of Florida, 2002).

7. Edwards, "The Manuscript," 202–19.

8. J. R. R. Tolkien and E. V. Gordon, eds., *Sir Gawain and the Green Knight* (Oxford: Clarendon Press, 1925), vi.

9. A. C. Spearing, *The "Gawain"-Poet: A Critical Study* (Cambridge: Cambridge University Press, 1970), 3–4.

10. Michael J. Bennett, *Community, Class, and Careerism: Cheshire and Lancashire Society in the Age of "Sir Gawain and the Green Knight"* (Cambridge: Cambridge University Press, 1983), 246.

11. See David Coley's chapter, "The Northwest Midlands and the Ricardian Court," in this volume.

12. Edward Wilson, "*Sir Gawain and the Green Knight* and the Stanley Family of Stanley, Storeton, and Hooton," *Review of English Studies* 30 (1979): 308–16; Michael J. Bennett, "The Historical Background," in *A Companion to the "Gawain"-Poet*, ed. Brewer and Gibson, 89; Andrew Breeze, "Sir John Stanley (c. 1350–1414) and the *Gawain* Poet," *Arthuriana* 14 (2004): 15–30; and Su Fang Ng and Kenneth Hodges, "Saint George, Islam, and Regional Audiences of *Sir Gawain and the Green Knight*," *Studies in the Age of Chaucer* 32 (2010): 257–94.

13. Bennett, "Historical Background," 75–76.

14. Michael J. Bennett, "The Court of Richard II and the Promotion of Literature," in *Chaucer's England: Literature in Historical Context*, ed. Barbara A. Hanawalt (Minneapolis: University of Minnesota Press 1992), 13–14.

15. Bennett, "The Historical Background," 80.

16. Gordon, ed., *Pearl*, xliii. See also Ethan Campbell's chapter, "Authorship: What Does the *Pearl*-Poet Tell Us about Himself?" in this volume.

17. Bennett, "The Historical Background," 71.

18. Bennett, "The Historical Background," 72.

19. J. R. R. Tolkien, "*Sir Gawain and the Green Knight*" (1953), in *The Monsters and the Critics, and Other Essays*, ed. Christopher Tolkien (London: HarperCollins, 2006), 73.

20. John M. Bowers, *The Politics of "Pearl": Court Poetry in the Age of Richard II* (Cambridge: D.S. Brewer, 2001), 41–56.

21. *SGGK*, l. 280.

22. Bennett, "The Historical Background," 89.

23. Malcolm Andrew, "Theories of Authorship," in *A Companion to the "Gawain"-Poet*, ed. Brewer and Gibson, 29–31.

24. Barbara Nolan and David Farley-Hills, "The Authorship of *Pearl*: Two Notes," *Review of English Studies* n.s. 22 (1971): 295–302.

25. William Vantuono, "A Name in the Cotton MS. Nero A.x. Article 3," *Medieval Studies* 37 (1975): 537–42.

26. Clifford Peterson, ed., *Saint Erkenwald* (Philadelphia: University of Pennsylvania Press, 1977), 9.

27. Clifford J. Peterson, "The *Gawain*-Poet and John Massey of Cotton, Cheshire," *Review of English Studies* n.s. 25 (1974): 257–66, and Peterson, ed., *Saint Erkenwald*, 21–23.

28. Bennett, "The Historical Background," 78.

29. Ad Putter, *An Introduction to the "Gawain"-Poet* (London: Longman, 1996), 28–37.

30. For discussion, see Michael Drout, Jonathan Gerkin and Scott Kleinman's chapter, "St. Erkenwald," in this volume.

31. Elizabeth Salter, *Fourteenth Century English Poetry: Contexts and Readings* (Oxford: Clarendon Press, 1983), 75–76.

32. Marie Borroff, "Narrative Artistry in *St. Erkenwald* and the *Gawain*-Group: The Case for Common Authorship Reconsidered," *Studies in the Age of Chaucer* 28 (2006): 41–76.

33. John Scattergood, "*St. Erkenwald* and the Custody of the Past," in *The Lost Tradition: Essays on Middle English Alliterative Poetry* (Dublin: Four Courts Press, 2000), 179–81.

34. Peterson, ed., *Saint Erkenwald*, 9.

35. George Lyman Kittredge, *A Study of "Gawain and the Green Knight"* (Cambridge, MA: Harvard University Press, 1916), 282–89.

36. Diane Speed, *Medieval English Romances*, 3rd ed. 2 vols. (Durham: Durham Medieval Texts, no. 8, 1993), 236–37.

37. Thomas Hahn, ed., *Sir Gawain: Eleven Romances and Tales*, TEAMS (Kalamazoo, MI: Medieval Institute Publications, 1995), 309–10.

38. Gillian Rogers, "*The Grene Knight*," in *A Companion to the "Gawain"-Poet*, ed. Brewer and Gibson, 369.

39. Rogers, "*The Grene Knight*," 369.

40. Rossell Hope Robbins, "A *Gawain* Epigone," *Modern Language Notes* 58 (1943): 361–66, and "The Poems of Humfrey Newton, Esquire, 1466–1536," *Publications of the Modern Language Association* 65 (1950): 249–81.

41. *Pearl*, l. 1154.

42. C. L. Wrenn, "On Re-Reading Spenser's *The Shepheardes Calendar*," *E&S* 29 (1943): 48.

43. See Joel Fredell, "The *Pearl*-Poet Manuscript in York," *Studies in the Age of Chaucer* 36 (2014): 1–39.

44. Antony Singleton, "The Early English Text Society in the Nineteenth-Century: An Organization History," *Review of English Studies*, n.s. 56 (2005): 91.

45. Richard Morris, ed., *Early English Alliterative Poems in the West-Midland Dialect of the Fourteenth Century*, EETS o.s. 1, 1864, vii, xx.

46. Morris, *Early English Alliterative Poems*, viii, xx.

47. Morris, *Early English Alliterative Poems*, viii, xx.

48. For further discussion of editions and translations of the *Pearl*-poems, including those specifically made for students, see Kenna Olsen's chapter, "Translations and Paraphrases," in this volume.

49. Sir Israel Gollancz, ed., *Pearl: An English Poem of the Fourteenth Century Edited with a Modern Rendering* (London: David Nutt, 1891), xiii.

50. Kittredge, *A Study of "Gawain and the Green Knight,"* 4.

BIBLIOGRAPHY

Andrew, Malcolm. "Theories of Authorship." In *A Companion to the "Gawain"-Poet.* Ed. Brewer and Gibson, 23–33. Cambridge: D. S. Brewer.

Beal, Jane, ed. *Becoming the Pearl-Poet: Perceptions, Connections, Receptions.* New York: Lexington Books, 2022.

Bennett, Michael J. *Community, Class and Careerism: Cheshire and Lancashire Society in the Age of "Sir Gawain and the Green Knight."* Cambridge: Cambridge University Press, 1983.

———. "The Court of Richard II and the Promotion of Literature." In *Chaucer's England: Literature in Historical Context.* Ed. Barbara A. Hanawalt, 3–20. Minneapolis: University of Minnesota Press, 1992.

———. "The Historical Background." In *A Companion to the "Gawain"-Poet.* Ed. Brewer and Gibson, 71–90. Cambridge: D. S. Brewer.

Borroff, Marie. "Narrative Artistry in *St. Erkenwald* and the *Gawain*-Group: The Case for Common Authorship Reconsidered." *Studies in the Age of Chaucer* 28 (2006): 41–76.

Bowers, John M. *The Politics of "Pearl": Court Poetry in the Age of Richard II.* Cambridge: D.S. Brewer, 2001.

Breeze, Andrew. "Sir John Stanley (c. 1350–1414) and the *Gawain* Poet." *Arthuriana* 14 (2004): 15–30.

Brewer, Derek, and Jonathan Gibson, eds. *A Companion to the "Gawain"-Poet.* Cambridge: D.S. Brewer, 1997.

Condren, Edward I. *The Numerical Universe of the "Gawain" Poet.* Gainesville: University Press of Florida, 2002.

Edwards, A. S. G. "The Manuscript: British Library MS Cotton Nero A.x." In *A Companion to the "Gawain"-Poet.* Ed. Brewer and Gibson, 197–219.

Fredell, Joel. "The *Pearl*-Poet Manuscript in York." *Studies in the Age of Chaucer* 36 (2014): 1–39.

Hahn, Thomas, ed. *Sir Gawain: Eleven Romances and Tales*. TEAMS. Kalamazoo, MI: Medieval Institute Publications, 1995.

Gollancz, Sir Israel. ed. *Pearl: An English Poem of the Fourteenth Century Edited with a Modern Rendering*. London: David Nutt, 1891.

———. "Introduction." In *Pearl, Cleanness, Patience and Sir Gawain: Reproduced in Facsimile from the Unique MS. Cotton Nero A.x in the British Museum*. EETS o.s. 162, 1923.

Gordon, E. V., ed. *Pearl*. Oxford: Clarendon Press, 1953.

Kittredge, George Lyman. *A Study of "Gawain and the Green Knight."* Cambridge, MA: Harvard University Press, 1916.

Madden, Sir Frederic, ed. *Syr Gawayne: A Collection of Ancient Romance Poems by Scotish and English Authors, Relating to That Celebrated Knight of the Round Table*. London: Bannatyne Club, 1839.

Mathew, Gervase. *The Court of Richard II*. New York: W. W. Norton, 1968.

Morris, Richard, ed. *Early English Alliterative Poems in the West-Midland Dialect of the Fourteenth Century*. EETS o.s. 1, 1864.

Ng, Su Fang, and Kenneth Hodges. "Saint George, Islam, and Regional Audiences of *Sir Gawain and the Green Knight*." *Studies in the Age of Chaucer* 32 (2010): 257–94.

Nolan, Barbara, and David Farley-Hills. "The Authorship of *Pearl*: Two Notes." *Review of English Studies* n.s. 22 (1971): 295–302.

Peterson, Clifford J. "The *Gawain*-Poet and John Massey of Cotton, Cheshire." *Review of English Studies* n.s. 25 (1974): 257–66.

Peterson, Clifford, ed. *Saint Erkenwald*. Philadelphia: University of Pennsylvania Press, 1977.

Putter, Ad. *An Introduction to the "Gawain"-Poet*. London: Longman, 1996.

Robbins, Rossell Hope. "A *Gawain* Epigone." *Modern Language Notes* 58 (1943): 361–66.

———. "The Poems of Humfrey Newton, Esquire, 1466–1536." *Publications of the Modern Language Association* 65 (1950): 249–81.

Rogers, Gillian. "*The Grene Knight*." In *A Companion to the "Gawain"-Poet*. Ed. Brewer and Gibson, 365–72.

Salter, Elizabeth. *Fourteenth Century English Poetry: Contexts and Readings*. Oxford: Clarendon Press, 1983.

Scattergood, John. "*St. Erkenwald* and the Custody of the Past." In *The Lost Tradition: Essays on Middle English Alliterative Poetry*, 177–99. Dublin: Four Courts Press, 2000.

Singleton, Antony. "The Early English Text Society in the Nineteenth-Century: An Organization History." *Review of English Studies*, n.s. 56 (2005): 90–118.

Sisam, Kenneth, ed. *Fourteenth Century Verse & Prose*. Oxford: Clarendon Press, 1921.

Spearing, A. C. *The "Gawain"-Poet: A Critical Study*. Cambridge: Cambridge University Press, 1970.

Speed, Diane. *Medieval English Romances*. 3rd ed. 2 vols. Durham: Durham Medieval Texts, no. 8, 1993.

Tolkien, J. R. R. *The Monsters and the Critics, and Other Essays.* Ed. Christopher Tolkien. London: HarperCollins, 2006.

Tolkien, J. R. R., trans. *Sir Gawain and the Green Knight, Pearl, and Sir Orfeo.* Ed. Christopher Tolkien. London: George Allen & Unwin, 1975.

Tolkien, J. R. R., and E. V. Gordon, eds. *Sir Gawain and the Green Knight.* Oxford: Clarendon Press, 1925.

Vantuono, William. "A Name in the Cotton MS. Nero A.x. Article 3." *Medieval Studies* 37 (1975): 537–42.

———, ed. *The "Pearl" Poems: An Omnibus Editions, Volume I: "Pearl" and "Cleanness."* London: Garland, 1984.

Wellek, René. "*The Pearl.*" *Studies in English* (Charles University, Prague) 4 (1933): 5–33.

Wilson, Edward. "*Sir Gawain and the Green Knight* and the Stanley Family of Stanley, Storeton, and Hooton." *Review of English Studies* 30 (1979): 308–16.

Wrenn, C. L. "On Re-Reading Spenser's *The Shepheardes Calendar.*" *Essays and Studies* 29 (1943): 30–49.

Index

Page references for figures are italicized.

Adam, 15, 17–18, *28*, 29–31, 36n30, 46, 51–52, 56, 62n38, 87
adaptation, 8–9, 81, 94, 148, 156–157, 174–175, 176–177n15, 249–250, 257–258
adornment, 4, 5–6, 10, 19, 50, 53, 77n53, 85, 101n3, 145–147, 149–150, 153n28, 155–163, 216
agency, 6, 69–71, 128–130, 132–133, 135, 151, 159, 162–163
Agnus Dei. See Lamb of God
alliteration, 3, 4, 68, 94–101, 103n23, 109–111, 122n68, 135, 250, 252–257, 268, 270
alliterative verse, 230
    alliterative long line, 3, 93, 95, 97–98, 110;
    Alliterative Revival, 117–118
Amazons, 84
androcentrism, 87
Anglo-Norman, 82, 90n29
Anglo-Saxon, 93, 104n42
animals, 4–5, 77n48, 127–130, 132, 134, 137, 138n6, 171–173
    eagle, 171–174

horse, 68, 146, 160, 170, 174, 176n7
    lion, 171–174
    whale, 68, 70–73, 75n22, 76nn37–38, 76n40, 76n42, 129, 131, 147–148, 209
    See also Griffin; Lamb of God
anthology, 9, 80, 217, 259n6, 272–273
Apocalypse, 13, 27, 39n86
Aquinas, Thomas, 46–48, 58n3, 59n11, 61n27, 61–62n34, 62n38, 69, 237, 243
Aristotle, 22, 68
Armitage, Simon, 1, 9, 176–177n15, 255–257, 273
armor, 131, 160–161, 266.
    See also Clothing; Shield
artes praedecandi, 14, 95, 237–240
Arthurian, 9, 81, 90n29, 111, 115, 160, 169–175, 250, 269
Audience, 2–3, 5–10, 15–18, 20, 22–23, 25, 36n33, 69–74, 77n59, 79–81, 84, 86, 90n29, 110–111, 114, 116–117, 120n22, 132, 145, 148–151, 157, 159, 169–170, 173–174, 176–177n15, 184–189, 190–191n10, 191n15, 199, 205, 224, 228, 231n12, 233n61, 240, 249, 256–257, 265–273

About the Contributors

Elizabeth Allen is Professor and Chair of the English Department at the University of California, Irvine. She is the author of *Uncertain Refuge: Sanctuary in the Literature of Medieval England* (University of Pennsylvania Press, 2021). She has written essays in *Speculum, Exemplaria, JMEMS, New Literary History, ELH*, and elsewhere on Chaucer, Gower, episodic romance, and other topics, including an essay on *Patience*, "'As Mote in at a Munster Dor': Sanctuary and Love of This World" (*Philological Quarterly* 87 [2008]) and *"Pearl* and Landscape," a contribution to *Approaches to Teaching the Middle English "Pearl,"* edited by Jane Beal and Mark Bradshaw Busbee. She is also the author of a book on exemplarity, *False Fables and Exemplary Truth* (Palgrave, 2005).

Jane Beal is Professor of English Literature and the Chair of English Department at the University of La Verne in southern California. In addition to editing and contributing to *Becoming the Pearl-Poet*, she has written *The Signifying Power of "Pearl"* (Routledge, 2017), co-authored and co-edited *Approaches to Teaching the Middle English "Pearl"* (MLA, 2018), and edited and translated *"Pearl": A Middle English Edition and Modern English Translation* (Broadview, 2020). She has written *John Trevisa and the English Polychronicon* (ACMRS/Brepols, 2012) and co-edited *Translating the Past: Essays on Medieval Literature* (ACMRS, 2012). Her edited volumes on the reception of major religious figures in the Middle Ages appear in Brill's Commentaria series: *Illuminating Moses* (2014), *Illuminating Jesus* (2019), and *Illuminating Muhammad* (in progress). She also writes poetry, magical realist fiction, and creative non-fiction. To learn more about her and her work, visit http://janebeal.wordpress.com and http://medievalpearl.wordpress.com.

Kristin Bovaird-Abbo is Professor of English at the University of Northern Colorado. Her areas of special interest include medieval language and literature, particularly Middle English and Arthurian studies, and she has published on Geoffrey Chaucer's *The Canterbury Tales*, Thomas Malory's *Le Morte Darthur*, the anonymous *The Knightly Tale of Golagros and Gawane*, and the anonymous *The Marriage of Sir Gawain*. Her current research project explores the effects of gender and class on depictions of the Arthurian character of Gawain in fourteenth- and fifteenth-century Middle English romances, particularly in terms of Gawain's interactions with women and younger knights, as a reflection of changing values among the English gentry. She regularly teaches classes on Old English, Middle English, History of the English Language, Linguistics, the Arthurian Legend, and J. R. R. Tolkien. Her wider research and teaching interests include linguistics, James Joyce, Victorian poetry, drama, mythology, and medievalism. In her free time, she enjoys hiking in Rocky Mountain National Park with her family.

John M. Bowers is an internationally known scholar of medieval English literature with books on Chaucer, Langland, and the *Pearl*-Poet. His articles span the range from St. Augustine to Shakespeare. Educated at Duke, Virginia, and Oxford where he was a Rhodes Scholar, he taught at Caltech and Princeton before beginning his career at the University of Nevada in Las Vegas. His work has been supported by fellowships from the NEH, Huntington Library, and John Simon Guggenheim Foundation. His Great Courses series *The Western Literary Canon in Context* was released in 2008. His latest book *Tolkien's Lost Chaucer*, based on his discovery of an unpublished, unknown book by J. R. R. Tolkien, has been published by Oxford University Press.

M. W. Brumit is an Assistant Professor of English, Catholic Studies Fellow, and Faculty Mentor for the Gregorian Scholars Honors Program at the University of Mary in Bismarck, North Dakota, where he lives with his wife Amanda and their four children. He earned his PhD at the University of Dallas, where he taught courses in the Seven Arts of Language and the Literary Traditions sequence, with a dissertation titled "From Plato to *Pearl*: Chaucer and the *Pearl*-poet in the Platonic Tradition." He contributes to the Chaucer Bibliography (published in *Studies in the Age of Chaucer*), reviews books for *Carmina Philosophiae* (the journal of the International Boethius Society), and has also published articles on Jane Austen and Robert Herrick. He regularly teaches Composition, History of the English Language, World Literature, and Introductions to Narrative, Lyric, and Drama.

Ethan Campbell is Associate Professor of English and Literature at The King's College in New York City. He serves as coordinator of the college's English major and Literature minor degree programs, both of which he helped to found. He is the author of *The Gawain-Poet and the Fourteenth-Century*

English Anticlerical Tradition (Medieval Institute Publications, 2018), which was based on his PhD dissertation from the City University of New York (CUNY) Graduate Center. He has also published scholarship on medieval drama, Wycliffism and Lollardy, and religious expression in both the Middle Ages and contemporary fiction. He is currently preparing an edition of a non-Wycliffite Middle English translation of the Book of Revelation to be published by the Middle English Texts Series (METS) as *The English Apocalypse*.

Trained in Comparative Literature, **Nancy Ciccone** holds the position of Associate Professor Emerita at the University of Colorado, Denver. Her specialization in the English Department ranges from classical to medieval literatures. Her most recent articles include "Dislocated Identities," in *The* Aeneid *and the Modern World* (2022); "Depression in Ricardian Dream Visions," in *Faces of Depression* (2021); "Now and Then: Ishiguro's Medievalism," *This Year's Work in Medievalism* 32 (2018). She continues to work on Medieval Romance and the representation of Practical Reasoning.

David K. Coley is Professor of English at Simon Fraser University in Burnaby, British Columbia. He is the author of *Death and the Pearl Maiden: Plague, Poetry, England* (Ohio State University Press, 2019), which focuses on submerged discourses of plague in both the Cotton Nero A.x poems and late-medieval English literature, and *The Wheel of Language: Representing Speech in Middle English Poetry, 1377–1422* (Syracuse University Press, 2012). David's work has appeared in such journals as *Studies in the Age of Chaucer*, *Exemplaria*, *The Chaucer Review*, and *JEGP*, and he has contributed to several edited collections, including *Approaches to Teaching the Middle English* Pearl (MLA, 2018) and *Premodern Ecologies in the Modern Literary Imagination* (Toronto, 2019). He is currently editing John Clerk of Whalley's *Destruction of Troy* for the TEAMS Middle English Text series.

Michael D. C. Drout is Professor and Chair of English and Director of the Center for the Study of the Medieval at Wheaton College, Norton, Massachusetts, where he teaches Old and Middle English, Science Fiction, and the works of J. R. R. Tolkien. Drout is the author of *How Tradition Works, Tradition and Influence in Anglo-Saxon Literature*, and *Drout's Quick and Easy Old English*, and he is co-author of *Beowulf Unlocked: New Evidence from Lexomic Analysis*. He edited J.R.R. Tolkien's *Beowulf and the Critics* and the *J.R.R. Tolkien Encyclopedia* and co-edited *Transitional States: Cultural Change, Tradition and Memory in Medieval England*. One of the founders and a co-editor of the journal *Tolkien Studies*, he has published widely on Tolkien, fantasy and science fiction, and medieval studies in journals that include *Anglia, Anglo-Saxon England, English Studies, JEGP,*

Modern Philology, Neophilologus, Neuphilologische Mitteilungen, and *Oral Tradition*. Supported by three grants from the National Endowment for the Humanities, Drout has co-developed "lexomic" methods of computer-assisted statistical analysis that have led to discoveries about Anglo-Saxon, Old Norse, Latin and Modern English texts.

Joel Fredell is Professor of English at Southeastern Louisiana University near New Orleans. He is the editor, in cooperation with the British Library, of an online documentary edition (with full facsimiles and transcriptions) of the sole surviving manuscript of *The Book of Margery Kempe*; and the editor, in cooperation with Cambridge University, of Wynkyn de Worde's early print abridgement of that text, both available at http://english.selu.edu/humanitiesonline/kempe/. Widely published on later medieval manuscripts in Middle English, French, and Italian, he also writes regularly on issues in the digital humanities. At the University of York, he spent a year as a Leverhulme fellow, and has held fellowships and research grants from the National Endowment in the Humanities, the Huntington Library, the American Philosophical Association and others.

Jonathan B. Gerkin is the sole English teacher at the Burke Mountain Academy in East Burke, Vermont. After years of studying medieval literature and theology under the tutelage of Professor Michael Drout at Wheaton College, Gerkin completed a Fulbright Scholarship in the Slovak Republic. He is now continuing his studies at Middlebury.

Grace Hamman is an independent scholar of medieval literature, writer, and podcaster who works to make the beauty of medieval literature and theology accessible to general audiences on her podcast, *Old Books with Grace*. She received her doctorate in English from Duke University in 2019, and her MA and BA from the University of Arizona. She has published on authors from Julian of Norwich to Jane Austen in scholarly and popular journals, including *The Journal of Medieval and Early Modern Studies* and *Plough Quarterly.* Currently, she is working on a book about medieval literary and artistic representations of Christ aimed for both academic and nonacademic audiences. You can find her online at https://gracehamman.com.

Kimberly Jack is an Associate Professor of English and Drama at Athens State University in Alabama, where she teaches Medieval and Renaissance Literature, Greek Mythology, Early World Literature, and Costume Design. Her research focuses on the rhetorical function of material culture as it relates to clothing and the body in Middle English literature, specifically in the works attributed to the *Pearl*-poet (or *Gawain*-poet). Her publications include "What Is the Pearl-Maiden Wearing and Why?" in *Medieval Clothing and Textiles 7*, "The Pearl-Poet" in *An Encyclopaedia of Medieval Dress and Textiles of the British Isles c. 450–1450* (Brill, 2012), and "Putting Sir Gawain on Trial" in *Creating the Premodern in the Postmodern Classroom: Creativity in Early English Literature and History Courses* (2008). She puts sartorial semiotic theory into practice on stage, designing and producing costumes for three live theater productions each year.

Scott Kleinman is Professor of English and Director of the Center for Digital Humanities at California State University, Northridge. He has published on a variety of topics in Old and Middle English language and literature with a focus on regional cultures in romance and historiography. He has published on topics such as Old English dialectology, Laȝamon's *Brut*, and *Havelok the Dane* in such journals as *Neuphilologische Mitteilungen*, *Studies in Philology*, *Modern Philology*, *Exemplaria*, and *Viator*, as well as contributions to recordings of *Cleanness* and *Piers Plowman* for the Chaucer Studio. He has strong interests in using technology for both research and teaching and is working to understand how the growing field of Digital Humanities can expand our knowledge of and access to the cultures of the Middle Ages. His recent work includes the development of the *Lexos* text analysis tool and the WhatEvery1Says Project, which text mines public and social media at scale to explore the public's view of the humanities.

Kenna L. Olsen is Professor of Medieval English Literatures and Languages in the Department of English, Languages, and Cultures at Mount Royal University in Calgary, Canada. She teaches Old and Middle English literatures and the History of the English Language. She is a collaborator on the *Cotton Nero A.x Project* (gawain-ms.ca) which, in partnership with the British Library, has made digitized images of the *Gawain*-manuscript available on the web. Within that project, Dr. Olsen was the editor of a diplomatic edition of *Cleanness* (2011) and a new critical edition of *Cleanness* (2014). She has contributed to other collections on the Cotton Nero A.x poems, including Jane Beal and Mark Bradshaw Busbee's *Approaches to Teaching the Middle English "Pearl"* (2018). Kenna also works on the literary participation of Middle English secular women (www.medievalmaterialgirls.ca), medievalisms, and ecocritical approaches to medieval English literatures. Her current research considers the incorporation of emerging technologies, such as digital immersion, in teaching and researching medieval English literatures.

Corey Owen lives on a small farm near Saskatoon, a former temperance colony, and he is an Associate Professor in the Ron and Jane Graham School of Professional Development at the University of Saskatchewan. He teaches communication, rhetoric, classical mythology, early Christian literature, and Latin. His peer-reviewed academic articles appear in *Arthuriana, The Chaucer Review*, and *Florilegium* as well as elsewhere. He is currently completing a monograph on the cardinal virtues in the works of the *Pearl*-poet.

Jonathan Quick is a doctoral candidate in English at Stanford University. He holds a BA in English and Classics, and an MA in English, both from Texas A&M University. He has presented papers on "The Bath Old English Gospels" at the 53rd International Congress on Medieval Studies and "Networks of Communication: The Lives of Manuscripts in Early Medieval England" at the International Congress on Medieval Latin in Vienna, Austria. He has been a Digital Humanities Research Fellow for the Center for Spatial and Textual Analysis (CESTA) at Stanford University, and he is currently the project lead for The Movement of Manuscripts in Early Medieval England, a digital humanities and visualization project. He teaches on topics in medieval English literature, medievalism, and history of the English language.

Mickey Sweeney is Professor of English and past co-director of the Honors Program at Dominican University in Illinois. She has written *Magic in Medieval Romance* (Four Courts Press, 2001) and edited, with Rosalind Field and Phillipa Hardman, *Christianity and Romance in Medieval England* (D.S. Brewer, 2010). Her peer-reviewed articles appear in *SMART, Enarratio, Arthuriana, Mediaevalia, PMAM, Essays in Medieval Literature*, and elsewhere. She is an organizer of the Illinois Medieval Association conferences, President of the Medieval Association of the Midwest, and guest editor of *Essays in Medieval Studies*. As she says, "First and only love, the *Gawain*-poet, but a researcher of magic, medieval romances, and Arthurian histories, too."

9 781793 646774